READING
VOICES

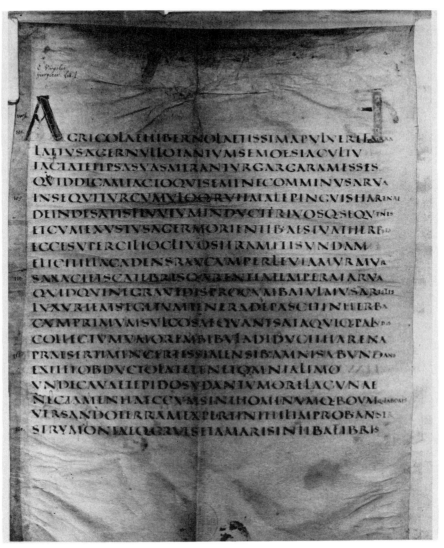

Virgil, Codex Augusteus (fourth century). Berlin, Staatsbibliothek, MS lat. F. 416.

Note. The curves of the returning wave overlap, the angular space between is smooth but covered with a network of foam. The advancing wave already broken, and now only a mass of foam, upon the point of encountering the reflux of the former. Study from the cliff above, Freshwater Gate. July 23.

Gerard Manley Hopkins, "Waves" ("Study from the cliff above, Freshwater Gate"), 1863. Courtesy of Mr. L. Handley-Derry.

A CENTENNIAL BOOK

One hundred books
published between 1990 and 1995
bear this special imprint of
the University of California Press.
We have chosen each Centennial Book
as an example of the Press's finest
publishing and bookmaking traditions
as we celebrate the beginning of
our second century.

UNIVERSITY OF CALIFORNIA PRESS

Founded in 1893

Reading
Voices

Literature and the Phonotext

● ▲ ■

GARRETT STEWART

University of California Press

BERKELEY   LOS ANGELES   OXFORD

University of California Press
Berkeley and Los Angeles, California

University of California Press, Ltd.
Oxford, England

Library of Congress Cataloging-in-Publication Data

Stewart, Garrett.
    Reading voices : literature and the phonotext / Garrett Stewart.
      p.   cm.
    Includes bibliographical references.
    ISBN 0-520-06877-7 (alk. paper).   ISBN 0-520-07039-9 (pbk.: alk. paper)
    1. English literature – History and criticism – Theory, etc.
2. English literature – History and criticism.   3. English language –
Discourse analysis.   4. Reader-response criticism.   5. Phonemics.
I. Title.
PR21.S7   1990
820.9′0001 – dc20   89-20518
                                                     CIP

Printed in the United States of America
1 2 3 4 5 6 7 8 9

Material from the Prologue and Chapter 3 appeared in "*Lit et Rature*: 'An
Earsighted View,'" *Literature Interpretation and Theory* (*LIT*) 1 (Fall
1989): 1–18. An earlier version of Chapter 7 appeared as "Catching the
Stylistic D/rift: Sound Defects in Woolf's *The Waves*," *ELH* 54 (Summer
1987): 421–61.

The paper used in this publication meets the minimum requirements of
American National Standard for Information Sciences – Permanence of
Paper for Printed Library Materials, ANSI Z39.48-1984. ∞

For N—
My Foreign Ear

Errata
for Garrett Stewart, *Reading Voices:*
Literature and the Phonotext

Page 2, line 9, should read:
called up is voice but only under suspension, a stratum of response located

Page 141, line 17, should read:
page, reading becomes a demystified but still palpable, still material, speech

Page 264, lines 12–13, should read:
"one." At the same time, the entire verb phrase itself, "were run" (not just
"—re run"), slackened and rushed enough in enunciation, is pronounced as one

Page 291, line 6 from bottom, should read:
wavering "reflux"—let us say, too *diaphonous*—ever to knock and jostle one

Contents

Acknowledgments

Formal work on this book began, backward, with a lecture in 1985 on verbal experimentation in Virginia Woolf for the Tudor-Stuart Club of the Johns Hopkins University, at the kind invitation of Sharon Cameron. As if to honor that original venue, I began systematically tracking the argument back to its Elizabethan roots. For advice on things philological along the way, my gratitude to Hans Aarsleff, Frank Gardiner, Paul Hernadi, and Seth Lerer; on matters philosophical, to Timothy Gould; and for assorted literary examples, to Kenneth Bleeth, Karen Cunningham, and Linda Kauffman. For subsequent opportunities to try out my sense of textual voicing on listening audiences, I wish to thank the Department of English at Stanford University and at the University of Utah. For timely and time-consuming help on various pieces and stages of the manuscript, I am indebted to Donald Foster, Sandra Gilbert, Richard Helgerson, and Jan Bowman Swanson, as well as to Paul Fry for the shrewd advice of his press reading. Special thanks go to Marie Borroff and Susan Wolfson, who so generously engaged with early drafts of my ideas on rhyme and allied effects in poetry and helped think them through. Thanks also to my expert research assistant, Jocelyn Lutz Marsh, and to Robert Pendleton and Donna Rudolph, who helped in preparing the index. Most of all, for the invaluable aid of a structuralist eye for texts, a polyglot ear, a firm critical hand, a gentle touch, and many an encouraging word, my greatest continuing debt is to my wife, Nataša Ďurovičová, to whom, once again, more than a book is dedicated.

Prologue:
Silence Speaking Words

The reader should be carried forward, not merely or chiefly by
the mechanical impulse of curiosity, or by a restless desire to
arrive at the final solution; but . . . like the path of sound through
the air; at every step he pauses and half recedes, and from the
retrogressive movement collects the force which carries him
onward.

Coleridge, Biographia Literaria, chapter 14

And strangely on the silence broke
The silent-speaking words

Tennyson, In Memoriam, 95.25–26

Reading voices. My title is a hypothetical proposition, a sentence. This book
is not concerned with our reading of voices, or the voices of our reading, so
much as with the reading that proceeds to give voice, or at least to evoke
silently such voicing: to evocalize. In view of this proposed paradox of a silent
textual sounding, the title is, at least at the start, rightly a question: Reading
voices? It derives from another, perhaps more fundamental, question: Where
do we read? This is the leading and alien question around which the following
pages have eventually been collected in response. Leading, because its adverb, *where* (if anticipating any answer less banal than "in the library"), points
away from the usual areas of consideration. Alien, because in the standard
inquiries into literary activity, the ruling adverbs or relative pronouns holding
down the interrogative slot in such a question have usually been, instead,
either "*why* do we read?" (the philosophical or psychoanalytic approach),
whom (the literary-historical or canonical), *how* (the interpretive), *whither*
(the sociological or political), *what* and *when* (the empirical), *what precisely*
(the linguistic or semiotic), or *which* kind or sort (the generic). Where, then,
does *where* leave us? The place of reading into which it inquires is none other
than the reading body. This somatic locus of soundless reception includes of
course the brain but must be said to encompass as well the organs of vocal
production, from diaphragm up through throat to tongue and palate. Silent
reading locates itself, that is, in the conjoint cerebral activity and suppressed
muscular action of a simultaneously summoned and silenced enunciation.

●   1

Semantic Excess, Somatic Access

Recent studies in semiotics have shifted attention from the body of literature to literary and cultural representations of the body per se, to the body as text, an impressed field of cultural signs.[1] The body in these pages will figure, by contrast, not as the inscribed site of meaning but as the passive register of inscription itself when silent reading processes a text as the continuous inhibition of the oral. Inwardly, reading voices only as a concerted veto of sound. Where we read to ourselves is thus the place, always, of a displacement, a disenfranchisement of voice, a silencing. It is the place where what is called up is voice suspension, but only under a stratum of response located between a merely evoked aurality and an oral vocalizing: the zone of evocalization. That this locus of reading should be insisted upon, to any theoretical profit, as the place of the body is, however, a relatively late development in the investigations here introduced. The very fact that these somatic implications of reading should have come so slowly to the surface in the course of research devoted to the play between phonic and graphic articulations should serve to demonstrate, for a start, how far the body, the reader's sensorium, has traditionally been kept from the field of literary concern.

The textual evidence for such investigations consisted at first in mere scattered instances of a recurrent but critically unnoted verbal phenomenon that came to seem quintessential to the deepest operations of literary language, not only in verse but in prose—and all the more so for the ease with which the phenomenon had tended to evade interpretive notice. These collected samples were simply this, instances without a principle, long before they started to provide answers to a central question. To hit upon the inevitability of the question "Where do we read?" needed steady prompting from the weight of this gathering evidence. The current project, then, was an exploratory and highly tentative attempt at practical criticism well before it became a work of theory. In the process, a good part of its early motive—to redress the eclipse of stylistics in literary discussion—encountered a more or less continuous frustration at the very inability of traditional stylistic analysis to account for the verbal slippages that had prompted the rescue mission in the first place. What emerged from this potential impasse was the approach which I will here be referring to, and soon defining, under the general name of *phonemic reading*. Its practice has to do not with reading orally but with aural reading. To authorize it as an even plausible procedure, however, requires considerable demonstration.

This approach, in its extremity of detail, is in essence oppositional, defining what it is up to in open contrast with what it is up against. Any inclination to sustain and extend the impetus of poststructuralist theory into the atrophied field of phonological analysis has a difficult allegiance to win in the ranks of deconstruction itself. Such an inclination cannot help but confront a widespread (if only implicit) "phonophobia" generated in the wake of the Derridean attack on the Logos. No longer disposed to hear the author behind the text, the Voice behind all inscription, we are at the same time (though not necessarily by the same logic) no longer encouraged to hear the phonemic counterpart to the spaced lettering of a text: counterpart, not content; for the phonemes are neither contained nor containable by script. Though inner audition need not in any sense subscribe to a myth of an originary Voice before the letter, still the resistance to a supposedly "undemystified" orality has created a veritable deaf spot in the tenets of even the most sophisticated reception theories. An exhaustive antimetaphysical philosophy of writing has thus hindered rather than facilitated a more responsive approach to the "phenomenality" of literary reading. The otherwise natural gravitation of stylistics toward the phonological stratum has in this sense been impeded (with a few notable exceptions, herein explored) by the very postformalist programs that ought to have renewed the energy of that tendency through an emphasis on linguistics as well as rhetoric. The question is no longer the presence (or index) of voice in text but, instead, the presence *to* evocalization of any text when read. No longer a metonymy of voice as *origin,* the idea of an "embodied" voice emerges as just the opposite: signaling the very *destination* of the text in the reading act, the medium of its silent voicing, sounding board rather than source. The recognition of such a somatic quotient in the reading of writing, though having nothing to do with the "internalization" of written ideas or ideation as such, nevertheless carries indirect but profound implications for the relation of subjectivity to text production, of consciousness to language.

Text Duality: Air/Ink Differences

In his influential distinction among locutionary, illocutionary, and perlocutionary acts, J. L. Austin considers respectively the meaning, force, and effect of an utterance.[2] At one point in *How to Do Things with Words,* Austin, working within the illocutionary formula "*In* saying x, I was doing y," illustrates exceptions to this model which are in fact not illocutionary at all, which carry no force beyond signification itself in the process of its own clarifying redistribution. "We use," he writes, "the same formula where 'to y' is to perform an incidental part of the locutionary act" (123). His only unqualified example of such an exception to the usual formula is the self-referential message: "In saying 'Iced ink' I was uttering the noises 'I stink'" (123). Adjective disintegrating to pronoun, noun conglomerating to verb, phrase mutated into clause: this homophonic burlesque seems deployed by Austin for its all but parodistic collapse – and instantaneous regrouping – of the signifying system itself, both its morphology and its grammar. What I will be discussing as the locutionary turmoil of ambiguous phonemic juncture is here perfectly illustrated in the sort of verbal gambit that falls – like so many of the poetic and fictional passages to follow – between comedy and referential chaos, between a joke and a radical breakdown of lexical yoking. Somewhere decidedly between: risking neither pole, risibility nor disintegration, but unmoored nevertheless from any discursive norm. Though this lies quite outside the category of a phrase's illocutionary force for Austin, such a radical ambiguity does bear indirectly on that intentionality in language which is his largest subject, involving not just a phrase's unwritten purposes but also the accidents of audition to which it is prey. Upon such phonemic contingencies as well as such layered purport, literary language often flamboyantly depends.

What distinguishes the "I stink"/"Iced ink" dyad or, for instance, the child's similar jingle "I scream for ice cream" from the problematics of homophony in classical linguistics is the lexical syncopation these lateral slippages entail. The sounding (silent or otherwise) of either half of the dyad does not simply mark an unexpected space in the paradigmatic axis (between phrasal clusters inscribed differently but pronounced the same); it marks a gap in the syntagmatic axis as well: a sliding of the blank between words; a perplexing, therefore, of syntactic contiguity along with lexical integrity. Such cross-lexical homophony dislodges "segmental" demarcation, producing in this way a sounding that enlists but redistributes the graphic void (the lexical interspace) as a signifying function: a cross-word puzzle, so to speak. The far-ranging implications of this lexical fraying and reweaving – one word at loose ends providing the fringe benefit of another – comprise the largest subject behind the smallest textual "objects" under investigation in this study.

It so happens that Austin's case in point was never transcribed in the philosopher's formal papers but comes instead from the lecture notes of his students, confirmed "from many secondary sources" (165). This is no surprise, since the power of the example, as a linguistic *distinction,* depends on the enunciatory precision of its divergent articulations. In the linguistic effects I will be examining in what follows, however, the lecturer becomes a passive *lecteur,* the reader silent and alone – for whom the force of words, their formal permutations beyond manifest content, may well reside in just such a co/incidental shift within locutional linkages. In such cases involving the homophonic ambivalence of lexical juncture, the text gives it one way – and only under pressure of silent enunciation does the phrase begin in the other sense to give. It may in this way give out at its borders, give up its double. The phonic will not hold fast within the graphic. Or, more to the point, the phonemic will not stay put within the morphemes apparently assigned by script. Differential rules thus interfere in the acoustic continuum, the lexical codes getting jammed in the message. When this transpires in the reading experience of a literary text, the effect is registered (upon the passive sounding of the reading body) as a semantic dissonance, a disturbance in the whole sequence of signification. Austin's homophonic farce is an extreme case, unusually pure in its ambivalence, unusually drastic in the semantic irreconcilability of its components. Poetic devices — rhyme, assonance, euphony — thrive ordinarily on something more like a middle ground, a hovering aural dispersion. In the literary text, a junctural or segmental blurring may operate as a more subliminal blending, a supple overlap without risk of lexical breakdown. In the passive *airing* of a text's unvoiced articulation, in the space between evoked but unactivated breath and the writing that incites it, emerges what Austin's example might lead us to call an "air"/"ink" difference, a friction that may at any moment thaw the iced fixity of scripted lexemes. Such a friction thus reads as a "dyslocutionary" tension between phonemic and graphemic signification.

There is another way to think of this. In any ordinary application of the figure/ground distinction to a written text, one would naturally consider the inscribed letters — or their grouping in words, their arrangement in printed lines — as the effective "figure" to the blank, inactive ground of white: the latter including junctural word breaks, interlinear spacing, and lateral margins, as well as less frequent gaps between paragraphs, sections, or chapters. At least within a normal syntactic span, phonemic reading (against this common sense) sensualizes the lexical interstices of such a ground, teases them into a kind of perceived activity, makes them continuous with lettering as a potential space of interloping semiosis, of wording. The distinction between foreground and textual backing is thus, as it were, rewritten — so that not only every letter, every phoneme, but also every junctural blank comes to figure (to figure morphemically) only by asserting its signifying function against the oppositional ground of a still potentially significant other. The result is a figure/ground relationship very much in flux, like the gestalt drawing that is now a vase, now two profiles facing each other in silhouette. A word, that is to say, may seem over, all said, its figuring function lapsing back to ground — when all of a sudden the next word just may, in waiting to emerge at the other side of the gaping ground, turn out to have been bound up partially, recursively, with the word we have just read, whose signifying function it now refigures at an unsettling off-angle to the tread of script. It does so only by incorporating and neutralizing, not by ignoring, the blank on which it has encroached. Here is one circumscribed form of that "retrogressive" moment in reading envisaged by Coleridge in the epigraph to this Prologue. Such is the tension—a play generated between words but negotiated between text and reader—such is the *recursive reading* upon which more literary effects depend than have ever been recognized in either literary criticism at large or the specialized domain of stylistics.

Sound Defects

For an ambivalent literary play of phonemes explicitly associated with the auditory status of written texts, we can turn now to our second epigraph, from section 95 of *In Memoriam:* "And strangely on the silence broke / The silent-speaking words." Tennyson, mourning the elegized subject, Hallam, finally has the heart to return to his letters, "those fallen leaves which kept their green, / The noble letters of the dead." What speaks in them, however, is only "love's dumb cry," mute no matter how lettered, how articulate. Hallam's voice is certainly not to be heard in his letters, neither in the whole documents nor in the graphic letters that compose them. All that speaks in or through them is the spirit of the man: "and strangely spoke / The faith, the vigor." Here is no phonocentric recuperation of speaking presence; the "thanatopraxis" (or death-work) of textuality is hardly accompanied by a voice or embrace from beyond the grave. Cued, instead, by the almost dead metaphor "spoke" is a reading effect: the uncanny transference of past energy into reception through mute textuality. Tennyson was said by W. H. Auden to have "the finest ear, perhaps, of any English poet."[3] On the present evidence, this would seem to include an inner ear for the phonic ingenuities—and ambiguities—of his own silent (because) textual phrasing. In listening with our best approximation of such an ear, we recognize that a segmental (and hyphenated) scriptive border between the dental and sibilant of "silen*t-s*peaking words" might allow for another audition, in this case a metalingual variant. To paraphrase Austin: When Tennyson writes "silen*t-s*peaking," he might implicitly be saying that "in writing 'silent-speaking,' I was also transcribing the noises 'silence-speaking'" (where *t* fuses with *s,* in what phonologists call "assimilation," to form a homophone of *ce* and then reduplicates, by merely sustaining, itself). If so, in this densely self-instancing case, the silent oxymoronic speakings of the *In Memoriam* text would enact as well as name their own evoking (their own "evocalization") of just that *speaking silence* which is textuality itself, posthumous or not, in its definitive divorce from oral presence. In Hallam's silent reach through text to the ear of the persona, and through his to ours, the aura of voice is displaced upon internalized enunciatory urges at the site of reception.

Through an invisible, an unscripted, finessing of the junctural gap between words, lexical autonomy is here eroded to the point where the chief function or "force" (illocutionary, dyslocutionary, or otherwise) of the wording seems to be the reconstitution of the very possibility of wording, of locution. Literary language is thus submitted in process to its own metalingual analysis. Sprung from the reflex of a phrasing upon its own phonic alternative, such conflicted lexical transitions repeatedly invite, without depending upon, the kind of thematization found in Tennyson—in ways and for reasons I shall explore in Chapter 3. There, too, the phonetic and phonemic distinctions relevant to this study will be further examined. For now, it is important simply to note that where phonetics deals with the precise calibration of the whole range of speech sounds (elaborately coded and traditionally identified within brackets), phonemics is concerned only with those sound "values," those structuring forms, which have a pertinent or paradigmatic opposition to other available sound shapes—hence a signifying function—in the morphophonemic structure of a given language. These pages will have far more occasion to identify phonemic than phonetic entities (the former in the usual manner, between slanted lines), because it is precisely the oppositional nature of such systemic sound "forms"—at the interchanged edges of lexemes—that constitutes my subject. In question is a reshuffling at those "segmental" borders within which internal lexical bonding is often indicated in linguistics by the "=" sign. When "iced ink" is transcribed yielding at its boundary to /ay/ plus /st/ = /ɪŋk/, for instance, the specialized phonemic sign language necessary for the coming deliberations is pretty well laid out.[4] One need only bear in mind that although audible phonetic sounds do not result from a text that is not read out loud, the "inner" articulation— or "endophony"—involved in silent reading not only actuates the whole range of phonemic differentials but latently engages the somatic or muscular activity (again, see Chapter 3) whose acoustic result phonetics is designed to chart.

Strictly speaking, at least when one is speaking strictly, there *is* a difference, a phonemic distinction, between "silent" and "silence" before a sibilant. Not much, but it is there. But not always there when, and where, we are reading. One deep ambiguity of literary textuality in activation may indeed be that it sends the rigor of such differences into remission. Reading is the displacing without forgetting of one word by the next in the syntactic chain. When this displacement operates a shade too quickly or too slowly—one word shadowed in passing by its neighbor, partly assimilated to it by recurring in it—the "will" to morphophonemic structure is thus found exerting its full, indeed overflowing, pressure on the written sign. At such moments, within the economy of grammar and the duration of reading, what we might call the twofold "rate" of exchange between words is upset; pace becomes unreliable, the toll on syntax increased. In such an aberrant grammatical economy, lexical expenditures are sometimes not entirely paid up at their seeming borders, held hostage there by a contiguous word—a case of language in arrears to itself, ransoming its own succession. Laterally entailed, that is, words do not speak, or get spoken, entirely for themselves. In this, the cross-lexical drift attests to a central apprehension of poststructuralist thinking: the metonymic or associational slippage by which a signifier is the mark only of another signifier rather than of a signified. The *t* of Tennyson's "silent-," for instance, marks in this sense not just the lexical border of a referential attribution synonymous with "mute"; as read, the /t/ sound represents the first half of another (composite) signifier (/t/ /s/) as well, otherwise the lexical boundary *ce,* determining thereby—as it happens—the noun form of that same signifier, "silence." With its increments plastic and detachable, the constitutive slide of the signifier, its intrinsic deferral of the signified, is exposed and diagnosed in such a crossing of lexical boundaries with rather drastic clarity.

The narrow brush with nonsense which these cross-lexical "assimilations" may involve is what links them to the transformative play of jokes, including the commercial wit of advertising slogans. Freud's examples of verbal conflations in his study "Wit and Its Relation to the Unconscious," such portmanteau terms as *famillionaire, anecdotage,* and *alcoholidays,* are contrasted with that sort of wit based on word division to be found in the play on *Rousseau* versus *roux* plus *sot.*[5] In the latter case, the joke depends on the word "cut up into its separate syllables like a charade" (647), whereas in the previous portmanteaus, the process of compression is explicitly related to "condensation" in the secondary processing of dreams. Freud reserves application of the other chief dream analogue, "displacement," for the kind of wit that turns not on combinatory mechanisms but on the wholesale substitution of one referent for another, as in traditional punning or double meaning. But considering the curious conflations, say, of "I stink" through "Ist (st)ink" into "Ic(e)d ink," certainly there is a "displacement" at play there as well. Through a lateral shunting of blanks and limital phonemes, such phrasing evolves through a dislocation of junctural markers as well as through a "condensation" of two possible lexical shapes within a single homophonic nucleus. Such a pun depends upon a partial and reciprocal, a sliding and transitional, composite: a phonemic layering and elision that resembles, in one way or another, the overlapping palimpsests of unconscious dreamplay.

What, then, is the relation of such a psychoanalytic model to the somatic registrations of phonemic reading? Refocused by Freud's theories of wordplay in relation to dreamwork, our leading question again asserts itself: Where do we read? What is the relation of suppressed oral articulation to the very different suppressions and conversions revealed in the unconscious? The most radical theory of the articulating body in relation to the psychic doubleness of portmanteau phrasings is found in Gilles Deleuze's commentary on linguistic "disorders."[6] Comparing the "esoteric word" (328) of Lewis Carroll and

Antonin Artaud in light of the combined failures of both "clinical psychiatry and literary criticism" (335), Deleuze refuses any facile identification of conflational, composite, or anagrammatic wordplay with the mental processes of schizophrenia. For him, Carroll's portmanteau terms are thin, skin-deep, whereas the violent distortions of language in Artaud rend surfaces, plumb depths, and recover the pulsating body from the externalizing artifices of an expressive aesthetic. The spasmodic clashing of Artaud's "breath-words, scream-words" (331) may be said, or rather felt, to bespeak the sieving, fragmented, dissociated body (Deleuze's attributions) of the schizophrenic, whose "values are exclusively tonic and non-written" (331). Phrased this way, the schizophrenic tongue may seem very far from the hypertrophic logic of articulation behind a segmental ripple like "Iced ink"/"I stink." There, problematized junctures induce dissociation only in the instantaneous transition to their reconstituted alter egos in the reader's recognition. Deleuze places primary emphasis on the fluid, amorphous body as the source of utterance, scripted or oral, rather than as the site of reception. "That is why it is insufficient to say that schizophrenic language is defined by an incessant and mad sliding of the signifying series onto the signified series. In fact, no series remains at all; both have disappeared" (334). Language becomes psychotic gesture. Most literature holds back from this, holds tighter. In the process of reading across those only marginally disarticulated slippages of juncture to which the following chapters are given over, though, the nonschizophrenic mind does undergo its own temporal dislocations. Attached to an articulating body passively processing words as vocables, the mind may well hear—in the inner ear of silent reading—no more (but no less) than just such a sliding of signifiers over signifieds, more particularly of phonemes over morphemes, in the ripple effect of evocalization. Whereas, in Deleuze's sense, the fluctuant schizophrenic body, pliant beyond articulatory distinction, creates a somatic *affect,* the way reading voices (that is, gives voice) in the coming examples is instead through a somatic *effect* at the site of reception. It is an effect that all but simultaneously breaches and rebuilds the integrity of lexical sequencing itself.

But the strained analogy to psychotic disruption does not simply go away. Rather, it is modified by a very different analogy—to that domain of publicly oriented wordplay that capitalizes rhetorically on the very anxiety (free-floating) over linguistic disturbance (free-form) which it is designed both to induce and then to "cure." This is the realm of the commercial (including journalistic) use of what are quite loosely called "puns," verbal contortions (including portmanteaus) that may themselves loosen up more than just dictionary reference, even grammar, indeed wreaking havoc at times with the whole alphabetic register. In this sense, rather than a psychotic breach, the aberration incurred—in that closed system previously discussed as the "economy" of syntax—is what we might call a default in lexical coherence: one, however, with an exchange value in its own right. Anyone's favorite examples will do, from ad copy to headlines to signposts to bumper stickers. Even as I write, southern California is suffering a drought for which the local public-awareness campaign has as its motto the interrogative pun, "Water . . . You Doing to Save?" A few years back there was the national magazine ad that not only put the homophonic "oomph!" back in the Tri*umph* sports car but spelled it out as a numerical and graphic pun on the formula for acceleration: "0-000mph!" Within the realm of sheerly homophonic rather than graphic dislocations, such punning is of course eye-catching as well as ear-catching, if for no other reason than that it throws the graphic out of joint through subvocal enunciation. There was the newspaper coverage of the apocalyptic boat-builder in New Jersey: "New Ark in Newark." Or the recent science fiction and slasher films *Alien Nation* and *Child Splay*. Typical of the British taste for punning ads and logos, there is the "Crispbread" hors-d'oeuvres cracker, which is either to be crisply (mimetically) enunciated or else its name ends up vocalizing the "spread" for which it is designed. Somewhere along the Oregon coast appears the artificially humanized name of a tourist curio shop, "Aunt Tiques." Or there is the chain convenience store logo, spelled by "assimilation" (or elision) as swiftly as its touted service, FASTOP—with an octagonal stop sign for an *O* into the bargain. More baroque yet, perhaps, is the Midwest turnpike franchise parodying the so-called Scandinavian ice cream fad, its boast and its brand name being at once "Hañ Dipped." And in my own hometown, a sign above a hairdressing salon, listing its proprietor as one Susan Light, identifies the establishment as "Light Shears Ahead." That double cross-lexical drift—across the first word break into the breaking up of the next word ("a head")—permits that extra twist of reflexivity which is often part of such jokes, here the lightning-fast play with ingeniously snipped edges.

The double take, indeed muted double threat—both somatic and linguistic—involved in such "catchy" cross-lexical punning is meant to be in every sense arresting. Grabbed, we are to stop short, go back. If we get it, they've got us: that's the logic. Sketched here is something, of course, like the logic of paranoia as well, activated by the practice of a quasi-schizophrenic reading, language now seen one way, now heard another, textual work or reading agent split apart at the seams. We've all heard at times the dismissive hyperbole "Puns drive me crazy." The idiom is telling. Puns induce an anxiety which modernism of course, as well as literature less systematically before it, moves to exploit, psychoanalysis to diagnose, and advertising to contain and recuperate. In the last case, as soon as we're "in" on the sellers' jokes, we are suddenly "with" them rather than against them; linguistic violence is itself marketable, its assaults converted to seduction. In between aggressive verbal salesmanship and psychopathology, one might say, with their shared reconstitution of the self as cognitive subject across the space of linguistic disorder, lies the literary "use," fully mobilized or not, of such disintegrative—become investigative—linguistic play or give.

Once again, literature may be found to operate as the continuous analysis of reading itself in both its somatic and referential dimensions. When we read to ourselves, our ears hear nothing. Where we read, however, we listen. Barthes has written: "*Hearing* is a physiological phenomenon; *listening* is a psychological act."[7] To amend this formulation about listening by calling it a "psychosomatic" act would be to derive a notion nearer to my premises in this book. Barthes's fullest (if indirect) theorizing of this, without naming the phonemic component in particular (because his subject in this essay is primarily the musical text), arrives with the closing paragraph; what is for the most part "listened to . . . in the field of art . . . is not the advent of a signified, object of a recognition or of a deciphering, but the very dispersion, the *shimmering* of signifiers, ceaselessly restored to a listening which ceaselessly produces new ones from them without ever arresting their meaning: this phenomenon of shimmering is called *signifying* [*signifiance*], as distinct from signification" (259). Extend the field of application from music to other forms of textuality, other forms of attendance, and the chief repeated (and italicized) tenet of his essay, "*listening speaks*" (259), should operate to rephrase—and so reassert—the notion that *reading voices*. In a better-known essay, "The Grain of the Voice," however, Barthes pursues such insights in a way that obscures what is of most interest to the present speculations about the body as the receptive (let us say from now on, the receptual) site of textual activation. "The 'grain' is the body in the singing voice, in the writing hand, in the performing limb."[8] There is a false parallel in this triad. What drops out is precisely that listening speech, that silent articulation, which would align a singer's voice or dancer's leg not with the upper limb of the writing subject, the textual source, but rather with the principal organs of textuality *as a performance medium:* the listening throat and mouth of the reading voice, whose "grain" is no less textured for being silent. In what follows, therefore, the acoustics of textuality will be isolated as just such a malleable "signifying" energy floated upon the counterplay of phonemes against graphemes within the order of signification. To listen in this way is to speak silently the turmoil of wording itself before and athwart the regime of words.

The Importance of Being Modernist

Qualifications aside, Barthes's pioneering work at this level has never been pursued in relation to literary reading in general—and is not destined to find its natural extension in a critical climate influenced in good part by his own partisanship on behalf of a far more specialized kind of experimentation in the contemporary text. The anticlassical animus of such a preference, the premium placed on the "writerly" rather than "readerly," tends to block a closer look at the manner in which "listening speaks"—or reading rewrites by revoicing—even in the classical text. Barthes is scarcely alone in truncating one lineage of his own thought. Upon much that concerns us here, two rather different historicizing trends have recently turned their backs. The shifting differential fundament of textuality is likely to be ignored by both an extrinsic and an intrinsic historical approach, by those studies reaching beyond but also by those keeping too tightly within literary practice. On the one hand, we encounter in certain historicist tendencies a dissolution of the literary instance into a system of cultural "inscription" and exchange, often an extralinguistic coding and transmission. This may amount to suppressing either the verbal particularity of the specifically written text or the "literary" quality, however defined, of the aesthetic document. On the other hand, within the study of literature per se, there is a bias toward a narrowly conceived literary history that, though occupied with the linguistic components intrinsic to verbal textuality, remains too epochal and irruptive in its masterplot. It is therefore too much inclined toward watersheds and convulsive turning points. In the process, it fails to do justice to the penchant in any period for phonemic counterplay as one of the very hallmarks of literary language. This is a phonemic tendency—a syllabic tending—very much in evidence across the whole course of literary practice, let alone open experimentation, in English letters. It is in the linguistic nature of the English language itself that this should be so.

Intrinsic historicizing, the latter approach mentioned above, is to be found, more or less undisguised, in some of the most challenging and influential poststructuralist theory of the last three decades. It manifests itself especially in connection with what we might term the "catastrophist" premise of a radical break(through) into modernism. In the writings of—to name names—Julia Kristeva, Barthes again, Jacques Derrida, and Michel Foucault, we encounter respectively a highly specialized sense of the "semiotic" (or countersymbolic), the "writerly" (or *scriptible*), the "grammatological" (or nonphonocentric), and the "literary" (or materialist-ontological) as the dominant characterizations applied to a modernist textual condition won by poetic insurgency. Enshrined thereby is a supposed antimetaphysical rupture in poetics of which each theorist is in various ways the champion. Kristeva sets the tone with her title *Revolution in Poetic Language*,[9] in which, as in all these writers, Mallarméan modernism is the pivotal moment, with Joyce in English literature arriving later to seal the fate of the new, an absolute rift with tradition. The trouble is, to take another English case, Shakespeare. Or Donne. Or before them, even Chaucer and Spenser. Or thereafter, of course, Milton. Shelley, certainly. Dickens, too. And so on. To treat the textual tradition in any language as merely the prehistory of a modernist overturning is to miss something in modernism as well as in its predecessors, something that phonemic reading is in part meant to disclose. Kristeva's approach through psycholinguistics ignores, for instance, the way in which literary textuality is permeated by her favored "pulsional" and asyntactic energy well before the concerted discontinuities of modernism. Turning to Barthes, the same can be said of that "writerly"[10] participation by the unsettled reader, often phonologically cued, which constitutes the modernist advent. From Shakespeare to Balzac, classical writing often illustrates the same effects — if far more sporadically. Within the precincts of readerly texts there are even to be found phonic texturings that point toward that "grain of the voice" which Barthes seems to adumbrate in several places as the ultimate destiny of modernist textuality. Derrida's literary history is, as we might expect, more allusive, glancing, and cryptic. We will nevertheless notice in Chapter 3 how much his sense of "modernity" in writing (Derrida's own quotation marks)[11] depends on a text's writerliness, its detachment from the presumption of a speaking voice, on discontinuities within any conceivable logic of *transcribed* utterance. It thus depends in part on precisely those reading effects against the graphic "grain" which these chapters are soon to chronicle and dissect across the range of one national literature — extending far back before any received definition of the "modern."

In the work of that fourth leading apologist of the new, Michel Foucault, the stratum of pure "literary" production is revealed only at the point of its volcanic eruption as avant-garde modernism. To vary the original title of Foucault's third book, *Les mots et les choses,*[12] words themselves in modernity become merely things, no longer the guarantors of a transparent and rational discourse. This same view of language, if never before so exclusive, must, however, have been available to writers well before Mallarmé — or at least this same fact of language on view. Instead of Foucault's narrative of advent, break, and redirection, we need (if only in one sense) to put modernism in its place. Instead of appearing as a deus ex machina from within the workings of language, the parturition of self-conscious "literature" from belles lettres should disclose its continuous birth throes in every period. Foucault's story is, to be sure, appealing in its elegant simplicity, even as it is the fullest attempt in recent theory to periodize the interrelationship of linguistic and literary presuppositions. Well before there was any attention in philosophy to what we now call "universes of discourse," there was the discourse of the universe, the language of nature, sometimes called "God's

Book"—in Foucault's phrase "the prose of the world." By the second half of the seventeenth century, however, with the inauguration of what is now known as the classical period, "the relation of the sign to its content" no longer appears "guaranteed by the order of things in themselves" (63). What Foucault calls "general grammar" arose to explain that relation, as well as ceaselessly to elaborate it. According to general grammar, all wording is propositional, discursive. No matter how far analysis proceeds, how deeply into the chinks and crannies of expression, no matter to what subsidiary articulations of the general grammatical process it is pressed, this classical theory of language still comes upon representation, a nominalizing function, a tendency for the smallest units of grammar to signify in and of themselves. Labial and dental sounds, for instance, were assigned in this theory particular representational values, as if they named and so divided up a certain sector of reality, softness and sharpness respectively (102).

At this level of micro-analysis, general grammar actually anticipated in its specificity the nineteenth-century science of philology that was to overturn its representational premises. And then again, after its own century-long preoccupation with the smallest units of linguistic operation, philology was itself to be turned inside out by the aesthetics of modernism, with its multiplication of esoteric sublexical curiosities. Coming round full circle to the almost occult increments of signification in general grammar, this modernist upheaval revealed in a new key the saturated representational nature of discourse—but now only through its reflexive presentation of language itself as a closed system. If language in its classical understanding was "nothing in itself but an immense rustling of denominations that are overlying one another, contracting into one another, hiding one another, and yet preserving themselves in existence in order to permit the analysis or the composition of the most complex representations" (103), then this general grammar finds its later counterpart in modernist poetic practice. For the latter is a linguistic field equally seeded (and no longer so deeply beneath a discursive surface) with "dormant nomination." During the interim period of nineteenth-century philology, as it anticipates the development of modern linguistics, "such analyses remained, in the literal sense of the word, 'a dead letter'" (103)—assuming the single letter as dead to reference, a mere differential in an arbitrary system. Late in the last century, however, the "enigma of the word" resurfaced, "reemerged in all its density of being, with Mallarmé, Roussel, Leiris, or Ponge" (103). This amounts to a modernist ontology of the syllable, even the single letter: "The idea that, when we destroy words, what is left is neither mere noise nor arbitrary, pure elements, but other words, which when pulverized in turn, will set free still other words—this idea is at once the negative of all the modern sciences of language and the myth in which we now transcribe the most obscure and the most real powers of language" (103). It is precisely this play with the "molecules" of language, this logic of pulverized recombination, that in Chapter 3 we will watch Foucault studying in the work of Roussel. There, language's "immense rustling of denomination" has become, with words no longer the names of anything beyond themselves, merely "that endless murmur in which literature is born" (103). Is and always has been. But, for Foucault, the emphasis is on a verbal production reborn into its reductionist destiny.

For Foucault's purposes, then: Mallarmé, Roussel, Artaud, Ponge, Leiris. For ours: Shakespeare, Milton, Dickens, Joyce, and all those before, between, and since. Even when conceived as a general mode of discourse, the nature of literary writing as signifying system is to be more than ordinarily opaque with respect to the signified, to be thickened, dense, excessive. What constitutes this excess of poetry and fiction is precisely its language, what used to be called its style. This is what we might now call, in light of Foucault's terms, the margin or residuum between the process of discourse and the sequence of verbalism—or, in Barthes's terms, that overflow of signifying beyond signification. As such, it is a supplement, an excess, that is often registered as a textual effect by the contrapuntal tempos of silent reading, where graphic and vocal patterns intersect each other, cross and discompose the text. Phonemic reading, as I am theorizing it here, stakes out the site of that discomposure. What modernism (in Foucault's sense as a new ontology of "letters" and, by extension, phonemes) serves to highlight is no more than what the language of poetry and prose fiction has by definition always allowed: the opacity, the turbidity, the heft and viscosity, the malleable materiality, in short the *thingness* of language. What modernist writing was born to acknowledge, if Foucault is to this extent right, to acknowledge rather than construct, must have been there in textuality all along—or else there would be no linguistic ontology to foreground. In this sense, the theory of modernist literature proposed by Foucault, as by Kristeva, tends to strip such literature of the very theoretical purpose that would constitute it, robbing the metatextual agenda of its own true object: all that, if rather too naively, has come first. This is another way of saying that a history of the literary must be fashioned so that literary language is observed to precede, and hence to necessitate, its own critique by Literature. Otherwise, what happens in Foucault and in Kristeva, as well as in Barthes and Derrida in related ways, is the fetishizing of a revolutionist modernism, a part-object severed from the historical body of textual production and ascribed a postmetaphysical cult value. No sooner are the representational assumptions of earlier textual production demystified than a countermythology of modernism—as itself inaugurating this demystifying move — rises in triumph: a turning point canonized as epochal break.

Back to Bases: A Churn of Phrase

Such skewing predilection for the modern within literary history is matched in its limitations from without, from the extrinsic realm of history at large, by that other current source of indifference to intensive linguistic reading alluded to above: the practice of cultural study under the aegis of a broader historical "poetics." It is certainly true that culture not only produces texts but produces itself in and through texts. Documented, it is itself a web of documents and representations, a con-text. Students of culture will not rest content with its literary products and manifestations, even its written records, seeking out as well its nonlinguistic expressions. This is of course the great critical legacy of semiotics. Too often, however, it comes at the expense of that equally important achievement of structuralist textual analysis: its unprecedented clarity about the "languageness" of the literary document in particular. Even if literature is not to be regarded as a privileged medium of textual production, ranking instead along with trial records, manuals, ledgers, and the rest, nevertheless *language* remains a central and unique instrumentation of culture. In recent paths of academic inquiry, however, what is unique to linguistic signification, as stressed and interrogated in the various projects of literary structuralism and poststructuralism, risks being rather summarily ignored in the name of all that motivates or devolves from texts — often called power, coercion, ideology. Much ground is being lost as the concept of textuality is stretched to cover anything that bears interpretation, a blanket sense of "reading" no more precise in semiotic terms than such a vernacular dead metaphor as "signs of the times." Against this tendency, what would be formalist about a return to textual theory is exactly what would equip it for registering the *forms* of cultural dissemination in both the literary instance and its alternative discursive modes.

In deed as in word, textual *meaning* is participial, progressive, transactive, the operation of signifying process in receipt by a reader. Language asserts as well as exerts itself in the interchange between a given social sphere and any particular text. Particular — and particulate: built up, constructed, even when not, in the literary sense, composed. Obliterating lines of demarcation between literature, other forms of writing, and other "legible" forms, though leveling elitist hierarchies, does no service to the larger project of cultural study. It thinks to win one case (against the hieratic autonomy of literary art) by destroying evidence for another, dismissing or minimizing those "higher" or more "resistant" modes of address upon which the stratified sociolects of a culture depend, its very habits of reception. To cast the recent critical trajectory in terms of early and late Barthes titles, it is as if one indispensable line of investigation has been derailed between *Elements of Semiotics* (1964) and *The Pleasure of the Text* (1975). In between would lie a rigorously linguistic attention to textual semiosis, the paramount sign function of our culture, as the occasion not only of a conceptual but also—at least in the literary instance—of a full sensorial response.

In between, then, is where we read, phonemically. There can be no doubt that, as reading "subjects," we come to a text already crossed (both it and ourselves) by other texts and that in reading we are constructed once more by such a textual intersection, placed in a new and composite subject-position, one that is set by historical, social, political, and ideological coordinates. Nor of course is there any doubt that these texts, coming to us in the first place traversed by other texts, are plotted in their own construction against coordinates historical, social, political, and otherwise ideological. Situating the textual encounter in this way is essential to any fully alert critical enterprise. But what, more precisely, of the *site* of reading, and why? What is gained by intervening between the made text and the cerebral procedure of its reception, between the situated text and the sighted reader? Let us assume again, tentatively, that the body is this site of silent reading, subtending all conception. It is a place not separable from the space of "understanding," though standing under it. Reading builds up the semantic possibility syllable by syllable, even when these syllables are still only phonemic pulsations on the far side of word formation. But why should this level of reading be attended to? Certainly not in order to recover some sensual ontology of music before language. Rather, it offers one way of knowing the specificity of the text, the irreducible fact of that particularized semiosis known as language and maximized in literature. This is a semiosis not only active but interactive, requiring the reader it at the same time positions and defines.

The read text in this sense is so far from a given, from being given to us, so little a product and so much a production, that language itself has offered up a new way of formulating it. An idiom, that is to say, has crept into usage which addresses, by phrasing, a need: a need to see our texts as kinetic, as machines of production. In a reversal of expected subject and object, we are just as likely now to say that "Dickens reads this way to me" as we are to say "I read Dickens this way." We do so in order to assert a textual communication that is not entirely passive (the text as read) but active (the text reading) and even, according to some psychoanalytic models, transactive (the text reading me). Short of the issue raised by this last notion—"Where am I read?" (with its implications for the unconscious as text)—the notion of a text appearing to read *itself* in process only returns us to the question "Where do we read?" It is now seen as a reciprocal consideration. In the text's "reading" one way or another, its reader collaborates in the writing. To answer "where" it is that readers find themselves doing so is once more to determine a site located, because negotiated, between text and reading subject, between the materiality of the text and the subjectivity of the reader – in short, negotiated in and upon the material body of the latter. And negotiated there in language, if not always in words – in language on the generative verge of words, churning, emergent.

To insist that recent approaches to cultural poetics should bear in mind the linguistic basis of those texts (including poems) that are in fact verbal is not to mythologize the hermetic "world" of literature. Such an insistence is not exclusively aesthetic, nor is it intended to ensconce, privilege, or fortify literature against the other productions of language. It seeks their common denominator, but precisely as literature tends to reveal it. Literature thus becomes part of the investigative apparatus of reading theory rather than its highest object. Such a view seeks to guard textuality itself from too sweeping a consideration as mere referential evidence, with no attention to its specific bases in language. What literary writing participates in without claiming as its own, what it points up within the operations of textuality at large, is the way in which linguistic information may also manifest itself as language in formation. What in this sense a text itself *reads,* and is silently overheard to do at the site of our own simultaneous reading, is the structure of the language from which it comes – from which it is heard to appear (indeed, *materialize* is just the word) moment by moment out of the phonic merger of contiguous syllables. To be placed on such hypersensitive alert to language itself by the literary function is certainly to resist the conservative holding actions of traditional stylistics, canon-bound, author-oriented, aesthetically biased, both normative and hierarchical. Among the foreseeable gains to be made by reconceiving the purposes of so-called stylistic study in light of poststructuralist linguistics would not be to recover the shibboleth of "style" and the methodologies of its specification from writer to writer but rather to retrieve the fact of writing itself – and precisely in its inseparability from reading – from amid the welter of cultural "inscriptions" now under scrutiny. This is the salvage operation going forward, under the name of phonemic reading, in the present chapters.

Worddivision

The materiality of such a reading has itself a past, a chronological dimension. We need, therefore, a less exclusionary history of "reading," a historicized semiotics not wholly intrinsic to literary "art," on the one hand, nor extrinsic to "language" as such – the two extreme forms just discussed. Still pending, then, is a historical sense of linguistic textuality as it passes (back and forth) from aesthetic to nonaesthetic registers, as well as back and forth from page to reader. One major turning point for such a historical understanding has already been carefully documented by the archival work on manuscript and reading practices in late antiquity and the early Middle Ages. Recorded in such scholarship is the advent, in effect, of a developing cultural defense mechanism against just the sort of phonemic reading "proposed" here — posited, that is, as inevitable. Reading at the speed of silence came late to the culture of manuscript transmission. There is a famous moment in Augustine's *Confessions* in which the possibility, in our terms, of a "text" apart from recitation first dawned on the young man. Arrived at Milan, Augustine puzzles over Ambrose's "reason" for reading "to himself" in an era when sounding words aloud was the norm — at least outside of the monastic enclaves of scholarship, where, as Marshall McLuhan reminds us, the "medieval monks' reading carrell was indeed a singing booth."[13] Pursuant to such speculation as Augustine's, as it seeks ultimately to define the very nature of consciousness in relation to the body, Cartesian philosophy will arrive well over a millennium later to set the terms of a profoundly influential dichotomy.

All philosophies of language, for instance, are necessarily plunged, to one depth or another, into the mind/body dualism. Notably, for our epoch, the philosophy of Hegel. In remarking on the power of alphabetic, as opposed to hieroglyphic, writing as a facilitator of abstract thinking, Hegel stresses the redundancy of sound to concept once the reasoning process has taken over. Whereas "people unpractised in reading utter aloud what they read in order to catch its meaning in the sound," more adept, more *literate* readers "need not consciously realize" the words on the page "by means of tone." While "the audible (which is in time) and the visible (which is in space), each have their own basis, one no less authoritative than the other," in "alphabetic writing there is only a *single* basis: the two aspects occupy their rightful relation to each other."[14] There is no need, Hegel would assert, to process the visible as audible, to decode it over any more time than a glance requires. Reading to himself, therefore, it would seem that Ambrose had long before divested his mind of an excrescence at the basis of alphabetic writing. An excrescence, an excess, a surplus, a bonus — one which literature, as opposed to other forms of writing, is slow to give up, and thus slows reading to reinstate.

The marginalization of the audible in Western text culture has, so we begin to see with Augustine, a history in its own right, not just a set of cognitive implications. Involved crucially here, within the broader transition from oral to written culture, is the specific history of word units coming into their own as scriptive rather than just vocal entities. Word/division is neither a founding nor an inviolable stance of textuality. Lexical juncture was an oral phenomenon, that is, well before a textual one, as can be seen from the first frontispiece, showing a typical Latin manuscript without marked word breaks.[15] In the resultant mode of reading, text "production" was indeed the act *performed* in reading, performed *upon* an inscription. To speak of this by way of such a theoretical anachronism only highlights what we might call a cognitive reversion incident to poetic language in the subsequent epoch of print rather than early manuscript culture. The diachronic ground gained in the medieval introduction of word division into script is ground always lost again, a grounding giving way, in the synchronic flux of any evocalized reading. Such reading thus generates a kind of metahistorical backsliding from word to word. In encounters with the texts of Shakespeare or Joyce, phonemic reading constitutes at times a relapse to the primitive status of a writing which, as it were, gave the decipherer no break. Phonemic reading—reading as we inevitably read—thus undoes that same economy of scriptive demarcation which writing, in imitation of vocal inflection, was only gradually to develop.

Phonemic reading might thus be said to replay, if not the birth of modern consciousness in something like Hegel's sense of the inward articulation of mind, then the birth of its localized correlative in a private, an inner, an asocial reading. In a written text, as it is augmented and recontoured by silent reading, we descend into the origins of the reading activity as we know it. From late antiquity through the early to late medieval period, the oral processing, if not delivery, of texts eventually metamorphosed into silent reading, with the parallel shift from composition by dictation, or self-dictation, to composition by writing. In the present state of civilization, ontogeny now recapitulates phylogeny, with each child or preliterate reader being tutored in what the culture had once to discover for itself: the liberating pace and privacy of silent reading, as historically facilitated by the innovation of marked lexical borders. Transformed at the same period in the Middle Ages, too, was the representation of reading in the visual arts, its earlier iconography having frequently included the pictorial trope of a dove hovering at the ear of a reader, suggesting audible voicing.[16]

It is hard to overestimate the contribution of textual word division to such historical change. In this light, those cross-lexical slippages actuated, whether intentionally or not, by a later literary writing generate an aural ambiguity that does indeed return writing to the condition of orality without the predetermined inflections of public oratory or private vocalization. Scholarship on the scribal tradition, as a matter of fact, often instances errors of transcription which have the form, if not the force, of poetic transformation. As one would expect, running words together without breaks runs the continuous risk of "assimilative" misreading. Discussing the career of Chrysanthus after his sudden death, one of Petronius's speakers in the *Satyricon* says "Quid habet quod queratur? Ab asse crevit," given by the Loeb translation as "What has he got to grumble at? He started with twopence" (the "as" a basic unit of monetary measure). At a late point in its manuscript history, this speech was anachronistically transformed by a Latin scribe to "Quid habet quod queratur? abbas secrevit,"[17] introducing the specter of a judging, discriminating, or rejecting "abbot" (the scribe's demanding supervisor?) into the pre-Christian context. Whether or not this ecclesiastic imposition on the Roman text is taken as a kind of direct dictation from the scribe's unconscious, its medium is still the shifting phonemic base of language. It is this very basis in the phonetic alphabet—especially given the fact that scribes regularly mumbled the undivided words out loud to aid in differentiating them—which permits the displacements that lead to junctural ambiguity. In the present case, for instance, it was enunciation which no doubt suppressed the initial distinction between a single and a double *b* in the transference from "ab asse" to the rewritten "abb = as se-."

Another "classic" example of scribal error, combined again of ecclesiastic transformation and syllabic malformation, happens to occur later in this same epic by Petronius. A curse is being delivered, a promise of sure vengeance—even "though you may have a gold beard like a god" ("barbam aureum habeas" [chap. 53]); the imprecation continues with a new sentence, "I will bring down the wrath of Athena on you" ("Athana tibi irata"), which a later scribe--mistakenly reading it as the wrath of Satan ("Sathanas")—was able unconsciously to co-opt for a Christian context. This misprision may have occurred, commentary suggests, because of the preceding *s* at the end of the "habeas," inducing the "dittography" of a false liaison.[18] This error—as literal *slip*—thus results from what I am equally inclined to call the *dittophony* of aural (in this case presumably vocal as well) text production. The point is finally that even when word breaks were introduced into the manuscript tradition and reading went internal, its operations under cover of silence, there remains a sense in which private text production is always a response to writing as "interpreted" by voicing. Writing is received first by the retina and then "copied," reconstituted as language, along the palpable surfaces of the vocal apparatus, however much inhibited by silence—and well before any secondary graphic recording that might follow. Reading is thus a transcoding, if not a transcription, of the graphic into the alphabetic, the scriptive into the morphophonemic—and all the while, of course, the linear into the syntagmatic. By speaking out loud in order to facilitate his graphic replications, the scribe merely ritualizes that detour through "reproduction" at the root of all reading.

In view of the unsteady link between the phonotext and its graphic determinants, the scribal epoch and the post-Guttenberg computer age enjoy at least one point of near—and illustrative—convergence. Those collaborative slips of eye and ear in conjoint dictation to the confounded pen of a scribe find perhaps their closest equivalent – across the many centuries since word division was introduced into textual culture – in the working interplay between cursor and space bar in the electronic operations of so-called word processing. Without the typewriter's mechanical interposition of the impressed page between the moment of input and the legible text, the fluid "screen" of one's thoughts is open to continual and virtually instantaneous self-revision. What we see on the computer's display panel is a cursor speeding along just fractionally ahead of the words we think – and think we are finished with. Precisely because such textual production is more completely at our "disposal" than any set of typed lines, its momentum remains at the perpetual mercy of a spacing that can lop and fob off a stray grapheme, make a word by breaking another, or, for instance, where "a void" is meant, "avoid" it by nudging forward the gap. In continual play is the cursor as "pace bar" sparring with a space bar for the disposition of the text. Letter by letter, the incremental articulation of words in syntagmatic sequence can, therefore, in their electronic manifestation, activate a felt relativism of word division that bears closest comparison, outside of technology, to the work of the inner ear in reading – for which of course "word processing" might also serve as another name.

To summarize these curious intersections of philology, technology, and the physiology of reception: in the modern encounter with texts, to read phonemically is to be reminded of the historical "necessity" of word breaks by the momentary chaos of their suspension or displacement. In this sense, the contingencies of computer "writing" can serve to visualize, precisely because they do not stabilize, the fluxions of such reading – of reading as such. With the history of word division in mind, to evocalize a text is therefore to travel a major cultural advance in reverse, and to do so in the private space, the lag or slack, between the scripted demarcations of a text and its aural processing. The perpetual risk of ambiguity being introduced into the system, however, since it would not be scriptive, hence visible, does not, as it did for the medieval scribe, so much require a deceleration in reading speed as incur an inevitable oscillation in the read field of wordplay.

Oscillation: another word, at times, for disturbance, dysfunction. From Hegel's phenomenology of mind to this somatic phenomenality of reading is a leap for which a quintessentially modernist passage from Virginia Woolf should provide some mediating intuition. With its unique struggle of mind against body, sickbed reading (even to oneself) struck Woolf as a rather astonishing reversion to the temporality of sound production, a dis-ease of the signifier – in other terms, a rematerialization of Hegel's "two aspects," aural and visual, as no longer a unified "basis." Sickness, for Woolf, rediscovers the invalidation of writing's solely graphic stratum. In yielding to the phonic grip of poetry, Woolf is transgressing a latter-day Hegelian law of literacy that will be formulated at its most rigid a little more than a decade later, in Wellek and Warren's *Theory of Literature,* whose authors dismiss as "absurd" any "behavioristic" attempts to deny what "all experience shows," namely, that "unless we are almost illiterate . . . we grasp printed words as wholes without breaking them up into sequences of phonemes and thus do not pronounce them even silently."[19] Of this supposed (and, for her, pernicious) norm, illness temporarily cures Woolf. By a calculated ironic reversal, she writes of "health" as if it played the role of foreign invader in her psychopathology of silent reading: "In health meaning has encroached upon sound. Our intelligence dominates over our senses. But in illness, with the police off duty, we creep beneath some obscure poem by Mallarmé or Donne"—those two modernists?—and the meaning, when it finally comes, "is all the richer for having come to us sensually first."[20] The Romantic valorizing of creativity as neurosis, of art as pathology, is enshrined once again at the center of a "modernist" aesthetic, but here as a manifesto for reading, not writing. Woolf moves from textuality to reception in order to speak about a troubling of sense by sensuality. In this fine madness of a reading at once debilitated and hypersensitized, phonology obtrudes upon script, delays the denotative by the delirious, keeps meaning at bay. It thereby induces a poetically restorative encroachment of sound upon cerebration. In fact, it does just what Barthes hopes for from textual "listening": it lets the forces of *signifying* out from under the watchful eye of signification. With the anti-body, so to speak, of silent textual processing no longer immunizing the mind against letters as the signs of sounds as well as of semic elements, reading finally for Woolf, and in more than the ordinary way, makes sense: aural before logical sense. What Saint Ambrose may have thought to escape, what Hegel theorized into subordination, Woolf turns round to embrace—and at her desk as well as upon her sickbed.

Idiom once again has it right, especially for literary texts: silent reading is not inactive or undirected: I read *to myself.* When John Russell, in *Style in Modern British Fiction,* attempts to expose the excesses of Stanley Fish's brand of "affective" or "reader-response" stylistics, he drives Fish's premises to what he considers their reductio ad absurdum: "Take his criticism to its ultimate application, that is, to the experiencing of *syllables* while one reads, and it will be seen to be overstated. The very attentiveness the mind gives to words will be to *portions* of words chiefly."[21] Yet this "ultimate application" of a response theory, in its very inevitability, is just what the present study is after. We will be examining the combined somatic and cerebral "affect" generated in the reader by the exertion of one syllable or phoneme upon another at its border. With the eye as "cursor" and the ear as "space bar," now making space, now barring it, such is the affectivity of writing occasioned but not contained by script. It invites an "affective stylistics" that—far more palpably than Fish ever intended by the title of his influential essay—does indeed locate "literature in the reader."[22] It is situated there, in me, as a linguistic fact of phonetic writing under the sway of inflection, of "phrasing" in the musical sense. And it is there in me as I am present to its meaning: dispersively, with no grounds for a totalizing integration. In breaking with the verbal "icon" of the New Critical enterprise, and in replacing it with a very different kind of kinetic "artifact," the magnitude of Fish's departure has to do with our own uprooting as readers. To process a text at full engagement may well be claimed "to use it up" (137), in the sense that its whole purpose is eductive: "It gets *you* (not any sustained argument) to the next point. . . . It is thus a *self-consuming artifact*" (137). At a deeper, because also more superficial, level than Fish explores, however, such an artifact "consumes" the readerly "self" as well—and in both senses: preoccupies and exhausts me, drawing me so far into the text, even while it is all surface from the start, and leading me on and astray so blatantly, that there is no stable position left from which an implied I can be said to *have been reading* all along. Literature thus takes (its) place "in" the reader to the exclusion of the existential "self," doing so—at the most rudimentary level of psycholinguistic operation—through the tremble and blend of what could well be called "affective phonemics."

Beyond a Stylist's Tics

"Style may be a *continued* solecism," Geoffrey Hartman has written.[23] For the purposes of the present investigations, however, style is less a continuous transgression than the continuous possibility of regression. Literary language often goes forward by marking the perpetual danger of a collapse back from structure into origins: into phonic and graphic bases together—or no longer together, which is more to the point. Literary textuality, when self-consciously foregrounding the relation of literature to language, may be read—which is a way of defining a certain kind of reading as well—as the continual confrontation, within writing, of the phonic and the graphic. A confrontation variously elastic or implacable, placid or explosive. At this point a graduated formulation is in order, one which should explain why so much of what follows may seem preoccupied with semantic denotation, with referential activity, however much carried out in the name of phonological analysis. For this is exactly where the anarchic possibilities of phonemic reading encounter directly, only to diverge from, a more familiar stylistics of motivated and thematized authorial effects. A threefold understanding, then: If (1) speech is the coordination of noise into articulate utterance, and (2) poetic language is understood to be a recovery in part of the acoustic aspect—

or a submission to the acoustic resistance – within the referential process, then (3) style as deviation, style as the drawing (forth, out) of language beyond regular limits, may be reconceived in one of its major aspects as the continually returning *challenge* of sound to sense.

Such a challenge is posed most directly not through the irruptions of musicality into meaning, since this is merely one classic reckoning of the poetic function in general. The challenge is triggered instead by the dragging of meaning back toward its source in a dispersion of phonetic material awaiting articulation. Significance at work, with its saliencies and evasions, its foregroundings and conversions, yields place to signifying. The pulse of language itself is thus heard beneath utterance, heard bringing itself to utterance. This sense of a regressive rather than transgressive style, this whole logic of textuality, immediately points up the denotative as well as the acoustic issues at stake. Hence the need (well before any thematized stylistics sets in) for a partly semantic surveillance of phonic modulation. Textuality submits to attention in this vein as the continual churn of wording beneath and between the chain of words, the rumble of utterance as it passes in and out of possibility, of potentiation. Where the first phase of formalism was concerned with the "roughening" – the estrangement or alienation – induced by style upon discourse, the microlinguistic attentions of this book will treat the narrower abrasions of language against itself. Whereas ordinary stylistics concerns the difference between what is said and what might alternatively have been expressed, the kind of aural reading undertaken here operates within the invisible differential between what is said and what is otherwise said. So it is that lexemes are not always taken at their word.

In this sense, phonemic reading moves beyond – or behind – "style" altogether. Its concern is more with linguistic accident than with aesthetic craft, the lottery of letters and sounds as they pour in and out of lexical molds. When segmentation no longer holds firm, a trans-segmental – by elision: trans(s)egmental: hence, transegmental – skid in either direction may occur to the inner ear in the blink of an eye, as we saw with "*silent*=*s*-(s)peaking." Phonemic reading in these pages will zero in on such effects as they zero out letters and breaks by turn, in a fluctuation of juncture that can never, by definition, be prescriptive. Even if we had external evidence that a poet like Tennyson calculated such a textual ambiguity at a given point, its reading effect would still fall under the category of linguistic accident. The conceivably strategic effect is no more certain of reception than is such an irrelevant distraction as this from Tennyson's own preceding line: "And strangely *on* the silence broke." Between the markers of manner and place, there flashes another phantom locative (short for "yonder") which earns not even a momentary foothold in the line's grammatical and contextual sense, even though its passing claim on the inner ear, if not the mind, is hard to deny. By contrast, phonemic reading of the more operable sort is densely overdetermined. Even though it catches textual utterance on the verge of radical dispersion, utterance on the cusp of mumble, it tends to honor both syntactic and semantic constraints – if and where it can.

Countless phonemic strays and filaments wash perpetually across any passage of verse or prose, neither premeditated nor preventable, relentlessly unattended, both irrevocable and at the same time unvocalized. Indeed, it is in the nature of phonemes to surrender all real discreteness to the rippling flow of speech. It is also in the nature of phonemes in a given speech act to blur at their borders, creating there the possibility of more paradigmatic choices than can simultaneously be made. This is what causes a systemic overload, as it were, in the differential process itself. Only when such an overload actively discharges a new morphological option, an alternate syllable or lexeme, does the phonemic *condition* take semantic shape, however momentary and malleable, as an effect in phonemic reading: an evocalization. Again: reading voices, but as a clausal proposition, not a participial phrase. The effect is not, as in Mikhail Bakhtin, a dialogism of voices, a fugal braid, but rather a weft of voicings tucked under each other's edges. These evocalizations are looped or cross-stitched, folded or seamed, across a loose fabric of morphological ambiguity. They inscribe there a dual logic of juncture, a dual logging of enunciatory options that eludes the ordinary purview of stylistic study.

Stylistics is a discipline of long standing, of course; phonemic reading only a hypothetical project of the current study, a hunch, a blueprint of tentative possibilities. But let me speak for a moment about the latter as if it were already established in full acknowledgment of its natural parameters – and thus in clear distinction from that "rival" methodology which it would in fact hope to revive, by revising, from within. Where stylistics operates always in view of the normative, phonemic reading engages the formative. Stylistics is concerned with the lexicon recruited by syntax, words arrayed in sequence; when it takes up the single letter, it is usually only to calibrate a recurrence or symmetry (such as alliteration) deployed to brace or inflect the syntactic structure. With a quite different importance accorded the letter as signifying marker, phonemic reading enters the perpetual dialectic between lexicon and syntax, their mutual tension and erosion. Stylistics studies the language act; phonemic reading intersects the action of lingual formation itself, its increments and transformations: the former is directed at *parole* (the speech act) in progress, the latter at *langue* (the whole structural fund of a given language) in its continuous but shifting provision for utterance. Stylistics is concerned at most with phonological patterns, while phonemic reading takes up their morphological implications, the junctural overlaps and detachments that both make and undo words. Stylistics in this sense examines surface structure; phonemic reading overhears its dual and often divided basis, the league and leak of acoustic matter delegated from word to word. Stylistics is distributional, phonemic reading differential; the one focused occasionally on phonetic units, the other on phonemes themselves as the fundamental increments of word formation. In stylistics the lexical code usually stays in place and only the message is submitted to examination. In phonemic reading, the lexical code remains perpetually in play. While stylistics might at times consider verse or prose "rhythm," phonemic reading depends upon the very tempo of cognition as it may actually imperil the order of syntactic contiguity. Stylistics is thus aimed at the sequential, while phonemic reading gravitates toward the segmental. Whereas stylistics tends in this way to establish and certify itself as a branch of poetics, phonemic reading emerges more as a subdiscipline of linguistics. At issue, in short, is the errand of meaning versus the errancy and hazard of signifying.

In all this difference from stylistics in response to a perceived spillage of syllables, I am not of course proposing a difference from everyday reading practice so fundamental and confounding that the very notion of reading as regularly understood, of reading as understanding, would become inoperable. *Reading Voices* contemplates a sensory — encroached upon a cognitive — processing of texts whose intermittent inevitability says nothing about the prevalence, feasibility, or likely force of its recognition. Reading voices primarily what it is told to by script: this is the commonsense objection to, or stopgap against, phonemic free play. Deviant voicing may occur, yes, but no one would or could in the ordinary sense "read" that way often or for long. One couldn't do so, that is, and still call it reading. Literature disallows it as much as any other textual form, though unlike others, literature may program — or if not, may openly tolerate — an occasional phonic counterplay on the near side of chaos. To note this in a critical discussion is thus to offer no alternate way of reading but rather to expose the alternating resistances that get in the way of reading, the energies that reading as we know it must for the most part override, counting as it does, as it must, on all the deafness one can muster across the stroboscopic — hence also strobophonic — flutter of textual sequencing.

Operating the Phonotext

In the work of Barthes and Kristeva, prominently, the understanding of a "text" is based on a model of production rather than communication. A text is seen to actualize its semiotic operations by the manifestation of "significance" through a linear and discursive succession of words: by the conversion, that is, of "genotext" into "phenotext," of some already sub-"textualized" (rather than intentionalist) "conception" into the surface phenomena of its lexical and syntactical realization. Working within the model of produced textuality as well, this book will consider that dimension of the phenotext which is regularly ignored in discussions of the phenomenality of reading. Ignored, no doubt, because it seems to open a less direct access from surface features to the foundational genotext — but ignored at some cost to a materialist apprehension of textuality's dual "phenomena." This underestimated dimension of textuality is what I will be calling the "phonotext," that articulatory stream which the interruption of script at lexical borders never quite renders silent, at least within a single syntactic period broken by no full pauses. This phonotextuality is inherent, it bears repeating, in the very nature of so-called phonetic writing. In alphabetic language, the "glyphs" are not of course pictograms but rather the indication (rather than transcription) of acoustic (though not vocal) signifiers; they are phonetic marks that become phonemic in a given language, as we have seen, only when they are lexically "relevant," when they mark "distinctive" or "pertinent" features in the construction of morphemes. Only such linguistically functional differences between sounds, such phonemic *values,* are engaged when reading operates at the level of — and so in the transitive sense may be said directly to operate — the momentum of the phonotext.

Everything here depends on silent pronunciation, on "endophony," even in the unspoken registration of a written text. This is just where phonemic reading comes in, where quite literally it intervenes. The silent sounding of a text of course often matches exactly, but often at other points crosses athwart, the lexical track of the inscribed text. As opposed to the "graphotext," what I am isolating under the name of the phonotext has precisely that degree of independence from the scriptive aspect of writing which allows for the kinetic, wavering tensions of phonemic reading — especially in a language of such orthographic irregularities as English. By contrast, one can imagine a purely graphic equivalent to phonemic drift that would carry no phenomenal charge — that would simply not be engaged by silent or sounded reading. "Though ostlers are long-lived, they must one day give up the ghost," for example, yields up no transegmental "ou*gh ost*" of its own. The single phoneme of "ough" — /o/ — does not disintegrate in reading — nor, if it did, would the short *o* of "ostlers" provide the needed vowel for the monosyllabic third term in question. In normal reading, that is, only such effects emerge as can be manifested by the slippery interdependence of phonemes and graphemes, not by their radical divorce. The phonotext is thus a materialized part of the phenotext, accessible only in phonemic reading.

It is within the activity — and activation — of phonemic reading that the exemplary case of the transegmental drift comes into play: exemplary because exposing most often and most clearly that unstable partition between lexemes which the blank between graphemes would attempt to secure. In Derridean grammatology, to be investigated further in Chapter 3, it is this blank that is meant to serve as the irrefutable proof that meaning is carried, even in speech, by the graphic (or "grammic") rather than phonic signifier. Without confuting in practice this theoretical claim, the read phonotext of any written "utterance" (still an entirely dead metaphor) nevertheless does move, always in motion as it is, to contest the articulatory reign of the blank, to render word division unreliable, contingent, dispersive. Generated only by the latent musculature of silent enunciation, the phonotext, then, is the general field of this study. Which is a way of saying that the subject of these chapters (the transegmental drift) is only part of its project (phonemic reading). Such a project can best begin by convoking earlier studies in textual "audition" and intertextual variants. Chapter 1 will therefore bring into dialogue perhaps the most suggestive experiment to date in phonologically oriented reading, the "microstylistics" of Geoffrey Hartman, with both the more sustained theoretical work of Michael Riffaterre in the semiotics of poetry and the less systematic investigations of Christopher Ricks into the impinging alternatives that inflect a line by their very exclusion as "anti-puns." Where Riffaterre is interested in the semic displacements by which a text's produced "significance" (as phenotext) is generated over and above its root "meaning" (as genotext), Hartman and Ricks confront at often closer range the manner in which an indeterminate signifying force underlies, and at times surfaces within, the syntax of a textual succession, obtruding lexical alternatives to the graphic text. Once this approach is extended further yet into the realm of phonemic alternatives subtending even lexical sense, the premises of their work will contribute directly to, and from different perspectives help to clarify, the possibilities of phonemic reading.

At various points in the research for this project, I tended to think of the particular effect under scrutiny, the transegmental ambiguity or drift, as a kind of "styleme," the smallest measurable unit of "style" (very loosely defined), a feature which would, to be sure, cause no few problems for the procedures of traditional stylistics. But given that style is itself unquantifiable, the very idea of a stylemic "unit" seemed to falsify the differential operations in question. The idea of a "styleme" simply did not claim the same status as, say, a "phoneme." Factor in reading rather than increment in writing, relation rather than component, the transegmental *effect* studied here is not quite a minim, even a quantum, but rather, again, an oscillation: a flickering instance of the phonotext at odds with the written manifestation of the phenotext. My concentration upon just such a narrowly deliminated (and liminal) function as transegmental slippage within the whole field of phonotextual effects—one among many, even as it provides their exemplary "border case" (where one word abuts and deforms another)—is meant, I repeat, by way of hypothesis. The sense to be tested is that phonemic reading can serve to read that moment of strain and give in a text when style is reduced to more rudimentary and still fluctuant processes of word formation.

Back again to Freud's example. It is the nature of a portmanteau like "alcoholidays" that its morphemic transgressions get recuperated by the logic of lexical coinage. The phenotext here is a word, but the genotext is implicitly a syntactic breakdown: in terms of transformational/generative grammar, a lexical collision at the level of "deep structure." This verbal invention thus derives from a dreamlike condensation or elision of "alcohol(ic) holidays" that flouts etymology to create not a shared syllable, not a lexical integer as unit, so much as a morphemic oscillation. At the level of the phonotext, another way to account for the portmanteau conflation of lexemes is to speak of a wavering displacement of one syllable by its double, a wavering that takes place— instates its displacement, that is—as a clear-cut superimposition of common morphemic elements. This of course is apparent at the level of the written as well as the phonic text, which is why the cut (and paste) is so clear. Unlike such homophonic puns as "holy" and "wholly," say, the reciprocal elision in Freud's "hol" from one lexeme or the other by simultaneous turn is a visible doubling up as well as a phonic multiplication. Its interest for phonemic reading, however, is its status as a mutual overlapping rather than a fixed span of overlap. In standard homophony, the phonotext "says" exactly twice as much as the scriptive level of the phenotext. By contrast, in the visible elision of a portmanteau, the pure doubleness is dilated to a morphophonemic biplay. The same is true of the more specialized case yet, the transegmental drift, even though its effect is never visible or clear-cut—never clear to the unaided eye in its lexical recutting—but available only to phonemic reading. The transegmental drift can thus be read as a cross-lexical homophony that shifts the very lexical boundaries upon which it depends, effecting condensation only by a displacement of the gap, operating with all the alogicalities and covert agendas of the unconscious. Such lexical drifting is activated only by a homophonic pun on silence itself, a double reading of the gap.

In this way, phonemic reading attends in general the slack between morphemic and sheer graphic structure: the play between. Its elusive limit case, the transegmental drift—the cutting edge, as it were, of the phonotext—is the more narrowly read crisis of lexical boundary in which paradigmatic alternatives for a morphemic unit intrude phonemically upon the read text through the contamination of adjacency. The transegmental drift defies the scripted, the visible, the graphemic form of words in sequence, defies especially their constitutive dependence on inscribed gaps, the very logic of junctural breaks.

This drift of the phonotext is therefore, as we have seen, not a component but an exponential interplay, less a microsegment than a differential segue, part one word, part the next. Such drifting is generated by diction under read duress from syntax, but in a way that puts syntax itself at risk. It undercuts the spaced succession of words by cutting across them at an angle oblique to inscription, generating in the phonotext an ambiguously inflected contiguity, severing and assimilative at once. Whereas traditional stylistics is the study of words (or sometimes, say, "rhyming" syllables) in sequence, phonemic reading acknowledges an in(ter)dependence, and hence potential discrepancy, between two parallel textual sequences: the march of script and the flow of unsounded voicing. The liminal case of transegmental drifting mobilizes this discrepancy as a lexical fluctuation, a junctural strain by which morphemes are not just neatly reconceived ("alco*hol*idays") but radically destabilized ("silen*ce/ts*peaking) by phonemic uncertainty. Whereas the smallest measure of style is the verbal *option,* the irreducible crux of phonemic reading is an *alternation* still in process as our eyes move across the text. In the extreme case of a transegmental slippage, this differential play is realized — both senses — as a problematic *tension.* The conjoint foundation of a text in phonemes and graphemes becomes instead a reciprocal con-founding of that very wording toward which they are meant to collaborate, a "graphonic" contrariness.

As this transpires, signifying falls between the cracks of wording. Null values are invaded by full, while adjacent ones are invalidated in their turn. Such is the contestation of style at its inner horizon, an affront by language itself at the bedrock of lexical segmentation. The transegmental drift is not an irruption of discourse into language, one traditional hallmark of style, but rather the breakthrough — through vanishing breaks — of linguistic materiality into style itself. The blanks that make wording possible are processed instead as a sequential mirage that dissipates into new mergers. Some very broad apprehensions (in every sense) may accrue to the narrowness of such attention. Acknowledging in this manner a reading eccentric to writing may finally provide one of the most convincing ways to localize the no longer metaphysical but no less mythologized status of writing, as a crisis of the decentered subject, in the work of Blanchot, Barthes, Derrida, Lacan, Kristeva, Deleuze, and others. In a melodramatic (often little more than metaphoric) scenario, writing in this way becomes the imputed emptying out of identity always incident to inscription, a traumatic alterity. It becomes indeed that proto-schizoid alienation from the presence of self to oneself necessitated by being presented — by representation — in language. Writing is thus variously the site (place) or scene (enactment) of otherness, dispersal, dis-integrity, annihilation: the permanent overthrow of the sovereign self, the "thanatopraxis" of revolutionary self-execution, the groundless skid of metonymic desire in an unconsciousness bereft of signifieds for its signifying desire, and so on. The emphasis is always on writing, on the letter, on script and its determinant blanks. Instead of the blank as inscribed void, a fatal hole in continuity, however, phonemic reading would give a different weight, a differential force, to the blank, one all the more subversive for being less figurative, more actively linguistic. The work of this book is thus to specify further many of the contentions of po*stst*ructuralist thought—as they come to be constellated around just such a graphonic fold as that reciprocal assimilation of the doubled *st* sound in the word itself.

Consider again the death of the subject in our revised sense of the "self-consuming artifact," that self-effacing fact of verbal art. The supposed neutral simulacrum of self, of the "I" who speaks, that sign rather than vestige both instituted and constituted by writing, that evacuated trace of identity, finds the best justification for its hyperbolical treatment as the lethal instantiation of nonidentity in the fact (actualized only by reading, not by script alone) of writing's own internal decenteredness, its difference from itself in process. This is a difference, often a morphemic deferral, produced by precisely that bivalent momentum of the phenotext, graphic and phonic at once, which can at any time materialize as a graphonic friction, a dyslocution. It is one thing to recognize that writing never says what one means. It is quite another to know that you can never be there where it does its saying. It is still another (perhaps even more actively disruptive) thing for a text not to say what it says, to be at odds with its own processes from within the logic of wording itself. Here may be the most powerful apparition of the unconscious in its full threat to reason and ego. In such a phantasmal mélange, words take shape by stealing it. Nothing hones to the expected efficiency of the communicative will. The most obvious identity crisis figured forth by writing is in this sense the lack of identity between its own material co-presences, the friction of phonemic against letteral articulation. In this sense to read (*lire*) could well appear to rescind the presumption of a coherent signifying subject (*abolir*) by abrogating the very rule of diction. Reading along a written sequence could thus sweep away the bracketing gaps that hold the lexeme in place, abolishing the tyranny of the blank by emancipating the stream of phonic continuity that is ordinarily regimented by the halting system of script: in a word, inter-dicting the law of the letter. In this sense, at least, the relation of the phonotext to the graphic stratum of signification—the relation of our reading to what we think we read—bears comparison with the workings of the unconscious, fluid, diffusive, perverse, beneath the discipline of conscious expression. With preternatural directness, the phonemic enactment of a text audits the voice of the other. Reading always with an alien ear, it brings the alien near.

This verbal *stream* in which otherness mutters to us is of course Virginia Woolf's experimental trademark. It is related to that dis-ease of reading in which, no longer policed by script, the sounds of language return again, encroaching on vocalization. Once more, then: reading voices. Wellek and Warren notwithstanding, countless silent readers of literary texts since Ambrose (and even well before) must have known this, must have heard it for themselves. Woolf's illness, like her art, simply takes this awareness to a certain limit in English writing. On the *other* side of which, though arrived before her according to a different agenda, glimmers the polyglossolalia of James Joyce. Past the early phase of the Joycean "revolution" and on toward the feminist bearings of Woolf's studied and heroic ill-literacy, as a final stand against the gender-straitened body of the positioned reader, this book of readings theorized — and of theorized reading — now makes its way. The support it gains not only from precursors at the intersection of literature, linguistics, and psychoanalysis but from moments of revisionary verbal responsiveness in practical criticism cannot be missed. Nor is it unencouraging to find that, in his role as poet rather than critic, one of our most astute and nuanced readers of acoustic play in English verse has just last year in the *New York Review of Books* (2 February 1989) published "An Old Counting-Game" poem in which numerals are sequentially deconstructed by way of transegmental phonemic junctures. That John Hollander should sound more like Lacan than like a mathematician in his assimilative biplay — his lexical as well as lineal enjambment — "Three: / The Real, the Unreal, and their dreamer, Me" is no more surprising than that he should be seeming to speak of alphabetic integers themselves in "Five: / Fie, vain, literal digits!" Such is the phonotext's ludic calculus of semantic transformation, otherwise its restless dreamwork of morphemic elision and dilation.

The textual evidence to follow is arranged in a graduated and interpenetrating relation with the theory that both grows from such examples and calls for more in clarification. Chapter 1 begins with a reading of a Shakespearean sonnet designed to contrast and extend a classic instance of New Critical methodology with approaches drawn alternately from late formalism and poststructuralism. Once having developed a vocabulary of intensive reading freed from the authorial orientation of New Critical stylistics, the chapter moves to apply its "phonemics" of the text to *Hamlet*. In turning from a sonnet to a stage play, the emphasis shifts from silent reading, of course, to a virtual prompt text for dramatic vocalization and, hence, to the different effects permissible within the range of such phonemic ambiguities as elision and liaison. At the same time, sonnet and play together offer a kind of proof text for our traditional idea of literary reading (or theatrical reception, for that matter), with its verbal expectations of kinetic variety, ambiguity, phonic density, and so on. Building on the Shakespearean text (whether privately read or publicly intoned) as a touchstone of literary signifying, Chapter 2, on rhyme, moves to proven phonological territory in order to isolate a phonemic widening of the rhyming unit — as an exemplary case of lexical slippage in the written text. The way is then prepared for the theoretical overview of Chapter 3, in which the divergent claims of such writers on language as Saussure, Jakobson, Jespersen, Derrida, Lacan, Kristeva, Barthes, Foucault, and Lucette Finas are weighed and negotiated under pressure of the evidence so far amassed about script's vocalic subtext. This forum on the graphic versus the phonic dimension of textuality paves the way in turn for the second phase of this study: a wide-ranging consideration of "ove(r-r)eading"—the reading of two words superimposed over each other at their adjacent edges — in the whole tradition of English poetry and prose fiction. Following a survey of such effects in verse from Donne to Dylan Thomas (Chapter 4), a comparable experiment is performed (Chapter 5) on three centuries of English fiction from Sterne through Dickens to Lawrence, including related material on homophonic wordplay in the Victorian popular press. This investigation of both dialogue and description in novels and their punning intertexts is designed to discover how much leverage on narrative prose can be achieved by the linguistic orientation of phonemic reading—before confronting, that is, the metalinguistic prose poetry of James Joyce (Chapter 6) and the very different phonemic modulations of Virginia Woolf's verbal wavelengths (Chapter 7). Throughout both parts of this book, on as many fronts and with as much focus as possible, the effort is to give theory back to literature by giving literature back to language.

I

PRONOUNCED DEFECTS
The Transegmental Drift

1   "To Hear With Eyes"

Shakespeare as Proof Text

O O O O that Shakespeherian Rag—
   T. S. Eliot, *The Waste Land*[1]

The first phase of my subject is that authorial idiolect, or "style," which has come to be the measure of literary language in English. Acoustically textured to the point of distraction, it is a verbal medium full of a phonemic fury of sound signifying not nothing—but signifying more energetically than any signified requires. This is a sense of the commanding "Shakespeherian Rag" that haunts all our literary writing and reading. When Eliot in *The Waste Land* spells out, stretches out, the incantatory Bardic name, he does so without the punning "hear" and "ear" which are there, nonetheless, to be read. But how read? The answer is obvious enough to elude most literary study: we listen while we read. Who can doubt it? How, though, to prove it? This chapter will attempt in some measure to close the distance between credence and demonstration.

It remains a humanist truism that literature speaks to us. The work of deconstruction might be understood to have resurrected the dead metaphor of such a notion in order to lay its ghost for good. Literature has no voice. It is text, not talk. But what is left in the wake of this widely successful campaign against phonocentrism? Let's take an extreme case. Who would deny that the rest of us read to ourselves differently from the case of a sighted reader deaf from birth? What then is it that we think we hear, or hear in thinking? Not the author's voice, granted. Yet if literature cannot be fairly said to speak to us, perhaps it speaks *through* us. Our being there in front of it is the precondition not of its existence but of its function. Or another way of putting our relation to a text: we speak to it, silently, in the loose sense of moving to a beat. A less extreme case. Imagine a cultural context within the use and dissemination of the English language in which the written words of that language, while referring to the same known entities or concepts as they do now for us, are nonetheless quite consistently different in aural quality. Easily done, since this

●   37

is of course the case with Elizabethan pronunciation. Readers silently ven-
triloquize a text according to the linguistic conventions of their time. To
borrow from Shakespeare's sonnet 23, the role of the reader is "to hear with
eyes." Texts are in this sense not begotten but made, produced in reception.
Such is the auditory leeway opened precisely by the lack of literature's *inherent*
voice. This chapter will eventually close in on a very particular and particularly eccentric effect, the transegmental drift: product of a phonemic operation off-center from the graphic signifier that occasions it. To attend to such
phonic drifting is to track the smallest node, in effect, of a deconstructed
writing's so-called difference from itself.

A "Writerly" Bard?

In Shakespeare's sonnet 15, the speaker, after a sustained contemplation of
transience in its organic aspects, summons a specular image, though entirely
undetailed, of his beloved young man, promising him, or it (his image), the
immutability otherwise stolen from the youth, from any and all youth, by the
violence of time: an "engrafting" of new vitality through poetry. I choose this
sonnet because it happens to have most of an entire chapter devoted to it, the
last and summary chapter, in Stephen Booth's *Essay on Shakespeare's Sonnets*
and to be thoroughly and expertly glossed in Booth's subsequent edition of the
sonnets. [2] These commentaries constitute a pair of interpretive texts (by any
other name) that together mark a kind of watershed in late New Critical
readings of our most read poet — and of poetry in general. To begin with, the
lyric in question:

> When I consider everything that grows
> Holds in perfection but a little moment,
> That this huge stage presenteth nought but shows
> Whereon the stars in secret influence comment;
> When I perceive that men as plants increase,
> Cheered and checked ev'n by the selfsame sky,
> Vaunt in their youthful sap, at height decrease,
> And wear their brave state out of memory;
> Then the conceit of this inconstant stay
> Sets you most rich in youth before my sight,
> Where wasteful time debateth with decay
> To change your day of youth to sullied night;
>> And all in war with time for love of you,
>> As he takes from you, I engraft you new.

Booth's compressed editorial gloss on the syntactic duplicity of the opening
lines is more expansively investigated in his *Essay*. The note in his edition of
the sonnets — to the effect that "under pressure of syntactical necessities

introduced by *Holds,* a simple subject-verb-object construction comes to be understood as if it had been 'When I consider *that* everything that grows'" (*SS,* 155)—is enlarged upon in the *Essay* in view of its reading effect, the dynamics of its processing. Shortly after Stanley Fish argues in *Surprised by Sin* for a cognizance of similar crossed signals in readerly responses to Milton,[3] Booth writes that this syntactic self-revision "requires an easy but total reconstitution of the reader's conception of the kind of sentence he is reading" (*ESS,* 181). There is, however, something more cannily to the point—or is it uncannily?—in Booth's own compression of this issue in his edition: again, "comes to be understood as if it had been." It wasn't, it only *seems* to have been; the first meaning cannot rest easy, but its necessary revision, in light of our already elapsed experience of the first line, is itself a phantasmal rewriting. If only implicitly, Booth here parts company from Empson. Though sensitized to "double grammar" in the sonnets, the favored Empsonian mode of analysis, Booth would apparently resist the notion that such vacillating syntax is ever finally "resolved" into stability and coherence. Instead of saying that what seemed to be the sense of the first line turns out not to have been after all, Booth intriguingly suggests that what seems in retrospect to be the reconstituted first line is still only an "as if." Retroaction in reading does not recast the original but only rereads it as it would *have* to have been, but wasn't, in order to permit continuity with the grammar that ensues upon and reroutes it. Rethinking is not revision; the "last word" on a set of lines does not supplant, only subdues, our first impression; what *is* is not necessarily what was.

To unload these implications from Booth's editorial gloss is to appreciate at how narrow and elusive a range he can detect what he has claimed in his earlier *Essay* about such snags in the "syntactic fabric" of the sonnet: the fact that they "do not merely describe inconstancy but evoke a real sense of inconstancy from a real experience of it" (*ESS,* 181). This too is an unusually suggestive phrasing, at least from the hindsight of contemporary discussion. Such double grammar in the sonnets does not mime inconstancy, or even thematize it, but *performs* it autonomously in the linguistic sphere. At the risk of "double reading" Booth himself—or paraphrasing, that is, from a vantage two decades further along in critical history, what it seems *as if* he meant—it must nevertheless be remarked that the "real sense" of mutability in the lines has little to do with grammar developing a mimetic analogue of transience based on floral and astral prototypes. Rather, the ephemeral *in* language is its primary experience, as "real," as material, as any other. Its evocation is at most homologous with the declared themes of the poem, not subordinate to them. In this latter sense, style does not "answer to" theme—except by enacting its counterpart in words.

Just this line of thought also serves to underwrite Booth's attention to Shakespeare's phonemic and syllabic as well as syntactic play in the sonnets. Pursuing this interest, Booth's approach demonstrates as much congeniality, if not direct allegiance, to the Jakobsonian as to the Empsonian tradition, with the former's more systematic commitment to (Booth's phrase) "phonetic and ideational interplay" (*SS,* 157).[4] Such a commitment is ultimately in the service of that iteration-within-difference which Jakobson has elevated to the very definition of the poetic "function," which thereby "projects the principle of equivalence from the axis of selection into the axis of combination."[5] Words are not just linked by syntax, by combination, but fastened, again, by that "phonic affinity" (among other features) which intersects and inflects the axis of contiguity. One word is selected over another from the paradigm of alternatives not just to fill a space in the grammar of progression but to secure an equivalence (or resemblance) with some other word previously set in place, as in the aurally looped sequence in sonnet 15 likening, as well as linking, "consider" to "conceit" through the intermediary syllabic matter of "perceive." The paradigmatic principle of *comparability* thus invades the syntagmatic chain of combination; equivalence dictates contiguity; sameness overtakes difference; language becomes poetic.[6] Style in this sense is always a particular intersection of the vertical paradigm of available alternatives with the horizontal sequence into which the *decidedly* chosen word will be dropped into position. Plotted by such choices in succession, the poetic is the crossing of the contiguous by the interchangeable.

Working back, like Jakobson, to the binary linguistics of Saussure, Michael Riffaterre's more recent investigations into the language of literature also concentrate on pertinent oppositions as they are spread out across the syntactic line.[7] For Riffaterre, however, equivalences that cannot *simultaneously* be pressed into the logic of sequence still address each other in an oppositional play that could never be fully accounted for by the scrutiny of those surface features regularly studied as "style." In essays collected under the title *Text Production,* Riffaterre demonstrates that it is in fact surface texture's structuring difference from its origin and alternatives, as perceived in the reader's own "production" of the text, that generates what another of his titles identifies not as the "semantics" but as the *Semiotics of Poetry.* In true formalist manner, style is sidelined by questions of *literariness,* itself in Riffaterre a kind of binary alternative to literalness: an avoidance of the explicit by figural displacement. True to semiotics, too, literary textuality is constituted by an array of associations that can be traced only through "signs" of meaning, clues, gestures, vestiges. Rather than searching out, as Saussure did,[8] the anagrammatical displacements of a Latin verse line — dismemberments of sacred or heroic names to be reassembled in the reading — Riffaterre instead looks for more obvious systemic disturbances that foreground the unsaid *as* unsaid, avoided, suppressed. For Riffaterre, "Saussure's stroke of genius . . . was to understand that the text's true center is outside the text and not behind it, hidden away, as victims of the intentional fallacy are fond of thinking" (*TP*, 76). When Riffaterre himself looks beyond rather than behind the text, however, what he finds is a veiled revelation far less encrypted than Saussure's anagrams. He finds a semiosis mobilized without being literalized. Rather than radiating centrifugally from some occulted core, the text is generated from point to point by its variance from a paradoxically external (and unwritten) center.

The relevance of this notion to Booth's edition of the sonnets grows quickly clear. The editor's scrupulous logging of those contemporaneous proverbs and aphorisms that "underlie" Shakespeare's sonnets, for instance, witnesses to an intertextual pressure which Riffaterre would theorize as the semiotically definitive relation of a given sonnet to its decentered matrix. More specifically, this relation is understood by Riffaterre as a semiotic reaction formation variously characterized in terms of denial, avoidance, suppression, conversion, condensation and displacement, all with their openly courted Freudian associations, including especially the return of the repressed. Already generated by the deflection of some received or proverbial formula, then, the text is further "converted" or "expanded" into readable units by local "actualizations" of this clichéd "source."[9] We encounter here the phrased, rather than tacit, semiosis of the *paragram*. "The model I propose for the lexical paragram is thus the expansion of a matrix. Since it is lexical, this expansion occurs in the form of words linked together grammatically, and is not phonetic or graphemic, as in Saussure's paragram" (*TP*, 77). Evident here is Riffaterre's tacit holding action against exactly the kind of phonemic reading which this chapter finds invited by the Shakespearean text—as the clear (if pulsing) signal of its literariness. The phonotext "produced" in this way, as we are to see, occupies a middle ground between the lexical/grammatical sine qua non of Riffaterre's method and the graphemic free association of an anagram. Between full semantic security and syllabic mayhem, then, lies the domain of phonemic reading.

A Riffaterrean take on the opening quatrain of sonnet 15, for example, might read the mentioned "comment" of the stars (their legibility as a sign system) to reveal the whole figural sequence of astrological reference in the text as the expanded variant of the proverbial notion that we *read our destiny in the stars*. Where Booth and others have noted the etymological hint of sidereal or astral observation in the sonnet's first verb, "consider" (from *con-* + *sider-*, *sidus,* star), a Riffaterrean semiotics of the text would take this verb as a "lexical paragram" providing for the astrological matrix its first "model" (the guiding prototype of subsequent actualizations) in the etymological sediment of a single syllabic cluster. Though Riffaterre himself does not very often pursue matters even to the level of the syllable, let alone its constituent phonemes, his method would seem to allow for this in principle. The end of sonnet 15 offers a test case ready to hand.

As the text moves into the monosyllabic tread of the closing couplet, one word stands out. The disyllabic verb "engraft" is a horticultural trope that at the same time marks the sonnet's deepest predication: the power of sonnetizing in and of itself. Booth annotates by paraphrase the likely pun on poetic engraphment: "'As time withers you, I give you new life (by writing about you)'" (*SS*, 158). He goes on to suggest, however, that to become operable the pun needs (intertextual) support from the opening of the next sonnet: "Despite a probable pun on *engraft* . . . and its Greek root *graphein,* 'to write,' . . . a reader presumably does not recognize this first of several traditional claims for the immortalizing power of verse (see sonnets 18 and 19) until the line is glossed by the first quatrain of sonnet 16, which is both logically and syntactically linked with this one." This ensuing quatrain insists that there is "a mightier way" to fight time than with "my barren rhyme," an image whose denial of fructification ("barren") seems to retract what sonnet 15 has proffered with its primary botanical sense of "engraft." It is only the punning double of this phrase, of course, that has instituted the "traditional claims for the immortalizing power of verse" in the first place, those claims which Booth finds suppressed beyond immediate recognition—except through the route of metaphor and its decoding. But the metaphor itself, even if we catch its general application, is not very clearly pointed. The "cutting" by which a graft takes place harkens back in its derivation to the Latin *stylus* on its way to the Greek root for *carve.* Booth is surely right in supposing the line to allude to the "practice of replacing the wasted limbs of old trees with slips that grow to be new boughs" (*SS,* 158). But if this allusion in turn alludes to the speaker's expressed hopes for the marriage and propagation of the young man, then it cannot be the speaker who is to engineer this new grafting of a scion. Not only won't the whole metaphor thereby come to rest where we expect it to, but the apparent transitive grammar of its vehicle is internally unsettled. If the speaker's meaning is that by writing about you I "engraft you new," then this can mean—following Jakobson's treatment of similar ambiguities of the predicate in sonnet 129—either that "I make (by engrafting) you *new* again" (an adjectivalized adverb) or "I graft you *anew*" (an adverbalized adjective). In neither case, however, does the figural logic, as governed by the transitive grammar, come quite clear. Does the speaker mean that I cross something with you, or implant something in you, or attach something to you, or otherwise extend you by means of something—or, if you are the sole direct object of the phrase, that I simply ingraft *you,* however that would come about?

And even in this last case, what could possibly be disclosed as the tenor of that metaphoric vehicle — or of any of the preceding grammatical alternatives, for that matter — except the whole of you in renewal? We are thus thrown back on the verb's punning application, which makes, albeit in its less idiomatic format, more syntactic sense after all. It does so precisely by its near-homophonic collapse of vehicle upon a tenor spelled out at last: the "graft" that is always "graphic" at base. But phonemic too, aurally overdetermined. The closing verb phrase thus manifests climactically in this sonnet — and not, we shall later see, for the first time — that graphonic interplay which will eventually come to dominate this commentary: as a test case for a micro-poetics of style beyond the lexically coded semiotics of poetry. The phrase "I engraft you new" can, in other words, just faintly be *heard,* be "produced" upon the inner ear of the reader (in what might be termed a para*phonic* variant actualized by liaison of the *t* and tacit elision of an unwritten *o*) as the phrase "I engraph t' you new." Or even as "I engraph t(o) you (ə)new." In either of these latter senses, it is an admittedly scripted communication (I write of but also to you) that exposes, in the very name of an atemporal epiphany, the apostrophic form of the entire sonnet as a textual fiction, a writing without any address beyond itself. Yet this is a scriptive fabrication whose confession comes about only through a phonic pulling against the grain of the very graphic lines that have let such an admission slip.

In his generally admiring review of Riffaterre's semiotic methodology, Paul de Man objected mostly to what he saw as a consistent sheltering of description from the deconstructive fact of sheer inscription.[10] This shortcoming is occasioned, on de Man's account, by Riffaterre's failure to attend closely enough to the master tropes of rhetorical analysis: namely, the pervasive *catechresis* (the alogical strain, paradox, or anomaly) of poetic figuration and the *prosopopoeia* ("giving face") that attempts to mask or naturalize it. In view of Shakespeare's explicit thematizing in this sonnet of such a giving (and preserving) of face through a nondescriptive engraphment, through sheer apostrophe, it is further worth noting that de Man bases his tropologically oriented critique of Riffaterre indirectly on Saussure's interest in the Greek root *hypographein* — or "signature" — as an important source for the "hypo-textual" variants of Saussure's inscribed anagrammatic ciphers (30). What de Man objects to in Riffaterre's retreat from such an admitted graphological emphasis is that the resulting method subserves without proper qualification "the determined, stable principle of meaning in its full phenomenological and cognitive sense" (30). But how stable is this principle? The burden of the present discussion is that, in the phenomenality of a text when read, cognition subtly diverges from direct semantic processing; inked letters enunciated to oneself often take thinking by surprise. A stress on inscription may be one corrective to a semiotics of description, but then so, on the other hand, is an emphasis on reception. The path through a text taken even by a resolute tropological reading, deconstructing all stable reference as it goes, will be phenomenologically impeded at every "turn," or troping, by the phonic as well as graphic materiality of the language in process—impeded, in short, by "text production" at the cognitive (if often subliminal) level. The full implications of this in connection with sonnet 15 we must hold for a few pages longer in abeyance.

Beyond Formalisms

For now, we need to expand still further the critical and theoretical context within which the play of phrasal alternatives in poetry can be addressed. We turn from Riffaterre's paragram (including here the "paraphone" as well) to the frequent stylistic investigations of two very different critics. In their divergent vocabularies and allegiances—the one a leading promulgator of poststructuralist theory in America, the other an inveterate British humanist—Geoffrey Hartman and Christopher Ricks each nurture in their work a sense of potentially subversive lexical free play that resembles Riffaterre's "agrammaticality" as the very definition of literariness. In "The Voice of the Shuttle: Language from the Point of View of Literature," an important essay from *Beyond Formalism,* Hartman skirts very near to Riffaterre with his idea of an embedded "seed phrase" bursting in various contortions upon the surface of a poetic line.[11] Like Ricks as well, Hartman is interested in the layered reticulation of a text (in the root sense of a textured fabric) woven upon a "silence" that will not quite stay put. In Ricks, too, this silence is every bit as "volcanic" as Hartman dubs it (342), and from it may erupt at any turn the rejected or dismembered phrases that might, alternatively, have gone to make it up: the matrix as cauldron. In Ricks's collected essays, *The Force of Poetry,* the ground of poetic meaning seethes with pressures upon it that do not quite become presences in it, the shimmering surface of a poetic line alive with tremors from beneath.[12]

　　Hartman's essay, however, is both narrower and broader at once. It proposes a complex interchange between the "microstructures of literature, entities studied by linguists" (341) and the largest narratological issues of mythic plotting. He moves, for instance, from such "cross-eyed" phonetic structures as chiastic alliteration to the fateful double cross of the Oedipus story. At its most provocative, in fact, his essay describes an even larger trajectory, moving from the space *between* syllables and words to that breathing space of "indeterminate middles" between "overspecified ends"

(339) which develops as a kind of structuralist definition of human life as plot. One of Hartman's examples of alliterative chiasmus, among several sound figurations he takes up, is the "famous pun" in *Paradise Lost,* "O Eve in evil hour." What Hartman does not do with this phrasing, this voweling, is instructively continuous with what he does. "To go from 'Eve' to 'evil' is a metaphor on the level of sound" (343), he writes, as if he were directly alluding to Jakobson's notion of echoic substitution in the axis of combination, his "figures of sound." Hartman's gravitation toward a "transformational poetics" of the "zero value" (341) is illustrated here between the bonded phonemic halves of *ev/il(l).* What, this particular sound figure of "etiological distancing" (338) asks us to ask, is the direction of causal descent? Which came first: the evil or its namesake? When Hartman suggests that the power of the line derives from the overtones of derivation itself, "the sense of a third term or matrix, a common root from which both might have sprung" (343), his (unmentioned) overlap with the work of Riffaterre (as well as that of Jakobson) could hardly be more direct. What Riffaterre would advance in answer to Hartman's question about the priority of Eve or evil might well be that the whole conundrum is materialized as the variant of a more overtly formulaic teasing with false etymology. The text is produced in this sense as the paragrammatic dodge of a pat aphorism like "The Eve in all evil," as in the comparable (if commonplace) punning of a bromide like "Woman means woe to man." In any case, it should be clear that Hartman is intrigued to read in such a case the projection of paradigmatic equivalences onto syntactically deployed paronomasia in a manner that certainly calls up the "conversions" and "expansions" of Riffaterre's semiotics.

Beyond this, there is in linguistics a more problematic sense of juncture or "zero value" ambiguously negotiated between words, which Hartman hints at but never pursues directly. Illustrating the "language jam in which we are stuck" (343), which is often enacted in poetry as a jamming at intersections, and drawing on Elizabeth Sewell's linguistically imprecise but suggestive notion of the "soundlook" of words (341), Hartman offers as example of junctural irony the title of Wallace Stevens's "Le Monocle de mon Oncle." Comments Hartman: "Technically defined the difference in sound is a slight distortion of quantity but primarily a matter of what linguists call 'boundary' or 'juncture'—here typographically indicated by 'monocle' dividing into two words, 'mon oncle'" (341). Once again, a poetic test case is generated from, in Jakobson's sense, a metonymic projection of sameness in a paronomastic domino play. Hartman's allusions there to the linguistics of "juncture," however, have an even more direct bearing on the present explorations than do his literary examples. Though none of his quotations is strictly ambiguous in its phonemic boundaries, he tangentially invokes a whole range of debate, as summarized in Kooij's *Ambiguity in Natural Language,* about the functioning of so-called suprasegmental phonemes — namely, pitch, stress, and juncture — to enforce lexical decidability. More so than with a chiming phrasal balance like "monocle" and "mon oncle," the classic problem for phonological "disambiguation" (the problem of telling where one word ends and the next begins) arises with such "minimal pairs" as "an aim" and "a name," "night rate" and "nitrate," "light housekeeper" and "lighthouse keeper" — or, for that matter, our inaugural instance from Austin, "I stink" and "Iced ink."[13] Such a phonic crux has sometimes been addressed not only by the general notion of "suprasegmentals" but by the concept of a sliding phoneme of "zero" value, a so-called zero allophone of internal open juncture (19). It is this linguistic feature to which Hartman may be alluding in his mention of "zero values." For many linguists, however, as Kooij observes, this offers a suspect account, a "fiction" (11) designed to rescue segmental autonomy. In the study of adjusted and suspended junctures, one is advised to recall Jakobson's postulate: "From a strictly articulatory point of view . . . there is no *succession* of sounds. Instead of following one another the sounds overlap."[14] In view of this fact, a purer example of junctural value under poetic pressure, one not requiring a footnoted disclaimer like Hartman's ("I am aware that 'oc' and 'onc' contain a different phoneme"[341]), would have been provided by another cryptic Stevens title, "United Dames of America." In this brief poem about political oratory, the title, in its outrageous homophonic spoof of "United Aims of America," becomes a virtual textbook example of ambiguous juncture in a minimal "pairing" — one phrase written, the other (silently) sounded.

We should now be able to return more alertly yet to the linguistically gauged plight of Eve in the garden, at exactly the point where Hartman himself broke off with her. The "zero value" reinvested with force is not just the lexical cipher at the morphemic boundary between syllables, "Eve" elided with "il(l)." Further, there is the actual liaison in speech that overdetermines both ends of the punning phrase. Given that its second vowel in standard pronunciation is /ə/, "evil" can be heard, by an ambiguous but just plausible fricative decoding at the syllabic juncture, as "Eve-ful(l)," the coined adjective tautologically spelling out the line's slippery pun in a more coherent manner than the nonword compound "Eve-ill." At the same time, the last remaining juncture in the phrase, the unstressed border at "evil/hour," elides its nearly voiceless *h* to form a chiastically voweled close to the phrase: "O Eve in *Evil Our.*" The ear thereby traces, across the sinuous assonant contortion of the very phrase, the dread lineage of contamination leading from that one evil hour to all our woe: a condensation of the poem's whole theme in a single phonemic lapse. Such shadows cast by one letter on its pertinent opposite, its ghostly afterimage, such phantasmal transformations between *v* and *f* for instance, or between *h* and its silent phantom double, would themselves be included, however, in Hartman's hedging analogy drawn from conjectural physics: "You probably feel as impatient with me, and all this talk about zero values, as Bishop Berkeley with Newton's infinitesimals. He called these entities, calculable only by Newton's theory of fluxions, the 'ghosts of departed quantities'" (347). My very slight "impatience," and I assume that of others, comes simply from Hartman's own, his itch to dart away from a further speculation on the linguistic—or call them semiotic—implications of the stylistic intricacies he puts under such intensive scrutiny. More even than his approach is inclined to tally, zero values count.

Larger questions are certainly at play, and at stake, in the structural, psychoanalytic, and philosophical reverberations of Hartman's essay than in any of the twenty papers collected by Ricks in *The Force of Poetry*. Yet neither critic pursues his speculations quite far enough for close readings to open upon a principle of textual generation. Ricks, for once, is almost as near to a delimited but genuine theoretical breakthrough as is Hartman. Indeed, Hartman's use of Berkeley's phrase "ghosts of departed quantities" reads like a paraphrase of Ricks evoking the poetic vanishing act of the "anti-pun." Words, phrases, syntactic understandings are momentarily enrolled only to be annulled by context, "surmised and then ruled out" (101). The phenomenon turns up everywhere in Ricks's essays, on writers from John Gower to Geoffrey Hill, being more or less implicit in his previous stylistic considerations of Milton and Keats as well. With Wordsworth's phrase "fleet waters of a drowning world," for instance, Ricks calls attention to the "anti-pun" on "fleet" as noun. The adjectival form of this monosyllabic "variant" (to recall Riffaterre's term) would, according to Ricks, "be careless or perverse if it were not positively (rather than forgetfully or willfully) setting aside the other sense" (101). He garners his characteristic authorial validation for this by quoting Wordsworth's definition of the poetic temperament as the "'disposition to be affected more than other men by absent things as if they were present'" (100). In what might well be taken as a "semiotics of poetry" capacious enough to embrace such contradictory semantic signals, absent definitions in Ricks's readings hover like ghostly revenants over the text, often with a sense of violent irrelevance. They create at once a linguistic siege and its own resistance.

Though Ricks would never put his case in strict linguistic terms, it is as though binary oppositions from the axis of selection bedevil the syntagmatic axis as phrasal impertinences—and must be staved off. In Robert Lowell, for instance, one semantic sense "gains its territory by fighting off" the invasive double. The denotation that emerges "means intensely by meaning the whole thing including its exclusion," a "phantasmal violence" (271) of "potent absences" and "vigorous spectral combats" (268). Poems "muscular with these ripples of solicited misconstruction," these "warring possibilities" (269), take their part in the "anti-sense" of a "violence-acknowledging non-violence" — a phrase which itself, read (aloud) without the hyphens, aptly enunciates (Ricks leaves us to discover) its own seditious converse. Without for a moment admitting the claims of any tradition of reading other than the line of Empson and Donald Davie, though with a few approving asides about some of Hartman's insights, Ricks is nevertheless very much in phase here with the shared perception in Saussure and Riffaterre that "the text's true center is outside the text." The intertextual variants are generated for him by a tension between legible surface and (Ricks's recurrent word) its indirect "force" of evocation.

Like Riffaterre, too, Ricks tends to minimize the acoustic in his lexical investigations. He is willing to hear a homophonic pun in Gower between "braieth" and "prayeth." And he will homophonically pun himself in assessing Gower's instance of pertinent opposition in the paradigmatic axis as an "air's-breath" difference (10) between plosives. But he does not generally seem alert to the possibility of what I would call the *antiphone* rather than anti-pun, that antiphonal or contrapuntal phantom latching upon lexical units and breaking down their integrity. If a critic were to grant that there is a phonic slippage of this kind inherent in language, an irresolute and disruptive drifting that destabilizes any given constraint upon the bonding of phonemes into words, then that critic would also have to face a fact about (to reverse Hartman's subtitle) literature-from-the-point-of-view-of-language. Such language is in some ways too heterogeneous and dispersive for an author-centered aesthetic like Ricks's, too freakish, eccentric, and insubordinate.

Antiphonemics

Returning to certain remaining effects in Shakespeare's sonnet 15 that depend on phonemic rather than lexical displacements should draw further into the open an important point of convergence between Hartman's and Riffaterre's respective methods. There is, for instance, the acoustic undercurrent that pulls upon the climactic personification of mutability in the poem: "Where wasteful time debateth with decay / To change your day of youth to sullied night." Again we find a brand of double grammar organizing, or disarranging, the line. Booth notes that idiomatic expectations lead us to imagine at first some contest *between* time and decay ("debate *with*" in the sense of "against"), a "false start" that must undergo almost immediate revision when "one realizes that time and decay are obvious allies" (*SS*, 158). Once more we encounter Booth's implicit reader-response criticism, though tied always to manifest linguistic signals in the text. This time Booth leaves the full upheaval of our response unexplored. The shifting ground of prepositional grammar pulls the foundation out from under the very possibility of opposition; in the blink of an eye we are yanked up short by the recognition, foolish to have forgotten even for an instant, that between time and its own process of decay there is no contest at all—that everything in life colludes with decay, which even as a sound pattern brackets and engorges the next line's "day." Moreover, within the vexed and self-corrective phrase "debateth with" is seeded not only a syntactic irony but an additional phonemic insinuation. For there is in fact a larger phonic frame in place here than that which encloses "day" within "decay," namely the encompassing bracket "DEbateth with deCAY." In Hartman's vocabulary this is a "decontraction" of the syllabic terminals that happens to install yet another "etiologic distancing" between the cause (those inevitably conjoined temporal forces) and the effect (doom). The figuration of decay-as-death is so overdetermined that it further generates a virtual ana-grammatic code (graphically in "DEbAteTH with," or again in "DEbAteth wiTH," and phonetically in "DebatETH with" and "DebatEth wiTH"). Over and above this, the genuinely *pronounced* effect, as it were, the one with more "phenomenal" charge, is the antiphonal hint triggered by the segmental detonation of "debaTETH (debaT/DETH)." Attuned to the text in this way, we can also hear another accordion-like play with phonemes that decontracts a matrix phrase and arrays it upon the lexical surface of the line as a paragram, if not quite an anagram this time. Concerning the phrase "the conceit of this inconstant stay," Booth's edition notes that it "functions like an oxymoron." It also may—may in a given reading—operate as a kind of phonemic pleonasm, its last two words standing thus as a paragrammatic decontraction of "incon-stancy." As such, this antiphonal overtone would only foreground by contrast an emphasis on the paradox of a fleeting "stay."

This kind of reading draws on a phonemic patterning evident elsewhere in the sonnet apart from any lexical transformation, though tampering nonethe-less with junctural value. An instance: "Vaunt in their youthful sap, at height decrease." If these words abut in silent enunciation with full phonemic distinction, then their very contrast is thus dramatized. On the other hand, the sort of dental "ambiguity" that permits the hint of "death" in "deba*teth*" operates in this case across the lexical segmentation effected by juncture. The chiastic arc of the whole line would in this sense be replayed, if quickly read, in the phonemic hinge between the noun of apogee and the verb of downgrade. No sooner said than done and gone, in this sense the phonemic matter of "height" might be felt to yield on the instant to the verb of its reversal. As with the season of youth it describes, so might the noun "height" itself provide the first impetus of its own undoing. Either way, articulated in full contrast or nudged toward elision, the phrasing could well precipitate a phonemic reading thematically cued by the logic of antinomy within evanescence.

Since such an effect would scarcely be as forceful, even if registered, as "inconstant stay" or "debateth with decay"—in their service as phonemic paragrams for "inconstancy" and "death"—we might rather leave the sonnet with a more emphatic example of microlinguistic compression, a dissonant actualization of arguably the poem's chief and deepest matrix. To hear as much in this opening line will require an exemplary recognition of the interplay between graphic and phonic signifiers in the "Shakespeherian" text: a *graphonic* tension. This chapter's inductive survey has so far followed out certain common strands uniting the stylistically alert editorial glosses of Booth, the semantic dismemberments and phonic reassemblages of Saussure in his anagrammatic phase, the structuralist stylistics of Jakobson, the formalist literary semiotics of Riffaterre, the renovated New Criticism of Ricks, and the "microlinguistics" of Hartman in that transitional period self-denominated as "Beyond Formalism" but not yet dedicated to the deconstructive enterprise. If these pages have so far succeeded in suggesting how Booth's interest in "phonetic and ideational interplay" could be linked through Jakobson's "figures of sound" to the embedded phonetic patterning of Saussure's studies, how at the same time Booth's deciphering of multivalent syntax derives straight from Empson's explication of ambiguous double grammar, and if these pages have further tracked a palpable connection between the relationship in Riffaterre of paragram to matrix and Ricks's preoccupation with the anti-pun, as well as between Hartman's finessed zero values and the manifold conversions and expansions of Riffaterre's system—if so, then we should be ready to back out of sonnet 15 by way of its first diffusive phrasing: a test of phonemic differentials in their (in every sense) *marginal* wordplay.

Sonnet 15 may be heard to turn the corner of its first line, to complete its initial grammar, by citing its own theme of mortality *under erasure*. In this way the first line becomes virtually the sonnet's last word, the inaugural transformation of a primal matrix. Represented in shorthand, the Empsonian ambiguity of grammar has so far been read to go like this: "When I consider (that) everything that grows / holds-in perfection (or holds still in its perfection), . . . then is when I . . ." What might be further said to operate here, at the level of the phonotext, is a phonemic as well as linear "enjambment" which happens to coincide metrically with the onset of the sonnet's next line. The first line runs on, and at its turning, so also—by grammatical doubling and revision—turns the phrase ("grows/Holds") that comprises its enjambment; turns, too, the phonic matter that frames (both internally and externally) the second word of that phrase. Like poetic lines themselves, lexical units are not cleanly sliced off at their borders but spliced together, edging into each other on the sly, the slide. If the far end of the word "Holds" tends, for instance, to erode toward a semantic ambiguity, it is the other, the near end of the same lexeme, that—more malleable still—leans toward surrendering its aspirated yet all but silent first phoneme. In so doing, it momentarily "sounds," rather than spells out, the most deeply secreted, because in every sense the most hopelessly clichéd, seed phrase or matrix from which the poem is generated: the brute truth about all life on earth, which always and inevitably "grows / (H)old(s)." That the poem never mentions growing "old," as it never mentions "death," is exactly the point. The *h* in "Holds" is functional, yes, but frail, is activated, but barely; it holds its lexeme in place, yet with the least insistence. Like everything the sonnet describes, this phrasing itself is mutable, wispy, dogged by its own negation—holding for a moment only insofar as it does not quite give out to "old." Establishing at the very start its semiotic "model" in the layered ambiguities, both grammatical and phonemic, of the first clause, the sonnet as paragrammatic variant—the sonnet as a conversion and expansion of a nest of timeworn truisms about the work of Time—would now, as we listen back over it one last time, be understood to go like this: "When I consider all growing things, and consider how in growing no thing can more than momentarily hold in—or hold on in, hold to—its own ripeness, how all things must therefore grow hold only to let go—in a word, to *grow old*—then I write poetry, this poetry, the text of you in youth."

The Shakespearean lyric text is thus dense not only with sonic patterning of all sorts, with lexical and grammatical ambiguity, with loaded rhyme, internal echo, even an anagrammatic streak at times, but dense also with what I have borrowed from Ricks's consideration of the "anti-pun" to call the *antiphonal* variant, spawned by a phantom enjambment between words. To sample just one more, earlier sonnet on the same theme of mutability, we note that sonnet 12 includes a lament for the cyclic passing of the summer foliage, "Which erst from heat did canopy the herd." The image of a "canopy," veil, or screen returns as an allusive trace in the next line's "summer's *green* all girded up in sheaves." This sonnet then closes with a tripled ligature that elides the twinned consonants *g*/*g*, *t*/*T*, and *s*/*s* across the sequentially enjambed gap between words. The result is again to depersonify the iconographic trope of Father Time—"And nothing 'gainst Time's scythe can make defense"—with an un-figural vernacular truism, the matrix under erasure: *nothing gains time* (against age and death).

Sonnets are of course, in verbal derivation, "little songs," sonnettes. In phonemic reading, however, enunciation as speech act is not the issue—but pronunciation as a linguistic fact decidedly is. Script, alone, cannot entirely exhaust its energies, and the unsettling excess—the *edgy* remainder—may operate as a return to differential origins from the seeming fixity of a written wording. To isolate this reversion as a convertibility in the literary object itself, a functional ambivalence generated in processing the "object" as "text," is the work of the phonemic reading begun here.

"Porches of the Ear"

As we move from the ambivalent materiality of Shakespeare's lyric lines to a theatrical text whose phonic undulations would be at least to some extent disambiguated in the voicings of any given performance, questions of inflection and pronunciation become more prominent, though not finally determinate. How to do justice to Shakespeare's intonations and accents has long been a debate in the performance aesthetics of his plays. On the evidence of a remarkable parody of such debate in Henry Fielding, we are led to think of it as an "eternal" topos in Shakespeare studies. In the eighth chapter of Fielding's *A Journey from This World to the Next,* the deceased narrator comes upon Shakespeare, our deathless dramatist, holding court in the otherworld, arbitrating debates over "ambiguous passages in his works."[15] The Bard is at one point asked to adjudicate a dispute about the accentual stress and pitch with which Othello's murderous line "Put out the light, and then put out the light," should be intoned, and so interpreted, in performance. A parallel reading of the two clauses is suggested on one side, then an emphatic singling out of the second as "THE light," the light of lights. The narrator himself joins the debate to suggest instead "the light . . . THY light," but he is soon impressed with another reading "very sophisticated in my opinion"; without designating it as such, he is drawn to the idea of a paronomastic slant rhyme: "Put out the light, and then put out THEE, light," where the fuller voicing of the *e* in "the" elongates the pause between words into a virtual comma, allowing the article to thicken into a homonym for the doomed second person — as if in venomous travesty of a cliché like "light of my life."

The celebrated oratorical richness of Othello's speeches might well have provided further evidence of phonic contouring in this chapter, but it is *Hamlet* that most exhaustively thematizes the wiles of language, the unction and poison of speech, in company with a texturing sound play that saturates nearly every scene. The "phonetic and ideational interplay" (Booth again) prevalent in the sonnets is every bit as much in evidence, though less often critically glossed, in a dramatic text like *Hamlet.* Says the Prince, for instance, to Ophelia: "Nymph, in thy ori*sons* / Be all my *sins* remembered" (3.1.88–89),[16] as if the monosyllabic "sin" could be purged by internalization within the very term for its remembrance in benediction. (And even here the paronomasia is not free from the transegmental drift of a widened internal rhyme ["ori*sons* / my *sins*"] of just the sort the next chapter examines in terminal positions.) More often in this tragedy, however, the role of paronomasia is to encode directly some overt and spreading contamination. This play about poison in the ear repeatedly submits its own phonemes to perverse dilutions and admixtures, the syllables split and spilt along the line. Rhetorician himself of these effects, Claudius would have his auditors intuit the leaking virulence of his nephew as the danger of one who would "envenom with his envy" (4.7.103), where the "etiologic distancing," as Hartman would call it, between imputed cause (desire, greed) and effect (pollution) is exposed in compression by the internal echo.

Again on the subject of a poisoning of ears, now literalized, the ghost charges that Claudius is the villain who "in the *por*ches of my ears did *pour* / the le*pr*ous distilment" (1.5.63–64). The syllabic figuration of these lines seems itself concentrated into a final phonemic juncture at the *p/r* of "leprous." Dell Hymes has suggested that poetry is often organized by a dominant nucleus of vowels transformed by consonantal variants.[17] Such a generative or transformational phonology, rather than grammar, serves to track euphonic and paronomastic effects back to a vocalic deep structure. This theory of the dominant nucleus may of course be subsumed to the notion of projected equivalences in Jakobson. A further example, with a doubled *o* sound more nearly equivalent in Shakespeare's pronunciation, appears in the internal slant rhyme of Hamlet's first soliloquy, where the sense of degenerate and unchecked luxuriance choking on its own excess is captured in a self-begetting thicket of sibilants: "'ti*s* an unweeded garden / That grow*s* to *s*eed. Thing*s* rank and gro*ss* in nature / Po*sess* it merely" (1.2.135–37). The paronomasia of "grows"/"gross" may well be accounted for as a long *o* nucleus framed by gutturals and sibilants and then projected along the axis of contiguity—not only as a nearly perfect internal rhyme but as almost a full homophonic pun.

In moving from this general paronomastic terrain of *Hamlet*'s poetry to a specific crux like "A little more than kin and less than kind" (1.2.64), we can see the particular utility of the "dominant nucleus" model—with its transformational deep structure—for any partial utterance depending for its full power on what goes unsaid as well. In this respect, the relation of this model both to the "transformational poetics" of Hartman, with its overdetermined poles and elided middles, and to the invisible matrix of Riffaterre's semiotic expansions begins to take shape more clearly. Attempting to cajole Hamlet into accepting both his uncle's rule and his kinship, Claudius has just addressed the hero as "my cousin Hamlet, and my son" (1.2.63). Realizing that these blandishments have no effect on Hamlet's black mood, Claudius has then wondered aloud: "How is it that the clouds still hang on you?" (1.2.65). Echoing the uncle's cozening syllabic chime in "cousin . . . son," Hamlet has then rejoined, "Not so, my lord. I am too much in the sun" (1.2.66), a reply which not only mocks the heliocentric tropes of monarchy but, in its homophonic pun, seems to suggest that the hero is on all counts too much in the *role* of "son" to suit him. Strategically lodged in just this larger field of phonetic reverberation is the famous ejaculation to which Hamlet now turns aside: "A little more than kin, and less than kind!" Taking "kind" as pitched between the meanings "natural" and "benign," between "of the kind" and "kindly," we thus overhear Hamlet mumbling at once about Claudius and about himself in a relationship too close for comfort, so near and yet so far: both incestuous, on the one hand, and mortally antagonistic, on the other. We are horribly more than cousins, he says, while I am far less than kindly disposed toward you, precisely for how far short you fall from the natural standards of your kind.

Then, too, as if the "more" carries with it almost a sense of prosodic quantity as well as spiritual quality, the weighted increase from "kin" toward what is here its virtual antithesis in "kind" passes invisibly through an unuttered but mediating third term. The complexities of the said circle the unsaid and entice it toward voice. Hamlet cannot name this transformation of the "kin" nucleus, nor even let slip a variant of its buried matrix, for such rancorous candor might consign him to final paralysis, spelling out the ambitious self-interest at the back of any revenge. Yet caught inaudibly between "kin" and "kind," or left in the lurch between them, lurks a ghostly overtone — lurks unheard, that is, by subversive reverberation, the tacit noun "king." More than "kin," "king" should be Hamlet's own title. Even in the silence between immobilizing polarities, the return of the repressed will out. Partly because the rhetorical schema of the line sets up the expectations of a guessing game ("What is a little more than kin and less than kind?"), we virtually await Hamlet's speaking the word "king" as a phonically clued solution to the puzzle. It may not seem accidental, either, that this threefold pattern recalls the triadic riddle asked of Oedipus by the Sphynx. The ultimate masterplot for Hartman's microstylistics is the elided maturation of Oedipus, the hero's internally truncated lifeline as an excluded middle between over-determined ends — in Oedipus's case, the overspecified terms of son and husband (of the same woman). Hamlet's case, too, is figured by the extremity of the elided middle in a lexical form, the nephew effaced between a parent's death and a denied inheritance. Moreover, such an impetus is fostered by a phoneme ($/g/$) that never even appears in the text, a transformative cipher kept between the lines because it is interdicted by the psychology of the speech. If so much can be incident to so little, what then about a letter not interdicted so much as let loose in disguise, under cover of a dictional gap? Such is the fluctuant force field of an actually inscribed, though phantasmally detached, phoneme: resulting not from the blanking out of (forbidden) words but the activated and displaced blanks between them. A closer attention to this latter (transegmental) effect will follow some further discriminations among types of Shakespearean sound play made operable across even a library copy as well as a theatrical experience of the "text."

Ghostly Play

Given the furious profusion in *Hamlet* of all sorts of lexical bucklings and permutations, it should be helpful to subdivide them on the way toward that most radical transegmental effect on which this discussion, as with sonnet 15, is eventually to concentrate. We will call their three chief manifestations, for convenience, "intralexical," "interlexical," and "supralexical" transforms. The least disturbing of the phonemic slippages, the one that respects most closely the lexical borders, if not the integrity of what they enclose, is the phonic tension that breaks down a word without breaking it open. To the examples already examined, we may add a double instance from the coda of *Hamlet*. About to become his own ghost in death, Hamlet commissions the retelling of his tragic history. Over the body of his friend, Horatio consecrates himself to this oratorical purpose:

> So shall you hear
> Of carnal, bloody, and unnatural acts,
> Of accidental judgments, casual slaughters,
> Of death put on by cunning and forced cause
> (5.2.380–83)

Before the transposition (or metathesis) by which "casual" is switched to "cause," the monosyllable "acts" has already passed to its apparent reiteration, but only as a momentarily detached morpheme immediately expanded as part of a new epithet for random violence, "accidental." And just as "acts" carries a metadramatic overlay of the elapsed theatrical experience that has been comprised thereof, even as these sequential acts are about to be retold in narrative rather than theatrical discourse, so might the inner ear additionally mistake the second syllable (if there is one) of "forced" in a way that transforms the whole word into the punning "foresaid." What would thus be phonetically fostered is a metanarrative hint of the play's own previously written and performed incidents ("foresaid causes" already "put on," enacted, placed on stage by "cunning" — or theatrical conning) as they are now to be cast up into report. Indeed, the earliest cause of enmity and violence mentioned in the play is the usurpation of Fortinbras's territory — "all those his lands, / Which he stood seized [possessed] of" (1.1.88–89) — by Hamlet's father, the King. When these holdings are alluded to again fifteen lines later as "those foresaid lands" (1.1.103), the meter openly invites the pun on a disyllabic "forced." The homophonic twist on "foresaid" is thus a turn of phrase that is arguably to be reversed five acts later in yet another retrospective allusion to all that antecedent bloodshed—beginning with the "foresaid" lands "forced" from an enemy of the state—that has led so inexorably to the play's funereal denouement. By even the differential minutiae of such a subtending phonemic webwork can a play's overall thematic symmetries be brought to light—and to bear on the text in production.

It is clear that "fore*said*" is a complete homophonic transformation of the word's second syllable, whereas "*acts*-idental" is merely a temporary (morphemic) deflection. Still, in regard to their retention of the outer boundaries of the lexical unit—however unorthodox their internal syllabic manipulation—both belong essentially to the first type of transformation (intralexical) under analysis. Neither of these effects outplays the lexical frame that generates it. There is by contrast, with the next category to which we move, the tendency toward a momentarily breached word boundary. Though this distinction does not necessarily emerge from the performance of the text on stage, it has considerable ramifications for a theory of phonemic free play. There is at least the *off* chance that such a lexical breach is operating in Hamlet's climactic speech in the graveyard. Coming round to his long deferred echo of the "To be or not to be" soliloquy, there is the capping disyllabic sentence: "Let be." The complete brief text of Hamlet's transfiguring acquiescence of course goes like this: "The readiness is all. Since no man of aught he leaves knows, what is't to leave betimes? Let be" (5.2.222–24). Across the syntactic accumulation of this thought, and in colloquial continuity with it, flashes the momentary idiom "what is't to *leave be*," as in to *let alone*. The thought holds, even as the syntax converts it into its corrective extension. No sooner said than undone, the second syllable of the fleeting verb phrase, "leave be," is absorbed into the adverb for early, "betimes." It is just then, in turn, that the very idea of *leaving be* is revoiced in the more capacious and relaxed alternative, "Let be"—where something may be coming as well as being put behind.

There is another way to upset the reading sequence without ripping apart a lexeme. Beyond (1) intralexical transforms—the single word either extruding another from a syllabic warp (the approximation of "son" in "cousin" or of "sin" in "orison") or twisting itself into a wholesale homophone ("grows"/ "gross" or, in a single pun, "forced" as "foresaid")—and beyond (2) interlexical displacements—one word shearing off from another for some momentarily transformed phrasal attachment ("*leave be*=times")—there is the related phenomenon of (3) supralexical conflations—two separate words fusing as the syllabic components of a third, a finessing of the zero juncture that creates both a new aural impression and a new semantic expression. This third category of effect tends to be less fleeting and diaphanous than such a junctural shuffle as "leave be=times," gone almost before it is registered. An illustration: after impugning Gertrude's "judgment" in her choice of Claudius (3.4.70), Hamlet in the next line refers to "sense" (for feeling, rather than intelligence) in his backhanded, punning acknowledgment, "Sense sure you have." With its almost inevitable elision (in the mouth of an actor) between *s(e)* and *s,* the phrase thus lets slip the very "censure" which the whole speech intends.[18]

We find another example of such lexical (con)fusion—somewhat more debatable in philological terms but present at least as a near miss, an anti-pun—in the opening lines of Hamlet's first soliloquy, "O that this too, too sullied flesh would melt, / Thaw, and resolve itself into a dew" (1.2.129–30). Backward to start with (if not simply pleonastic), since thawing would be expected to precede melting in any normal process (or at least to be indistinguishable from it), the second line's at best tautological series serves to invite another sense of "resolve" that dislodges the image altogether from the overdetermined context of deliquescence.[19] Conjured here, if only in words, is the *resolution,* even for suicide, that Hamlet cannot otherwise summon. Nor is the deepest desire expressed in the line further dimmed or appeased by the completion of the figure with "into a dew." Obviously, Hamlet speaks metaphorically, but the metaphor is itself double-voiced and returns a literalism from its underside. A reconstituted lexical bond resolves the scripted article and noun into a disyllabic homonym. With certain philological reservations about the precise anglicizing of the French word in Elizabethan English, the result is nonetheless that the wish fulfillment of a suicidal "resolve" commits the self to an overtone of life's final adieu.[20]

As I began this chapter by suggesting, "Shakespeare" in these investigations is not a proper name so much as the common term for a literary property: for a certain euphonic, polysemous roughening of the textual surface which has become the very norm of verbal *wit* in English—a virtual thinking in words and word sounds. Shakespeare is thus the password for that definition of the literary within which the writer by the same name wins his preeminence. If Shakespeare is a field of textual phenomena, rather than the source or hero of a private literary idiolect, then traditional stylistics does indeed stand in need of revision by a more impersonal categorization of perceptual (or receptual) effects, as with the thumbnail taxonomy of lexical and phonemic mutation here in progress. In this regard, to distinguish a Renaissance reading of, or attendance at, *Hamlet* from a modern-day counterpart (not equivalent), while locating both within a developing experience of the Shakespearean text, should only confirm our sense of Shakespeare as a receptual rather than a biographical category. On balance, there is certainly as much phonic density in the Shakespearean texts we read in their modern English "translation" as in the "originals"; it is just otherwise distributed, located along different orthographic axes. Sounds may differ, but the sounded density remains, and remains in the form of an instigation to what we can only call *thick reading*. Since it all depends on how you say it, no matter whether out loud or to yourself, the "Shakespeherian Rag" is thus recognized all the more openly here for what it all along has been: a reading *effect*.

In the phonemic mutations discussed so far, we have noted three modes of morphophonemic transformation still bounded by the logic of lexical parameters: (1) intralexical—the homophonic syllable, the part echo, or the full homophonic pun; (2) interlexical—the momentary breaking-off of a phonemic cluster as free vocable; and (3) supralexical—the outright fusion of adjacent but lexically discrete morphemes in a new third term. In addition to these is perhaps the most common, potentially the most disruptive, in practice the most muted, and in criticism certainly the least discussed of all the phonic convolutions of Shakespeare's language—or of any other writer's. This is the transegmental drift that leaves at least one of the abutting lexemes no longer intact. Staying a while with *Hamlet,* we can now draw into the open some examples of this fourth, aurally diffusive category, as already noticed in sonnet 15 in the glancingly asserted "engraft (t')you (a)new" or, more faintly and fleetingly, "grows (h)old/s." This fourth type of (transegmental) mutation is characterized by the vanishing act of a single phoneme—backward or forward, by ligature or elision—in transit from one lexical unit to an adjacent one. It therefore constitutes an ambiguation of juncture at the level of the single phoneme rather than a mobile and adhesive morpheme or lexeme. Its exemplary leverage in this study derives from its refusal to respect even the morphemic, let alone lexical, borders on which traditional stylistics depends.

The spectral elocution of the father's ghost offers illustration within *Hamlet's* thematic of defiled hearing. With well over half a dozen iterations of the call to Hamlet's audition—including "List, list, O list!"—massed behind it in the first scene, the ghost's indictment of Claudius climaxes the motif of hearing with the synecdoche "ear of Denmark":

> 'Tis given out that, sleeping in my orchard,
> A serpent stung me. So the whole ear of Denmark
> Is by a forged process of my death
> Rankly abused.
>
> (1.5.35–38)

In performance—given that our hearing, along with the hero's, has been whipped into febrile attention—we could barely help catching for a split second the drift, the rift, the junctural upset of "serpent's tongue." It is a spectral anti-pun from a ghost's own mouth.[21] Close upon, closing upon, this mere flick of the tongue is the syntax that infinitesimally shifts its ground and shuts out the pun's very possibility, putting the second hissing sibilant back in its place as frontal alliteration. For a moment, though, in this metalingual irony of phonemic ambivalence, we eavesdrop upon the revelation not only of murder but, proleptically, of the forgery of report that follows — and for which the same villain is to blame. Hamlet is, after all, a play where death's sting is very much in the tongue, both in the surviving report that falsifies the crime and in the posthumous obligations that giving voice to it entails.

Beyond this reflexive ambiguity — a quintessential slippage in this play of ghostly phonemes — there are other sorts of aural conversions at lexical intervals. Conducing to reintegration in a new word, they do so within a plausible new syntax as well, as "serpent's tongue" does not. Says the ghost to Hamlet: "I could a tale unfold whose lightest word / Would harrow up thy soul" (1.5.15–16). Few actors could manage, or would trouble, to disambiguate the junctural slippage and ligature of "whose lightest" into "whose slightest." Equally difficult to keep from activation is the flickering counterphrase hovering over the next dire consequence of which Hamlet is warned by the ghost, whose story would "Make thy two eyes like *stars start* from their spheres" (1.5.17; my emphasis). Again a drifting, this time backward, of a sibilant, this time doubled, creates an auditory elision. From this telescoping of the syntactic gap is released, by an ambiguity of the dental d/t sound, the equally likely "stars dart": in a sense the momentaneous effect of the cause of "starting" in the first place. Phrasing becomes an etiology on the run, microscopically (or microphonically) contracted. The pressure of the unsaid matrix behind this strained kinetic phrase — the etymological link to "startling" — is not quite sufficient, that is, to suppress the transegmental alternative, since it too operates within the semantic paradigm of functional choices.

Upon the ghost's first exit, before he meets with Hamlet, it is Horatio who describes how "Th' extravagant and erring spirit hies / To his confine" (1.1.154–55). The erring of a phonemic ghost, too, in the root sense of wandering (hear *errancy*), is also at play here. Eventual English teachers, among others, learn somewhere on their way to graduate school, usually on the occasion of an aphorism from Pope, that the word *erring,* if pronounced as in *error,* is in fact a mistake, since it should rhyme, for instance, with *deferring.* But this softening of the vowel sound had not yet taken place by Shakespeare's time,[22] and so the polysemy of this line from *Hamlet* is closer to pure segmental ambiguity than the educated theatergoer might today expect. "Extravagant and erring," given the etymology of "extravagant," thus comes bearing a redundancy that is partly done away with by the antiphonal drifting of the *d* into a reduplicating liaison — and hence into a transforming consonant in the unwritten but aurally unavoidable "extravagant and daring." Two paradigmatic axes are involved here, one linguistic, one contextual. The phonemic alternation is allowed only because the lexical alternatives of "erring" and "daring" are also operable, in context, within the binary system of semantic and thematic choice. In their slippage they still fit the sense.

A close parallel in phonemic contour to this sliding recombination of dentalized phonemes returns us to the play's motif of the violated and defiled ear. The new king is attempting to poison Hamlet's reputation by accusing the Prince of poisoning Claudius's own. Not only does the usurping monarch claim that rumors "infect" Hamlet's ear (4.5.90), but he shortly adds that, as a result, the diseased Prince never hesitates "our person to arraign / In ear and ear" (4.5.93–94). Performed as prompt text for the "ear," there would again be an immediate doubling and liaison at the consonantal borders of the two particles, the preposition and the conjunction. An infectious drifting from word to(ward) word would thus discover in this emphatic, this tautological repetition of the noun "ear" the fractionally displaced paragram of an idiomatic matrix or cliché, "in near and dear." As never more exhaustively thematized in Shakespeare's work, the ear indeed is in dis-ease.

With wording itself out of joint, *Hamlet,* then, is a play whose preternatural quality is partly conveyed by the spookiness of its sepulchral echoes. If poison is to be poured in the ear, the ear must have porches. Since even the casual is causal, acts can't be accidental, which goes for linguistic acts as well. By its very nature, here its verbal nature, what envy does is to envenom. This is a play where cousins are cozened by the name of "son," where unkind kin vie for kingship, and in whose garden all that grows is, by acoustic contagion, gross. "Shakespeare" thus names a verbal field where words perpetually fertilize each other, sometimes in decomposition, crumbling and recombining, surrendering the envelope of their separate definition to mix, blur, and confound even their own lexical identity. One thing leads to another, lends to another. Paronomasia narrows to an interplay between (in the sense of *across*) words, across their segmental breaks: again, wordplay as word-splay.

A Never-Fixed Mark

If paronomasia is the prototypical instance in Jakobson's definition of the poetic function, how then do these transegmental flashes and dodges either fit or revise that definition? One might say that they simply project comparison into combination, equivalence into sequence, at an angle of less deflection from the vertical, or paradigmatic, axis, so that the equatables or alternatives are overlapped within a single equivocation. But this adjustment of Jakobson's definition still fails to account for the unsettling effect *in reading* produced by these disjunctive lexical overlays. By contrast with such equivocal contiguity, the echo of "grows to seed" in "rank and gross," for instance, is separated almost as decidedly as end rhyme, falling indeed in a separate line. This sort of chime quite audibly lifts words from sequence and stacks them on top of each other in the mind's ear, leaving the grammar intact. In such cases, the chain of succession in syntax remains the baseline upon which phonic recurrence is projected as a secondary feature. In the transegmental dislocations we have been examining, however, syntax does not remain a stationary grounding. With "stars (s)tart" (as a far limit of paronomasia in almost pure, undelayed doubling), if we hear them "start" and "dart" at once, we do so by an infinitesimal shift within the same grammatical collocation: "stars (s)=t/dart." By just this logic, however, the very axis of succession itself seems suddenly destabilized, the combinatory logic of semantic production no longer secure. At issue is not just a choice within the lexical paradigm, since "start" emerges as if by stealing a sibilant from the preceding plural. That its loss is not syntactically noted, that the plural stays put, does not mean that one axis has not encroached on the other. If straight paronomasia is the quintessential projection of equivalencies from the axis of selection onto that of combination, then such transegmental slippages might instead be read in part as the reverse projection of successivity back upon the axis of alternate selection. It is this spectrum of substitution, kept preternaturally active, that is now the operable though malleable baseline. Upon this shifting ground the previous security of grammatical sequence is mapped in all its sudden oscillation and vagrancy.

Whether or not the transegmental drift is taken to skew or directly to invert the coordinates of the poetic function as rendered by Jakobson, it does tend, as suggested earlier, to shadow the individual speech act (*parole*) with its basis in language itself (*langue*). As against signifying practice in other semiotic systems, language is based simultaneously on two stages of difference known to linguists as "double articulation." The phonic raw matter of speech is differentiated into a set of oppositions pertinent to a given language, as, for instance, the functional distinction in English between *d* and *t*. Upon this system of distinctions is mounted the difference between various bondings of phonemic matter into the units known as morphemes and lexemes, as in the functional opposition between "start" and "dart." This all takes place within the paradigms of the *langue,* before being further caught up in the metonymic linkage that bonds word to word in such a syntactic chain as the intransitive present-tense predication "stars start" (or "dart"). The options of the *langue* that continuously stand waiting for the selections of *parole* are ordinarily subsumed entirely to the final signifying function of any coherent grammatical utterance. That segmentation which undergirds the morphophonemic structure of the lexeme, in other words, is usually ignored—*sentenced* to suppression—once the lexeme passes into continuous utterance. If we take the transegmental drift to project this normative march of the horizontal, or metonymic, sequence back into the paradigmatic axis, we must understand it to do so in a way that causes a temporary regression or breakdown, a reversion from selective speech to the dormant fluctuation, even turmoil, of language. "To hear with eyes" can in this sense be an audition of flux and irruption beneath and between the graphic signifiers on the page. The study of such disruptive moments becomes the monitoring of linguistic differentials as they impinge upon and disintegrate the sureties of *parole,* a study of *langue* itself — or "languageness" — as the return of the repressed.

It is a return to which the Shakespearean phonotext is endlessly hospitable. Among the widely noted puns on "Will" in the sonnets, there is this often-glossed moment from sonnet 136: "Will will fulfill the treasure of thy love, / Ay fill it full with wills, and my will one." Booth remarks on the "gradual revelation, increasing overtness, and mounting crudity of the pun on fulfill" (*SS,* 470), though not the play on affirmation as identity — the economy of an "Ay" for an *I* — that further crystallizes the self-nomination of "Will." Nor, in a transegmental mode, has anyone noted a related punning effect on Shakespeare's first name, Will's "will = full-"ness. As a lateral gambit of the text not contained by normal lexical borders, this effect emerges as a seeming impulse asserted from within that autonomous model of desire which is language itself. It is no accident of literary history that this telescoping process of one word from two finds its homage by reversal in Joyce's own later play with the last name of Will's wife, Ann Hathaway, decontracting it into a homophonic willfulness all its own: "If others have their will Ann hath a way."[23]

At least one such effect in the sonnets is even pitched explicitly between the claims of eye and ear, of script and presumed utterance. "Why is my verse so barren of new pride?" asks the persona of sonnet 76, lamenting that his lines are not given to "quick change," to "new-found methods, and to compounds strange?" Before even bringing the interrogation to a halt, however, the Shakespearean text has instanced its own quick-change artistry in the "compounds strange" of a segmental regrouping, as it asks why "every word doth *almost tell* my name?" (emphasis added). Though Booth notices in a later paradoxical figure from this same sonnet, "Spending again what is already spent," that there is a "muffled pun" (read: a muted junctural breakdown, otherwise an intralexical drift) evoking the "compound(s) strange," as it were, of "a = gain," and though he elsewhere glosses the verb "stell" for "to carve" in its relation to writing (to *stell,* to *steel,* to *style* [*SS,* 172–73]), neither his nor other commentary registers the transegmental "inscription" by which "almost tell" — that dead metaphor of vocal utterance — becomes (more accurately, in textual terms) "almo(st) stell." Here is the transegmental ligature of an entire diphone rather than single letter — and this carrying a suggestion about the graphic rather than phonic imprint of poetry (a hint partly complicated, of course, by the aural form in which it reaches us).

We are listening, after all, to the same writer who, as dramatist, puts such a phonic drift into the voice of the chorus in *Troilus and Cressida*. After Ulysses's speech about the wanton and sluttish wiles of Cressida, the lascivious "language in her eye," a choric voice announces, by way of equivocal enunciation, "The Troyans' trumpet" (4.5.64) — where the expenditure of the sibilant breath famously blares out the phonemic and moral slur "s = trumpet." There is even an internal literary history, or intertextual lineage, ensuing from this morphemic joke within the sequence of Shakespearean drama. Two years after *Troilus,* in the next of the tragedies, Iago slips almost unconsciously into the same pun, uttered in soliloquy by a subliminal logic of association. Looking on at Cassio taking Desdemona's hand, he has begun hatching his adultery plot when Othello's arrival interrupts and refocuses his scheming. Putting himself on alert with "The Moor! I know his trumpet" (2.1.178),[24] Iago is also implicitly congratulating himself on having conceived his stratagem to recast the doting wife in the role of whore. This is, after all, the same "Shakespeare," the same punning field, that resuscitates the chronicle of the ancient "King Leir" as a privileged testing ground for that intensified blind willfulness which is "kinglier" only by tragic definition — a vein of wordplay, turning elsewhere on the "Roya*l* /EAR" (1.1.139) of the king's attention, that is further exploited in Jean-Luc Godard's film version.[25] This is, as well, the same Shakespeare, the same homophonic field, in which a dialogue between Romeo and Juliet, where the notion of sinning lips is thrice on their lips (1.5.107, 108, 109), is followed by Juliet's renowned rhetorical question at their next meeting; as precipitated by the liaison of a sibilant and enhanced by the iambic emphasis on the second syllable, Juliet's phonemic lapsus will often be heard from the stage as the thematic distillant: "What sin a name?" This ambivalent lexical s/play asks as well as answers that deeper question about Shakespearean verbal pluralism: what's in a word? Nothing that cannot slip past in the happy fault of a redistributed lexical caesura, a dropped and recovered downbeat in the syncopated rhythm of the "Shakespeherian Rag." Even when not uttered from the stage, the written page has its own phonemic enactments, its own plays-within-the-play of reference. In that famous sonnet about love's necessary unalterability (sonnet 116) — to take a last reflexively thematized example — the very negation of a love so constituted rises to haunt all protestation from within the fickle signifying system of "a(n) (n)ever-fix'd mark," one mark after another on the track and trail of desire.

But why — one may ask again — should the author of *Romeo and Juliet, Hamlet, Lear,* or the sonnets be called upon to begin these proceedings?

Shakespeare serves to "authorize" the phonemic reading of this study not in his role as the poet who first posits the modern (lyric) subject—as in the convergent claims of Anthony Easthope and Joel Fineman—but rather as the writer and performed playwright alike who positions us before a certain kind of literary textuality in English.[26] Shakespeare has come to be read as if he taught us how to read, as if his texts are the wellsprings of those specifically literary inflections of language that are at once most prized and most often appraised in the processing of a poetic text, whether by reader or critic. The term "Shakespeare" thus stands in retrospect as the primary manifestation of that sustained and extreme verbal originality, that driven invention, density, and obliquity, which is literary language. With "his" lexical and syntactical eccentricity, concatenation of imagery, and sustained verbal opacity, "Shakespeare" names an exemplary case of that working of words beyond their referential service which has come to be called poetic. And, by circular reasoning, whenever we discover such literary "values" in a single text by Shakespeare, they only serve to confirm again his priority, his mastery, and his influence. The exemplary status of Shakespearean textuality resides therefore in the fact that such textuality defines for the act of reading not predominantly the modern discursive subject but, more decidedly, the modern subject-position of the reader, adrift amid a constant play of signifiers, a subject split, doubled, ambivalent, layered, elided, and in flux, moving forward only by doubling back, proceeding by reprocessing, reading by rewriting. If grammar, and certainly rhetoric, work to sustain this discursive positioning, at the same time there is something in what we might call the fact of the linguistic that also serves to contend with and contest the subjective grounding of utterance—equivocating it through the fluctuant wash of a phonotext polyvalent and unspeakable. The phonotext, in short, cannot be englobed or totalized as voice.

It is in this sense that the "enunciation" of discourse needs qualification by its always contingent "evocalization" as text. Poetry as produced *language* inflects and bedevils, strains and unfastens, poetry as discourse. The reigning ideology in any period may be one of containment, but the material base itself is always insurgent. This insurgency is what, in and of itself, we call literary, as well as what is often meant by the Shakespearean preeminence, or priority, within the history of literariness. In this closed conceptual circuit, the objectivity—the material basis, the inscribed signifiers—of a text, processed in the receptual "subjectivity" of reading, induces as secondary effect of their effects the very subject-positioning upon which the reading in the first (never fixed) place depends. Given what we have come to expect as readers of literature in the modern English tradition, it is precisely as readers rather than as psychological agents that the Shakespearean text reads us in the making, which is another way of saying that it makes us in the reading. Stylistics has traditionally explored the "structuring" activity in only one sense: the authorial manufacture of the text. A concentration of the phonotext would, by contrast, entertain literary production as a *construction of the reader,* in the double genitive sense (both "by" and "of"): denoting text production on the one hand and subject formation on the other, a twain that never fails to meet—but never for more than a word or two, for one word on the verge of its relation to another. Shakespeare provides, then, less the literary-historical than the prototypical starting point for the present attempt at a phonemic reading of the transegmental drift—that structural biplay which is an exemplary instance of the fluctuations of literary discourse. This reading procedure, with its emphasis on the somatic as well as psychic dimension of the positioned subject, needs now to extend and deepen its reserve of examples before theorizing further the place of the voiced body in the "subjective" space of reading.

2   Rhymed Treason
A Microlinguistic Test Case

Syntactically seditious, lexically anarchic: an arc of echo across unbonded, nonconfederate syllables—contaminating in the process that bastion of conservative poetics, the regularized forms of metered rhyme. Without in the least backing off from the claims of Chapter 1, we should now be able to watch certain of the verbal operations examined there as they get mobilized in a unique sort of rhyme, one engaged just fractionally before an echo is usually thought to set it. In play at such moments is the phonetically rough left edge (rather than merely typographically ragged right) of the rhyming cluster, an edge abrasive and absorbant: a lexical edging back. To move from the "unwritten" cross-lexical biplay in Chapter 1 to one of the most canonically inscribed of poetic features—end rhyme—should get the discussion, if only temporarily, back on common "stylistic" ground. But as the classic touchstone of poetic surplus, rhyme will also serve here as a test of phonemic surfeit, of segmental overflow.

We may begin with a radically unorthodox and entirely "modernist" rhyme, one that does not even adhere to the protocol of line endings. In Gerard Manley Hopkins's "Wreck of the *Deutschland*," the line "She drove in the dark to the leeward" finds a rhyme for its last syllable, *ward*, only across the enjambment of the two subsequent lines: ". . . night drew *her* / *D*ead to the Kentish Knock."[1] This is a leeward as much as a wayward rhyme, one that will go any way the prevailing wind takes it. Driven here to the point of morphological mayhem is a dismembering rhyme that treasonably betrays both lexical and metrical borders, resting on what might be termed a double enjambment: first between words, "w=[h]er," then between whole lines, "er/=D." A rhyming cluster edging or lurching backward is common enough, as we shall see, but an echo toppling forward like this is rare indeed.

To begin with the spectacular exaggeration of the latter is meant to throw into relief the overlooked frequency of the former.

It happens that three of the most important contemporary essays on the question of rhyme—William K. Wimsatt's "One Relation of Rhyme to Reason," Hugh Kenner's "Pope's Reasonable Rhymes," and John Hollander's *Rhyme's Reason*—all highlight the logic behind the nonincidental coincidence of sound, the variable semantic overtones that rhyme sends into reverberation.[2] I certainly do not mean to discount the possibility of thematic links afforded and forwarded by rhyme, even though I will not here be pressing such points. This chapter is designed, rather, to register a break at times with rhyme's authorized grooves or tracks. Implied by "rhymed treason" is the kind of lexical insurrection that results from the overlapping, and so undermining, of word boundary in certain transgressive—namely, transegmental—rhymes. There are, it thus seems, more echoic constellations than normally admitted which need not be seen to be heard, nor even intended in order to be read. As a matter of fact, the whole argument from intentionality goes by the board if, within the undeniable return of acoustic material, we hear not only more than ever bargained for but more than can plausibly be absorbed within a given prosodic economy. Rhyme, that is, turns traitor to its own expectations, revolts against its own formulas, when its acoustic mass disturbs into recurrence more phonemes than the apparent verse contract requires. Rhymes generated by such systemic excess may be accidental, even counterproductive, but there nonetheless, audibly, they are. Thrust into the foreground by the force of echo, detached from the sole authority of syntax, such loosening through recurrence creates a fractional backsliding in a given line. Rhyme, in short, does not always toe the line ends.

More Than Meets the Eye

For the present purposes, the truancy of certain rhymes will help delimit by contrast a primary normative locus of phonological attention in the study of poetry, one too narrowly restricted to the regularities of meter and lineation. Then, too, rhyme offers an inviting experimental field on which to explore the sometimes discrepant work of graphemes and phonemes in literary (e)locutions—precisely because of its own long-acknowledged division of labor, at times, between eye and ear. From the "new"/"true" rhyming couplet of Shakespeare's sonnet 15, for instance, down through Yeats's rhyme in "A Prayer for my Daughter"—"yet not"/"distraught" (ll. 17–18)—there is a kind of rhyme that honors only the requirements of the ear, not the recognition of the eye. At the other extreme, of course, is the hypertrophy of lexically complete homophonic rhyme—called, after its more common French occurrences, *rime très riche.* An example from Chaucer, in whose Middle English such effects proliferated, is the homophonic and all but homographic echo in "The Legend of Cleopatra" of "liven *may*" with "rose in *May*" (ll. 612–13). By contrast, the nature of English orthography often prevents the instant recognition – unless pronounced – of such a subsyllabic homophony as Yeats's "n*ot*"/ "distr*aught.*" There is another way, as well, in which the graphic can mask or occult the phonic; homophony may go unnoticed in its full sweep because of lexical format itself, regardless of spelling. Certain phonic recurrences thus slink between ortho/graphic units as a surreptitious link. With the previously discussed tension between graphic and phonic signification in mind, consider now the common denominators of the following rhyming couplets, distributed across seven centuries of English verse:

> For thus saith Salomon that was ful trewe,
> 'Werk al by conseil and thou shalt nought rewe.'
> (Chaucer, *The Miller's Tale,* ll. 421–22)

> KNOWLEDGE. Your Five-Wits as for your conselors.
> GOOD DEEDS. You must have them ready at all hours.
> (*Everyman,* ll. 663–64)

> Sans-foy his shield is hang'd with bloudy hew:
> Both those the lawrell girlonds to the victor dew.
> (Spenser, *The Faerie Queene,* 1.5.5)

> And lovers' houres be full eternity,
> I can remember yet, that I
> (Donne, "The Legacie," ll. 4–5)

> Sees by degrees a purer blush arise,
> And keener lightnings quicken in her eyes.
> (Pope, *The Rape of the Lock,* 1.143–44)

> Some hungry spell that loveliness absorbs;
> There was no recognition in those orbs.
> (Keats, "Lamia," ll. 259–60)

> Came tamely back in front of me, the Drover,
> To suffer the same driven nightmare over.
> (Frost, "Our Singing Strength," ll. 44–45)

There are rhymes more or less apparent to the eye in every pair of lines except those from *Everyman,* where the imperfect mating (almost slant rhyme, even by contemporaneous standards of pronunciation) remains in a sense true to the eye only by being visible as a near miss. At first glance, the rhyming matter of these couplets would run as follows: "tr*ewe*"/"*rewe*," "counsel*ors*"/ "h*ours*," "h*ew*"/"*dew*," "eternit*y*"/"*I*," "ar*ise*"/"her *eyes*," "abs*orbs*"/"*orbs*,"

"Dr*over*"/"*over.*" As such, the phonic consorts are not more exact than those in Shakespeare's "*new*"/"tr*ue*" rhyme, for instance—just more visibly so.

But they are something more as well, something *in addition*, in lateral (and not immediately visible) accretion. They produce a different difference, as it were, between eye and ear. Rather than defying the eye, they simply offer more than meets it: a broader band of rhyme than appears at first glance. No handbooks or commentaries on rhyme pay any notice whatever to this ac-cretive swath of rhyme, this magnetic force that pulls into its field stray phonemes. Yet it would surely seem that the audible—or, if unspoken, at least the aural—effect of these rhymes should properly be reschematized as fol-lows: "*trewe*"/"nough*t rew,*" "counse*lors*"/"a*ll hours*" (or even "counse*lors*"/ "*all hours*"), "blou*dy hew*"/"*dew,*" "eterni*ty*"/"tha*t I,*" "a*rise*"/"he*r eyes,*" "ab-sorbs"/"tho*se orbs,*" "Dr*over*"/"nightma*re over.*" All but one of the rhyming pairs (where *dy=hue* actually "predicts" *dew*) happen instead to begin with a lexeme that is answered by a transegmental phonemic cluster never gathering to a new semantic or lexical unit—but nevertheless urged upon the ear (even though unusable by syntax) by the preceding lexical model. Broadened from the rhyming minimum, these transegmental accords do not in any way render a more "perfect" rhyme—just a more dispersed one. They are not simply to be grouped with the condensed repetition of that *rime très riche* on "may" and "May" noted before in Chaucer's "Legend of Cleopatra." In that same tale from *The Legend of Good Women*, we also find examples of the more common *rime riche*. Such rhyme adds an initial consonant to the mere sufficiency of the closing vowel (or vowel-and-consonant) cluster, as in the parallel syllabic rhyme "u*saunce*"/"obey*saunce*" (ll. 586–87) and even the subsyllabic recur-rence of "a*tones*" in "s*tones*" (ll. 638–39). Between such "rich"—such fully invested—echoes and the minimal return of ordinary rhyme falls an additional accord—one unidentified in scholarship but detectable in the reading act. It falls there by falling between words, a richness whose enhancement comes by way of an extract from the adjacent term: a lexical lending as blending. In "The Legend of Cleopatra," as it happens, we do find such a compromise or median rhyme when mention of the queen's "purple *sayl*" is sounded against the "strokes" of the oars "whiche that wente as thikke a*s hayl*" (ll. 654–55). This rhyme also includes a semantic redundancy capable of functioning in the larger sense of the line—as if, for instance, the oar strokes were exactly as rapid in their flailing as is the flapping of her windswept sail. Semantics aside, this cross-lexical echoism has passed beyond the formulaic densities of either ordinary or rich rhyme by falling between (as well as overshooting) them. It boasts a richness in excess of the minimal accord without being constrained by the delimited syllabic envelope of *rime riche* proper. It generates in this way a destabilizing excess born of phonemic subtraction from the lexical precursor. Such a rhyming pattern, intended or not in a given case, is often nevertheless inevitable, given the nature of English "word processing." Or call it a rhyme only if it is taken as an intended aesthetic effect, an inadvertent echo otherwise: there it remains, between words, between them and the reader. There it is, after all, in Chaucer's "liv*en may*"/"rose *in May.*"

The aesthetic acceptance of *rime riche* in both French and English poetry of Chaucer's day would in fact tend to encourage the sort of transegmental or assimilative echoes — as active rhymes — found in Chaucer's *"for age"*/*"forage"* ("The Reeve's Prologue," ll. 3867–68), where the charm of rhyme is not dependent on the avoidance of direct echo. This may in turn argue for the intentional force of Chaucer's *"sayl"*/"a*s hayl.*" Aesthetically validated rhyme or not, however, the echo would be no less operable in the phonotext if the same line endings were found in Shakespeare, Milton, or Keats, poets in a modern English tradition not inclined to the symmetries of *rime riche.* Whether such later poets would have noticed these marginal phonemic assimilations and settled for them regretfully, or whether — in certain cases, from poet to poet and verse to verse — writers from Shakespeare to Tennyson, say, would have actively courted the increased textural possibilities provided by such a drift of acoustic iteration, this question need not escape the realm of sheer conjecture to justify consideration of the effects themselves. In roughly the place of rhyme, they offer more of the same, even if the same as different: formal rhyme lapsed (backward) to irruptive chime. It might be argued that such cross-lexical slippage is merely an aleatory offshoot of English morphophonemic structure, a risk of word division that has no formal place in English poetics between Chaucer and the modernist extravagance begun, roughly speaking, with Hopkins. Still, the inevitable slack within that locus of heightened phonemic sensitivity induced by rhyme might well serve to detect, once again, the roots of modernist disruption long before its systematic and canonical practice.

The issues raised by all such lateral play within rhyme begin in well-established theory and quickly move to test its limits. According to Jakobson's definition of the poetic function, rhyme shows forth as the most visible form of the "poetic" in a structural sense. To be sure, rhyme markedly projects equivalence from the axis of comparability ("profound," say, in its likeness to "resound") into that of combination (the sequence that laces them together as part of the same syntactic progression). Further, rhyme serves to activate the dead metaphor of *axis* itself as a real graphic figuration. The imagined horizontal armature of combination appears broken-down, pieced out, and stacked up, length upon length, metrically calibrated, until the vertical axis becomes visible (for the reading more than the seeing eye) at the right margin.

Granting that end rhyme thereby graphs equivalency as a vertical line of descent, at right angles to metered lineation, what then happens when this stacked axis of visible (or sometimes only phonic) accord becomes just slightly staggered, terraced, or tiered? Such variously telescoped echoes are certainly to be distinguished from the mere rhyming of a two-syllable word with the complete sound elements of two parallel monosyllables (usually called "polysyllabic" rhyme). The effect of a tiered rhyme, instead, is enhanced by the interlocking of two adjacent words at their border, whether for the augmentation or the concentration of the rhyme. The result is usually to widen the rhyme by attracting the closing phoneme(s) of a bordering lexical unit, by ligature; alternately, by elision, a contiguous phoneme may draw off its phonetic double (exact or approximate) in a way that isolates the rhyming matter into a more discrete node of echo. The linkage of words is performed, that is, either through an aural ligature – an acoustic holding over of one sound – or, instead, through a knotting up that bonds (in effect, by shortening) the phonemic span. In either case, a related musical term, the *tie,* would seem adaptable to poetic scansion as an invisible notation that overlaps and blurs words at their edges. Echoes generated in this way are the most purely phonic of all rhymes, defying even the intervals of script in order to forge an equivalence from the graphically discrete increments of combination.

Derrida's expansion of the category of rhyme to cover all the contingencies of iteration in poetry begins with a grammatological perception very close to the tenets of Jakobsonian structuralism. "Rhyme – which is the general law of textual effects – is the folding-together of an identity and a difference."[3] Jakobson might rather stress the unfolding, the displacement of identity into difference along the track of the consecutive. But from Derrida's perspective, rhyme is certainly an exemplary codification: an identity within difference that derives from the simultaneous orchestration of chance and design, of randomness and rule, precipitating from its first term a difference never predictable in advance, a deferral of return along the axis of advance. But a crucial aspect of all this eludes Derrida's comment, if not always his notice as a "practical" critic. The axis of syntactic sequence, whether subdivided into metrical lineation or not, also involves another crucial difference within sameness: the homophonic ambiguities of junctural distribution. In tie rhymes, the axis of contiguity becomes the axis of perpetual recombination, a lexical successor recruited in part as adjunct or increment rather than merely neighbor of the word before. Difference is thus generated from within the sameness of the lexicon itself (a word's or syllable's supposed acoustic identity with itself). The options of rhyme are transformed (whether widened or compressed) whenever the boundary matter of one lexeme is recruited in this way for a new morphological combination, whenever it is invisibly *con-*

scripted into the phonemic mass, but not graphemic integrity, of an adjacent word — regardless of whether any new semantic melding results. With a single word failing in this way to retain its phonic matter untainted by acoustic contamination, its role as rhyming unit may well be either to annex or to exile a phoneme or two in order to maximize its sameness in recurrence. The differential shifts within the increments of a syntactic sequence are thus, in short, projected as the sameness-within-difference of a rhyming play capitalizing on just such fraying segmentation.

Shakespeare's verse deploys or exploits — or permits, or at least fails to prevent — such drifting rhymes in both initial and echoing slots. When "In the old age black was not counted fair" is rhymed two lines later in sonnet 127 with "But now is black beauty's successive heir," the closural adjective of the first line predisposes the third to a homophonic (nongraphic) rhyme not just on "fair"/"heir" but on "fair"/"successi*ve heir*," the latter possibility based on the suballiteration of *f* and *v*. Shakespearean rhymes also frequently work in reverse, anticipating across two words a spread of sound heard only *in retrospect* as pattern, here again at the added distance of an alternating rather than couplet rhyme: "Thou art as fair in knowledge as i*n hue,* / . . . And therefore art enforced to seek a*new*" (82). In sonnet 3, the expressed desire that the young man should reproduce so that his face should "form another" is contrasted in rhyme to that selfishness which would "unbless so*me m*other." In this case, the transegmental drift of the rhyme is subtractive rather than accretive, signifying alternatively in the process — by way of that most loaded of psychological puns — both the woman he should inseminate and the genetic other and double he would sire. The arguable presence elsewhere in Shakespeare of that first example of a rhyming increment, that fricative adjunct in "fair"/"successi*ve hair,*" is entertained in a recent article by Debra Fried that offers one of the first signs in Anglo-American criticism of a willingness to surrender (at its edges) the hegemony of the word as a stylistic unit.[4] This is the case even though in her essay, "Rhyme Puns," Fried nowhere discusses the implications for rhyme at large of that poststructuralist "overdetermination, indeterminacy and phonemic play" (99) to which she is so steadily alert. On the subject of old age in sonnet 68, Fried seems at first simply to agree with Booth in an instinct "to audit 'hair'" as well as "heir" in "signs of fair" (97), but it is her own gloss on his remark that further identifies the mechanism of "elision" (97) by which this audition is encouraged. To the catchall category of elision (rather than liaison) she also attributes her most striking later example of a rhyme pun, the "stroke of eight" that clangs against "wait" in Housman's poem about a hanging, *A Shropshire Lad* 11, only to knell further with overtones of the "stroke of fate" (97).

The guiding thought of this chapter is that the demonstrated presence of even semantically *un*motivated and irrelevant rhymes will provide a stronger phonotextual basis for assessing and theorizing the effects of those lexico-syntactic "puns" and other combinational duplicities more decidedly fore-grounded in the reading of literary writing. This chapter is thus designed as the laying of a groundwork—but precisely in order to demonstrate the shakiness of the textual foundation, the indeterminacy of graphemic shape when phonemically processed. From line to line, the unchecked match of rhyme in the paradigmatic axis can unlatch the syntagmatic, unfastening the locks of juncture from word to word. As it happens, traditional phonological structuralism appears to converge with deconstruction upon just such eccentric echo—that special case of rhyme which begins in departure from itself before projecting its difference elsewhere for iteration. The particular usefulness of these tandem rhymes in following out such lines of convergence between formal patterning and aleatory free play—following them straight into the previous impasse of stylistics, into questions of "voicing"—is that these (like all) rhymes speak, as it were, for themselves. They isolate the phonotext in operation. The cross-lexical slippages in Chapter 1 often had to be subsumed to meaning in order to emerge at all from the undulation of English phonemes. In the case of transegmental rhymes, however, meaning need not be invoked for the effects to be functional. Their randomness is thus dependent on no referential or thematic likelihoods except the undeniability of phonemic recurrence itself. What the ear hears in rhyme requires no surplus of meaning: this is the general rule. If transegmental effects can thus be readily admitted in association with already rhyming syllables, where no syntactic or semantic demands constrain the ear's acceptance of such phonic transformations, then their wider existence outside of rhyme, latent at least, must be allowed. The following chapters will elaborate on this corollary proposition after the present chapter lays the necessary groundwork. It must do so by situating its specialized demonstrations against the larger backdrop of received opinion about both the phonetic routine and the semantic machinations of rhymed verse.

Echonomics

Rhyme's reach, its breach, its treason: an accord syllabically heretical, (s)cryptic in the sense of being suppressed by writing. Such an echo is experienced only by voicing, either on waves of audibility or in the echo chamber of the mind's ear. In all his extensive scholarship on verse echo, including "polysyllabic rhyme," John Hollander tends to disregard, outside of comic verse, what we might term *polyphonemic* rhyme, operating as it does without syllabic check.[5] The closest his own evidence draws him to such a phenomenon is with the off-rhyming couplet from Geoffrey Hill taken up in an important recent essay: "Patience hardens to a pittance, courage / unflinchingly declines into sour rage."[6] Quite apart from echo, the interest of the first two lines for Hollander rests with the way in which they implicitly develop a linguistics of their own generation through those "fabulous etymologies" by which poetry often operates: what he closes his essay by calling "chronic synchrodiachronosis" (133). Just as the ablauting of "patience" into "pittance"—with "forbearance shrivelling into its own pit"—has a metaphonetic dimension, so with the "diachronic" implications of "courage" as it "declines" to "sour rage," as if the adjective-noun phrase "were a suffixed, /au/- grade form, as it were, reflected in some latter day satem language" (129). Nothing, however, is said by Hollander about another (at least as likely) transegmental anti-pun—or antiphone—of "sour rage": the slightly less assimilative but semantically operable "sour age."

Hollander's own rhymes in the self-exemplifying verses of *Rhyme's Reason* do incline to such transegmental effects. After reading dedicatory verses that rhyme "I f*ill a*" with "anc*illa*," we later encounter Hollander's explicit attitude toward polysyllabic rhyme in a reflexive pronouncement: "A serious effect is often killable / By rhyming with *too* much more than one syllable" (14)—as in "This d*imeter* / Would l*imit her*," or in such later rhymes as "So p*ure a*"/ "caes*ura*" (18), "s*eem a*"/"ottava r*ima*" (17), "*a dime*"/"par*adigm*" (18), "up*on it*"/"s*onnet*" (20–21). In extreme form, "polysyllabic" rhyme tends toward what Hollander refers to in *The Figure of Echo* as *rime équivoquée* (from the French tradition of the *rhétoriqueurs*).[7] Illustrated by Hollander with Théodore de Banville's "perfectly punning" lines, "Dans ces meules laques, rideaux et dais moroses, / Danse, aime, bleu laquais, ris d'oser des mots roses" (32), this is what Walter Redfern in *Puns* calls "holorhyme," the complete homophonic nexus—again illustrated from the French: "Gal, amant de la reine, à la tour Magne, à Nîmes / Galamment de l'arène alla, tour magnanime."[8] Redfern adds in further demonstration a triple rhyme from Hugo—"*mémorable*"/"*même au râble*"/"*mais mort, hâble*"—along with the risible polysyllabism of Byron's "pukes in"/"Euxine" (100). Short of the drastic equality of the equivocating echo or holorhyme, the drifting or sliding rhymes that play to ear over eye—or, rather, that play off eye against ear—may be said to span a gap in two directions, down *and across*. They are thus found bracketing the horizontal as well as the vertical axis, cutting loose from the syllabic paradigms of standard rhyme as they break with the lexical modules of the syntagmatic sequence.

Before Hollander's *Rhyme's Reason*, Wimsatt's influential essay had also consigned polysyllabic rhyme to the category of humorous extravagance, to the "double or triple rhymes of a Butler, a Swift, a Byron, or a Browning." His interest lay instead with rhymes more subtly "logical." Building on Wimsatt's approach, Hugh Kenner, in "Pope's Reasonable Rhymes," distinguishes between "incongruous rhymes" and those "normal rhymes" that seem more indissolubly "mated."[9] Kenner argues that in early Pope the former are reserved for satiric effect, the latter for "the realm of law" (82), asserting those "banal congruities" (83) that carry the force of received truth. One might take as an exception the early satiric passage from *The Rape of the Lock,* which Donald Wesling, in *The Chances of Rhyme,* has singled out as a supreme example of "chiastic rhyme."[10] The disarray of the pandemonium described is nevertheless organized by close semantic correlates. "Where wigs with wigs, with sword-knots sword-knots strive," it is inevitable that "Beaux banish beaux, and coaches coaches drive" (1.101–2). The semantic distinction between purpose and sheer impetus implied by *strive* versus *drive* is parodically blurred within the rhyming format by the reciprocity of a sibilant elision — "s = (s)trive" — and a sibilant liaison — "s = drive." This interplay is then re-echoed two lines later with the summarizing "Sylphs contrive it all," subordinating the crisscross purposes of Pope's preceding couplet to a nucleus of first cause in "cont*rive*" — the "hypothetical morpheme" (Hollander's useful concept), or homonymic root, of *drive* and *strive* together.

Pope, master of the rhyming couplet, is the recurrent test case in criticism for interpretations of semantic and phonic accord. From the present vantage, when such transegmental slippage serves to inflect a rhyming pattern with some kind of referential bonus, questions of intentionality seemingly ruled out by the contingencies of English phonemic structure return intriguingly to the fore. Yet all one needs to allow is that the active lexical ambiguity and thematic force of such a tiered rhyme in the following example from Pope's "Essay on Criticism," for instance, is produced in the phonotext as we read, however the words that allow its lateral play may have come to be there on the page in the first place. The subject is Homer as source of inspiration: "Thence form your judgments, thence your maxims bring" (l. 126). From Homer take your lead: this is the imperative logic organizing both halves of the chiastic line, with the second half inverting the placement of verb and object after the adverb. The result is a plosive transegmental ambiguity across the drift of sibilance: "thence your maxims (s)p/bring." The suspicion that what is being described is a spring or fountainhead, a fluent source, a wellspring of wisdom, is soon confirmed by the fulfillment of this cross-lexical hint in the rhyming line: "And trace the Muses upward to their spring" (l. 127).[11] Furthermore, if this undoubted tier rhyme between "s = bring" and "spring" is allowed by double grammar to supplant effect with cause even in the reading of the first line (the sense of "flow [from]" replacing "draw [from]"), then it would only ratify — at the level of rhyming logic — that very aesthetic "maxim" later to be articulated by Pope: "Men must be taught as if you taught them not, / And things unknown proposed as things forgot" (ll. 574–75). Forgetting is here the very sign, in reception, of what is partly suppressed in the written text. The rhyming word that merely repeats the implicit by surfacing it—that spells out the unwritten vocable cloaked by its preceding scriptive alternative—can therefore be read to reverse the combined letteral forgetting of both an entire hidden "matrix" (a cliché like "the well of inspiration") and in particular the verb itself, "springs," that connotes such a source phrase. When that fore-stalled verb actually emerges into the letters of the text for the next line's rhyming slot, it is, like wisdom itself in the formula of that later precept, inculcated as if merely recalled to mind. It appears, in other words, as something we full well knew to—but immediately forgot to—expect, some-thing we might well have deduced from the phonetic as well as the didactic context. Upon its arrival, we take it as given, given already by the phonic uptake of the preceding terminal wording. Pope's transegmental rhyme thus instances here—yes, whether he knew it or not—the whole didactic logic of his rhyming style.

Recurrent Tendings

In retreat from a premature and compromising *semantics* of the transegmen-tal, however, in which only those echoes would be heard that are put to work, let us return now to the formative stages of that rhyming tradition in English out of which Pope develops his more systematic and masterly effects. In the "General Prologue" to *The Canterbury Tales,* Chaucer, portraying the cum-bersome headgear of the Wife of Bath, matches the mention of this burden with the described red of her stockings. He does so in such a way that the transegmental anticipation makes her costume seem all the more of a piece, the finery "upon hir *heed"* suited to the "hoosen" of "scarlet *reed"* (ll. 457–58). Of the Miller, along with the fact that "he hadde a thombe of gold, par*dee,"* we hear that "a blew hood were*d he"* (ll. 565–66). Moving into "modern" English, we find several kinds of transegmental rhymes in Spenser. There are those, like the already mentioned "blou*dy hew"*/*"dew,"* that seem like a phonetic analysis by decontraction, among which should also be included "*b*rood"*/ "we*re wood"* and "b*e (h)ealed"*/*"*conc*ealed"* from *The Faerie Queene* (1.5.20, 29). Other transegmental rhymes can of course entice us with a semantic evocation. In *The Shepheardes Calender,* for instance, there is the hint of a "rhyme pun" in the way that "lyftes him up out of the loathso*me my*re" (l. 92), though anticipating the rhyme word "admire," looks back to "so hie" at the completion of the preceding (and, we now see, incremental) couplet, which yields to the new rhyming pair by the addition of an /r/ to its recurrent vowel sound. The effect on the transegmental instability of the succeeding couplet is to suggest that "the loathsome" can operate as a generic noun for that out of which one can only be raised "(h)igher": lifted, that is, "out of the loathsome (m)yre." Again we confront a semantic appropriation of syntactic form, managed by transegmental adhesion or assimilation even while motivated by rhyme: an anti-pun sprung by eccentric recurrence.

One inevitable result of this chapter's collection of evidence is to suggest how often, how inevitably, this *will* happen. Transegmental rhymes in Donne, for instance, can be as inconsequential as "do*th us* / *thus*" from "A Valediction: Of the Book," but we move closer to an active semantic drift in "A Fever." Beyond the title's homophonic overlay of a single adjective, *afever*, the speaker's "persever" rhymes with his insistence that he would rather "owner be" for "one hour" of his beloved "than all el*se ever*" (ll. 26–28). What needs primary emphasis here is that, quite apart from any functional lexical severance and regrouping, the ligature of the *s*, permitted by the elision of the *e*, at once widens and tightens the rhyme. It does this regardless of whether we hear the phantom repetition of the word *sever*. Neither does the effect (given the transitional and not entirely regularized status of *then* and *than* in early seventeenth-century comparatives) depend upon whether one hears a functional double grammar in the expressed wish to own her an hour, and *then* (thereafter) to sever all else, all other ties. If the transegmental audition of rhyme seems to open the floodgates of such syntactic as well as phonemic rearrangements, to trigger major ambiguities by the least pull on a single word, this no more certifies than it denies the existence of the widened rhyme in the first place. It needs only to be heard to be believed, not recovered by meaning (any more than does rhyme in general). Precisely because the undisputed existence of rhyme in no way depends upon thematic correspondence, we are approaching the problematic operation of the transegmental drift within precisely this area of overdetermined (but not semantic) stress, the manifest (but not necessarily meaningful) sound play between lines.

To be sure, following Jakobson again, we can acknowledge that rhyme is merely a special case of the poetic function in this regard. Phonetic recurrences do not respect syllabic — even lexical — boundaries, since even the simple matter of alliteration is, in its own way, the cryptic anagrammatizing of a line. Returning to Donne with the stylistic work of David I. Masson in mind,[12] we find that certain not uncommon pararhymes, often associated with a more immediately perceived terminal rhyme, approximate the "circumsyllabic sequence" noted by Masson in a paronomastic shift like Pope's "Why feels my *heart* its long forgotten *heat*?" Related to the "circumsyllabic" paronomasia — or *accord riche intérieur* (170) — explored by Masson in such a quasi-anagrammatic bracket rhyme as Donne's "*give*"/"prerog*ative*" ("A Valediction: Of the Book," ll. 44–45), or the more complex example from his Holy Sonnet 6, "pur*gd of evil*"/"*devil*" (ll. 13–14). In such tercet rhymes as we find in the preceding century in Herbert's "The Sacrifice" or Crashaw's "Wishes," the strain on invention and variety leads, as one might expect, to an unusual ingenuity in the recruitment—or felicity in the accident—of proximate phonemes within the rhyming span. An obvious ligature in Herbert's text gains hold on the phonic orchestration of "o*n high*"/"to d*ie*"/"compa*nie*" (ll. 233–35). In Crashaw's "Wishes," one notes such transegmental augmentations (followed by dilutions) as "*lye*"/"morta*l Eye*"/"Destiny" or the more obvious phonemic declension of "*grows*"/"Morning *Rose*"/"bein*g owes*" (ll. 34–36), with the homophonic bond between the first and second lines reduced to a circumphonemic bracket in the third. Again, this density of syllabic and phonic overlay can obviously spill over into semantic play. In Crashaw's "Wishes," rhyme enters the semantic field almost by way of a tautological circle:

> Life, that dares send
> A challenge to his end,
> And when it comes say *Welcome Friend.*
> (ll. 85–87; Crashaw's emphasis)

In the interplay of liaison and elision, one can hear—even see—the reduplication as either "dares *send*"/"hi*s end*" (allowing for the slight difference of the *s* of *his* as a voiced /z/) or "dares s*end*"/"his *end.*" In the latter case, especially, the reflexive gauntlet thrown down by life to its own death is captured by the sense that our "daring to end" is the be-all and end-all of the circumlocutionary notion of "daring to send" an invitation to one's own death in the first place.

Rhyming Pares

No doubt the most widely recognizable example of such subtractive, reductive, or distillant rhyme, where phonemic matter progressively falls away to expose the homophonic core, is George Herbert's famous tercet rhyming in "Paradise." From the first stanza forward, the poem blatantly capitalizes, so to speak, on the sublexical increments of its rhyme. Announces the persona in gratitude to God, "I GROW" like those trees "in a ROW" that thus to "thee both fruit and order OW." The remaining triadic, eroding rhymes go as follows: "CHARM"/"HARM"/"ARM," "START"/"TART"/"ART," "SPARE"/"PARE"/"ARE," "FREND"/"REND"/"END." In *Vision and Resonance,* John Hollander terms this process "metonymic" echo, which would seem to imply the synecdochic detachment of part from whole. Herbert's poem makes "typically brilliant use of metonymic rhyming sequences to stand for the conceptual sequences they describe, the central device being one of seeming to extract each rhyme of a tercet from its preceding one, the corresponding trope in the poem being one of pruning" (130). Hollander stresses "phonetic derivations" but admits as well the presence of "graphemic or scribal ones," since the reader "cannot audibly chop *c* from a *ch* cluster any more than he can prune *w* down into *v* by removing half of it" (130). What, on the other hand, the ear *can* do (though Hollander does not mention this) is actually to register the ampersand joining "hand & ART" in the central stanza: "I START"/"and TART"/"& ART." This would serve not only to vocalize it (silently) as *and* but also to soften the extracted "art" into a more nearly homophonic rhyme with the preceding line: *d=tart/d=art*. In resistance to this, one might well imagine that the conjunction, unlike its appearance in the preceding line (or in two later instances), is here rendered nonalphabetically, nonsyllabically, to avoid just that dental accretion which would spoil, by overcrowding, the clean descent of the rhyme.

Elsewhere, however, the de-escalation of the rhyme is not so strictly policed. A ligature may indeed, though rendering slippery a single rung in the contracting ladder, work to highlight its governing structure. In the move from "judgment*s* SPARE" to "prime and PARE" in the next stanza, for instance, the elision institutes the pruning back of the verb, the paring away of its lexical excess, even before the compound verb "prune and pare" is dropped into the rhyming slot. And the elision operates in such a way that the "metonymical" link emerges almost as an etymological association—synchronic and diachronic at once—as if *paring* were the slowly disclosed first cause of anything *spare*. In the closing lines of the poem, another transegmental augmentation of the end-stopping "end" (as in Crashaw's "Wishes") also subserves rather than subverts the logic of the poem:

> Such sharpness shows the sweetest FREND:
> Such cuttings rather heal than REND:
> And such beginnings touch their END.

Read phonotextually as well as visually—in other words, read rather than glanced at—the last line's opening "And" touches its own "END" by the diacritical variation of a single letter. Further, the closing evocalized rhyme "REND"/"theiR END" returns the last verse to the already mistaken idea of rending (actually a nurturing). Lexical slack becomes spiritual lapse: the transegmental overtone of the phonotext staging here, at the poem's metalexical climax, a miniature ritual of resurgent doubt exorcized by a prelapsarian faith in God's spiritual gardening. The idea of rending, that is, returns only as a phantom antiphone, denied at the lexical level by the visible or graphic logic of the whole poem, itself a teleological model of paradisal ordering and destination. Such is the return of a repressed religious doubt under the erasure of formal coherence. It is a spiritual hesitation put in its place by the last fluctuant move of a grand, malleable, and pervasive design, a Creation in little.

Whether paring away to a phonic module or modulated by adjacent matter into a broader base of rhyme, such jointures are a recurrent, an irrepressible feature of rhyme—not only down through Pope but on into the next century, where the hegemony of rhyming verse begins to give way, regular echoes becoming marginalized as comic or satiric extravagance. Well before the Romantic decline of neoclassic rhyme, however, between Herbert's extreme experiment and the regularization of rhyming couplets in the eighteenth century, falls Milton's masterly variety in verse forms and acoustic schemes. In "Il Penseroso," for instance, the thematized acoustics of the rhyme "noise of folly / most melancholy" (ll. 61–62) seems to justify the phonemic self-consciousness of the elision of fricatives, purifying the rhyme to "of (f)*olly*"/ "melanch*oly*." Even the blank verse lines of *Paradise Lost* do at one point happen to incur an exact lexical recurrence—though not a rhyme, exactly. The moment is also acoustically thematized in a way that releases a transegmental irony. Hollander's *The Figure of Echo* contains a fine extended gloss (43–44) on this passage in which Sin cried out "*Death*" as proper name in one line and two lines later, by inversion, "back resounded *Death*" (2.787–89; Milton's emphasis). Writes Hollander: "Hell's return of the word is the sound of revulsion from caves whose hollowed emptiness" becomes "a physical locus of echo," no longer pastoral and affirmative. The sonic contours of the scene capture all this and, I think, more. The resounding caves, filling their void with the name of all mortal voiding, do not register solely in the exact chiming of "*Death*"/"*Death*." Taken as exposition, this is the sign of echo more than its work, but Milton in fact gives both within the immediate sound play of his phrasing—even if we don't hear the potential ricochet of "dead" in "re-soun*ded*." Given the dental assimilation in both halves of the rhyme ("ou*t* Death" and "resounde*d* Death"), the second, answering phrase begins to stutter with its own inward echo. What we may well finally hear is the rumbling and ungrammatical *resound-d-deth,* a formal if garbled present tense (as in Shakespeare's "*debateth* with decay") for the eternal re-verb-eration of the abstract substantive *Death,* its deafening process in and across time.

Echoic Cleavings

As we move forward from Donne, Milton, Dryden, and Pope—each authorial surname merely the place-name here for the site of certain phonemic contingencies—into the frequently comic or satiric echoism of Romantic poetry, we come upon the exemplary syllabic ingenuity of Thomas Hood's light verse. There is the overt polysyllabic and cross-lexical spread of "dis*honour*"/"left *on her*" or "pit*iful*"/"city *full*" from "The Bridge of Sighs." In reverse, the rhyme word in Hood can of course be anticipated by a collision of two predecessors: "mornin*g c*loud / so sweet and loud" ("False Poets and True," ll. 8–9). By means of ligature, the conflation of the voiced and unvoiced stops produces a covert emergence of the adjective from its denominated source. Oppositely, by elision, the *abab* rhyme in "Queen Mab" captures, partly through such sonic dispersion and recurrence, the ubiquitous magic upheaval of earth, sea, and sky: when "raging flames comes scorchin*g round*" and, two lines later, "serpents crawl along the *ground*" (ll. 30, 32). The first rhyming cluster could genuinely be heard—in its semantic, its syntactic, context—as a homophonic alternative for its actual scripted form; as verb phrase, that is, "come scorching ground" would fall into place in the larger grammatical frame. No less suggestive, even though not passing through any such moment of semantic availability, is a tiered rhyme from one of Hood's noncomic poems, "The Workhouse Clock: An Allegory," in which the persona wishes "that all the Good and *Wise* / Could see the Million of hollo*w eyes*" (ll. 73–74). The contrast between the blinkered vision of complacent morality and the emptied stare of malnutrition and despair seems actually to hollow out the rounded first phoneme of "wise" on the way to the contrasting "w = eyes." In a graphic play between signifier and signified, these "eyes" thus appear visibly severed on the page from the *w* of the supposed "wisdom" that might appreciate and help appease their deprivation.

Byron's rhymes are often deployed in such a comic mode, whether in the explicit self-reference of *Beppo,* with its polysyllabic rhyming of "person" and "for rhyme, to hook my rambling *verse on*" (st. 52), or in *Don Juan,* with the proleptic rhyme of "al*l ears!*" with "some *leers*" (9.78).[13] Wordsworth would not seem to be this sort of poet, and he isn't, nor even a poet particularly inventive in his manipulation of rhyme, and yet a similar anticipatory echo haunts—there is no other word for it—a late sonnet, "The Column Intended by Buonaparte for A Triumphal Edifice in Milan." As the attentive soul "hears combats whistling o'er the ensanguined heath," the couplet is rounded off only by an eye rhyme in "What groans! what shrieks! what quietness in death!"—a rhyming pair that nonetheless reveals the very sign of "death" fluttering visibly across the windswept "ensanguine*d (h)eath.*"

According to Donald Wesling's account, in *The Chances of Rhyme,* of the rise of modernist poetics, Romantic writers are situated at the irreversible crossroads of the rhyming enterprise. Opposed (like many of the Romantics) to the notion that "rhyme is the whole being of poetry" (132), Wesling nevertheless studies it as a signal ingredient of poetic transformation over time, a limit case for euphonic recurrences and regularized schematic patterns. Wesling's is as much an essay on modernism as it is on rhyme, using the latter as a touchstone for the more dispersed and experimental forms of "markedness" in the poetry of the last two centuries. If, on Wesling's showing, rhyme is most productively understood as a special case of literary "defacilitation," then it may well appear that transegmental echoes—where the text is roughened to the point of lexical disjunction, retarded to the point of double take (when the effect is noticed at all, that is)—is a special case of defamiliarized devising. Transegmental accords expose the whole manufactured fabric of rhyme by drawing upon the phonemic additions or subtractions always incident to it—but rendered more graphically extreme in such cases across the zeroing out of the scriptive space between words. By being less overt than ordinary rhymes, by being in fact mostly invisible to the unaided (the unauditing) eye under the normal constraints of syntagmatic or lexical expectation, the echoic recurrence based primarily on liaison or elision thus lays bare the entire machine of rhyme's artifice. Since Wesling's book deploys rhyming practice as an index to modernist ferment, its commentary does indeed naturally gravitate to Romanticism as a watershed moment for the "chances," both local accidents and historical fortunes, of rhyme. If in Romanticism rhyme gradually loses its definitive hold on the poetic imagination, the transegmental drift further loosens the syllabic autonomy itself upon which rhyme has usually, in principle, been centered. The tendency in transegmental rhyming, more than in its polysyllabic cousin or even in certain rare forms of *rime équivoquée,* is to denaturalize the lexeme itself, even the syllable—to disperse both into their phonemic minims, their linguistic constituents. This microstructure of echoism thus falls into line with the other eccentric and elaborately reticulated sonorities of Romantic practice.

Keats's *Lamia,* one of the handful of self-conscious Romantic experiments in rhyme, was written under the immediate influence of Dryden's rhyming couplets. Though most of the paired rhymes sound more neoclassic, more cleanly paced and clipped, the following couplet precipitates a curious transegmental ambiguity; it describes the supernatural dispensation by which Lamia's beauty is "unassailed," in her invisible doings, by "the love-glances of unlovely eyes / Of Satyrs, Fauns, and blear'd Silenus' sighs" (1.102–3). In the grammatical scattering of the second line, the intended sense is probably that Lamia is safe from the stares of such unlovely eyes as those of satyrs and fauns, as well as being spared the sighs of the drunken Silenus. Yet the misleading serial grammar of this line—along with the strong association of blurred or bleary vision (as well as of dull-witted drunkenness) in the adjective "blear'd"—encourages, at least subliminally, an elision of sibilants resulting in the extraction of a more exact echo: *"eyes"/"Silenus' sighs."* This tautological echo, after all, would only operate to establish cause for the graphically stated effect, since it is the escape from all eyes that liberates Lamia from the insult of anyone's lecherous sighs. In a famous passage from Keats's earlier attempt at rhyming couplets, *Endymion,* the rhapsodic and rather vaporous description of the "Cave of Quietude"—

> O happy spirit-home! O wondrous soul
> Pregnant with such a den to save the whole
> In thine own depth.
>
> (4.543–45)

— is redeemed by the telescoped sibilance ("wondrou*s s*oul") that releases the transegmental *rime riche* (or its near miss) on *oul* and *(wh)ole.* Hearing this right off as a kind of redundant homophonic pun reveals from the start the sense of totalizing fecundity (or "whole"-ness) infused within the spiritual term "soul."

There is a more dramatic, and more typically Keatsian, threading of such effects in the "Ode to a Nightingale," turning on a rhyme that has been much debated in Keats criticism without any account of its transegmental dislocations.[14] The knelling of "forlorn" that works to "toll me back from thee to my sole *self*" serves in the process to defy the fancy as a "deceiving *elf*" (ll. 71–74). In the transitional context of "magic" and "faerylands" from the preceding stanza, one may (half) hear "soul's elf" for "sole self." Echoing this, the exact belling rhyme in "deceiving elf"—that castigated and excluded alternative—both endorses such a directly polarized anti-pun and at the same time rectifies it in a single stroke of denounced imaginative escapism. Against the sensuous drifts of the ear, the inscribed rhyme may be taken to reconsolidate a genuinely sole or solitary "self" as antonym of "elf." The speaker's asserted subjectivity is construed as an integral being rescued from the invasive—here homophonically obtruded—threat of a preemptive double, phantasmatic and deceptive. Such an audition of the phrase explores in effect the underside of just the sort of critique leveled by Donald Reiman at "repetition of sounds" in even the "greatest poems" of Keats and Shelley. In a chapter on Shelley's style, Reiman alludes to Keats's alliteration in "sole self," quite apart from any hovering pun on "soul," as "a bit heavy-handed."[15] Such heaviness is, on my hearing too, exactly the first impression created by the phrasing—and not just by its written sibilants but also by the heft of another *s* in the gap of homophonic transformation between the words. This is an extra burden that works to fracture the collocation under its own phonic weight—and by shearing force to generate a momentarily ambiguous slippage.

When Wesling moves forward from the Romantics, the lack of attention paid by his overview of rhyme's "chances" to such elusive phonemic displacements prompts the unqualified historicizing of a sentence like this: "The off-key consonant rhymes of Dickinson, Owen, Auden, and the later Yeats are clearly deliberate dishevelments, attempts to cut the sound sweetness of most high Victorian rhyme, except Browning's" (120). Browning, however, cannot so easily and singly be exempted from the post-Romantic nostalgia for euphonic chiming, partly because of the phonemic mutations his prosody shares with the other more stately or harmonious Victorians. In "Youth and Art," Browning rhymes—or his text does, arranging the echo without authorial veto—"rankles" not just with "ankles" but with "her *ankles*" (ll. 42, 44), a *rime riche* obstructed only by juncture. The same ear—ours, if not Browning's—for the embedding of one lexeme within the span of another has, two stanzas before, generated a rather more Keatsian word play. Reminiscent of the manipulation of lexical subclusters in "Not to the sensual ear, but, more endear'd" from the "Ode on a Grecian Urn" is Browning's "For spring bade the sparrows pair," as if—beneath the transegmental alliteration here—the natural imperative of such creatures were the homophonic verb form instinct in their name. So, too, Browning's colloquial dexterity with bold polysyllabic rhymes may be enhanced by a transegmental nudge, as in this from "A Grammarian's Funeral": "what i*t all meant*"/"by ins*tallment*" (ll. 106, 108).

Such tactics—or accidents—readily lend themselves to the contrapuntal harmonics of a high Romantic legacy, even while they afford a different sense, and a broader history, of "deliberate dishevelments" than Wesling intends when he lists Browning as a modernist forebear. There is a phonic disarray, a discord within lexical sequencing itself, that is (paradoxically enough) native to rhyming metrical accords. It is to be detected, as we have been seeing, from Chaucer through Pope to Byron and Keats—and beyond. We find it in simple form, semantically neutral and unobtrusive, forming no gratuitous new lexemes in process, in a rhyme like Arnold's "smoother r*eed*"/"shall h*eed*" from *Thyrsis* (ll. 78–79). The elision of the liquid *r* and the suppression of the aspirated *h* smooth the very strain of the rhyme to a purer homophonic core. In American verse of the period, Dickinson's irregular rhymes can readily tap into this phonemic instability. In "My life closed twice before its close" (J 1732), her text mounts, or at least permits, such an effect in portraying those mortal separations that, when they "twice be*fell*," are "all we need o*f hell*," that last portentous noun seeming to yawn from within the verb of simple occurrence, "befell," while making good on its inactive etymological underside of plummet. So can Tennyson, "sweetest" of the high Victorians, demonstrate this vein of phonic shifting, even within the regularizing constraints of the *In Memoriam* stanza. Tennyson's persona subscribes there to the belief of Hallam, that former poet of "diver*s tones*," that "men may rise on stepping *stones*" (ll. 1–3). Beyond the already "rich" echo beginning with the consonant *t,* the special aptness of this rhyming tie (or tiered rhyme) rests with the lingering, though entirely nonmorphemic, hint of "tone" in "stones"—apt, because the very agency of human betterment in this elegy is allegorized as the surviving inspiration of the dead poet's "silent-speaking" voice.

Lines like this suggest why any periodization of rhyme should be pursued cautiously. Certainly it is too easy to limit the notion of "dishevelment," as Wesling tends to do, to a modernist aesthetic — or even to exclude the poets of high Victorian sonorities from textual disturbances incident to inevitabilities in the language itself. Tennyson rhyming may at times sound like T. S. Eliot avoiding it, or Shelley like Stevens. The Romantic energies of oblique rhyme are much in evidence as they inflect the complex scheme of the second stanza of *Adonais,* which unfolds from an interrogation (addressed to Urania) about the conditions of death: "where was lorn Urania / When Adonais died?" (ll. 12–13). The answer is conveyed by a set of rhymes that seem so deeply contaminated by the matrix verb "die" that they proceed almost involuntarily to reveal its third-person singular form, first by means of a transegmental adjustment of juncture and then by a syllabic disintegration of the lexeme. Urania sits "with veile*d eyes,* / 'Mid listening Echoes, in her Para*dise*" (ll. 13–14), and there, a line later, "Rekindled all the fading melo*dies,*" with rhyme an aural form of such rekindling. Two centuries before, Donne's "Who though from heart, an*d eyes* / They exact great subsi*dies*" ("A Valediction: Of the Book," ll. 43–44) displays a similar ligature securing a widened spread of rhyme. It does so, however, with none of the semantic charge that Shelley's lines manage at once to bury and to detonate in those echoes from *Adonais,* when the past tense "died" seems to saturate the transegmental rhyme scheme with supernal traces of a still present dying.

Even more crucial to the thematic resolution of its text is the closing aberrant rhyme of "Mont Blanc." In the speaker's apostrophe to the absconded power source of the mountain, the title's potential pun on "Mon Blanc" (for the imaginatively impregnable blank of nature when received into the mind) is at last thematically — and transegmentally — foregrounded:

> And what were thou, and earth, and stars, and sea,
> If to the human mind's imaginings
> Silence and solitude were vacancy?
>
> (ll. 142–44)

Even before the rhyming word, the emptiness that threatens is felt in the lurking specter of "dearth" in the first juncture, "an*d earth.*" Adducing the final echo to illustrate how the highly irregular and displaced rhymes throughout "Mont Blanc" subserve the thematic emphasis on that "sound no other sound can tame," those voices issuing from the heights and recesses of power, William Keach, in *Shelley's Style,* asks whether the trisyllable "vacancy" can "belong in the rhyming sequence with 'thee' and 'sea.'" His answer: "It both does and does not: the '-cy' suffix rhymes with 'thee' and 'sea', but imperfectly because it is rhythmically unstressed and because it is attached to the root *vacan(s)*."[16] The poem's last word thus "seems both to yield to and to resist the rhyming power of the compositional will" (200). The "imperfect" rhyme might on this account be said to introduce a dissonance into the whole consort of rhyme, a precarious reverberation from its own subjunctive fear ("What if?") of a spiritual nonaccord with the physical universe. But Shelley's closing lines are framed as a question, to which one possible response is that the mind does indeed rhyme with the universe. And so does "vacancy" rhyme in its own way as well. Keach characterizes it simply as "unstressed," unlike "and sea," a trisyllabic word that would get no terminal emphasis in the normal (nonversified) pronunciation of its last syllable. But more than the imposition of an iambic measure helps to secure Shelley's final accord, perhaps the single most arresting transegmental echo in the whole Romantic period. In the first of the two would-be rhyming lines, that is, there is an encroachment not just from phoneme to phoneme across an ambiguous syllabic break but from word to whole word. Emerging there—from within the very vacancy of spacing as transcended alone by *reading*—is, after all, the full, the overfull, rhyme of "stars *and sea*"/"vac*ancy*."

Though this effect may *sound* closer to a polysyllabic rhyme out of Byronic satire than to lyric high seriousness, it is deployed by Shelley as part of the unsettling urgency of the closing question. Neither the textural nor the metatextual resources of rhyme are exhausted in elevating the imperfection of one word to a metaphysical crux, to a problematizing of language in its power to order phenomena. Since the problem is itself bipartite, concerned with the interrelation of mind and nature, that component of the rhyme which establishes the ground of the latter ("earth, and stars, and sea") should be given equal weight with the noun of potential subjective decimation ("vacancy"). Phonemic undecidability has thus located the crisis, rhyme courting the danger the text's fluctuations can move to cure. It is in this sense that the topography of the rhyming phrase *describing* the natural landscape enters upon the *inscribed* metadrama of the closing rhyme. A disjunction between sight and sound privileges yet again the power of unseen harmony in the poem. In so doing, it anticipates the unorthodox rhyme word to follow ("vacancy") by exercising the lexical blank ("and-sea") for meaning. And it is precisely the *graphonic* force of this syllabic play, the intervallic transformations of its phrasing, that makes Shelley's largest metaphysical point for him. In the sweep of the mind over "stars, *and* sea," the very syntactic interval or break—requiring "conjunction"—rules out the facile fusion which would chime too closely with an imaginatively impoverished "vacancy." It is thus in

Shelley that we come to hear how Mon(t) Blanc remains perpetually available to be filled in by imagination's various engagements with the gap. Blanks represent hiatus, not void, a secret source in nature mated to a waiting hollow in the mind, a source imagined yet again as fecund, reverberant, eternally renewed.

Rays of Iteration

Hopkins's rhyming practice, as part of his larger system of grammatical torque and lexical strain, may be taken to mark one point of transition from nineteenth-century sonority, or its comic opposite, to a more irrregular modernist texturing of the line. In a literary history conceived apart from influence, Hopkins leads through the early poetry of Joyce to the gyrating phonotext of *Ulysses* and *Finnegans Wake*. At the same time, in a way that recalls the starting point of these chapters in a Shakespearean "hearing with eyes," James Milroy's study of Hopkins introduces "gradience," its most comprehensive term for the poet's concatenated sound effects, at the conclusion of a chapter entitled, with a phrase borrowed from Hopkins, "Read with the Ear."[17] The term "gradience" is accompanied by an example directly pertinent to the transegmental effect, both in rhyming patterns and elsewhere. Its subsequent exposition, however, offers an unusually compact example of the artificial limits imposed, even in linguistically oriented criticism, upon hearing with the ear. The example, from stanza 26 of "The Wreck of the *Deutschland*," is "The down-dugged / ground-hugged / grey," and Milroy uses it to illustrate his claim for "gradience" as "a kind of extended 'rhyming'" (148), the later term including internal as well as terminal echoes — assonance, consonance, and so forth. If a potential auditory recurrence actually threatens the lexical integrity of the graphic sequence, if it operates out of phase with the lettered sense, it is regularly suppressed. Hence the second hyphenated phrase, "ground-hugged," is said by Milroy to "abandon" (148) the *d* alliteration, when precisely what seems most Hopkins-like about the mounting sequence and its gradient escalation is the alliterative identity-within-difference, the incremental variance, provided by the ligature between *d* and the consequently less aspirated *h* in "groun-d=hugged."

Only in Hopkins would one tend to find such a phrase in a syntagmatic rather than paradigmatic relation to its alter ego, each collocation the phonic paragram — or internal slant rhyme — of the other as actively manifested in the text. In the case of "lee*ward* / dre*w her* / *D*ead," the dismembered rhyme with which this chapter began, Milroy is enticed only by the expectancies, the exigencies, of rhyme to find congruence around the acoustic edges of the scripted lexemes and lineations that produce this perverse (transegmental) enjambment. By contrast, supplemental rhyming matter at the other end of

terminal phrases—that is, occurring between lexically banded terminal syllables and the preceding phonemic (but sublexical) material of a given line—
slips past Milroy without comment. Such effects thus miss their chance, in
Milroy's hands, to illustrate a larger phonic principle of Hopkins's verse. In a
mode of "gradience" reversing the manner of Milroy's previous example, there
is a typifying internal rhyme in "The Starlight Night." From the two words
"diamond delves!" is thereby generated the possessive collocation "elves'
eyes," where the internal echo is either precipitated by the former phrase or
"delved" from within it. Either way, it is produced by an elision at the double d
juncture—as if the "inscape" (Hopkins's famous term for the inner contours of
both language and things) of "delves" is discovered as the very haunt of elves,
playing phantasmatically within its verbal borders—Keats's "s/elf" in a new
and pluralized phonemic habitat. The effect in linguistic terms remains a
transegmental slippage *between,* however, rather than an inherence within: a
swallowed d here, as above a forwarded d in "ground-hugged." Hopkins's end
rhymes, as well as such internal echoes as we have just examined, also benefit
from a similar phonemic motility, including the bidirectional drift from "The
Escorial" where "Gothic *grace*" rhymes with "engemming *rays.*" The assimilative liaison of c with g releases "race" to a closer slant rhyme with "rays,"
while at the same time the preceding g from "engemming" slides both out from
under its velar bond in *ng* (/ŋ/) and across the lexical hiatus to expand
("enrich") the rhyming nucleus just distilled. It is again as if the radiance of
"rays" were somehow part of the inscape of "grace" to begin with.

The metaphysical suggestion there is achieved by precisely that auditory
physics which Joyce, in *A Portrait of the Artist,* will call the "rays of rhyme"
(218)—and which he will exploit by means of transegmental ingenuities from
his early poems through to the embedded rhymed verses in *Finnegans Wake.*
The satiric passage in *Ulysses* in which Bloom compares Shakespeare's
ingenuity to the routine rhymes of ordinary poets, who in effect gull us with
such dull rhymes as "gull"/"dull" (*Ulysses,* 125), exemplifies a negative
standard for Joyce's own less prepackaged rhymes. In "A Flower Given to My
Daughter," Joyce's early text sets in echo to "Frail the white rose and f*rail are*"
the line "Whose soul is sere and p*aler.*"[18] This tendency has mutated by the
time of *Finnegans Wake* into such full-blown polyphonic rhyming in his
italicized verse inserts as "philos*opher*"/"top *of her*" (47.1–2), "from *on
Hoath*"/"up*on Oath*" (175.14–16), "s*tory ends*"/"*orience*" (418.29–30), or the
more blatantly false rhyme "red her"/"feather" (383.12–13). At one point in
the *Wake,* the semantic pressure of rhyme actually triggers a phonemic
slippage just before the terminal syllable, when "*At Island Bridge she met her
tide*" is answered a line later with "*The Fin had a flux and his Ebba a ride*"
(103.1, 3), the latter inevitably eliding to "his ebb a ride."

In between Joyce's early poetry and the late interpolated verses of the *Wake* comes the famous villanelle in the *Portrait*, its preparation laid in the younger Stephen's earlier bursts of compositional free play and phonemic progression. From the first, Stephen interrogates his own half-conscious effusions. In a daydreaming manner he has concocted some doggerel lines: *"The ivy whines upon the wall / And whines and twines upon the wall"* (179). But immediately he asks himself, "Who ever heard of ivy whining on a wall?" The reader "hears" more than this, however, and hears it in a literary-historical context that expands our sense of the verbal dispensation within which Stephen's inchoate word-spinning is to be understood. Hopkins's poetry had not yet been published, so there is thus no question of direct influence. Along with Lewis Carroll, however, Hopkins is the great forerunner of the Joycean portmanteau term. As with the transegmental logic behind Hopkins's port-manteau wording from "Inversaid," the phrase "turns an*d twindles*" arranged to reveal its appropriate overtone of "dwindling," so too with Stephen's *"And whines and twines upon the wall."* Beyond the probable free association of "whine" with the "vine" of ivy, dental ligature parallels dental elision to generate across the combinatory logic of syntax, and even of lexical articula-tion, the approximate equivalence of "d=whines" with "d=twines."

It is the same ear for covert phonic accords beneath scripted patterns that culminates in Stephen's morning composition of his villanelle, including the tandem rhyme of *"will of him"* with *"seraphim"* (217; Joyce's italics). Stephen's self-consciously shaped exercise in rhyming schemes is characterized in its final rendition by what his accompanying stream of consciousness prose calls "liquid letters of speech, symbols of the element of mystery" that "flowed forth over his brain" (223). The contradictory signals of "letters" and "speech" track the graphonic play not only of the villanelle but of Stephen's whole verbal imagination—half incantation, half inscription—as it is captured here in its transit from mental conjuration to the act of transcription. It is in this way that his poem "sent forth its rays of rhyme: ways, days, blaze, praise, raise" (218). That last word is heard circling round in its own homophonic rhyme to the very metapoetic trope of "rays" initially devised to figure the echoic process itself. It is, moreover, this same radiation of *a* sounds (*ai, a, ai*) that seems finally to lie behind the transegmental paring back (through elision) of that rhetorical question four times refrained: *"Are you not weary of enchanteD Days?"* The poem's self-examined array of rhyme is one mark of a poetic indulgence whose overcoming in the later style of Joyce is here virtually glimpsed—for a split second, a split monosyllable—in the technique of its own phonic deconstruction. Not for later Joyce the measured luxurious recur-rences of such lapidary rhymes, with their enchanted and enchained string of incantatory *a*'s.

As early as the *Portrait,* Joyce steps back from the celebratory securities of this aesthetizing view, even while he employs the transegmental mechanism that foregrounds it in the elision of "enchanted (d)ays." His text manages, if momentarily, the play between graphic and phonic signification, between typography and sonority, that begins to expose and unravel the over-schematized rhymes of the villanelle. His junctural ingenuity serves at the same time, in a passage of more mysterious mellifluity yet, to offer a liquefied lettering of speech in a covert vocalization: "A *soft* liquid joy like the noise of many waters flowed over his memory and he felt in his heart the *soft* pea*ce of* silent space*s of* fading tenuous sky above the water*s, of* oceanic silen*ce, of* swallows flying through the seadusk over the flowing waters" (225–26). Here are the rays of an interior slant rhyming that has naturalized the strained phonic gradience of Hopkins within the lyricism of a distended modernist syntax. It is in a prose-poetic passage like this, rather than in the anachronistic finesse of the villanelle, that Joyce begins to cut those stylistic grooves that will produce the graphonic cacophony of his later works.

"A Matter of Nice (S)pacing"

The great follower of Joyce in this phonemic hypertrophy of verbal texture is not Beckett, his heir in so many things, but Nabokov. There is the character (and novel) whose name is a telescoped phonetic transcription of the meta-linguistic account of his very conception: punning (punnin') as *Pnin.* And the subtitle of a later novel blends transegmentally with the main title in a manner that summons in advance the mirror wor(l)ds of the plot: *Ada; or, Ardor,* as if the first two words together, name plus conjunction, spelled the verb form "Adore." In the text of *Pale Fire*—half poem, half novelistic gloss—a phrase like "limp blimp"[19] plays less obviously, but no less functionally, with a collapsed junctural irony. Beyond the internal echo of the phrase, its abutting rhyme, is the reciprocal (and transegmental) subtraction of immediately adjacent phonemes, which in their very articulation can be said to take some of the plosive air out of this "limp (b)limp" of a phrase.

The closeness of this collocation, for instance, to the quasi-onomatopoetic word chains in Hopkins—as might be continued, say, with *simp, skimp, pimp, primp, pimple, dimple,* and so on—begins to suggest a common denominator between the two writers (along with Joyce) in their sense of textual incre-ments. James Milroy relates the manifold devices of Hopkins's internal accords and "complex phonetic play," including "alliteration, vowelling-off, *skothending,* assonance and internal rhyme," to "the old word-game whose object is to progress from one word to another . . . through a series of words formed by changing one letter of the previous words" (105). Sometimes called "metagram" (to borrow the term we will find Raymond Roussel adopting in allusion to just such games) and related to classical rhetoric's "metaplasm" (the transformation of a word by addition or subtraction of a letter), this is exactly what Nabokov in *Pale Fire* calls "word golf," illustrating it by the challenge to transfigure "live" into "dead" in just five moves, passing through "lend" (262). This is not only a metalinguistic allegory for that easing over from life into death which guides the novel's whole plot trajectory, nor in addition simply a parable of the "lending" and borrowing of letters that indeed negotiates the transformation between these monosyllables, but also a deeper-going reflexive commentary on the textual conditioning of any thematically momentous transit: as always, in some sense, a mere play on words, a cumulative interchange of signifiers lent out within the economy of difference.

More explicit play with juncture—not just with such eroded borders as in "limp blimp," but with the actual segmentalizing and recombining of terms—might be called a metaplasm of the blank itself, a plasticizing of the lexical gap. By such means, for instance, the obscure word "grimpen" becomes in the course of a given line the textual tool itself, a "Grim Pen" (l. 368). And for a latter-day instance of Hopkins-like "gradience," we find on the first page of *Pale Fire* "the gra*dual* and *dual* blue / As *night* u*nites* the viewer and the view" (ll. 17–18). Phonemic play is there doubly thematized as the graduation of visual tonality in one line and as unison through nondistinction in the next. Such is the inscape of coincidence (of lexical coincidings) in Nabokov's anything but fortuitous chiming. It is related to the prose play in the preceding novel, *Lolita,* on one word differentiated into two, a game that deconstructs the very psychoanalytic model of the erotic situation: "The rapist was Charlie Holmes. I was the therapist—a matter of nice spacing in the way of distinction" (2.1)—or for that matter, of nice distinction in the way of spacing.

In *Pale Fire* Shade and Kinbote, the poetic and editorial genius initially bifurcated for analysis, seem ultimately to converge—at least to the extent that each aestheticizes the verbal accident, the happy fault, the balletic slip. Both revel in a delectation of the verbal weft which is "based upon / A feeling of fantastically planned / Richly rhymed life" (ll. 968–70). The allusive twist here on *rime riche* notwithstanding, the actual rhymes of Shade's poem evoke something more subversive and unconstrained than "Echo's fey child" (l. 968). There is a weird fatalism as well as whimsy at work, which turns reading itself into a kind of paranoia. It is an apprehensiveness curiously matched by Kinbote's replotting of the poetic text as his own prolonged flight from death into textual immortality. To submit to the text as an occasion of paranoia is no longer to trust your senses. Words can't be relied on to stay in their scripted place. Their constituent phonemes may at any moment contract new allegiances, forge new words, or if not words, then unprocessed but palpable new sound configurations that subtend or overarch the lexical boundary without stabilizing any alternative phrase. Single rhyme words in the poem of *Pale Fire* may extend themselves backward in this way, in tandem rhymes reminiscent of Hopkins—though with less mannerist contortion, more comic snap. Nabokov's approach to the mystical coincidence latent in rhyme or echolalia is primarily through a transfiguration of the mundane. His rhyming inscapes are for the most part vernacular rather than baroque. Both phonetically overdetermined and liberated at the same time from the predictable boxing off of the prescribed syllabic unit, such treasonous rhyme quickly puts the reader on nervous alert. A given rhyme may already be upon us, so to speak, before we realize it, as in the thematized paranoia of an erotic snare when Shade, confronted with an unknown woman's "freckled hands, tha*t rapt* / Orchideous air," immediately "knew that I was *trapped*" (ll. 771–72). The context is of course heightened by that portmanteau "orchideous," a parodistic coinage by which the effect of revulsion is recognized as inextricable from its hideous floral cause. Otherwise thematized, the complex echo can be timed to a scene of mirroring in which the slippage between words is reciprocal, impossible to pin down: "the mirrors *smiled,* / The lights were merciful, the shadow*s mild*" (ll. 361–62). The rhyme gets the better of itself coming or going. Either an elision extracts "mild" from "smiled," or, if a liaison is instead felt to thicken the sibilant in the first line, then another liaison may work to extend the rhyme backward in the second. Such undecidable phonic drifts are only the more pertinent in this case for rendering ambivalent the exact dimensions of the echo, since smiling is simply a metaphor in the first place for the ameliorated mirror image in soft light.

Less perfect thematic matches may also result from interlexical phonemic slippage. These may destabilize further the reading effect, given that their phonetic overdetermination is neither confirmed by the scripted letter nor possible to shake off altogether. In the following pair of examples—"*dance*"/ "its s*tance*" (ll. 913–14); and "*stress*"/"woman'*s dress*" (ll. 951–52)—the closeness of dental phonemes connives respectively to extend and contract the rhymes (and in both cases to intensify them—in the first case, by elision; in the second, by liaison) across adjacent but gaped sibilants. In another place, a dental sound may itself provide the shifting piece of the subliminal phonemic puzzle: "no *doubt,*"/"lef*t out*" (ll. 307–8). A minimal ambivalence of dental sounds can elsewhere abet a classical instance of what Wimsatt, Kenner, or Hollander might all agree to call rhyme's reason, despite its unorthodox procedures. To wit, the question about "what dawn, what death, wha*t d*oom / Awaited consciousness beyond the tomb?" (ll. 175–76). In another ambiguity of dental articulation, again associated with death, a drifting *t* functions in a lexically seditious mode in Shade's false "syllogism," the contention that (his italics) "*other men die but I* / *Am not another; therefore I'll not die*" (ll.

213–14). At such loaded moments, the very otherness of language—every signified sliding into the signifier of yet some other referent—betrays the self into exactly the excision it would protest against. The couplet following this serves to gloss such a metalinguistic condition more directly than might at first appear, unless one is reading already with an unnerved ear:

> Space is a swarming in the eyes; and time,
> A singing in the ears. In this hive I'm
> Locked up.
>
> (ll. 215–17)

With that threefold repetition of the *I* sound (or /ay/ diphthong) in the preceding syllogism, Shade might well be punningly implying that the space of identity is "a-swarming in the I's," just as time is "a-singing in the ears." Given the stress on first-person pronouns, there is also, with "In this hive I'm," the momentary phonemic expectation of "In this I've . . ."—what, come to believe? This to one side, though (as, indeed, it is in the horizontal axis of syntax), there follows that last contraction into the monosyllable "I'm," a phrasing dislodged by elision from its antecedent rhyme: the actual predication of identity thus drawn forth from the enforced conjunction of time ("and *t*IMe") with space. By the very trope of rhyming inscape, as it were, the self is herewith imaged as enhived by the joint envelope of space and time, shape and duration. The *textual* self is similarly localized by the specific linguistic processes of eyed shape and heard duration—in short, by the *graphonic* nature of textual manifestation.

This habit of phantom lateral play finds a phonemic free agent ready (as the text's own anagrammatic formulation phrases the movements of a ghost at one point) to "sidle and slide" (l. 554) at will. The penchant for transegmental edgings and dodges comes to a climax marked by rhyme at exactly the pivotal moment of Shade's strangely displaced elegiac poem, in which the poet himself dies momentarily in the course of mourning his daughter. In so doing, Shade confirms his metapoetic instinct that the cosmos is not chaos but organized, rather, along the lines of those verbal differentials and hidden echoes that make for life's "contrapuntal" poetry (l. 807). On the brink of extinction, his is an epiphany of "topsy-turvical coincidence" (l. 809), of sameness within difference, a reticulated "web of sense" (l. 810) that makes "ornaments / Of accidents and possibilities" (ll. 828–29). Precisely at this turn, this recognition of interlinked contingencies, Shade's poem dips into its only illicit polysyllabic rhyme. With "possibilities," that is to say, the poet rhymes "S*ybil, it is* / My firm conviction," setting up a testament of faith whose declaration is interrupted and unfulfilled. Its point is nevertheless obliquely made in this self-instancing happenstance of artificially cohering rhyme. In the strained lexical disrespect of such farcical rhythm, Shade has fortuitously achieved what he has evoked a few lines before as "Some kind of link-and-bobolink, some kind / Of correlated pattern in the game" (ll. 812–13). His radically cross-lexical and low-comic rhyme on "possibilities" merely exaggerates into the open—into the multiple syntactic openings it bridges—those sly elidings that have intermittently characterized his rhyming habits and that are now erected into the logopoetic microcosm of a world to which, after almost leaving it, he finds himself restored.

It is left to his clinically paranoid commentator, Kinbote, to enter upon a closer analysis of cross-lexical effects, here those found in a variant manuscript passage of Shade's poem framed on a canonical Popeian rhyme of mortal imperatives. It is a traditional rhyme as seasoned and deep, if not as closely homophonic, as *doom/tomb*. "Do objects have a soul," he wonders, "Or perish must / Alike great temples and Tanagra dust?" (231). Though Kinbote does not mention it, there is yet another dental elision in "*an*(d T)*anagra*" that helps foreground all the more clearly the "*anagram-matic*" consciousness at work in his subsequent decipherings. Reshuffling this very line, Kinbote targets instead the next lexical juncture to find the name of the assassin buried in the subsyllabic ash heap of "Tana*gra dust*?" Mocking the "pedestrian reader"—one slavishly dedicated to metrical feet?—who may balk at this over-reading, Kinbote wonders rhetorically "how many such combina-tions are possible and plausible," offering two that are not: "'Lenin*grad us*ed to be Petrograd?'" Or the trisyllabic: "A prig *rad* (obs. past tense of read) *us?*" (231). Neither work, the one because its phonetic form (the long *u* of *used*) does not submit to metamorphosis of this sort, the other because the requisite *a* in *rad* appears in a word no longer in the *langue* and, hence, unsoundable in any *parole*. Like the Nabokovian text itself, whose surface tension Kinbote's dementia is established to travesty, his paranoia does set certain limits to its provocations.

Even the editor and anagrammatical exegete who finds Gradus lurking in the syllabic modules of "Tanagra dust" is bested by the bizarre alphabetical transcriptions of the poet's daughter, Hazel. She has spent time in a haunted barn engaging in coded conversations with a "roundlet" of light (188) that answers intermittently to her recitations of the alphabet, selecting out an apparently random sequence of letters. "The barn ghost," writes Kinbote, "seems to have expressed himself with the empasted difficulty of apoplexy"—some kind of lexical dysfunction?—"or of a half-awakening from a half-dream slashed by a sword of light" (189). In Nabokov's version of *The Wake,* this language of dreams, its condensations and displacements, is reduced to an alphabetic shifting and regrouping, a mass of "meaningless syllables which she managed at last to collect . . . in her dutiful notes as a short line of simple letter groups." They are given by Kinbote as follows: "pada ata lane pad not ogo old wart alan ther tale feur far rant lant tal told" (188). We can find intact lexemes like "lane," "pad," "not," "old," "wart," "tale," "far," "rant," and "told," though in context they don't register as units of signification, as words; they are contaminated by the nonce syllables around them. In explicitly linguistic terminology, Kinbote insists: "Divisions based on such variable intervals cannot but be rather arbitrary" (189). He does, however, sense that "some of the balderdash may be recombined into other lexical units making no better sense (e.g., 'war,' 'talant,' 'her,' 'arrant,' etc.)." The urge to "seek a secret design in the abracadabra," with its echo of "seek" itself in the adjective "*sec*ret"—the admitted need, one might say, for the phonic to submit to the symbolic Law of the Father as "pa data" (rather than "pad ata")—is followed by the confession that "I abhor such games; they make my temples throb with abominable pain," an admission which involves not only the frontal rhyme of "*ab*hor" with "*ab*ominable" but an additional part-echo based on the intervalic redivision—the transegmental drift—of "*throb* w*ith ab*ominable."

Despite this "pain," and the apparently contagious sound play of Kinbote's own retrospect, "I have braved it," he writes, "and pored endlessly, with a commentator's infinite patience and disgust, over the crippled syllables in Hazel's report to find the least allusion to the poor girl's fate. Not one hint did I find," nothing at all "that might be construed, however remotely as containing a warning, or having some bearing on the circumstances of her soon-coming death" (189). She in fact dies exactly midway through the poetic text by drowning in a partly frozen lake, "a crackling, gulping swamp" (1. 500), whose very designation would require, if orally rendered, either elision or a gulping exaggeration of the repeated *g* sounds. Moreover, the lake in which Hazel dies is located (by way of an aural rebus) in the alphabetic void—not even a functional lexical gap—between the towns of "Exe" and "Wye" (1. 490) when pronounced as the phonetic names of adjacent alphabetic characters. The "variable interval" guiding Kinbote's researches into the ghost's code is thus in and of itself the clue to Hazel's fate, and precisely in its semantic contingency, its nonsignifying mobility. The "certain sounds and lights" (1. 346) that the young girl tried to parse into an articulate message, calling up perhaps the auditory and visual collaboration of ordinary language, thereby offers a clue to the textual allegory of her end. She has suffered a vanishing into and between script, a death by letters—merely because of their phonemic and graphic constituents, shifting and imponderable as they may be. The clue was there in the impenetrability of the alphabetic code itself. Suicide or not, her death *as represented* is made to depend on the sheer accident of phonemic sequence. Whatever stabs we may take at it—as, for instance, when thinking that we perhaps hear an admonitory "do not go" or "not to go" in "pad not ogo," or finding by elision the closural note of "tale all told" in "tale . . . lant tal told"—remain undecidable.

Even if we suspect that this fateful message is a premonition not of her own death but of her father's, by Gradus's bullet in Shade's own neighborhood lane—"*Pada* ata *lane* pad *not* o*go*"—we are still responding to a carefully staged allegory of textual excision. In something of this sense the unevenly numbered last line of the poem, "Trundling an empty barrow up the lane," passes away into absolute blank—unless, as the textual notes suggest for different reasons, we return again to begin rereading the 998 lines leading up to it. It is, to be sure, a Joycean circular echo like Molly's "Yes" looped back to "Stately" or, in the *Wake,* "the" attached back to "riverrun." But the circularity of Shade's poem defies all rules of proximate rhyming accord, so that "lane" carries us back to the poet's projective identification with the death of a bird against his window in the opening line:

> I was the shadow of the waxwing slain
> By the false azure in the windowpane;

The false "azure-in" is what gives false "assuran(ce)" to the bird so slain. Other such phantom mirror words hover over this passage as well, including the grand homophonic accident that allows us, in the antiphone "waxwing*s* *s*lain," to hear pluralized the designation of the species (as well as the waxen "wings" for which it is synecdochically named). This same sibilant drift also releases by elision (and grammatical license) the past participal of "lie," as in the wings of a flying body having "lain" against the windowpane upon fatal impact with it—with the additional passing suggestion, in an anti-pun on the participial form of "lay," of the wings as s/laid out. In the retrospective rereading urged by Kinbote, this transegmental displacement of "waxwing*s* (*s*)lain" would thus only free up a more perfect rhyme with the long-deferred closing "lane."

This is again the "division" of "variable intervals" which was the real secret message of the barn ghost's code, its cryptogrammatology of the scriptive break. And as with daughter, so with progenitor: an author's "issue" or product (represented partly by Nabokov's own brainchild in Shade himself) passes from supposed existence into textual sequencing, from living voice to the material processes of graphic and phonic succession. In lateral play here is the "interval" (Nabokov), or, as we will see, *brisure* (Derrida), or signifying gap (Lacan), that floats meaning over the void—the void between words—and listens there for the voice of the other, surfaced in permutation. It is in this Nabokovian sense that literature and the self it enshrines, whose doom it seals, whose immortality it assures, is merely so many marks aswarming before the eyes, marks whose traces are at the same time singing upon the inner ear—a silent singing variably assigning its notes to meaning.

In something of a Nabokovian reflexive mode, poet-phonologist John Hollander, in the twelfth stanza of his recent poem, "Summer Day,"[20] offers an exemplary instance of what we might designate as a "phonemic trope" in rhyme—otherwise, his "figure of echo"—a braiding of end rhyme by which "Twilight and meaning, darkness and rising hope," having "Stretched out across my path a twisted rope," are followed, after a night of sleep, by a day in which "I trip over last evening's trope." The peculiar twist of such a "rope," beyond the proleptic etymology of troping as turning (as well as the etymologically false association of "twilight" with "twist" or "twill") is that, by liaison of the preceding participial /d/, the word's original appearance phonemically prefigures—as if by the logic of a midsummer night's dream— the dentalized alternative $t = rope$.

With dozens of examples gathered behind us, we can begin to recognize the full leverage offered by graphonic eccentricity upon the whole structural logic of rhyme. In this light, the linguistically as well as thematically "ironic" rhymes of Hopkins, Joyce, and Nabokov may be read all but explicitly to dismantle the artificial protective barrier in the previous English tradition, at least after Chaucer, between the low comedy of polysyllabic recurrence (Byron, Hood) and the lyric sanctity of tastefully restrained echo (the Shakespearean "line"). In turn, we can finally arrive at a definition of rhyme itself, in its play of discrepant matings and matched divergences, that actually includes, at its lower limit, the category of transegmental dislocation. The peculiarities of cross-lexical rhyming may in this way be found to reenact the general nature of terminal accord across the intervals *within,* rather than between, phrases. Implicit in this understanding, to begin with, is the nature of rhyme as an exemplary, even definitive, case of the poetic function. Taking the term "rhyme" in the broadest sense of recurrence and symmetry, phonic included, one could well characterize poetry, indeed literature as a whole, as "rhymed discourse." On this view, transegmental reading, insofar as it reads a certain (telescoped) logic of rhyme, might carry with it a rather pointed understanding of the literary condition itself as a reading effect.

All traditional rhyme, as normally conceived, puts difference at a safe and stabilizing distance, removes the recurring syllable or phonemic cluster at least as far away as the next line, and often farther. Rhyme thus plots either partial echo or phonic ambiguity, both aural factors, as graphic ones. It inscribes linguistic similarity and difference so that, up and down the page, gaps loom; the very loom of the text gapes; distances need to be crossed, convergences secured. For rhyme to work along this vertical axis, the ear must overcome the compartmentalizations of the eye. So, too, with the horizontal axis in the event of transegmental rhymes, as well as the case of transegmental drifts per se as a liminal variety of "self-rhyme." That is, in graphonic slippage apart from end rhyme, lexical rather than linear spacing—prone to Nabokov's "variable intervals"—is defied and finessed by new hearings of a phrase, evocalizations that construe divergent vocables from the visible given of script. When the structure of terminal echoism draws on such transegmental effects, then, it does not just enhance or spread out the possibilities of phonic accord; it explicates the very mechanism of rhyme within a single reading span. When, for instance, an isolated word(ing) rhymes vertically with another, *and then some,* that something more, that overplus, that increment borrowed by lateral proximity, accrues to a rhyming difference within the lexical structure of either phrase—a difference from itself as written.

To hear how this works is to encounter the physical medium of rhyme: that median field which provides the space of transference between one line and some next (or later) one by which—not *in* which—the chiming effect is to be activated. For chiming is after all an effect, not a fact. Rhymes are not read; rather, rhyming is a way of reading. This second chapter has hereby progressed to the point where we are thrown back upon the question that preceded even the first: Where do we read? Rhyme makes the answer unusually clear. It is not *found* on the page but, rather, *founded* through the activity of the inner ear. Rhymes are less induced upon than produced within our "reading," where such reading is taken to be a process and not a received text. In a word, a double one: reading *effects.* Part of that process, in the processing of any kind of literary text, involves our passive auscultation, a listening *in* on our own latent articulation. Treasonous one may say, certainly transgressive, offbeat—if transegmental rhymes (by any other name: tie rhymes, tier rhymes, terraced or tandem rhymes) operate apart from or beyond visible repetition (as in mere "eye rhymes," say), then they prove the rule of the ear once again. But of the *inner* ear, the decoding and remembering ear—as the instrumentation of a sequence rather than the organ of a unified perception. What end rhymes prove first of all, then, is the differential linguistics of all textuality. No single inscribed word can rhyme in and of itself. It must appeal (rather than peal) across a distance defined by difference even when processed under the sign of similarity. That distance, however, though visible as space, is essentially blank as text: it is merely the space between lines. In the vertical axis of the textual plane, the line one might draw between two rhyming termini may best be thought to inscribe the base of a triangle whose apex lies above the text at the site of reading. This is a reading which therefore only exists through the differential relation between these two points, separated cleanly by the space of lineation.

Less cleanly, because overlapped upon the same space, appears the contracted auto-echoism of the transegmental drift. Rhyme's constitution by difference — by the relation of one grapheme to its close phonic alternative — is intensively played out in the miniaturized compass of the transegmental effect, whether as part of a larger rhyming pattern or not. The relation of "rover" to "drover," "drive" to "strive," "end" to "send," "round" to "ground," "eyes" to "sighs," "rays" to "grace," "rapt" to "trapped" — to reconvene a few of the terminal densities scanned in this chapter — would amount to much the same relation as obtains in rhyme even if only the first of each pair were actually to appear (as graphism) anywhere in the text, the other left to an overtone contingent on some impinging phoneme. With enunciation thus encumbered by contiguity, such an adjacent, dislodged phoneme — catalytically activated at the level of the phonotext in the generation of a new though unwritten word — could therefore be said to precipitate the rhyming of a single lexeme with its own silent, layered evocalization. Alongside the traditional modes of end rhyme and internal rhyme, then, is the additional category of interstitial, or intervalic, rhyme: sprung to begin with from a word's resounding off itself in the slack — become play — between it and its neighbor. Such is the word in play with that difference from itself imposed by phonetic — become phonemic — context.

Mediating between two such hearings of a single phrase, negotiating their indeterminacy, triangulated by them as site, is again the reading body, medium of textuality as a phonic if not auditory phenomenon. Such triangulation resembles what Chapter 6 will borrow from Joyce to call "polysyllabax." In sum, reading alone voices rhyme, including that always imperfect but no less rich rhyme instituted between inscribed and evocalized signifiers in the same phrasing. The task of the next chapter is to work away at the conceptual objections to just this sense of text production, this "heretical" reintroduction of phonism (not, to be sure, phonocentrism) into the differential traces of textuality. Hearing reading voicing would otherwise have to take place over and above the distracting murmur of theoretical dissent.

3　　The Ear Heretical

A Theoretical Forum on Phonemic Reading

It is time to stand back from examples. The theoretical plateau of this chapter follows from a study of loosened end rhymes as a limit case for phonemic drifting. Such lateral accretions produce an instability within programmed iteration that redefines the marginal units of recurrence. In the usual case of an aural, whether or not oral, reading of rhymed poetry, the reader, so to say, looks to the sound of rhyme. We know where to look; metrically speaking, one can count on rhyme. If one hears there, here and there, more than expected at the ends of lines, it is because rhyme has edged back into the precincts of a language whose combinatory progress is less predictable in its rhythm of equivalences. This is the textual space of a less codified phonemic succession, the jagged terrain occasionally inflected in its own way by the transegmental drift. We need now an account of that unstable terrain – and that continuous potential for inflection – within the broader parameters of its theoretical field. The remaining chapters will then turn to a selection of textual moments in poetry and prose that should thus be more fully understood to read the structure of a certain structure – namely, language.

But that structure has itself warranted, in approaches associated more or less indirectly with literary analysis, many quite different readings, ones whose points of opposition as well as of potential consensus (at least on the ground of phonemic versus graphemic form) need to be followed out rather closely. From descriptive linguistics to structural linguistics – or, in other words, from phonetics to phonemics; from structuralist linguistics on to deconstruction; next, in turn, from the deconstructed or decentered text to the split subject of psycholinguistics; from this sense of the "unconscious structured like a language" to the renovated "semiotics" of a subliminal matrix or genotext somehow actively in touch with the bodily rhythm of speech production (a looping back, as it were, to articulatory phonetics at a new level of poststructuralist speculation); and on from this recorporealized linguistic substratum to the polymorphous pleasures of the read but no longer primarily interpreted text; this is the plan of a chapter that needs to ground itself at the start in the rigor of phonetic taxonomy.

The language of linguistics registers with keen, even colorful, precision the microturf of phonetic skirmishes flaring up as one speech sound, refusing to settle (in) for mere contiguity, struggles for dominance over another or induces its mutation. Concerning the boundary disputes and border conflicts between words, phonetic specificity tends to breed both terminological histrionics and clarifying analogy. Ballistic movements, morphemic onsets and offsets, open-vowel attacks, explosion, release, rests, constrictions, stops, residual breath streams, beat strokes and back strokes, false divisions, taut versus loose nexus, intrusions as well as occlusions, "diphthongizing diminuendo," even "vanish" used as a noun: these are just some of the terms that monitor the ceaseless interrelationship and relativity, the mutually implicated biplay, the virtual *dramaturgy*, of aural sequencing. In one extended survey of phonetics, for example, the factors most directly bearing on the literary phenomenon of the transegmental drift are enumerated by R.-M. S. Heffner under the heading "fusion," including such subcategories as "dynamic displacement," "doubling," "reduction," "omission," "glides," and "linking."[1] Yet the very rigor of distinction in phonetics is devoted to accounting for the functional "arrest of fusion" in a given communicative instance. Phonetic study is therefore less open to issues of cross-lexical vacillation than is the related consideration of morphemically pertinent *phonemes*. A case in point: in illustrating his claim about the disambiguating "initial element," Heffner writes in his subsection "Boundary Marks" that "no English form begins with [ŋ]." This axiom takes us back to the functional ambiguity, discussed in Chapter 2, in Hopkins's rhyme of "Gothic *grace*" with "engemmin*g rays*." The "dynamic displacement" of juncture itself is possible only if the fusion can be founded on a simultaneous "fission" of [ŋ] in "engemming": its splintering into the "allophone" /n/ plus a more overtly articulated /g/.

According to the narrowest precision of phonetics, there would nevertheless be operative differences even between "engemming rays" and "engemming grays" that would rule out all active undecidability of lexical juncture. Such boundary adjudication, so to speak, is what linguists label phonetic "analysis," the ear's ascertaining of morphemic structure, its pinning down of word breaks. According to the sheerly formal alternations of phonemic structure, however, the pertinent alternatives—by the very logic of potential pertinence—may be felt to impinge more energetically upon the given scripted phrase. As we process the phonotext in silent reading, that is, the paradigm is kept in an overcharged and unstable relation to the ongoing syntagmatic sequence. Though ambiguity can most often be hammered into submission by phonetics, in phonemic reading, by contrast, the weaker alternative remains something of a felt option even when—and often because—such reading is not constrained by one or another probable oral inflection. In moving from the descriptive linguistics of phonetic sound to the structuralist basis of phonemic differentiation—in short, from description to classification—we therefore find that the formal play of signifying units is more potently mobilized within the allophonic leeway of the latter system, a system, unlike phonetics, whose discriminations do not exhaust the uncertainties upon which poetic writing thrives.

Apart from critical junctures of lexical ambiguity, phonetics is certainly quick to admit that its calibrated speech sounds often overcode any functional difference, as language, between the "stimulus-response value" of given linguistic units.[2] But at another level of language production, of verbal "stimulation," the received "value" of literary phonemes becomes a matter of more freedom and more interchange in the *circuit* (rather than mere sequence) of stimulus and response. Literary language induces its own aural (if silent) feedback, not so much to thicken itself into "literariness" as continually to "reanalyze" the medium called "language" on which it is staked. In phonemic reading as practiced here, then, what is read is language itself, its deepest transformative logic, not just its given textual manifestations. In the semiotic terms introduced and reviewed in the Prologue, such reading engages genotexture as well as phenotext—in particular, the mutable phonotext subtending all script. We read language held in never more than partial check by meaning. Or put the other way round, so as to anticipate the Derridean turn, we read literature as the continuous critique of meaning. Not as a methodology, exactly, but rather as a working experiment, we read it here—as is seldom done—quite literally word by word, often word for (another) word.

What follows first in this chapter is intended mainly to concentrate theoretical issues scattered across or merely tacit in the previous two chapters. Derrida on Saussure's "general linguistics," Starobinski and Lotringer on the special case of Saussure's anagrammatic speculations—these complementary matters will offer the structuralist touchstones, both normative and eccentric, by which to consider, among other things, the unexpectedly related hypotheses of diachronic linguistics about the historical effect of junctural undecidability. From this anchoring in the formal linguistics of these separate schools, we can then move forward to the linguistic implications of post-Freudian psychoanalysis, Kristevan semiotics, Barthes's "grain of the voice," and other diverse ventures in avant-garde writing and reading—each as they bear in turn upon the elusive but illustrative function of the transegmental drift, that exemplary limit case of phonemic reading. With all this in mind, we will finally circle round to Derrida again to find in the graphonic interplay of just such a drifting aural signifier a further sense of that "supplement" so crucial to the deconstructive understanding of differential formations. Getting straight exactly what the transegmental phenomenon takes by way of clarification from this whole complex intersection of discrepant and often conflicting methodologies, as well as what it yields in connection with the most debated issues in the contemporary understanding of the textual condition, is the combined business of the present theoretical overview.

Hearing a Difference?

Oscillating ambiguously not only between words but between text and reception, the "dyslexia" of the transegmental effect consists in an aural activation that impedes mere scriptive processing. Derrida's frontal assault on the primacy of voice in language might well seem to render any reading-with-the-ear a theoretically groundless pastime. If one recognizes, however, why the phoneme need not suffer the same fate of banishment from textuality as does the voice, such an acknowledgment secures a considerable phonotextual foothold within both the practices and the axioms of deconstruction. From such common ground it should be apparent how deconstruction in no way necessarily prohibits the reconception of style, of voicing (not centered and authorial but, rather, textual, receptual) at the site, along the very track, of those irreducible differences upon which a science of grammatology is also mounted. So far from being at odds, deconstruction and postformalist stylistics are inherently compatible, both in theory and in application. This is because deconstruction, in retrieving literary language from phenomenology, gives it over entirely to the regimen of a textual analysis.

An essential fact about both primary and secondary articulation—that they must be understood as sign systems derived from sound *pattern* rather than as a transcription of actual speech—is what makes possible the Derridean intervention at the very starting point of Saussurean linguistics. According to Saussure, as summarized by Derrida, the utterance of a vocable does not produce signification through sounds per se, but through a "sound image," which appears in the authoritative English translation of Saussure's phrase "image acoustique" as "sound pattern."[3] Highlighted here is an aural configuration with no contradictory hint of the visual. Still, Saussure's emphasis leads not so much to a phonational grounding for language as to a *phonotational* one. It is for just such reasons that Derrida is drawn to Hjelmslev's "concept of *form* which permitted a distinction between formal difference and phonic difference, and this even within 'spoken' language" (57). It is here that Derrida introduces the notion of the *trace* as the very formation of such differential form. Functional—that is, formal—opposition emerges in the paradigmatic axis not by a phonemic difference in sound but by the unheard trace of the alternative. This trace bears the sheer form of difference, emptied equally of sound and of content, dematerialized. We do not, we cannot, hear the difference itself, yet with it alone, not with the sounds that may be thought to determine it, does meaning rest. Linguistics is thus concerned no longer with the pertinent opposition of phonic matter but with the semantic pertinence of opposition itself. This is difference not as between presences (sounds, for instance), but difference as the perpetual deferral within a network of signifying alternatives and alternations. One of Derrida's several summary formulations of this issue: "By definition, difference is never in itself a sensible plenitude. Therefore, its necessity contradicts the allegation of a naturally phonic essence of language" (53).

Acoustic production — material, substantial, *full* — only becomes language, speech or otherwise, with the introduction of breaks, fissures, cuts. In other words, absence is the catalyst of the system of traces that converts the activity of sound into the formal pattern of speech. "*Spacing* (notice that this word speaks the articulation of space and time, the becoming-space of time and the becoming-time of space) is always the unperceived, the nonpresent, and the nonconscious" (68). In phonetic terms, one can think of spacing, the exemplary nonphonic marker, as the switch point between the "offset" of a terminal phoneme and the "onset" of its successor in the next lexeme. Whether "in-between" a blank and a letter or "between" one letter and its alternative, linguistic difference is famously spelled *différance* by Derrida, evoking not only the formal "differential" of the trace but also, since the coinage is itself unsayable *as* different, its perpetual "deferral" of presence or voice — its operational basis, rather, in an "arche-writing" (68). It should be obvious how central this notion of the marked break in speech is for the present phonotextual investigations: this "joint" that (in Derrida's remarks on "la brisure" [65]) is both fracture and hinge, rupture and juncture, split and pivot — what I want to call the "double bind" of juncture.

Of Grammatology has thus deconstructed the metaphysical premises of Saussurean linguistics by introducing the proto-scriptive gap in order to erase the misleading metaphysical gap between the sensible (phonic) and the intelligible (semantic). All becomes properly semiotic, a tracery of signs, a differential notation. But in the sense that such a deconstruction is taken to reconceive language in a graphic rather than oral image of itself, it must be admitted that grammatology leaves out a theory of textuality as a *reading effect*. To include such considerations of speech in textual reception would reinstate, would indeed reinscribe, the phonemic stratum. It would be returned not as a dimension of full presence, never more than the mere trace of speech in writing. Rather, phonemics would be reinscribed within textuality in such a way as to account, for instance, for the power of Derrida's own entirely *writerly* coinage, *différance*. We might say that the antilogocentrism of this term renders it not a full neologism but rather a *neographism,* being already the homophonic double of an existing word which haunts it "under erasure."[4] Coined in part, as Derrida explains in *Speech and Phenomena,* to cover those two simultaneous differential chains that are mutually activated in language, the phonemic and the graphemic, the term *différance* enacts the formal interchange "between speech and writing and beyond the tranquil familiarity that binds us to one and to the other, reassuring us sometimes in the illusion that they are two separate things."[5] Contrived, therefore, to illustrate the fact that written characters—as integers of meaning—have no inalienable bond to sound, still the coinage derives its effect from our tracing an *apparent* (alphabetically marked) difference back to its emptied vocal center. Its whole force as pun, as reading effect, thus depends after all upon invoking (evocalizing) the phonemic determinants of language—if only in deferral and under erasure.

Let us grant that, once grammatologically rethought, literary language is always more "writing" than speaking. Nonetheless, at a text's receiving end, the "productive" (Riffaterre's sense) "presence" (the common, not the metaphysical, sense) of the reader, as well as the potential or "passive" (the linguistic sense) presence of an articulating voice, together emphasize the "reembodied" nature of textual inscription in the work of enunciation, whether latent or out loud, whether stopping short at the mere rules of pronunciation or bringing them to voice. A close *reading* of Derrida's *différance*—as a scriptive detour within phonic equivalence—thus leads us not so much to the confirmation of his theories as to the source of the original confusion they are meant to reduce. To understand textuality as text *production,* in other words, is to isolate the phonocentric temptation. Script has so often been mystified as transcribed voice, as encoded speech, in part because it seems to meet a speaking voice halfway. I don't mean halfway between author and reader, the text as silent interface. The voice of the author has nothing to do with, or in, the textual circuit. Reading, rather, provides a tacit halving of the distance between someone else's text, that someone long gone, and *one's own* voice. We can *read back* from text to voice in only one direction, not back (behind it) to origins but back out from the page into the locus of the text's production as evocalized. That words on a page make us *almost* hear the sonic "patterns" conveying their signifieds as the productions of a latent voice, if only our own, offers one probable explanation for the lure of logocentrism—as well as the motive for deconstructing it. Yet, as we shall see later, the proliferation of Derridean critique in literary studies tends to undermine this illusion of voice without fully acknowledging what prompts it in textual (rather than metaphysical) terms. In this sense, what the principle meaning of *différance* itself defers, often deters, from consideration is the role of the phoneme in that uncertainly fissured and fused stream of signification which is the read text.

This is a tendency rather than a tenet of the deconstructive agenda, however, since Derrida himself does make room, as noted earlier, for a certain oppositional play "between speech and writing" under the rubric of *différance* as well. This same interplay or tension will surface in his recent commentaries on Joyce. More than elsewhere in Derrida's work, the Joycean inference of "voice" (indeed, of multilingual pronunciations) within the very deferral of any such voicing by script will allow the return of a certain phonemic response to literary language – though certainly not a phonocentric one – into the field of verbal analysis. This is exactly the aspect of Derrida's practice as a reader that has been too little understood and pursued in the Anglo-American adaptation of his theoretical views – with a notable exception in the work of Geoffrey Hartman. One does need to begin any overall account of the "phonotext" roughly where (that is, in *Of Grammatology*) Derrida begins his critique of "phonetic writing" (23), parting company with the Saussure of a remark like this: "The linguistic object is not defined by the combination of the written word and the spoken word: the spoken form alone constitutes the object" (31). The present study would take exception to, and so take off from, this same statement in Saussure – but not so as to follow Derrida to his full reversal in arguing for the exclusive priority of "arche-writing." To proceed toward a receptual theory of the phonotext requires a more limited contradiction of Saussure. Concerning the writing at issue here, often an extreme (but exemplary) case of literary textuality, I would claim that, whatever the "linguistic object," the *textual* object, produced as read, is exactly "defined by the combination of the written word and the spoken [that is, speakable] word," though unclouded by what we have already seen Derrida reject as that "tranquil familiarity" which can delude us into thinking that writing and speech remain readily distinguishable at base. Rather, their bond is a never stabilized compact, the shakiness of its terms being exposed when the usual maintenance by suppression it involves – by which all sense of the spoken is subordinated and contained by script – is suddenly abrogated in the act of reading. The scriptive warranty of lexical autonomy may then frequently be breached, words rent by jostling divergences, syntax itself unraveled in the slippage of difference.

Given the curious transegmental effects (including tandem rhymes) so far examined, this book might well seem determined on a course of very special pleading. Why the insistence on putting forward not a collaborative stylistics of diction, syntax, and phonetics but, instead, a highly particularized approach to the phonotext as a system not only of differences but of intervals –

intervals as the sine qua non of difference? In all this, the specialized evidence is meant to prompt larger considerations. The transegmental drift simply exacerbates to the point of unprecedented clarity a leading fact about all language, a fact that much literary phrasing is meant in other ways to foreground as well. Language lives, and breathes, on the skid. I don't mean primarily to be holding out for the *dulce,* even the *utile,* of the transegmental drift, an effect so dubious and ephemeral, in fact, that the words constituting it could be said either to take it or leave it. That the transegmental trace must be heard to be believed, however, is exactly what suggests a theoretical utility to these slidings and elidings between words. Such a purely differential effect can gain a corrective purchase on the very deconstruction that would evoke "difference" (however spelled) in the process of subordinating its phonic seductiveness. If the present field of exemplification seems unusually narrow, then, it is because I am trying to drive a wedge. I want to assert enough leverage on the deconstructive critique to free up its analytic power from the single-mindedness of its anti-Saussurean (and hence, ultimately, antiformalist) bias. The linguistic refinement displayed in Derrida's apprehension of textuality, deconstruction's unprecedented grasp of the *play* of literary language (play in the sense of alternation, oscillation, give) — indeed, its naming of this play as the founding condition of the trace — ought to be, though has so far not proved, widely enabling for an intensive reading of the literary text. In fact, one line of Derrida's thinking could lead, more or less directly, to what I have been characterizing as phonemic reading: a continuous response to those traces highlighted in literary language as a drift of functioning differentials.

Anagrammatology: Words Sup on Words

In assessing the Derridean corrective of Saussure, one must include Saussure's notorious divergence from himself. Alongside the *Course in General Linguistics,*[6] there is the Saussure who tentatively put forward, but never into print, his very special theory of linguistic relativity in the putative "anagrams" of ancient poetry. Jean Starobinski has edited Saussure's notes on the anagram in *Words upon Words,* and Sylvère Lotringer's extensive review of this volume follows out even more fully the irreconcilable divergence between this never-completed work and the *Course,* in light not only of deconstruction but of post-Freudian psycholinguistics.[7] In his commentary, Lotringer proposes to show that general linguistics, with its deference to normative signification, could emerge only if "armed" against the implications of the anagram — on guard, in other words, against "the irruption of the signifier on the scene of writing" (2). Lotringer is able to seize upon the implications for self and subjectivity in the discontinuities of Saussure's method for reasons having to do in part with Saussure's recurrent emphasis of the proper name, usually of a deity or hero. This is the "hypogram" hiding *behind* the verse line or hovering *above* it—or, in Starobinski's formulation, lying *under* it (*Les mots sous les mots*) or, yet again, in the words of his translator, mounted *upon* it. The poetic line thus unfolds under the aegis of that name, sponsored by a "presence" beyond the text. In Lotringer's ironically loaded, logocentric phrasing, the divining of the name is regularly its *divinizing* (5), the accessing of a plenitude both linguistic and metaphysical. Saussure's first full-scale example is "Taurasia Cisauna Samnio cepit," which he advances as "an anagrammatic line containing the entire name of Scipio" in the rearranged phonemic dyads "*Ci*sauna" + "ce*pit*" + "Samn*io*" (16). This is an anagram, if at all, in no exhaustive sense, for many of the line's letters, hence sounds, fall away in the face of the erratic logic of recombination. What results is Saussure's specialized notion of the "hypogram," an absent "theme word" that deliberately organizes the line *from without,* like an absconded prime mover.[8] Causation, intention: these were crucial for Saussure. As they increasingly slipped beyond proof, he despaired of shaping his studies into a definitive work, withholding them finally from publication. The fear was always that the verbal interplay, unmotivated, decentered, if you will, would lapse to rhetoric, to decoration, to mere "style." In this context of a heavily *worked* if cryptic agenda, the danger signal was always the specter of asemantic sound *play,* a superficial density characterized by the term "paronomase" (18) which Saussure retrieves from its contemporaneous obscurity only to relegate again to inconsequence. Up to a point, nothing sounds more like Saussure in his charts of phonic recurrence than the work of David Masson, cited in Chapter 1, on "free phonetic patterns" in Shakespeare—"free" from semantic obligation, "free" therefore from the snares of intentionalism. Saussure, however, tried to recover these snares as a safety net, underwriting with the logic of causality an otherwise willful gaming.

In linguistic terms, all Saussure insists upon in order for the hypogram to serve as an appreciable function of the verse, rather than just the reshuffling of single alphabetic characters in the narrower sense of an anagram, is that the shifting sublexical unit of measure be diphonic rather than monophonic, composed of at least two sounds in sequence. This insistence, however, is the very point of attack in poststructuralist commentary: the supposedly vulnerable underside of Saussure's instinct for textual permutation. In regard to this sticking point in any allegation of a phonocentric bias, it must be remembered that Saussure lays his stress upon paired or linked phonemes more on account of their credible perceptibility than their acoustic primacy; he emphasizes their reception *as language,* unfolded in time, an enunciable linear procession—however interrupted—rather than a sheerly graphic puzzle. It is for this reason, a lineated duration, that Saussure insists on the diphone: the smallest registrable unit of sequence. On the other hand, the sense of progression clearly does not imply a continuous or unbroken flow of sound, merely the necessity of one "sound image" appearing (determiningly) before or after another.[9] Based on the diphone as the smallest increment that could effectually enter into covert bondings without surrendering itself wholly to the random, the result nevertheless remains a linguistic order irregular, ridged, interruptive. Since nothing in the principle of the diphone prevents the hypogram from overriding grammar and even morphology, one might take the anagram's aberrant rewording to mark the transgressed limit of that signifying continuum based on external open juncture, on lexical closure and punctuation, on decisive spacing and breaks. The law of the diphone could never, in other words, succeed in normalizing the anagrammatic moment within discourse; rather, the diphone anchors itself, just barely, against the exploding surface of that discourse.

For Lotringer, however, as for Derrida, the elevation of the diphone as first principle seals Saussure's pact with the textually conservative nature even of the anagrams. On this showing, the diphone, once insisted upon, becomes a policing agent: "The inter-position of the diphone is a summons to the linear order which will have its consecration in the *Cours*. The *Anagrams* weren't published: linguistics was born of that exclusion. We would suggest that Saussure's reasoning unreason proposed in fact the suppressed foundation of all that he elaborated subsequently" (8). But how conservative can the diphone be if it conserves only itself, relinquishing all else we take for granted about speech? How conservative, when it resembles so closely the polymorphous language of schizophrenia that Deleuze finds, for instance, in the displacement of the "difficult" consonants *r* and *l* of the English word *early* across a number of French expressions used in connection with time by his "schizophrenic student," including such anagram-like dispersions as "suR Le champ" and "dévoRer L'espace"?[10] Though stationed amid the directional stream of speech, the diphone is an *overreaching* agent. Its clusters mark, by stepping off, the spaces that need to be neutralized in order for the anagram to emerge. Once a free agent, in other words, the separate phonemic unit of the diphonic sequence enacts a textually disjunctive function, one whose possibility depends on the graphic apprehension of the very sequences it overleaps, the spaces or gaps whose ordinary structuring presence it only confirms by momentarily ignoring.

The general bearing of all this on the phenomenon of the transegmental drift should be growing clear. In such lexical slippages, a wording discrete and consecutive is tightened to the ambivalent segue of equivalence, the different fashioned on the trace of the same. Like the Saussurean diphone, the linguistic unit at issue in the transegmental effect—we might name it the *duophone,* constituted as it is by ambiguous phonemic ligatures—also calls the syntactic sequence into question. Yet the transegmental drift, whether eliding a letter or sliding one forward (or back) along the lexical chain, does, through its mutation of the diphone itself as double integer, also fuse a new unit on either side of its formerly bonded phonemes. Words break apart, syntax breaks down, but still no single phoneme—unless it also comprises in itself a lexeme (as with the article *a*)—ever breaks away entirely. The "deconstruction," though powerful, is not exhaustive, since the results are held within the realm of a reading effect, a factor of process. They must remain in play within the very system they assault, eroding it without removing themselves from it, a structure of oppositions passing in and out of lexical pertinence.

This "duophonic" nature of certain unexpectedly active synchronic oppositions, however, finds a curious parallel, as it happens, in the field of historical or diachronic linguistics. The contingencies of articulation—in particular, its lateral instability—make it prone to shifts over time in the same manner that it is prey to flux in a given utterance. Diachronic linguistics is illustrative here through just this homology with textual play. Otto Jespersen's landmark study in linguistic evolution, *Language: Its Nature, Development, and Origin* (1922), privileges voice over writing in this regard as the more fluid agency of historical transformation. Jespersen pays special attention to the infantile stages in the development of symbolic language, "sketching the linguistic biology or biography of the speaking individual" as in certain cases it models the development of the entire lexicon over time.[11] For our purpose, his most interesting studies of children's verbal fumbles, the "lapses and blendings" of semiliterate speech, concern the segmental ambiguities he classifies under a subheading called "Word-division," the hyphen proving its own point about phonemically indeterminate juncture. "Children will often say *napple* for *apple* through a misdivision of *an-apple*" (133), in what amounts to a transegmental blending truncated by aphaeresis. Or there is the pure transegmental drift of "some-ice" mistaken for "some mice." French examples include *un tarbre,* starting from *cet arbre,* and *"ce nos* for 'cet os,' from *un os"* (133). The junctural decision making in these cases, erroneous or (over time) transformative—the effort at what linguistics elsewhere terms "disambiguation"—is designated in Jespersen as "analysis." Lifted to the historical stage of language change, as "meta-analysis," it is rewritten by a transegmental fusion of Jespersen's own: "I have ventured to coin the term 'metanalysis,' by which I mean that words or word-groups are by a new generation analyzed differently from the analysis of a former age" (173). The British place-name of "Riding," for instance, "as a name of one of the three districts of Yorkshire is due to a metanalysis of North Thriding," meaning "third part" (173). Jespersen includes a further list of such lexemes as *napron, nauger,* and *numpire* that eventually, through recurrent use preceded by articles, gave up their first consonants to become, as in "*an (n)*apron," the words we have in modern English. One of his examples, the transformation of *a naddre* into *an adder,* can in fact be checked against that poem by Chaucer which provided early evidence of tandem rhyme in Chapter 2. In the tale of Cleopatra from *The Legend of Good Women,* we find the archaic version of the noun nested in an alliterative sequence of internal rhymes: "A*non* the *n*adderes go*nn*e hire for to sty*n*ge" (1. 699). And for a contemporary example of language change in the making, through the faulty analysis of consonantal "doubling," there is the solecism "advance degree" for "advanced degree," which I have actually seen spelled out in an advertising circular from Ford Motor Company (as if the Ph.D. were a way to getta head).

What is so distinctive in Jespersen's sense of that "metanalysis" by which we have come to lose such a lexical form as *nadder,* and with it, for instance, the chance for the particular consonantal alliteration of Chaucer's literary use of the word, is the role played by childhood—in other words, by marginal literacy—in linguistic change. Poised on the verge of fully mastered articulation, aware of grammatical bondings between articles and nouns, say, but not yet in control of vocabulary, the child, in Jespersen's view, is likely to find itself precariously adrift in the (transegmental) flux between diction and syntax. Within the diachronic "biology or biography" (8) Jespersen sets out to chart, we could say that ontogeny not only recapitulates but actually precipitates the phylogenetic transformations of language. In Julia Kristeva's terms (soon to be explored), the lingual vestiges of "semiotic" (or prearticulate) motility are glimpsed here in their still ambiguous and incomplete assimilation to the "symbolic" order, caught in vexed lexical junctures on the speaker's way toward full segmental mastery. The tricks of the ear thus take priority over the written "tongue," troubling its lexical reception, motivating its historical transformation.

As suggested in the Prologue, it should therefore be possible to conceive poetry, literary textuality, as the resynchronization of such a potential for diachronic change. Poetic writing, dependent as it regularly is on the phonic contours of language, invites a running junctural "analysis" kept open from word to(ward) word. Literature thus foregrounds without fossilizing those paradigmatic scrambles—sometimes historically determinate—that get disposed along the syntagmatic line. The tendency toward lapse and blend, toward phonemic lag and syllabic overlap, is always present, regardless of its force for change within the etymology of a given word. It resides in the differential synchrony—and syncopation—of a written text still haunted by the subarticulate undertones of a potentially more disruptive transformation, a junctural shifting supposedly forestalled by its very institution as text. The reader's registration of a transegmental effect depends upon this continuous latency of mutation, rarely of full lexemes but rather of diphones (triphones, and so forth) abutting each other in syllabic collisions or sundered by juncture. To recognize this is a way of acknowledging that in certain cases the structuralist axis of syntagmatic succession seems to compact and replicate the axis of historical change over etymological time. Diachronic shifts thus have their textual counterpart in synchronic drifts. In this way, the de-familiarizing ambiguity of articulation in the phonotext performs its own "metanalysis" in process, rewording script by silent listening.

Despite the implications of diphonic — or duophonic — juncture for diachronic linguistics, it is still the structuralist process of differential significa-tion to which the anagrammatic excursus of Saussure retains its most reveal-ing relation, if only by default. The time has certainly come to say it: one can finally believe neither Saussure's evidence for the anagrams, by and large, nor the theory of their generation. What is alone persuasive is the emergent linguistic principle of "consecutivity" by which he hopes, and fails, to con-strain both evidence and theory within the limits of credence, within a system rather than a random field of play. The limits of sequence placed upon the syntagmatic latitude of the anagrams thus make for a somewhat retrenched, but ultimately more progressive, account of reading practice as text produc-tion.[12] Jonathan Culler has written: "The interest Saussure's work on ana-grams has provoked comes in part from its practical dramatization of the tension between finding and positing meaning."[13] For Lotringer, a more provocative debate would have to do with *who* is responsible for either the finding or the imposition. Which is a way of asking about the theory of the psychic apparatus behind such verbal play: whether in fact the Saussurean anagram did come closer than the *Course* could have permitted to a subject split wide by the discontinuities of the signifiers through which it assembles meaning. This is also obviously an inescapable question, psycholinguistic rather than phonemic, for any emphasis on the reading *effect*. Upon whom? Upon what kind of subject?

Puns Spun: The Weave of the Unconscious

For all the kaleidoscopic discomfitures of its signifying energy, Saussure's anagram is still, from a poststructuralist vantage, found burdened with an unexamined complacency about the signified. In Lotringer's form of this objection, the "Saussurian anagram inhibits the circulation of desire by constituting a nominal reserve in which the subject remains caught" (9), a reserve of nomination, the sacred or at least mystified name. The specter of a constrained or inhibited subject, or reader, thus spurs a necessary deconstruction of the proper name. Such a deconstruction sees its fullest statement in Derrida's essay on the name of the French prose poet, Francis Ponge. The study appears under a portmanteau title that, in French and in English, happens to illustrate a transegmental principle of conflation itself undermining the integrity of the name. In *Signéponge/Signsponge,* the French for "signed Ponge" loosens by liaison the word *éponge,* while in English the elliptical syntax "(he) signs ponge" releases in fuller grammar, again by a kind of liaison, the aphoristic clue to the whole project: any sign will sponge off essence, will seem to absorb presence.[14] As regards the tensions between phonemes and graphemes in the work of alphabetic writing, it is typical of the distance between Derridean practice and theory that the localized punning implications of his title, its fortuitous disruption of juncture, carries even more telling suggestions for the free play of the signifier in inscription than does the book-length meditation on aleatory and irrepressible nomination that accompanies it. For unlike the case of the graphological coinage, *différance,* with its complete homonymic collision, the differences among *signe/éponge, signé/ ponge, signé/éponge,* even *"signé, eh! Ponge"* (101) do not so much depend upon as precipitate the graphic differentials or blanks, let alone the orthography of doubled or inserted letters, by which the spread of punning is determined. In such paradoxical, such contra-dictional, graphonic biplay, it is the *imaged* "brisure" upon which all punning activity "hinges" as *heard.* There is a moment in Ponge's own manipulation of a silent phoneme, as glossed by Derrida, that gets to something of the same linguistic depth. The unavoidable imbrication of description with inscription is so often foregrounded in Ponge that his own wordplay follows suit in the (transegmental) conversion of "nature" to "gnature" (122)—a name for the textually engendered world that, even as name, bears peripherally with it, under never more than partial erasure, the dismembered morphophonemic trace of its materialization as sheer "sig=n=ature," sheer sign.

The onomastic basis of the Saussurean hypogram, by contrast, privileges the "nominal" to the point of mystification. It makes axiomatic the wholeness of the reading subject—according to Lotringer—before the reintegration of the maimed name of the Other, reified and often deified: the hidden name of hero or god that "solves" the anagram. The argument concerns a displacement of implied presence forward from, as well as out behind, the text. To piece together the name is tacitly to name our own relation to the logocentric basis of the text—our relation as subjects, as subject to it. We participate in the text as interpreters before the mystery, dedicated in advance to the reproduction of the phonic substance of its dismembered body; our subservience is that of acolytes at a sacrament, a linguistic transubstantiation. Otherwise, we as readers would confront in such texts the explosion of all names, all words, in a leveling polysemy of the trace, a war of competing emphases, the fray (in every sense) of wording itself. In his one explicit allusion to the *Grammatology*, Lotringer registers how Saussure's claims for the anagrams, if pressed, would "in effect wrest the phonic substance away from that logocentric tradition (Derrida) which elevated voice to the ideality of meaning" (3). Derrida has himself pursued this toppled status, this dethronement of voice, not so much as a tumbling into the unconscious but rather as that fall, slip, lapse, that original and perpetual discontinuity, which, in Lotringer's terms, too, *defines* the unconscious: in *Of Grammatology* he writes, "Within the horizontality of spacing, which is in fact the precise dimension I have been speaking of so far, it is not even necessary to say that spacing cuts, drops, and causes to drop within consciousness: the unconscious is nothing without this cadence and before this caesura" (69).

Here of course is the dreamwork of Freud, its condensations and displacements, reread through linguistics. And at the heart of that linguistics, at the base of the Saussurean revolution (according to Lotringer and Derrida both), is a Janus-faced subject—conscious and unconscious at once, seemingly unified and ultimately split—whose contradictory positioning is brought to the fore in the reading of anagrams. In arranging to refer away textual motivation to a sacred or mystic nomination, to foist off on the name of a ritualized and transcendental signified all the deferments and deflections of what Lotringer calls the "phonetic gram" in its dance along the line, Saussure's attempted redemption of reference does no justice to the fractured nature of the text that produces this name. It is a text whose operations, aberrant and oblique, are in fact the staging of that name's coming (up) to consciousness from the words *under* words. The break *into* speech is thus a discontinuity at its point of origin, founded as it is on a lacunary slide. In resistance to this, the discoursing subject of the anagrams—and, by intersubjective extension, the reader as well—is shielded from the slippages of language by the Saussurean sense, as phrased by Lotringer, that "in the linguistic game, the subject of the enunciation does not have to be unconscious—language is unconscious for him" (5).

The psychoanalytic premise of Lotringer's critique is, more or less directly, Lacan's "agency of the letter in the unconscious." It leads us to the Lacan of verbal practice as well as theory. Christian Metz, in *The Imaginary Signifier*, compares the polysemy of language to the unbinding of psychic energies in Freud and then offers a punning passage from Lacan's *Ecrits*, never before translated into English, about the word as a nodalization of various meanings. Though not stressed by Metz, these are meanings that intersect the phonemic rather than semantic level of the word, unfurled there by segmental permutations. "'The word,' according to Lacan, 'is not a sign but a node of signification.'" As instance, Lacan gives *rideau* for "curtain," subsequently stretching it out "as pun" to *"Les rides et les ris de l'eau* [the wrinkles and smiles of the water], and my friend Leiris mastering [*LeiRIS DOminant*] these glossolalic games better than I can."[15] Walter Redfern, in his intermittent diatribe in *Puns* against the self-regarding cryptograms of French avant-garde literature and theory, castigates none other than Leiris for the quasi-anagrammatic conversion, in *Mots sans mémoire,* of *syllabe* to *sybille.*[16] It is, however, the sibylline power of the syllable that is just the point of such a memoryless *mot, bon* or not, its power to unveil new meaning from its own folds, its own refolding. Two pages later Redfern has turned his attack against "Lacanism," singling out the notorious (and typifying) "homophonic" logic (in French only, he objects) by which "le nom du père" and "le non du père" are related, let alone "Les Non-Dupes Errent" (80).

To claim, however, that the mind works in puns—in slips, parapraxes, glissades, elisions, and the like—is not to say that this can be demonstrated through the stylistic equivalents of these fluxions and functions. Lacan's rhetoric in this regard can never be more than evocative, never be conclusive. At the same time, since the play and displacement of verbalization is the very scene of the psyche for Lacan, punning does not merely package an argument but, rather, enacts it. The Name of the Father, for example, institutes the Law of the Father, the interdict, the psychically enunciated "no" to desire; hence *le nom* slides over into *le non.* In this paronomastic parable (it could never be more), the name *is heard as* a negation in the very instant of its designation. After Lacan and Derrida together, one could propose that all attempts of the *nom* to cover (for) an inevitable nonidentity (with) offer a deferring to naming that is never more than a deferring of the named. Taken this way, still a homophonic pun cannot prove the point, nor even argue it. It can, though, foreground the instabilities and splits attending upon language—and thus attending any attempts to prove in or with language the existence of a subject otherwise constituted.

This is the usual force behind the effrontery of Lacan's vaunts, including such famous punning manifestos as *l'être* seen comprised entirely of *lettres* or the portmanteau coinage *lalangue,* which is not another name for *la langue* but instead for something else, something other and prior, to which, in a non-name, *lalangue* gives voice. It is no longer *the langue,* even the language in which it is written, no longer one among many *langues* (French, say), but a shaping of sound previous to the fall into Babelized difference, a lingualism unspecified by syntax or lexicon. In lingual execution as well as in reference, a pun like *lalangue* bears closest comparison to the *semiotic,* rather than *symbolic,* stratum of language in Julia Kristeva's unorthodox distinction, a phonatory impulse before logical articulation. Indeed, the systolic nature of the coinage—that vibratory, palatalized effect produced by the syntagmatic telescoping of article and noun—catches perfectly the sense of a sound poised precariously on the threshold of referential or symbolic language. Before exploring the Kristevan parallel in more detail, we might simply note that *lalangue,* as *almost* a word, seems both to share with such punning as *nom/n* a phonemic basis and with *l'être* versus *lettre* to tap into a transegmental process that performs the deconstructive logic of signifying slippages. This is the metonymic skid that never allows signifier to catch up with a fixed signified.

But what does it really mean to *predicate* meaning in this way? Text production: the inscription, the *con*scription, of readers into the tread and skid, the separations and parings, the irregular restless s/pacing of *langue.* This is *langue* in its perpetual and never-completed realization as *parole,* as systemic *sons* made over into specific *sens.* The matter admits, however, of a more rigorous linguistic description than is usually offered. In mishearing— which is to say, in reading—*éponge* in *signé ponge,* for instance, or *lettre* in *l'être,* writing falls, stumbles, back upon its own double articulation. Primary articulation is voluntary, "stylistic"; secondary articulation subsists precoded, built into the word shapes of the *langue.* Upsetting this clear distinction, however, transegmental drifts transform, in the process of merely choosing, the lexical units they deploy; spacing becomes itself a module in the secondary stage of articulation, not just a partition after the fact at the primary level. A two-staged account of reception as well as of enunciation must therefore be developed, a double system not only of message production but of text production. If reading is construing, then we might call this reading function, in its reactivation of the twofold articulation of language, a *double construction.* It operates by the graphonic tension which in effect plays secondary off against primary articulation long after the former would ordinarily be silenced by lexical selection: call it the return of the repressed, of unconscious and involuntary phonemes, within the awakened but not orally engaged "voice" of the reader.

Phonocentrism is superseded entirely here by a decentered articulation. The uttering subject is gone from the authorization of the text, zeroed out at the point of origin. At the point of destination, then—or, rather, not *then* but *instead* (there is no *prior* to the advent of reading-as-producing)—at the point of destination, a decorporealized phonemic base is rematerialized by the still latent body of the reading—but the reading *what?* the reading self? the reading subject? the reading mechanism? This reading function processes inscription not as enunciation but, rather, as language in action. Writing is revealed as sheer writing, poetry or prose as a *text,* but a text formally constituted at its base, rather than at any tenable source, by differences *between* phonemes and graphemes as they bear on the double articulation of the system they jointly establish. Whereas Derrida demystifies Saussurean linguistics, even its glossematic revision, by deconstructing the "metaphysical" distinction between phoneme and moneme (or, in other words, between the ontology of the sensible versus the intelligible), I would want to locate elsewhere the brush of meaning with *sense,* with corporeality. At the locus of text production as a site of reading, texturing there the double construction of the semiotic fabrication, the dualism of mind/body returns already stripped of its metaphysical load. It returns not as a dualism at all but as a functioning difference within the (already contradictory, idiomatically deconstructed) "mind's ear" of the reader. It returns there as the very operation of the phonotext.

Metagrammatology

If the theory advancing a psycholinguistic foundation for the text produced in this way carries conviction, then the condition of such textuality must take precedence over any of the vicissitudes of literary history, including the championship of modernism in poststructuralist theory. Like early Foucault, like Barthes and Kristeva, Derrida in *Of Grammatology* is an inveterate advocate of modernist writing, even though he would seem to join Hjelmslev in departing from the retrograde devotion to the phonic stratum in its first great theoretical movement. Such is that Russian formalism which, in its "attention to the being-literary of literature, perhaps favored the phonological instance and the literary models that it dominates. Notably poetry" (59). On the other end of the spectrum from this implicitly logocentric formalism and the traditional texts to which it is in service lies the radicalized and irreducible textuality of a modernist writing practice: what Derrida follows Hjelmslev in calling, by a strained nesting of his own grammar, "the purely graphic stratum within the structure of the literary text within the history of the becoming-literary of literality, notably in its 'modernity'" (59). Derrida admits that this attempt at a "recaptured parity of substances of expression" taps a "vulgar" rather than purely differential "concept of writing" (55), an intuition "popular" (59) rather than scientific or formal, and that it holds no real interest for his own level of analysis. He retains the concept of the scriptive in "arche-writing," he admits, "only because it essentially communicates with the vulgar concept of writing" (56). This communication has in fact been too effective at times, for in the widespread extrapolations from Derrida's work, the graphic insistence, the relentless stress on the *inscribed* (too often the "vulgar" sense as well) trace, has often held sway among his followers, closing their ears to the silent but effectual *forms* of acoustic difference and deferral in literary writing. Against this tendency, the transegmental drift offers itself as a more revealing syntagmatic instance of that "'dialectic' of protention and retention" (67), that liminal waver of anticipation and holding over, which founds the trace as more than a tracery of letters and which can be silently heard—beyond the grounding of any Voice—to keep language awake on the productive edge of wording: a continual syntactic emergency sprung by that many a soundless slip between (always somewhere between) page and lip.

Derrida's preferential sense of the modernist *telos* of literary history can best be appreciated by the example of one of those defiantly experimental "writers," no longer an author in any traditional sense, who left an inaugural imprint on French modernism. We turn, then, to a writing agent all but fanatically nonmetaphysical—and irreferential—in his practice but one whose activity nonetheless qualifies more than confirms Hjelmslev's stress on a "graphic stratum" favored in the modernist program. The fiercely self-conscious "process" of Raymond Roussel's early texts begins in the structural logic of phonemic equivalences. Instead of settling for a homophonic unity of effect, however, where one sound cluster would be heard in another's grammes, the Rousselian experiment spreads out the graphically masked phonemic replicants along the length of an entire text: a case of writing *as* sheer process. In the quintessential form of these early texts, a cryptic statement initiates a narrative line, and the only logic by which the text then moves forward is dictated by the—desire is the wrong word, except as it is internal to language—by the impulse, let us say—to end exactly but unrecognizably where it began. Subtending the sequence of lexemes as a syntagmatic fluctuation, where the spaces between words can be recruited, bridged, syncopated, redistributed at will, this superimposition of "process" upon sequence—of *perceived* equivalence within the deceptive autonomy of orthographic difference—serves to isolate the very production of textuality as against its manifestation as script.

An entire "plot" is often in this way erected on a transegmental model—where, in a sense, it takes a whole text to bridge the gap between words. To give a concocted English-language example for economy's sake, imagine a short critical text that begins "Joyce, he annoys!" and then works itself round to a celebration of "Joycean noise." Or, indeed, a French sequence beginning with "Vraiment rousse elle!" ("Truly a readhead, she!") wheeling round to "rêve Raymond Roussel" ("dreams R. Roussel"). The idea is not to generate a set of discrete puns but to pun on the very failure of discreteness in language, to capitalize on the verbal penumbra that hedges round every supposed integral vocalization, a phantom trace at once evoked and revoked. The split nucleus for such word play may occasionally be formed by a phonemic variance within a single vocable. This is all it takes in *Impressions d'Afrique* (1910) for Roussel to construct an entire narrative around verbal clues inscribed on a billiard (*billard*) table as they set in motion the story of a notorious plunderer (*pillard*). Such random free play strikes to the heart of the arbitrariness of primary, not just secondary, articulation — as does Paul de Man's deconstruction of a similar *billow/pillow* rhyme in Shelley.[17] Forging a textual chime, the phonemic differentials testify at the same time to the referential dissociation between signifier and signified. The phoneme as trace becomes in this way a synecdoche for text production at large.

For his first and last extended venture in literary criticism, Michel Foucault, in his recently translated book on Roussel, studies the "process text" as underscoring "the sovereign role of chance in the interstices of language," an "effect" quite removed from "the order of style."[18] Foucault sees the "process" as a kind of obsessively proliferated rhyme, but his commentary takes no notice of individual couplets in Roussel's verse texts, where the premises of homophony are repeatedly tested. It is no surprise that such lexically dismembering rhymes in *La doublure* as "d'une voiture"/"ouverture," "saccades"/"des *arcades*," and especially "sec*ond doigt*"/"endroit"[19] come very near to the tandem rhymes discussed in Chapter 2. Foucault is interested in the more elongated as well as displaced chiming patterns which make the "process" texts seem bracketed by a concatenation of "antiwords" (33), each the "negative copy" (30) of the other, no original given privilege. In this respect, the "process" bears resemblance to the materialized visual pun on scriptive punning itself in Marcel Duchamp's anagrammatically titled film *Anemic Cinema* (1927),[20] where a spiral of script on a rotating disk — including such self-referential verbal transforms as the chiastic "esquimaux aux mots exquise" — literally put the spin on words. This later surrealist play with the hallucinated junctures of an alter language is indeed very close to Roussel's experiments in the "process" text. Duchamp's pseudonym, with which he "signed" *Anemic Cinema,* was *Rrose Sélavy* (for a swallowed "Eros, c'est la vie"), and he closes a brief pamphlet by that title with a Rousselian deconstruction of "literature" into "Lits et ratures."[21] Writing about the wordplay of Robert Desnos on the word *éphémère,* the surrealist Aragon also sounds remarkably close to Foucault on the molecularization of modernist phrasing. According to Aragon, Desnos has "pored long over these syllables which ring out like a legend. . . . He has descended philology's silk ladder in his search for the meaning concealed by this word at the heart of its fertile images."[22] Desnos is then quoted on the conversion of the trisyllabic *éphémère* into its alphabetic rebus, "F.M.R.," and then, in a more Rousselian mode, into its homophonic doubles, "Les faits m'errent" and "Des faix, Mères" (103). The English translator's version of Aragon's subsequent commentary is especially ingenious: "Ephemeral, F.M.R.L. (frenzy-madness-reverie-love), a fame really, ever, merrily, Effie marry Lee; there are words which are mirrors, optical lakes toward which hands stretch out in vain" (103).

In the strict early form of the "process" narrative, Roussel also gives, like Desnos and unlike Duchamp, each form of the wordplay. Both halves of the vocalic nuclear fission are thus (di)splayed to view, so that recognition is itself demystified, trivialized. A phrase like "Eut reçu pour hochet la couronne de Rome" is never left to insinuate its own dismemberment and reassemblage; the text moves instead toward some quasi-narrative justification for eventually spelling out "Ursule, brochet, lac Huronne, drome" (43), a phrase dispelling its phonic double even as it replicates it in different scriptive shape. Roussel himself explicitly saw the "process" as related to the game of "metagram" (25), where words are gradually transformed by the replacement of single letters (in rhetoric, the metaplasm). In Derridean terms, his texts expose the local "sponging-up" of phonemic material from one lexeme to the next in a serial displacement along the syntactic chain. So much textual space has elapsed between these two avatars of the same phonotext, we might say, that the bizarre *rime très riche* has become impoverished and nonnegotiable, neutralized by distance. The text at such points reads like a primed but undetonated pun, a play so free there is no payoff.

Closer than Duchamp's puns to Roussel's "process," then, are those distended echoic "glosses" of Leiris which were no doubt being alluded to earlier in that homophonic homage by Lacan. In the 1939 text, "Glossaire, j'y serre mes gloses" ("Glossary, where I store my glosses"), collected in *Mots sans Mémoire,* Leiris's alphabetic list of matrix terms is submitted to vocalic and semantic expansions of the sort that translate "VOCABLES" itself into "vos câbles, pour échapper à vos caveaux" (113). Often there is no strict homophony, even at the start, but rather a dilation of the syllabic matter across a very free semantic paraphrase. The latter strategy is often organized around a phonic bracket, as when "JOUISSANCE" is virtually anagrammatized into "jusqu'où (en jouant) se hissent mes sens?" (94). Or the pattern may be controlled by metathesis or chiasmus, turning "LIMON," for instance, into "mon lit" (96) or, less precisely, "LAGUNE" into "une langue" (96).[23]

As a matter of fact, Roussel's "process" may best be understood as an experiment in commutation at the very crux of linguistics. Paradigmatic "equivalences" or pertinent oppositions, ordinarily resolved by the very choice of words—and then set in motion along the axis of grammatical alternatives—are instead kept afloat at syntagmatic peril. This binary impertinence virtually undoes the semantic regime of language, reshuffles it into a dreamlike virtuality. Anticipating the vocabulary in *The Order of Things* used to describe the modernist literary revolution, Foucault sees the "process" as one wherein an initial grammar is "pulverized" (43) and reconstituted in the "syllable-droplets of a polyphonic language" (60). Roussel himself puts it this way: "I decided to take a sentence at random from which I drew images by distorting it, as though I were taking them from the drawings of a rebus" (41). The most systematically "processed" example of these "homonym sentences" (17–18) offered by Foucault is the nucleus (extracted from a folk song) "J'ai du bon tabac dans ma tabatière" transformed into "Jade, tube, onde, aubade en mat à basse tierce" (41). The phrase "I've got good tobacco in my tobacco pouch" thus spills over and out into the serialized non sequiturs "Jade, tube, water, mat, object, to third bass" — by no logic of plot, narrative, or signification, only by a phonemic filiation internal to language, strained and attenuated at that. But the stratagem is clear. The syllabic spin on one word sets up a phonic chain reaction that spirals along the nexus of syntax, relooping its linkages. The vowel sounds that end the first half-dozen words, despite the (silent) scriptive consonants that round off half of them, open an oral force field that seems to magnetize the largest aggregate of subsequent material capable of morphophonemic bonding into a new lexeme. By ligature, the attracted phonemic particles are either held over (as if geminated into renewal) for the next lexeme — "J'ai du b-" splitting its dental sound into d/t to generate "Jad(e) tub(e)" — or displaced backward: "-on tab-" become part of "onde aubade."

In the irregularities and risks of these regroupings, what dictates the pattern of recombination is the internal logic of *langue* as it spews up *parole* — but also (and this neither Roussel nor Foucault discusses) the power of reading itself to motivate the reconstitution of the chain. The reader can participate in the metagrammatic game only if his or her listening ear allows the inaugural dilation of one lexeme — reduced suddenly to mere phonemes — to linger for completion by the rest of the lexical material it now needs. Absorbing all it can at once, the reading ear must fend for itself from then on, submitting to the impoverishment of sense in its effort to catch up, to complete each phonemic move with a syllabic clustering capable of building supplemental words. The initial insolvency, that is, the expenditure of one word in augmenting its predecessor, forces each new sound into a phonemic parasitism, by which it leeches what it needs from the paradigmatic disarray in order to keep up the syntagmatic momentum. In all this, Foucault's interest in Roussel seems as exemplary as it is peculiar. Well before his exhaustive investigations into the discourses of culture, Foucault here submerges himself in a radical undermining of the culture of discourse. He studies in Roussel the human mind's very acculturation to language as signifying function. Roussel becomes the exception that only proves the rule, recirculating the ingredients of meaning without closing them off in an interpretable text: a mere procession of sounds slotted randomly into meaning, one by one, one upon the other, overlapping, slapdash, contiguous but maddeningly inconsequent. In narratological terms, the collapse into the oversameness of metaphor, of likeness, as postponed by metonymical dilation, would here be a collapse into the same once more, only different.[24] The metagrammatic variants, like a reverse Rosetta stone, give not one message in two languages, with the resulting spur to decoding through cross-reference; rather, the "process" text gives two phonemic messages in one scriptive form, waiting for a second inscribed formation to confirm the doubleness by seizing upon its alternative spelling — as upon a long-lost twin. This reunion scene, however, has no textual site, is consolidated in no single verbal space. With its leveling of reading effect into textual function, of impact into sheer process, it is a pun split wide and gone flat.

From a psycholinguistic perspective, there is certainly no chance for a stable subject-position in Rousselian text production. No reader can anchor the lexical and semantic drifting in a way that could possibly naturalize its doubleness. Indeed, no imagined speaker could be thought to *intend* both versions of the metagram in a single utterance, as a single subject can, for instance, be thought to *mean* a pun. The enunciating subject of the pure "process" text is split from inception, decidedly ruling out the phonocentric myth of authorial presence, a voice behind the wholesale syntactic shakedown. In "ordinary" written language, the link, say, between *lac Huronne* and *la couronne,* distanced from the possible friction and perceived *frisson* of a pun, would be a negligible fortuity of "phonetic writing." Any junctural undecidability would ordinarily be "disambiguated" by context without even coming to consciousness. But when we enter upon Roussel's hypertrophied textuality, with its unique strain on, and analogy to, mental processes, we enter a different verbal regime. What is distinctly *literary* about the metagrammatic games of Roussel is precisely the metalinguistic torsion within discourse they produce, a vertiginous instability that refers every word away to the variable procedures of wording. Roussel's metagrammatic maneuvers, straining the very notion of wordplay to its limit, nevertheless explicate once and for all the force of transegmental punning within a scriptive system. We may call it, once again, the return of the phonemic repressed.

For Foucault in *Death and the Labyrinth,* Roussel's homophonic chains, as they double and travesty each other, are likened not to phantom voices but to "mirror" images, as were the ephemeral words of Desnos by Aragon. In this they stage the relation of death to life; they inscribe, that is, by being no more than script, the relation of simulacrum to vital reality, of verbal ghost to the living body of utterance. True to Foucault's double title, the labyrinth, become a hall of mirrors, becomes a tomb: what Derrida would see as the underlying "thanatopraxis" of all textuality exhumed and laid open to view in a quintessential modernist instance. The implacable face of every text becomes a death's head, a death said. At the origin of the "process," writes Foucault, is "a repetition that is always anticipating itself; it acts as a mirror in relation to death[,] . . . life repeated to death" (162). If the mirror within the labyrinth is to serve fully as a figure for the depersonalizing (which is to say, killing) otherness in language, however, it can be only in a more or less Lacanian sense. The mirror is that figure of self in specular alienation from itself used to mark the transition from the imaginary to the symbolic, from a presumed plenary fusion of body and voice into the mere traces necessitated to express, and in the process surrender, just that union, that plenitude — to externalize and thereby deconstruct it. Script materializes the lacunae in speech that are at once created by and make for the activity of consciousness. Foucault comes close to such a perception about Roussel when he writes, in a way that calls up both Derridean and Lacanian presuppositions, that "it's the reserve from which words flow, this absolute distance of language from itself, which makes it speak. . . . It is the very edge of consciousness. It shows that at the moment of speaking the words are already there, while before speaking there was nothing" (39). The differentials by which language operates, if they include spacing as well as paradigmatic alternatives between phonemes, are therefore a matter of successive and conceptualized breaches sprung from an inaugural gap. They take part in a metanarrative on the very nature of language and the irrational, utterance always stretched thin across that abyss from whose silent mumbling emerges the pressure of alternatives, the ceaseless Voice of the Other. Deconstruction and psycholinguistics here meet again on the divisive ground of the rent and emptied center, as marked out — and, in Roussel's most illustrative feats, overleapt — by transegmental inscription.

Roussel's affront to ordinary poetics, to rhetoric, to style, his joint confounding of message and code within a strenuously scriptive (as well as, or because, obsessively homophonic) semiosis, invites some attempt to align his eccentric textual practice with the study of variation-by-"paragram" in Riffaterre's *Semiotics of Poetry*. Roussel's "process" is, as Riffaterre might say, certainly one of "conversion," but so relentless and unchecked that it undermines the principles of variation on which a normal, communicable semiosis of poetry is based. Roussel's texts are ferociously literary, letteral, without being in the least traditionally poetic. Unlike the paragrammatic conversion and displacement of the poetic text, Roussel's play with the metagram, having no rhetorical intent, avoids no cliché (in Riffaterre's sense) because it courts no original idiolect, aspires to no style. It displays the "languageness" of the literary in a way that forbids the poetic: a *parole* randomly sorted into *langue* and then metamorphosed beyond easy recognition. The metagrammatic text is systemically overdetermined but referentially arbitrary. Rather than generating a Riffaterrean paragram, it spawns ultimately a sentence that is more like an anagram (or hypogram) of *itself* — but of itself as different, alienated at base, uprooted at the point of semantic implantation and narrative departure. Signifying force in Riffaterre's semiotics comes from a tension between what is literally said and what is repressed by that phrasing. Roussel's texts, by contrast, short-circuit such a signifying system by extruding everything as surface play. The variant appears in the text along with its seed phrasing, each a variation of the other but without a real matrix – except in the pure phonemic substratum – and no model to establish priority in the forms of conversion. Semic variants at the level of primary articulation are reduced to the mere function of secondary articulation, polysemous and irresponsible, un-governed by any semiotic principle in the message at all, only the sequential code of the *langue*. Sequential – and irreversible.

This is the inarguable common ground of a Riffaterrean semiotics and a Rousselian metagrammar of literature. It is related to what Paul de Man remarked in his omnibus review of Riffaterre's work as the latter's conservative devotion to the "phenomenality" of the text as experienced, "its accessibility to intuition or cognition."[25] Pointed out here is what separates Riffaterre's "semiotics" from the extremity of Saussure in his anagrammatic phase. "What Riffaterre has done is to re-lexicalize Saussure, and no amount of emphasis on the mechanics of the procedure will undo the weight of this gesture" (26). To put it another way: only by extending the diphonic to the scope of the lexical could Riffaterre succeed in (de Man again) "assimilating, through the media-tion of the reader, phenomenal intuition to semantic cognition" (22). In line with de Man's critique, there is a rare moment of phonotextual – indeed, transegmental – audition in Riffaterre which confirms the primacy of the lexeme in the very process of allowing its momentary disintegration. A sonnet of Mallarmé's is the subject, including the line "Avec ce seul objet dont le Néant s'honore."[26] After two pages of commentary, Riffaterre observes the sole instance of cross-lexical homophony I have found noted anywhere in his work, "a pun to top it off" – or, in Ricks's terms, an anti-pun, since a complete alternative grammar is never activated by it. Riffaterre hereby registers the way "*Néant s'honore* sounds like *néant sonore*" (18), so that the idea of nothingness taking pride in objects is doubled by the idea of "sonorous nothingness." The fact that sonority itself at the level of the phonotext, silent enunciation, is what catalyzes this phrasal self-transformation, this evacua-tion of one phrase by its double, goes unmentioned. Typically, though, the threatened referential anarchy of this liaison is fended off by the immediate reassertion of a lexical alternative to the dissolving reflexive phrase, one that not only shelters the overall sense from disruption but renders it thematically efficient.

Faced with this signal departure from Riffaterre's semiotic norm, one might infer from it what Lotringer did from Saussure's excursion into anagrammatic reading: that an entire system (poetic semiotics here, linguistics previously) is based upon the exclusion of just this sort of textual permissiveness. If Riffaterre were to hear texts consistently "produced" at this level of phonemic free association, the paragrammatic structures of his method might soon find themselves in irreparable disarray. De Man's point about a "re-lexicalizing" retreat from the Saussure of the anagram is thus clinched here by counterexample. I stress this sense of Riffaterre's referential conservatism because it helps, in turn, to situate Roussel somewhere about halfway between Saussure and Riffaterre, committed to uninterrupted linearity but not to lexical stability, permitting the counterintuitive intrusions of phonemic latency upon visible script even within the relentless phenomenality of an *audited* text. In response to such texts, then, we need a "phenomenology" of the listening eye: a theory of the reading body in its silent activation of the voiceless but evocalized text.

Bodying Forth

Since Roussel's dramatic breakdown in the semiotic premises of signification returns us to the undulations of the language itself, it cannot help but raise issues of vocality upon which language is in one sense based. The "process text" therefore facilitates our commuting between two very different definitions of semiosis, that of Riffaterre and that of Julia Kristeva. On her account, semiosis has a decidedly somatic dimension, originating as it does in the maternal core or matrix, which she calls the "chora," a zone of vocal production that precedes articulation by providing its raw material. Demarcated thereby is an amorphous stratum of vibratory sound production, a phonation without phonemics, a lingual impulse before language. It is the origin and fund of all speech, rather like the "reserve" described by Foucault, and it is even materialized in scripted language as a vibratory pulse, a phonic counterpoint, in certain of the definitive modernist poets Kristeva studies in *Revolution in Poetic Language*.[27] In characterizing their experiments, she uses the very term, "pulverizes" (51), that Foucault applies to Roussel's language; it names for Kristeva the way in which the breakthrough of the semiotic into the symbolic disintegrates the logic of the signifier, let alone the signified, and drops the symbolic order back into that roiling phonic source that language exists to regiment. It is something of this heaving, sieved depth that Roussel's "process" may be found to extrude—and rethink—on the very surface of his texts. Such a momentarily disclosed and arbitrarily marshaled assertion of raw signifying energy is therefore a disturbance at the threshold of language and the threshold of consciousness at once. It is activated, I stress once again, through the body's as well as the mind's encounter with the text—through a reading effect that passively evokes even without engaging the phonatory apparatus by which script passes (not back but over) into speech. This Foucault, though ignoring, has moved us into position to understand.

Before we pursue further this receptual effect, it is important to look again, and warily (as we began doing in the Prologue) at the historicizing strain of — and strain on — such linguistically oriented readings of modern poetic and prose discourse as those of Kristeva and Foucault. Literary history tends to fade away when the focus is too narrowly aesthetic, charting a monolithic development climaxed by a radical upheaval at the end of the nineteenth century. But what else might explain a Roussel or a Joyce, a Mallarmé or a Pound, besides the inherent aesthetic mechanism of language itself, delved to new depths? An indirect (and, I find, partial) explanation has recently been offered by Friedrich Kittler, philosopher of media history, who traces the decline of Romanticism to the invention of phonographic storage media.[28] After centuries of uncontested and unexamined discursive preeminence, the medium of print was suddenly challenged on precisely the ground Romanticism held dear: the power of literary language, that privileged subclass of print, to evoke and incorporate the sounds of nature in textual evocation (or even simulation). With the beginning of phonographic technology, argues Kittler, literature lost not only its recording or storage monopoly but also its unquestioned supremacy as a representational medium. The sounds of the world, including voice itself, could now be far more closely approximated by a mechanical mimesis. Kittler thus recounts the history of a competitive and embattled advance in communications media, one innovation superseding the transmissive capacities of its forerunner, with post-Romantic print surrendering much of its representational authority to phonographic recording. Literature, Kittler claims, fled from the arena of its own dwindling prestige into a more resolute bookishness, a foregrounded textuality, an abdication of mimetic obligations, especially as regards the speaking voice — fled, in short, into the brandished textuality of early high modernism. But to Kittler's revisionist departure from Foucault's autonomous teleology of language theory, there is yet another counterresponse in return. Kittler may well be right about Derrida's failure to account even tacitly for the place of phonography in the origins of structuralist (differential) linguistics, with its dependence on the minute calibrations of language's phonemic materiality. If phonographic recording can be said to have lent empirical substantiation to the division in modern linguistics between differential values and sheer acoustics, this alone may justify the present theory of phonemic reading even after a full absorption of the grammatological critique. But is the historical causality as linear, after all, as Kittler suggests? Is it necessarily the case that literature as a whole, faced with the phonographic erosion of its mimetic empire, necessarily beat a retreat into an opposite, mute, purely graphic conception of itself? Where was the competitive spirit to compensate literature's anxiety? Is it not likely that modern literature instead attempted to preempt its partial eclipse by sound recording with its own syncopated phono/graphy?

In the case of this study's first example, as drawn from J. L. Austin, if "I stink" were to be given along with, or in place of, "iced ink" in a phonographically recorded utterance, ambiguity could either be maximized or prevented by the voice assigned to its articulation. Writing is different. It institutes a different difference. On the page, a transegmental provocation like "iced ink" is set by inscription; it cannot be ambiguous in the same way as it might be in a recorded speech. It is definitively inscribed, decided—but, then again, not quite. The phonic momentum that interrupts its lexical contours and aurally redistributes its spacing is not there in the phrase, not scripted. But it exists—in the phonotext. It is brought to bear only in the ungraphed phonism of reading, as it could never be so obliquely in sound recording. This is a way of acknowledging that the evocalization of transegmental alternatives is not sonic at all but phonemic. And such evocalization is only one among many ways—if perhaps the one with most theoretical edge—for texts to face down the phonographic advent through a stereography (one might say) of their own, with one word inscribed, its homophonic double copresent as the trace of a lateral displacement. Surrendering its supposed hold on the body of the world's sounds, literature makes an adjusted claim on the passive body of a reader voicing: voicing, that is, under erasure.

As an inevitability of "phonetic writing" that tends to be recruited by the opacities of literary style, such phantom stereography is to be found, of course, in Shakespeare as well as in Joyce or Woolf. As a shoring up of literary vocalization against the mimetic triumph of sound recording, its late nineteenth-century exaggeration may well be read as a specific stratagem of modernist inscription—recruited, concentrated, and explored as never before. And this, quite possibly, from within the newly defensive presumption of a nonphonocentric, purely text-based aesthetics of inscription. The modernist gambit would then read like this: lest phonography preen itself on a wholesale advance over literature, it must be noted that there is a more supple and striking (e)vocalization—bivalent rather than simply ambiguous—available to the scriptive text than can be found in the straightforward naturalism of acoustic recording. On this reading of media-historical anxieties at the level of material signification itself, literature did not so much back off from phonography as attempt to trivialize and overshadow it with an increased reliance on its own textual graphonics.

At this stage in surveying the theoretical implications of phonemic reading, questions obviously begin to regroup again around the idea of the reading effect and the reading subject. If speech—that is, language—does not originally reside in the body as talk and become dematerialized when given up to script, then is it the other way around? Does writing alone vest language with the only substantiality to which it can ever attain, the material substance of script? If speech is not the voice of the body but, rather, a special case of writing, then is writing the sole body of the voice? Opposing sides of such questions are debated by Denis Donoghue under the headings of "epireading" and "graphireading."[29] The first coinage comes not from *epi* but from the Greek *epos,* for speech or utterance. "Epireading is the reader's form of compensation, making up for the tokens of absence and distance which he finds in written words" (98). Nothing could be farther from the Derridean position, except that the "tokens of absence" are at least recognized as such — before the attempt is made to overcome them. The restoration of text to its human context in "epireading" includes the tracking back of script to its origin in an authorial voice, as well as the leading on from referents into the world they call up. Epireading thus "interprets experience in terms of voice, speech, utterance, *logos* understood as action and for that reason dreads the reification and idolatry of language" (151).

To this method Donoghue contrasts the preoccupation with graphic signifiers, with text as scriptive system rather than mediated voice. It is a tradition that for Donoghue runs (down) to the present day from its most illustrious culprit, Mallarmé, through (quite selectively and variously) Derrida, Barthes, de Man, to its last gasp in Lucette Finas. In this tradition, on Donoghue's understanding, the author is so violently excised from every textual consideration that the vacuum thus opened draws off the reader as well.

Though not mentioned by Donoghue, there is a particularly clear instance of the former position in John Vernon's *Poetry and the Body,*[30] which locates its titular conjunction at what seems to me the wrong end of the semiotic continuum between signification and reception; it thus makes the link between textuality and materiality more metaphoric than it need be. Indeed, Vernon's resistance to the tradition of Mallarmé, in favor of the bardic line of Whitman, recalls Donoghue's characterization of Mallarmé's own resistance to vocal plenitude: "If the word were to be defined as spoken, the sovereign author could not suppress himself in its favor; he would be dragged into the poem with every audible breath" (155). A deconstruction of the *authoring* (never mind the *reading*) subject does indeed take the wind out of inscription, robbing it of that "marriage of flesh and air" (2) which Vernon sees as the essence of poetry in the Whitmanesque tradition. By contrast, the work of this chapter would find the materiality of signification located in a script wed to the *possibility* of phonemic articulation as its very definition. It is only right that a conception of the body should return to our notion of literature through such a back door, should return through at least—if no more than—the *possibility* of reading aloud. Vernon wants something more, but something less plausible. In championing the poets of song rather than scribble, chant rather than jot, Vernon insists on his position that "language is the shadow of speech" and that, in poetry alone of all writing, such speech is bodied forth again in a fuller utterance, supple and sinuous, a "dance" (58) of form. What is never admitted is that no matter how far these impressionistic figures (and they recur frequently) may carry the field of concern away from poetry as an acknowledged text of writing, the dance of its flexed and corporeal form could never be more or less than choreo*graphic* at base.

For the present claim that texts are ultimately produced by the latent mouthing of the reader's body there is, beyond intuition, a considerable weight of scientific evidence. In a study concerned less with psycho- than with physio-linguistics, *Silent Speech and Silent Reading,* Ake W. Edfeldt investigates the process of unvoiced reading by analogy with that hypothesis in the latter part of the nineteenth century which conceived "thinking to be more or less restrained speaking or acting."[31] So too reading. Summarizing decades of elaborate mechanical and electrographic experiments designed to test the muscular responses (of larynx, pharynx, tongue, palate, lips, and so on) during silent reading, Edfeldt concurs in the evidence that reading is a kind of blocked or inhibited speaking, accompanied by suboral "vocalizations." Such findings, one presumes, are exactly of the "behavioristic" sort we have watched Wellek and Warren dismiss in the Prologue, and yet they are invaluable in any full-scale phenomenology of the reading act. Wellek and Warren, of course, invoke the "literate" reader as a standard for nonphonemic reading. It may be, instead, that we can define literature itself as precisely that textual practice whose impedances to the flow of sheer script recover within reading some of the lapsed powers of illiteracy. According to the experimental findings summarized by Edfeldt, one should more properly speak of silent reading rather than of silent listening, with an emphasis on passive vocality rather than on the figurative mind's ear. With auditory subordinated to motor habits, the reading process becomes more somatic than imaginary. Implications for specifically literary reading emerge only when Edfeldt's findings suggest that the more stumbling blocks a dense or difficult text throws in the path of comprehension, the more silent vocalization is likely to be produced. Such is the conjunction of activated text and passive anatomy, however, that an approach like John Vernon's in *Poetry and the Body* never takes up.

It does surface implicitly as an issue, only to be at once foreclosed, in one of the most influential theories of fiction to have gained currency in the last several years. We shall return in Chapter 5 to the potential application of M. M. Bakhtin's "dialogism" to the dualisms of transegmental oscillation in prose. For now, it is Bakhtin's understanding of the temporal and spatial coordinates of the textual site (as well as the narrative situation) that momentarily raises the possibility of a theory of evocalization. In Bakhtin's account of monologic (epic) form dispersed into the heteroglossia of the novel, he stresses an analysis of the "chronotope," the "time-space" of fictional form.[32] He then attempts to extend this bipolar determinant deep into linguistic structure, on the one hand, and out into the realm of reception, on the other. Besides the general temporal and spatial relationships pertinent to representation and plot, there is the level at which, for instance, nouns of person, place, and thing are rendered metonymic, syntactic—hence cast into sequence, into time. Such a metonymic factor inherent in grammar must also be said to meet its extrinsic reduplication in the serial pace of reading. In designating the "chronotopes of. . . the listener or reader" (252), Bakhtin skirts very close to Riffaterre's later position in regard to the reader "creating" (or producing) the text: "We are presented with a text occupying a certain specific place in space; that is, it is localized; our creation of it, our acquaintance with it occurs through time" (252). Just a sentence before, he has also suggested that in our response to "the external material being of the work," its status as an inscribed system of signifiers, "we not only see and perceive it but in it we can always hear voices (even while reading silently to ourselves)."

That last remark, however, cannot be taken in the spirit of the present investigations. Bakhtin's figurative sense that we "hear voices" has undergone no deconstruction. Pointing away from the reader at this point, it is openly phonocentric, for Bakhtin adds in clarification that "we always arrive, in the final analysis, at the human voice," always "come up against the human being" (252–53). This confirms his sense that both writer and reader inhabit a chronotopic world (or worlds) different from the represented world of the fiction, less dialogic, more "real, unitary" (253), and that the novel is the point of intersection between the author's time-space and ours. One thing to say about this is certainly that it has overstepped the bounds of *textual* theory. For a moment, though, if only in passing, Bakhtin seems to have alluded to another chronotope given voice at the receiving (or creating) end of the text, a voice generated not by its origin in the spatiotemporal realm of the author's world but produced instead by the activation of the text's material basis as a signifying system. This is the chronotope of the reading rather than dictating voice, of the reading that voices "even while reading silently to ourselves." It is the "time-space" inscribed by both the duration and tempo of reception in the dialogized locus somewhere between scripted text (in a phonetic alphabet) and the enunciating inner voice of a reading subject. Marked out in this way, again, is literature's double construction at the reading site.

Earsay

In contrast to such mystified "epireading" as we find at times in Bakhtin or Vernon, Donoghue closes his survey of "graphireading" with an extreme case of avowedly Derridean commentary by Lucette Finas, including the fullest quotations from her work yet translated into English. The way she replays a text involves the modes of transegmental reading more often than anything else I have seen in criticism—outside, that is, of a few phonemic flash points in untranslated sections of Louis Marin's book on autobiographical "voice."[33] Finas identifies herself (in Donoghue's translation) as interested in "the repercussion of the smallest shift, whether graphic or phonic" (192), while in fact her emphasis falls on the phonic "discomfiture" (her word) of graphic expectations. She calls it "cacophony," and is ready with illustration. Mallarmé's "Yeux, lacs avec ma simple" is heard to "trip up" eyes other than those it names, one phoneme following too closely on another for lexical discretion: "lac(s) avec, Lacavec, where, as a further chasm can be heard *les yeux là, caves,* those abysmal and cavernous eyes." The slide is not just in Mallarmé's verse but in Finas's own prose. She edges from chasm to abyss, from phonological figure to theme—as if the text knows no distinction between a verbal lacuna and a described lake. Finas is rarely so open (though, even here, not explicit) about the linguistically reflexive bent in her readings, a procedure by which the contour of sound remodels the semantic content. Indeed, she is elsewhere less insistent even about the subversive malleability of phonemes; in her chapter on Paul Claudel's prose poem, "Décembre," the prosodic term "hiatus" (rather than the figurative "chasm" earlier) is introduced to characterize "contr*ée et* ce"—without mention of an elision blurring over the internal caesura.[34] Just as often, though, Finas will actively pursue the phonic shuffling beneath the graphic mark, as in a passage on Mallarmé's "Salut"—not translated by Donoghue—where a line like "Solitude, récit fait toile" is traversed by the bidirectional "liaison" that dissolves it into such a variant as "Solitude, récif et toile." It is a liaison both "indicated and contradicted at once" (122)—in other words, written off by script even while sounded out. Such a textual listening is often, as here, unattached to any thematic logic. Following the title of Finas's collection of essays, *Le bruit d'iris,* it is the unprogrammed and cacophonous "noise of the eye" that is her most original subject, a poststructuralist equivalent, in effect, for Gertrude Stein's "sound heard by the eyes."[35]

In a methodological note (not discussed by Donoghue) to her reading of Mallarmé's "Salut," called "Interdicted Plays, Forced Rapprochements," Finas portrays her readings as "a process of integration by disintegration at the boundaries of the supportable," drawing on the manipulated sonorities of a "broken text," the "tremors" and "rebounds" of the "phonic zigzag" (126). She specifically rejects any suspicion, however, that her commentary is "playing according to Saussure," in any way "searching for some hypogram(s)." There is certainly no dispersed Orphic theme word here to be reconstituted, and yet no reading could be more reliant on the diphonic principle of Saussure's within the domino play of collapsing syllabification. Every bit as much as Saussure, Finas is committed to following out the text's "dilapidating of syllables and sounds" (125), her own chosen verb form serving in this case to negate the text as lapidary inscription, to chip away at any presumption of its marmoreal stability. Finas has thus brought to fruition the libertine threat, the diphonic free association, that passed under unspoken censure by Saussure as he left the anagrammatic studies behind. While denying all comparison to these studies, Finas nevertheless makes good on Saussure's checked promise of the open text. At the same time, she distances herself from the Freud of the *lapsus,* the loaded slip, and hence liberates the quasi-oneiric iridescence of language from any secretly prescribed agenda in the unconscious, as straitening as the Saussurean anagram in its way. In recapitulating the effects she proposes to disclose in a text (or generate from it) — "to retrieve (or produce? that's a question)" (124) — her stress is placed, as in no other literary commentary, not even Derrida's, on such transegmental shuntings and "generalized rhyme" as "hormis l'y taire" turning into "militaire" (123), "salarie" into "qui sale a ri" (127), or the slide from "s'honore" into "sonore" (126) that recalls Riffaterre's one unpursued foray into the possibility of a phonemic as well as a lexical matrix.

In the single essay on Finas's work that has been translated into English, Christian Prigent aptly compares her "echolalic throbbings"[36] with the "mechanism" of the Roussel text (45). Finas finds, in Mallarmé particularly, a kind of perplexed lexicon given to the "stroboscopic ebb or flow" (47) of syllables and sounds. Explicitly alluding to Kristevan semiotics, Prigent locates in Finas's readings "an anamorphic torsion of the pheno-texte" striving for "an access to the prodigious or monstrous theatricality of the geno-texte" (47). Though unexplored in his commentary, this approach to literary textuality inflects her own discursive emplacement as analytic agent. Throughout her undoing of Mallarmé's "Salut," Finas also deliberately undoes her own expository position. She speaks of her labors with an italicized first person pronoun (*Je*), as if it were a foreign word even in French, and always in the third-person singular, as in the glossed elision of "*I* detaches 'sept' from 'cette écume'" (my emphasis in translation). Only in view of such pronominal foregrounding can one appreciate the full force of Roland Barthes's vocative gambit in a revealing preface to her work, "Question de tempo," subtitled "*à Lucette Finas.*"[37] Such a preface *to* her — couched in the form of second-person address, a little epistle — might seem quaint, curiously avuncular, even patronizing, were it not heard to utter its commendations from a station (in respect to Finas's *Je*) equidistant from its own textual surface.

In this late essay, Barthes thus seizes the occasion to review and condense many of his own most challenging textual postulates. As in Finas's writing, Barthes's I-Thou pattern speaks out of nowhere and to no one, a dialogism without voice. He shares her interest in the tempo of reading as it guides the production of the text. He is especially intrigued, further, with the notion of "excess" (151) in Finas, an excess that various speeds of reading struggle with or shake loose, according to "the *battue* (the beat) of the text" (152) — the text, in other words, as performed. This "excess" is what Barthes sees as the chief contribution of Finas's readings, her instinct for those "oppositions of intensity" (152) left out of the binary calculations of structuralism. Finas finds an impertinent overplus haunting the pertinent opposition, and since this finding is in the reading, not strictly in the text, she, according to Barthes, "turns reading itself into a text" (153). When such a text of reading is in turn read, Barthes goes on to imply, the question of the reading subject comes into focus. Pushing beyond structuralism, the reader reads herself as structured by the reading, polysemously. This is what Finas no doubt means when, in the last paragraph of her chapter on Mallarmé, having rejected both Saussurean and Freudian premises, she returns to the lure of the "psychoanalytic siren" — only to turn it on its head by offering that "the text of Mallarmé, instead of being, itself, analyzed, analyzes" (131). This is where the reader comes in — comes in for deconstruction, as well. Reading the modernist text, reading the writerly, is a participatory decentering; by letting the tempo of reading remain undetermined in advance, contingent, variable, Finas puts herself, her *Je,* under the textual sway. As Barthes's own text summarizes it in grammatical address to her(s): "In opening up the tempo of reading, you are therefore opening up the subject. Your reading is therefore, to my mind, strictly materialist, more materialist than many materialisms which announce themselves as such" (153).

Its material base is, of course, that of the signifier, in perpetual counterpull between phonic and graphic demarcation. Read by her, that signifying insurgency by which words are spent and replenished on the run operates through the disruption of the linguistic continuum with wellings from the semiotic pulse below, from *lalangue,* from an acoustic latency of pure excess, unimpeded, unshaped. Having no access to the regimen of script, this is a super-fluency before language, in part genotextual, in part expendable. In this sense we might want to say that textuality enacts as well as lays bare a contradiction.

In the rhythmic tempo of the modernist text, as read by Finas, the bleeding between lexemes accomplished by evocalized script—by predication and (let us say) verberation—highlights a phonotexture that seems at once origin and "supplement," the trace as both basis and dividend. Such an effect—so often a homophonic phantom in her reading, its very "materialism" half disembodied—emerges as just what is left over (and, in most readings, left out) after phonic impulses are channeled through script along the ruts of words, the route of syntax, the routines of the sign. It is the remainder after *lalangue* is pieced out to *la langue* in order to be activated as *parole*. One thus confronts head-on the variance of the genetic from the heterogeneous premise, the primalist from the supplementalist doctrine, by understanding the phonemic trace as an excess *at the source.* "Graphonic" reading would measure, then, a surplus inherent in the fund of semiosis—as the very definition of its emergence into symbolic script. This emergence not only leaves traces, it *is* the trace in its first instance, the first nudge of mumble into utterance. For all the interknit distinctions upon which language is mounted, the originary (though never fixed) difference—that of language from murmur—is what marks the path of prelingual phonation on its way to phonemic articulation. Difference is first measured, therefore, from that primal voicing against which any functioning vocable, or its constituent phonemes, must be thrown into relief. That throwing, that veering, that verging is therefore the trace in the making.

I have used here the Derridean term "supplement" not lightly but with the same idiomatic sense to which Derrida appeals in order to vex it into reconception.[38] In the Western tradition at least since Plato, and most overtly in Rousseau's *Confessions,* writing has been considered the "supplement" to speech, subsequent, ancillary, denaturing. With Saussure, at last, emerged the definitive structuralist science of that subordination, under the founding premise, as we have seen, of "acoustic pattern." Derridean grammatology does not simply avert this elevation of speech over writing, it tends to reverse it. Language is not possible without spacing. Spacing is not acoustic in speech production. On this score alone, language has at base a spatial or graphic, rather than just temporal and phonic, dimension. Defying the traditional assumption, therefore, Derrida finds in spoken utterance something more like the supplement of the gramme. My whole project in aural reading begins, in one sense, by accepting the Derridean reversal (itself unfixed) of origin and supplement—as a quintessential case of the deconstructive agenda in action: a reciprocal overturning of priority rather than the rigidifying of a new hierarchy. In this spirit, the "graphonic" relativism of phonemic reading finds in the process of subvocal text production a uniquely *perceived* instance of the mutual supplementation of gramme and phone. In the full paradox of the

Derridean supplement, the inner is constituted by the other, the outer, and identity defined by difference. An important parallel follows from this. Let us accept that speech—as language rather than as sound—is differentially defined not from without, by writing (as its secondary transcription), but from within, by the gramme (as its formal principle). It may then emerge that reading—understood not just as recognition but as cognition—should be defined as a response not merely to graphemes but to their difference as—as well as their difference from—phonemes.

At its transegmental crux, then, the phonotext is produced as follows. A phrase has been written where no succession of sounds has been made. A word is read with no presumption that a voice either preceded that textual mark or can be elicited from it. Yet a voice is brought *to* it, one that often produces an adventitious, potentially submorphemic "sound" even when the written word is over—a voiced though silent sound, one that sticks, whether borrowed in advance from the successor or lent to it in the aftermath of the lexeme it has already served to complete. The phonemic "supplement" is thereby created, created upon the trace of a grapheme, but no sooner created than expropriated, incorporated, internalized, made constitutive, changing one root or pluralizing another, say, but in any case found momentarily inherent in—rather than adhering to—a lexeme to which it has no graphic attachment. This inherence is the very "production" of the lexeme as difference—but not just different from the word as written; activated here is instead that (both morphophonemic and grammatological) difference *within* that structures only by opposition. The phonemic supplement is thus actually recirculated through the written word as the revealed dynamic of its generation: its deviance from, and so deferral of, alternatives. In this sense, a given word is distinguished from its near miss—and phantom double—by that very binary logic which the principle of the supplement leads us to rethink at a more paradoxical level. One word's difference from its alternatives in the paradigm is thus kept before us, as a signifying principle, by a given word's shifting difference from its successor in the syntagm—and this by way of that phonemic supplement which co-opts the gramme of the blank in its transit to a new lexical bond. Such transegmental drifts, exposed as they are by phonemic reading, isolate in this fashion—at the level of a single linguistic feature rather than governing principle—the full paradox of the *internal* supplement. In literary reading, especially, such drifts operate, in short, to sustain the structuring "versus" of binary opposition as a viable register of the final, never-finished text.

But the reading mind doesn't stop with this partly somatic turbulence of wording within meaning. In Finas's phrase, the receiving mind doesn't just listen to the noise of the eye. It processes. It concerns itself with the pronounced *effect*. It *reads*. Which brings us round again to how, and why. By pressing the act of reading to the outer edge of coherence, Finas serves to demonstrate a textual conservation, if not conservatism, at the base of even the most radical reading projects. She only goes so far, so far out. The distance she gains on more subservient readings, ones more deferential to the supposedly *given* text, only marks a far perimeter within which the text continues to *function*. Her maneuvers are curtailed only by the value she implicitly places on such continuance. The hold of language upon Finas's readings, even as it relaxes back into *lalangue,* is still strong. Syntax undergoes a rending — but not a complete surrender. Why it does not, could not, is a question whose answers spread wide across interpretive practice.

It would appear that there are three phases of coherence which Finas sporadically reimposes on the textual decomposition she performs: the syntagmatic, the mimetic, and the reflexively thematized, the last two often accompanying each other. These three phases of reading are neither defended nor even confessed. Yet they bind her, if loosely, to an inescapable logic of interpretation nonetheless, however much she protests against it in the name of a freer reading. Though *langue,* or momentarily even *lalangue,* irrupts into *parole,* the law of "speech" is not abolished. The message regroups. New words slip in on the coattails of the vanished. Language unveils itself as mere traces, but it remains language nonetheless. Lexical segmentation may shiver to bits, but the phonetic shards are reheard as a new syllable; the lexicon is consulted for a new morphological opportunity, the syntagmatic axis kept intact — at least for a moment, even if no stable double grammar emerges. That is the first kind of normalization to which the ear's heresy submits: grammar, in short, is maintained. Not only mitigating disruption, the second kind of normalization renders it imitative — if only (and here we move to the third type) imitative of itself as text. When "lacs avec," rather than allowing its first *c* to be silenced, asserts it in a segmental ligature with the adjacent word to form (evanescently enough) the word "cave," its play with the lexical abyss is called "cavernous." All three persistent normalizations are here on view: a sequence minimally cued by grammar that is also a mimesis of the phantom referent, hollowed and resounding, and a thematization of the verbal blank.

Finas's work is too semiotically sophisticated to have much converse with mimed signifieds per se, so the opportunities for style-as-enactment are usually rooted reflexively in the signifier alone. Wordplay is ordinarily able to reproduce only the play of its own words. Nonetheless, the three recuperative moves (syntagmatic, mimetic, and reflexive) do find themselves operating at times together. Shattered, gaping, or set loose, syllables reconvene as words, while the loosening, gaping, or shattering — figure it how you will — is recovered by the textual mechanism as part of the reconstituted message. It is, further, a message that is regularly folded back upon the text in the form of a metaphor for its very textuality. In other hands than Finas's, or upon other ears, what is as much dutiful as willful about this procedure, what continues to respect the contract of interpretation between text and reader, would come clearer sooner. And could too easily be dismissed. Finas holds the line partly by obscuring it. Which is why I labor into the open the assumption of her procedures, or, more to the point, their inevitability. There is no other way to read. This is not because we are autonomous subjects reading our confirmation in the order of a totalized text. On the contrary, it is because, as constituted subjects, as never better than italicized *I*'s, we are defined precisely *as readers,* processors of signs. Texts, deconstructed, ask of us, in reading, the very work that in every sense makes us up.

An analogy dawns between Derrida's critique of phonocentrism and Finas's critique of the psychological subject, as elucidated by Barthes. Both attacks take too little account of the adversarial provocation: the respective appeals, physical rather than metaphysical, of voice and person. Those appeals happen to converge. They are two different formulations of the body as site — what we can call writing's *productive supplement* in becoming text. Neither authorial source, on the one hand, nor envelope of identity, on the other, this is the bodied site as heterogeneous locus: the body before the book, the body in place. It is because we hear overtones of our voice when reading to, and out of, ourselves — I have argued — that we are tempted to posit a sense, or sanctify a relic, of voice in text. It is because we have an "articulated" anatomy, upon which are strung vocal chords, that we read in this way, read *in* our own voice. Though our body is not a subject, nor even the outer form of one, it is often most of what we think we can demonstrate of one, as proof of one. This assumption, too, must no doubt be resisted. But it must also be recognized as a particular chimera of reading. The body is our guarantor, especially in "going out of ourselves" (never quite) in reading the words of another, the Other. Situated before a text, whatever its "voice," I have *mine,* whether I activate it or not; and if what I think I am reading is sayable (that is, meaningful), out loud or not, then it easily confirms my powers of reception as those belonging to me, to an I. The readerly leaves me be, comfortable in my mastery of it. The writable (which is certainly not to say, the exclusively *scriptible* in Barthes's postclassical terms) — the text in whose production I participate — instead exposes me to incoherences, exposes my own, or that incoherence which is no longer to be called "me" at all. The body's vocal apparatus thus colludes in a reception of texts in a manner that keeps that body in its place, no longer coincident with person, no longer *identical.* Just as the phoneme, properly recognized, can assist in the deconstruction of the Voice, so can the body (as the site of a voicing), properly occupied in reading, attend at the decentering of the very subject whose warranty it ordinarily provides.

Epicentrism

Midway between Donoghue's polarized concepts of "epireading," named for the *epos* of voiced presence, and "graphireading," named for the scripted signifier of all textuality, falls the spectrum of response we have been reviewing: a *semiotic* reading in Kristeva's sense; a Lacanian reading sensitized to *lalangue;* and, by way of Finas, an exploitation of the text in its full phonemic and syllabic fluidity (even though she is consigned exclusively to the "graphic" dimension by Donoghue). Into this space between polarized camps falls also a paradoxical concern for the "grain of the voice" in "vocal writing." I allude there to Roland Barthes's remarkable last two pages in *The Pleasure of the Text,*[39] as well as to the essay specifically titled "The Grain of the Voice" which I considered in the Prologue—as both would seem to anticipate the signal phonemic interferences in Louis Marin's restoration of the "excommunicated voice" of textuality. Though Barthes outlines in *The Pleasure of the Text* an aesthetic of vocalized textuality, his remarks never specify their implicit assumptions about the scene of reading. *"Writing aloud,"* Barthes suggests, "is not expressive; it leaves expression to the pheno-text, to the regular code of communication; it belongs to the geno-text, to significance; it is carried not by dramatic inflections, subtle stresses, sympathetic accents, but by the grain of the voice, which is an erotic mixture of timbre and language . . . the art of guiding one's body" (66). By the end of the paragraph, one guesses, Barthes himself is attempting something very much like writing *aloud,* illustrating the "whole carnal stereophony" (66) of such textual production: "It granulates, it crackles, it caresses, it grates, it cuts, it comes: that is bliss" (67). Barthes here has moved well beyond even Empson's feel for literary language as texture, as skein, as skin, "whose flesh has the character of the flesh of an organism."[40] When Barthes stresses "the pulsional incidents, the language lined with flesh" (66), he is speaking, if we may say so, less metaphorically, for he has in mind the very "muzzle" of enunciation.

For Barthes, *"writing aloud* is not phonological but phonetic" (66)—in other words, more phonic than phonemic, its energy not yet bound up in units of signification. Not *entirely,* no, but at the same time incapable—in any given textual manifestation—of entirely avoiding the symbolic in the flow of its vibratory semiosis. So, after all: phonemic reading. Silent but material, such reading is disciplined by the laws of combination while at the same time freed by those of equivalence. So where does this leave us as readers? Donoghue would give us too little room. Between *epos,* as voice, and *graph,* as mark, we need a third term, a third position—a site, all but a breathing space, for the reader's silent voice. A name for such a position seems implicit, as a matter of fact, in an alternate etymology of the term "epireading"—indeed, in the etymology we are likely to expect from the term at first glance. We ordinarily encounter that prefix *epi* in its derivation not from the Greek noun but from a flexible Greek preposition. We find it, for example, affixed to two English technical terms, one philosophic, one meteorological, that contribute to modeling a revised notion of the *epitext* in the ear. I have in mind "epiphenomenon," a secondary, derivative phenomenon, and "epicenter," a point somewhere above a decisive locus. In literary-critical terms, a phenomenological reading is of course bipolar, the text at the intersubjective center of an alignment between the consciousness of the author and of the reader. A decentering of the text, not to mention of subjectivity itself, breaks the axis, cancels the alignment, spins the text off into an eccentric orbit of its own. No phenomenological access remains available, except through the processed materiality of the signifiers. But an epiphenomenal approach—to the text as evocalized—is still possible once the text is recognized to transmit through the channels of its enunciation, and no more than mutely at that, only the voice of the reader. It is a voicing generated from his or her (if there is gender left at all in the reader as voice rather than person)—we had better say from *its,* from *my*—shifting stance toward the writing it activates. It is a stance taken up in part by my upper body's perch over the page—in other words, in the readerly epicenter of the decentered text.

From such a site, as well, the epiphenomena of textual generation may be said to jump off the page at me. It is this notion of reading as an open apprehension, rather than as a suppression, of perceived verbal ephemera that would connect with Hartman's allusion to "saving the phenomena" (or "the appearances" [xv]) in his book-length encounter with Derrida, *Saving the Text,* a "saving" that is not rescue so much as recognition and account. Part of this very "apparitional" dimension of reading is what he calls in the title of his second chapter "epiphony" (33)—and calls for in the imperative subtitle of a later section, "Look with thine ears" (128; from *King Lear*). Throughout, Hartman posits as a central agenda of literary reading the effort to reverse print's tendency "to blind the ear" (142). For Hartman, the "words of a text, in their silence, are but divining rods to disclose other words, perhaps words of the other . . . and critical reading allows us to describe that interiority, to estimate words as words, to see them as living in and off us" (142), subjective and parasitic at once, waiting for us to effect them. This is their phenomenality, and only reading of a certain intensity and give can retrieve it from neutralization: "And that is why poetry makes its curious alliance with critical reading, in order to reactivate the ear" (142). Early on, and despite his own later suspicions about a Derridean resistance to the privilege of the oral in

Joyce,[41] Hartman tries to dispel the assumption that his allegiance to the ear is in any sense an anti-Derridean position, insisting that what may appear as the derogation of the phonic in Derrida is instead a more radical insistence on it — but on a phonic energy uncontainable by script. The "cadence" of the phonic element, that is, "cannot be encased in grammar or meaning. It falls through, into, both" (14).

Very much in the spirit of the present study, then, Hartman acknowledges that the phoneme can drop out of syntactic regimentation only to resurface by fractional displacement. Such material "fallout" constitutes exactly that aspect of textual phenomena most in need of "saving" — not so that writing should thereby be revalorized as "stored speech," that old myth of transcribed voice, nor because such a process in any way confirms the timeworn assumption that "written speech puts sound on ice" (42) — indeed, as Hartman has it, "the phonè is more sphinx than phoenix" (44) — but because writing itself, broadly understood, can be generated phonematically only in its manifestation as reading. Hartman is thus the least likely of those Anglo-American critics engaged with Derridean deconstruction to subsume textual productivity to sheer inscription within a logic of the trace. In the terms of Hartman's closing chapter, "Words and Wounds," it is just the impossibility of doing so — the impossibility of fixing meaning, even the locus of meaning, in script — that makes for the "wound" of "equivocation" (129), the double violence both caused and supposedly cured by literalism, by letteralism, by the stable and bounded sign. Further along, Hartman writes that "closure is a sealing with healing effect" (150), a boundedness that lulls anxiety. Yet literary writing is there to refuse this calming, this balm; art "creates limits that prove to be liminal. In poetry this 'sense of an ending' embraces rhythm, rhyme, and caesura: what happens toward the end of a line, or rhythmically within the line, until lineation itself is affected" — or, as I would add, what happens even toward the ends of words, until both lexicality and syntax are themselves affected, one might even say infected, by the wound of ambivalence. This seems much the sense of Hartman's own appended remark: "The compounding or tmetic disjoining of words is also involved" (150–51).

The problematizing of linguistic juncture is thus at the microlevel a rebuke to closure, whether of lexemes or even of single morphemes. Such resistance to closure is a lateral friction that appears in the phenomenality of the text as performed, an interference that can be preserved only in reading at a certain pitch of responsiveness. To draw the notion of the "wounded" word more closely into the orbit of this study in connection with such transgressed closure, one may contemplate a Derridean parody of the Logos in its descent into time: a miniature mythography turning on a single model of the universal lapse, or cadence, of the Word into the mutable world, of speech into writing.

The trace of the morphophonemic Fall I have in mind is manifest, diachronically and synchronically at once, in that etymological trajectory which has transformed the sacrilegious exclamation "God's wounds!" (subjective as well as objective genitive, let us say) by euphemism into "His wounds," by elision into "'S wounds," by liaison and exaggerated voicing into "Zounds," and eventually into a rhyme with—and virtual echo of—the sound of the word "sounds" itself. By such contraction and displacement, such *coupure,* the archetypal wound is made flesh in read writing. What the genealogy of an idiom has done in this case over etymological time, at another level intensive silent reading—from the epicenter of the subvocal body—cannot help but do over the space of a line: in every sense such reading lets things slip. In Hartman's terms, reading in this degree opens itself to the literariness of textuality by "saving" any number of such epiphenomenal slips, recuperating them syntactically even in their full ambivalence, making them tell.

With the receptive epicenter of textual production thus hovering above the page, reading becomes a demystified but will palpable, still material, speech act—silent, reclusive, unmastered, but *placed.* To such a place we will next, yet again, let textual evidence direct us. If, in doing so, we extrapolate a major Derridean paradox to the level of text production, such embodied reading will stand disclosed as the very "supplement" of that textuality for which it is also the necessary condition. Prepared as we are, then, by a number of linguistically oriented theories indirectly related to the evocalizing of one word over the edges of another, to the lap and palpitation of the acoustic stream, to the reading of phonemic overlay within lexical sequence, we are ready now for a return to the phonotextual fray—and to that graphonic interference, that silent vocal feedback, which it everywhere entails.

II

OVEREADINGS

4   Graphonic Tension in English Poetry

Re: reading. In the case of phonemic reading, always potentially a rereading on the spot, a double taking, one sound overtaking another in sequence. Such reading-over is only in this sense an over-reading, trans-segmental, transegmental. For this recursive reading, then, that is thus also a rewriting, read: **over**eading. All we have to do, and cannot help doing, is to listen as we read — not listen *to* but listen *as* our reading. Do this, and the letters list and slip, push and are shoved, fan out or vanish, pun on themselves or double under. The words formed on the run by these letters overlie each other through aural coincidence, the overlapping of graphically indicated phonemes (by elision) or their holding over (by the ligatures of liaison or gemination) from one word to the next. Having already located such slippages in the textual system, indeed in the lexical code itself, first within a broad spectrum of transformational functions in Shakespearean verse, and then within a wider field of phonemic exercise in the habits of English rhyme, and having further considered the linguistic and textual implications of such slippages for a revisionist theory of reading, we are now ready to survey — across the whole range of English literary texts since Shakespeare — the variety and functions of such evanescent effects in action, in context, in force. This is a matter, and a manner, of reading the unwritten, of unwriting the word.

"By Parting Have Joyned Here"

Even by comparison with the typographic exaggerations of Herbert's rhyming triads discussed in Chapter 2, it is Donne among the immediate successors of Shakespeare who offers the most arresting reactivations of the lexical code from within its own erosion. Donne texts everywhere demonstrate the hold that semantic sense has on the textual sensorium: the reader's relentless tendency to control the phonemic in the form of the morphemic, to bracket free play by syllabification. Despite *appearances* to the contrary—despite lettering and spacing—even Donne's penchant for monosyllabism subserves the interdependence rather than the discreteness of lexical sequencing. His words are often overrun by each other, under mutual siege. In this sense, Dr. Johnson's famous definition of the metaphysical conceit—"heterogeneous ideas...yoked by violence together"—points us toward an equivalent violence at the morphophonemic level. In a transegmental thematization of lexical yoking that amounts to a "metaphysical" troping of juncture under the sign of an amorous coupling, Donne's knotty epigram "Pyramus and Thisbe" portrays two lovers who, by parting "love and fear," have themselves "joine*d here.*" In "Love's Exchange," the persona's emphasis is placed on how the woman "knows my pains," a necessary condition lest that "tender sha*me* *m*ake me mine ow*n new w*oe." The geminated consonants only begin to articulate the phonemic subtext, the transegmental reading effect, of these lines. In a semantic echo of "paines," the two yoked vocables "shame make" may well release the syntactically extraneous "ache." At the same time, the lover's recognition of the speaker's pain ("she knows") is transegmentally echoed—as "my known"—along the antiphonal slope of "mine own." The line thus instates a mating of reciprocal empathies across a syntax otherwise engaged. Then too, once "mine" is layered upon "own" to form the unwritten "known," so may the blending of *n*'s and *w*'s serve to condense the last three monosyllables; they may thus be overead upon each other in a metrically aided imbrication that elides out "new" altogether, muting the "e" (to /ə/) in one long-drawn groan of enunciation: "ow*n n*(əw) *w*oe."

It should be growing clear that the overead text is related to a sense of "overheard" vocalizations, but only in a special sense. We eavesdrop, but only on our own inner voicing as it sorts through the phonic strata of written language—often in excess of semantic necessity, sometimes of semantic capacity. Texts can be tongue twisters even when the tongue is not in motion; a line of poetry can depend for its effect on plosive alliteration when no lips move. Impedance is a textual as well as a vocal category, as is smoothness, as is flux, and so forth. We might, indeed, think of it this way: words as well as other structures have their own "eaves." To try listening from within such an extension of their basic framework is to overhear the inner workings of linguistic as well as textual structuration. Words have eaves, at least extended edges, abutments; making claims on adjacency, they have leanings and allow easements. The overead text as an overheard text is in this sense the registration of the passive phonemic incursion or overlap across adjacent sounds—not *if* they were realized by enunciation, but only in the continuous conjecture of the *as if*. Literary language is not conditioned by voice; rather, vocality remains its persistent conditional, a modality in abeyance.

Miltonalities

In moving forward from Donne into the later seventeenth century, it should be useful to refocus the notion of textual vocalization on certain major texts of the English poet for whom all texts, including his own, came to exist only as a system of phonemes, no longer letters. The blind Milton will not prove anything per se about sighted writers or sighted readers. Nor will his blindness prove anything about the way his verse sounds or should be sounded. Yet can we doubt that, in the tragic fortune of his blindness, Milton became preternaturally alert to one of the intrinsic rather than fortuitous dimensions of text production — its phonic texture? Milton would be worse than useless here if our investigation of his verbal effects were construed to suggest that all poets really take dictation from their own voices and that his need for amanuenses was only a special case of the general phonocentric process of composition-as-utterance, of text-as-transcript. We can, however, come at the issue differently. What is indisputable about late Miltonic composition might well illuminate what elsewhere must at least be held open for investigation. If what we hear in Milton's verses resembles, albeit at times in a more concentrated form, what we register in the contours of much English poetry, or in his own work before blindness set in, then the exceptional facts in his case suggest an overdetermined version of a phonological bias prevalent anyway in English poetry. Milton's texts thus become invaluable as the exemplary intensification of a tendency. It is certainly appropriate in this regard that the famous sonnet on his blindness (Sonnet 19) should provide a transegmental example in the opening line: "When I consider how my light is spent." The elision that transforms expenditure into confinement is confirmed by binary opposition in the second line, with its image of the mortal prison's "dark world and wide," as well as enhanced by the possibility of a more compressed rhyme with "bent."

Beyond such local effects, Milton happens to be the only writer in this book to have another book entirely devoted to his techniques of lexical contraction under metrical duress, "the cutting out or slurring of a syllable in the flow of speech."[1] This is the general subject of Robert O. Evans's *Milton's Elisions,* in which the metrical effects of verbal contractions are explored and debated. A prevalent technique in Milton's prosody for sustaining a metrical pattern across what amounts to a surplus of graphically indicated syllables is what Evans, alluding to Robert Bridges's borrowing of the classical term, calls "synaloepha," defined as "the suppression of hiatus (that is, vowel clash) between words by the cutting out or partial reduction of a vowel" (7). A typical, typographically indicated example from *Paradise Lost* would be "th' Ethereal sky" (1.45). Well beyond the purview of Evans's analysis, however, are those homophonic elisions, graphically counterindicated, that are found bridging other lexical gaps than those turning strictly on the hiatus of consecutive vowel sounds. In a cautionary speech by Michael in *Paradise Lost,* female lasciviousness is imaged as the urge "To dress, and troll the Tongue, and roll the Eye" (11.620). In conjunction with the implied etymology of "trollop" in "troll," there is the transegmental ghost of "droll" (an archaic intransitive verb, functionless here) in "an*d roll.*" It is part of what we might call a phonemic lubriciousness that—by internal echo with the dentalized overdetermination of "and troll"—unifies the image of promiscuous degeneration through a kind of lexical lowest common denominator.

The transegmental phenomenon is, of course, not confined to a version of elision or to its counterpart in liaison. By simple conjunction it can create from two whole words a third. In *Samson Agonistes,* when the hero blames himself for his sexual ensnarement by Dalila, characterizing himself as "vanquisht with a peal of words" (l. 235), we overead the overt seductiveness of "a=p(p)eal" in the explicit denomination of a sound. Direct lexical punning of this sort—stable in its perfect ambivalence, poised exactly between the graphic and the phonic—is less frequent, however, than the passing graphonic ambiguity, lexically operable for only the split second of a sheared lexeme. This can be a fleeting evocation, *in* sound, of a murmuring whisper of sound: a phonemic mimesis. There is the image of a swarm of flies in *Paradise Regained* that, no matter how many times it is beaten back, still "returns a*s oft* with humming sound" (4.17). It is a buzzing hum whose very sibilance we can scarcely avoid *reading,* though we can never see it in the line as written. In *Paradise Lost,* forewarning of God's "ire" (2.155) were it to be loosed again to fan the "grim fires" (2.170) of hell, the smooth-spoken Belial reiterates the idea of divine retribution twice over, as "rage" (2.170) and then again "vengeance" (2.173), before, three lines later, enfolding effect back into cause for the segmentally ambiguous "Cataracts o*f Fire*" (2.176). Adam later, lamenting the "only consolation left / Familiar to our eyes" (11.304–5), contrasts this narrowed human scope to the unlimited power "Of him who all things can" (11.309). Despite the strange intransitive syntax of that last clause, the touchstone of divinity evoked by it is clearly omnipotence, a limitless enablement ("all things can"). At the same time that other chief attribute of the deity, omniscience, is made to seem consubstantial with the text's very phrasing through the momentary hint (by liaison, and despite the wrong verb number) of "all things (s)can."[2]

Elsewhere, in Satan's fleeing from God's immediate "ken," there is the image of the archangel as "he wings his way / Not far off Heav'n, in the Precincts o*f light*" (3.87–88). Or the more loaded phonemic irony of Eve's meditation on the apple as "the Cure of all, this Fruit Divine" (9.776). This obverse prolepsis for the subsequent *cause* "of (f)all" is an irony further supported by the Latin overtone of "cure" as "care" or "trouble,"[3] which also appears through repetition in Belial's speech about the fallen angel's only hope in death: "our cure / . . . sad cure" (2.145–46). In such a manner *Paradise Lost* establishes a phonotextual system in which a phrasing like "With Serpent error wand'ring, found thir way" (7.302), already etymologically redundant (*errare:* to wander), can never be entirely free of "serpent terror" — and one in which phrasing itself may be all the more readily thematized. In his response to Abdiel's speech about the "Word" by which "the mighty Father made / All things" (5.833), a universe "named" by the language of fiat, Satan scoffs at this notion of created origin. He instead asserts his own being as "self-begot, self-rais'd" (5.860). His semantic stress on self-generation does not, however, quell the homophonic overtones of that phrasing, for in Satan's hubris we may also hear him claiming to be, through his own incarnate Word, "self-phrased." Beyond this, the additional ironic sense of the fallen archangel as "self-razed" would surface as an unsuccessfully repressed self-indictment, a Miltonic slip of his own fallen tongue.

Whatever Milton may or may not have recognized about his demonic allegiances in *Paradise Lost,* Blake himself was certainly of Milton's party at times, and knew it. And worried it. In an essay called "Re: Naming MIL/ TON," Thomas Vogler evokes the breach or bisection of the precursor's name in the title plate of Blake's poem, going on to suggest that the bardic or Urizenic domain of patriarchy is contrasted with the zone of Beulah, whose "rhythmic babble" anticipates the "prelinguistic, semiotic *chora* described by Kristeva."[4] In specifying what we might thus characterize as Blake's "Beulalangue," we can turn to the lateral biplay of an ironized transegmental drift in the *Book of Thel.* The title figure, anxious about accepting the mantle of human existence, stays sequestered from the toils of mortality in the unpotentiated sphere of Har, a place-name of obscure and undetermined origin. Its etymology might seem, in isolation, a monosyllabic irony, a pun (on "are") that exposes the entirely *pre*existent limbo (bordering on nescience) of Thel's state, the otherworld of all those things that *are not.* Once activated by the verse line, however, its thrice-repeated place in the refrain "vales of Har" (plates 2.1, 2.10, 4.22) seems finally to measure as well as to mourn Thel's timorous flight from the demands of being. By the time she has "Fled back unhindered till she came into the vales *of Har*," we may well have recognized her symbolic purlieus as a realm removed forever and *afar* from life's immediate vale of tears. Such vocalized irony taps the semiotic flux beneath the symbolic regimentation of diction without collapsing back into it; its sheer phonic undulation is recuperated by the phonemic order of pertinent differentials as soon as it begins to slip away. By the very fact of irony, of human perspective, the dream of an unfallen invulnerability to the world is mocked by the iambic twist of what might otherwise be read as a linguistic symptom of that otherworld's own amorphous evocation.

Esemplastic Voicings

For all this, Blake is by no means the most venturesome of the Romantic poets in these transegmental instigations. One thinks immediately of Shelley, then of Keats. The earlier generation of Coleridge and Wordsworth is also given to such phonemic bridgings and slips. Minor poets, too, make certain phonemic tendencies of the period baldly apparent, not just the punster Thomas Hood but Robert Southey as well. In a little-known, comically exaggerated, but in some sense quintessential Romantic text, Southey's 1823 "The Cataract of Lodore," we encounter "In Rhymes for the Nursery" (so the subtitle has it) the description of "Sounds and motions for ever and ever . . . blending," including a stupefying cadence of textual sounds designed to simulate, and finally subsume, the cascading of nature. Almost a dozen lines of dyadic participles — many alliterative, like "Flying and flinging" or "Turning and twisting" — give way to over twice as many pairs of such internally echoing participles as "threading and spreading," "pouring and roaring," "waving and raving," "foaming and roaming." The pattern then fans out to triplets: "Dividing and gliding and sliding," followed relentlessly by "And falling and brawling and sprawling, / And driving and riving and striving" — and so on, through more than another dozen lines of mixed pairs, triplets, and fourfold rhymes tumbling out in a deluge beyond all nursery patience or mnemonics. Cataractic phonology matches the steady plunge of a waterfall in a remorseless fluency of effect, including that transegmental tightening of the chime at the lexically reflexive juncture of a "riven" word in "And driving and riving" — which can thus be taken as two of one or two of the other. Either way, first by elision, then by ligature, internal rhyme converts to exact echo.

Coleridge certainly shares this Romantic instinct for phonetic iteration, especially in an imitative descriptive context, though he never carries it to anything like these lengths. When "Bard Bracy" is asked to address Sir Leoline in *Christabel,* he speaks like the poet he is, describing a dove "Fluttering, and uttering fearful moan" (l. 535) so as to stress the containment within one word of its own released echo. Coleridge is elsewhere capable not just of such insistent paronomasia but of unreserved homophonic punning even more ingenious and strained than Hood's. Coleridge was indeed a self-conscious exegete and theorist of such wordplay, as well as an avid practitioner in both prose and verse. There is a densely punning passage in his 1821 letter to James Gillman that includes two transegmental oddities as lexically defiant as almost anything in Joyce. First there is an aside involving the bilingual deformation of "Poor dear Jew!" into the French "pour dire adieu," with its junctural elision of a weak vowel (or synaloepha), and then (in connection with a wound Coleridge has suffered, and with apologies for his "Punarhoeia") the English liaison of "leave it's card on your arm."[5] The pronoun "it's" in that clause is punctuated with the apostrophe despite its possessive form; it is then glossed by Coleridge as if the apostrophe were a transegmental signal: "Now that last Pun, my dear fellow! is I admit, rather *obscure* [itself presumably italicized for its play on "cure"]—but if you will imagine a various reading in the margin, 'leave it scarr'd', all becomes clear as a Thames Fog." Coleridge had indeed planned an "Ode on Punning" as well as an essay on the subject, had defended Shakespearean wordplay, and had at one point in his notebooks tossed off the trisyllabic punning aphorism "Anymadversions of an Author's meaning now a days pass for animadversions."[6]

This leads us inevitably to wonder what signs of this hypertrophied verbal imagination might be visible, or audible, in his poetic texts. From such puzzle-like breaks with spacing—or spacings of the break—as that which converts "its card" into "it scarred," what crossovers are possible in a general verse practice very far from comedy or verbal farce? Any such homophonic alternatives, if mobilized in poetry, would indeed readily find theoretical justification in Coleridge's account of the Shakespearean oxymoron, whose meaning remains "unfixed and wavering."[7] Likewise, the pun that plays between meanings, especially the phonic doublet that does so by playing between lexemes as two alternate aural segmentations of the same sequence of letters, seems a perfect instance of imaginative instability, "still offering what is still repelled, and again creating what is again rejected" (104). This is very close, in fact, to Christopher Ricks's characterization of the "anti-pun," of which there is a twofold, phonemically sprung instance (not mentioned by Ricks) in a reiterated line from the *Ancient Mariner:* "With throats unslaked, with black lips baked" (ll. 157, 162). Until he "sucked the blood" of his own arm, the Mariner was "mute" with drought, unable even to hail an oncoming ship. Twice over, though, the straining toward speech is actually there to be heard in the enunciatory torsion of "lip*s bake*d"—a "mute" liaison phrasing exactly that active preterite which is ruled out by being swallowed up in the past participle. At the other end of this doubled refrain we may also hear a transegmental antiphone in which the impossible, the paradoxical "s = unslaked" holds out a mocking chance of relief from within the very source of feverish desiccation.

Or take the famous passage in "The Eolian Harp" added some two decades after the poem's original publication (here as printed in the Errata):

> O! the one Life, within us and abroad,
> Which meets all Motion and becomes its soul,

> A Light in Sound, a sound-like power in Light,
> Rhythm in all Thought, and Joyance everywhere
>   (ll. 26–29)

In textual terms, what exactly dictates the "rhythm" of this "thought," what syncopation and elision, what contrapuntal beats? Here it is worth examining the most direct evocation of the wind harp's seductive melody, whose "long sequacious notes / Over delicious surges sink and rise" (ll. 18–19). This is a music characterized in the next line as a "soft floating witchery of sound," where the slackening tendency toward elision in "soft floating" only enhances the airy delicacy of the described notes. With actual semantic force, too, a hint of immanent will slips into the collocation "delicious *surges*" by way of elision at the sibilant juncture. This further argues for the shading of personification in the archaic term "sequacious," which in musical parlance indicates only a strict metrical succession but which in its larger range of denotation (now obsolete) refers to the easily led, the intellectually tractable, the ductile, the pliable, the readily moulded. To the will of the wind, to the "urges" of that nature which is "within us and abroad," to the very breath of life which alone these notes make audible, they are at the same time subservient, dutifully attuned. It is worth recalling here that moment in the *Biographia* placed as an epigraph to my Prologue, where Coleridge describes the course of reading itself as a wavelike pattern resembling "the path of sound through the air." In this sense, his poem of Eolian visitations might well be meant to identify the "sink and rise" of wind as a trope not only for vocal production but for the very pulse of even silent reading.

The real crux of Coleridge's passage, however, is the metaphysical tenor to which its symbolic wind song is vehicle: the unifying interpenetration of "A Light in Sound, a sound-like power in Light." These "figures are technically oxymorons," writes M. H. Abrams early in an extensive investigation of the "cognitive infrastructure" organizing the lines.[8] He sets out to broaden that received reading into an awareness of the larger scientific context of the "figures" provided by Coleridge's studies of optics and acoustics. Revising Newton's holdings on the properties of light, Coleridge came to believe that sound and color were coefficients of each other: " 'Color is Gravitation under the power of Light while Sound on the other hand is Light under the power or paramountcy of Gravitation' " (166). Sound, in other words, is light weighted toward a kind of palpability. Though Abrams does not develop his argument in linguistic directions, his researches can help to draw out the transegmental play—the ligature of "alight" in the image "A light in sound"—introduced before the more scientifically couched corollary of the answering notion, "a sound-like power in light." Abrams does note in the first half of the line a deliberate echo of divine fiat as well as of post-Newtonian physics: in the uttered Word that brought Light. This should only confirm a sense of the lines as playing in their own right between sound and light, sound and the medium of vision—between, in one sense, listening and script, phonic and graphic signification. The phonic ambiguity offers, in short, a reflexive analysis of reading itself under its alternating "paramountcies" of eye and ear. Taken in this way to name the procedures of its own decoding, "A light in sound" becomes "Alight in sound" in the double sense of "brought to light" in sound (lit, lighted, imaginatively kindled) and descended, settled, or come to rest therein (alighted). The past participial form, *alight* (for *alighted*), is already obsolete by Coleridge's day but not therefore less operable as a poetic overtone. If the first version of this transegmental meld only spells out the sense of the oxymoron as scripted ("a=light" as implying "lit in"), the second (the archaic "a=light" as "descended") seems to evoke what Abrams demonstrates (though without mention of the wordplay) as the primary allusive intertext of the line: that theoretical hypothesis which sees sound as light virtually weighted down by a gravitational pull. What Coleridge called the "reciprocal neutralizations" by which the particular qualities of a thing arise in proportional relation to other properties co-present in the object would thus seem to apply as well to that reciprocal elision and reinstatement of the junctural break that determines the morphemic proportion—and, hence, lexical properties—in this perfect aural ambiguity. The "rhythm in all thought" has thus become the rhythm of reading with the ear, an access to the space of imagination beyond the constraints of sheer mental demarcation. Here is that profound coefficiency of light and sound, of eye and ear, in all reading that will not be more subtly—or more indirectly—addressed in English letters before Stephen's meditation on the reciprocal modality of the visible and the audible in the "Proteus" section of *Ulysses*.

Coleridge the extravagant punster, Coleridge the scientist of optics and acoustics, Coleridge the philosopher of the imagination and the fancy all meet on such a textual terrain. By not resting content with the "fixities and definites" which he claims in chapter 8 of the *Biographia* ("On the Imagination, or Esemplastic Power") are manipulated by fancy without that resynthesizing power of the imagination, lexical transmutation of the sort we have examined "dissolves, diffuses, dissipates." It erodes, in particular, the readerly threshold between eye and ear—between a written sequence and a malleable phonic sequacity—to produce the transegmental or esemplastic reassemblage "alight." In this sense, the poem's titular symbol itself, the wind harp—a structure of taut lines awaiting the breath (or inspiration) of the wind, a material symbol of a latency whose music is potentiated only by the breath of "vocal" performance—is therefore a "meet emblem" (to borrow Coleridge's phrase from this same poem) of the poem itself, this and any poem. It is an object whose parallel lines are activated only by an inner (at least) enunciation that manifests the two senses of "sequacious," submissive (to creative urges) and sequenced. This is the pliability (within progression) of passively voiced script. The poem, like the wind harp, is thus a model for that "one life within us and abroad" which is the metaphysical touchstone of this whole conceit of collaboration between the natural and the constructed. The conceit is extended, and so reinforced, by the entirely nonmetaphysical fact of silent reading — as in its own way a responsive internalization of the outer text by a voice held always "within us."

The subjective (as well as subvocal) interanimation of textuality is part of the thematic of empathy which energizes an even more pivotal phonemic biplay in Coleridge's "Dejection: An Ode." In the concluding stanza of the ode's revised address to the generalized "Lady," the feminine Other, in which her freedom from despondency is actively *willed* by the morose persona, an apostrophe to sleep is generated out of the desire to spare her the wakeful "vigil" from which he suffers: "Visit her, gentle Sleep! with wings of healing" (l. 128).[9] In the speaker's originating "wan and heartless mood" (l. 25), he must admit that "I see, not feel" (l. 38) the beauty of nature's forms. Feeling is, from this second stanza on, the negated and unsaid impulse of the text, its vanished power. It nevertheless hovers — in the drift of a wavering fricative — behind the climactic phrase "wings of *f*(h)ealing," manifesting the psychic cause of that blessing's transferred effect. The more familiar(izing) — and re-socializing — phrase, "wings of feeling," denoting that uplift which *is* feeling (by way of what Christine Brooke-Rose calls the "genitive metaphor") is thus the unsaid cliché whose paraphonic activation is here a self-fulfilling prophecy of the speaker's own restoration, the repeal of the "heartless" by empathy. To vary Wordsworth, feeling comes in aid of healing — and vice versa.

Wordsworth himself is, of course, not a poet of such luxuriant phonic texture as Coleridge nor a writer (despite his name) with the same punning bent. Yet segmental ambiguity still operates in the Wordsworthian text, in both overt and more elusive ways. When, in the narrative poem "Ruth" from *Lyrical Ballads,* Wordsworth's eponymous heroine, deserted by her lover, goes mad and is summarily "in a prison housed" (no external agency mentioned for the passive verb), it is a metaphoric as well as literal internment from which the mind, well before the body, achieves release. As with the image of the "prison house" everywhere in Wordsworth, what is required is that the imagination break itself free. True to form, Ruth wanted neither "sun, nor rain, nor dew, / Nor pastimes of the May" (ll. 200–201), for, as suggested by the pun on "pastimes," all these joys are recoverable by memory: "They all were with her in her cell" (l. 203). Permitted by the iambic rhythm, though jolting the syntactic parallelism—unshackling, that is, its semantic grip-lock—is the transegmental sense that this ·beneficence of nature is so far internalized that it floods the "inner cell" of her spirit (as one might say, "they were all with her innermost soul").

There are other phonotextual effects, just as suggestive, which do not so neatly fit the iambic cues of the given graphic script. By contrast to the clear-cut homophony in "Ruth," the rhetorical question on which the whole consolatory logic of the "Intimations" ode turns—"What though the radiance which was once so bright / Be now forever taken from my sight" (ll. 179–80)—leaves only the least trace of "from *eye*-sight" in the metrically divergent "from my sight." The (not unwelcome) result is that the difference between "my sight" (figurative as well as literal) and "eyesight" is thrown open to question in the space of an ambiguous lexical juncture. It is, in fact, at exactly this climactic turn of the poem that sight is redefined as a faculty of spirit, paraphrased later as "the faith that *looks* through death" (l. 189; my emphasis). Hence the rhythm of the verse might seem to have muted but not entirely suppressed the earlier transegmental pun, "fro/m eyesight," as an impertinent equivalence to that keener incorporeal seeing which the ode is striving to define even in the midst of its nostalgia for present and unmediated vision. It is the soul's sight, the mind's-eye-view of retrospect, in particular, that permits each of us (as recovered "seer blest") to envision the "immortal sea" of our origin, "And see the Children sport upon the shore" (l. 168). What in the general sense of these lines is there to veto the probability of the antiphonal phrasing "children's port," designating the threshold of life, the harbor of all arriving and unfettered energies? This is indeed the textual equivalent of those "intimations" the ode has set out to trace, fallings from us, here phonemic shavings, vanishings.

A similar instance, but harder yet to disambiguate—especially if read aloud—is also a case that illustrates more directly the interrelation between expressive sequence and lexical order or, in Paul de Man's terms, between rhetoric and grammar. This is the opening line from the short lyric, "The Solitary Reaper," whose junctural ambiguity, like that of the "in her"/"inner" pun in "Ruth," operates within a strict iambic format. Two of the three vocative gestures toward the reader in the opening stanza of "The Solitary Reaper"— "Stop here, or gently pass!" (l. 4) and "O listen!" (l. 7)—tacitly identify the reader as inhabiting the same space as the "Highland Lass." Depending on how we hear the poem's opening line—"Behold her, single in the field"—this stationing of the reader is either implicit still or actually explicit. Either each reader, by a transegmental blend (across the aspirate), is isolated as a lone "behold(h)er" on the landscape (even as the momentarily fused noun form can also describe the lass herself), or else (the more "obvious" reading) the scripted imperative grammar asserts itself simply to enjoin our role in beholding. Either way, our identification with the reaper (herself perhaps a beholder too) extends to the figurative sense of reading as its own version of garnering in solitude. Moreover, from a theoretical perspective associated originally with a critique of Romanticism, that epoch's entire aesthetic of imaginative manifestation comes into focus in this arguable ambiguity on "behold = (h)er" — as involving both subject and object, both rhetorical addressee and paragrammatical denomination. As we saw in Chapter 1, Paul de Man makes the figure of prosopopoeia, or its special case of apostrophe, the touchstone for a deconstruction premised on the working of literary language as a figural "giving face" to absence. This is a sustained rhetoric of the literary which he insists — against Riffaterre's more representational semiotics — must be understood as the activity of sheer inscription rather than description. We have at hand a peculiarly compressed test case. That apostrophic gesture, "Behold her," constitutes an address to an always, in one sense, absent reader who, even when present to the words of the text, beholds never more than words. If and when this conjuring gesture is heard to collapse, from a mere accident of inscription, into either the actual designation of (rather than summons to) the onlooker's role or into the correlative designation of the posited viewer's posited object — "beholders" each and all — we are that much more likely to perceive the latter, and our relation to "her," as sheerly a function of marks on a page, marks variously "realized" under the opportunistic laws of lexical convention. If so, we here confront a quintessential instance of poetic address — poetic inscription — as the reciprocal nullification, through mutual evocation, of both the referential object and the textual subject, the latter a reading "I" as implied vocative object "you." Retreating to the graphic security of script alone, to retrieve "(You) Behold her" again from the phonotextual ambiguity of "Beholder" is thus to give rhetorical face once more to the sliding effacements of grammatical metonymy: to effect, by insistent apostrophe, the very prosopopoeia of prosopopoeia. Wordsworth's line offers in this way a troping of the trope dependent entirely on the material inscription of the written text and its syncopated production as read. The self-"dis-figuring" inscription analyzed in de Man's deconstructed *rhetoric* may therefore be further isolated and unstrung — according to the present deconstructive *linguistics* — within the dyslocutionary force of phonemic reading.

Unheard Melodies

Rather like the "Eolian Harp" in Coleridge, with its rows (or lines) of latent instrumentation waiting to be breathed upon, Keats's sculptural symbol in the "Ode on a Grecian Urn" may at one point be more directly an emblem of poetry as text, as inhibited vocalization, than has been recognized. Everyone finds in this ode a parable of art and imagination. But when the musicianship pictured on the urn, as in turn rendered by the ode there*on,* is characterized as producing "ditties of no tone" (l. 14), there would seem to be more textual auto-commentary at work than just wholesale aesthetic meditation. In texts, as in plastic representation, "melodies" are not less melodious for being "unheard" (l. 11), for keeping the silence of their unspoken vocalizations. Rather than being generated for the "sensual ear" (l. 13), the unintoned "ditties" portrayed on the urn's surface are registered solely in the mind—yet registered as music, not just as the idea of music.[10] Then, too, Keats has even more in common with Coleridge than this may so far suggest. In his correspondence he is a homophonic punster as well, who gives Coleridge's "any-madversions" a run for its money—for its lexical short-changes and syntactic overdraft—with his complaints about the "{hie}*rogue*glyphics in Moors almanack."[11] In that rebuslike syllable, Keats's drifting phoneme (carried by the grapheme *gue*) doubles by liaison for the *g* of "glyphs" (just as the *r* of "hier" could have been made to operate in this way with the fuller spelling "hier-rogue-glyphs"). Such "rogue glyphs," loosed by phonemic slack, can, as in Coleridge, certainly inflect the graphic contours of a verse line as well. In the "Ode on a Grecian Urn," for example, there is a transegmental overlay in the very thought that art's idealized and wholly imagined music would not pipe or pander to the "sensual leer," to that fevered gaze of desire that animates the male lovers on the urn. From this we infer some sort of sensory luxuriance apart from aggressive sensuality: a rarefied state which the line, by thematically positing, also phonemically enacts.

In Keats's "Ode to a Nightingale," we have already noted the critically debated rhyme on "sole self"/"deceiving elf," with a potential homophonic ambiguity at the sibilant juncture that returns more unmistakably in *Lamia,* where the title creature is either "some penanced lady *elf,*" or, if not, "Some demon's mistress, or the demon's s*elf*" (1.55–56). In the multiplicity and logical contradiction of these lines, an uncertainty turning on identity-versus-possession would readily serve Keats's purpose. So with the proleptic irony of Lamia uttering her first words in the poem "for Love's sake" (1.65). As we saw in Donne's "Love's Exchange," the elided underside of the possessive "Love'*s* *s*ake" sounds a warning of that "ache" which attends the possessiveness of love in the tragic remainder of the narrative. In Lamia's own description of Hermes' nymph, the fourfold repetition of her going about "unseen" (1.96, 99) also impresses a narrative logic upon transegmental ambiguity: "From bow'd branches green, / She plucks the fruit unseen, she bathes unseen" (1.98–99). The virtual redundancy (for the sake of rhyme) in "branches green" is rescued by the sense of it being precisely their leafage which creates the "branches' screen" that provides her privacy (recalling Shakespeare's "summer's *green*" in Chapter 1). Such is Keats's ear for the thickening textures of the literary tradition.

In the second part of the poem, well after Lamia has taken up with the hero, Lycius, the climax is precipitated by the appearance of his stern mentor, Apollonius, at the wedding feast. Once within sight of his pupil's bride, the dry rationalist begins to puzzle out the mystery of the snake lady, her embodied ambiguity. The task is described as a "knotty problem" that "had now begun to thaw, / And solve and melt" (2.161–62). It is another highly Shakespearean moment in this poem. Keats would indeed seem to be consciously alluding here, and in the process normalizing, Hamlet's famous sequence, "melt, / Thaw, and resolve," while retaining a related pun on resolution in "solve." It is a pun that is submitted in Keats's line to a transegmental drift as well. Holding the place at once of rational "solution" and of metamorphic "dissolution" (as immediately restated in "melt"), the punning lexeme gives out laterally. In a silent voicing of the line, that is, the slight sibilant hiss of "And solve" is all that is necessary for the inner ear to generate, following the dental sound, the near equivalence of "An*d* (d)(i)*s*olve." Elsewhere, evidence of Keats's revisions also supports such a transegmental audition of his texts. The well-known change in the "Bright Star" sonnet— from "feel forever its warm sink and swell,"[12] describing the pillowing breast of the speaker's love, to "feel forever its soft fall and swell"—has everything to recommend it, including the transegmental echo in "soft *fall an*d" of the snow's "soft *fallen* mask" four lines earlier. Also in favor of the change is a no doubt unwanted transegmental possibility in the original: the hint of "swarm" welling up from "warm" as if by way of a transferred epithet confessing the persona's inundation by erotic thoughts. It is in the very nature of such phonotextual tendencies that they come unbidden—and must sometimes be avoided by rephrasing, just as the reader must at times censor their irruption in order to keep to the track of sense.

Keats's odes are a rich field of such effects at their most openly activated, however, as we began to see in Chapter 2. The famous fifth stanza of the "Ode to a Nightingale," which begins with the speaker admitting that he has "been half in love with easeful Death" (l. 52), closes with his imagined relation to the nightingale's song once he has given up consciousness: "To thy high requiem become a sod" (l. 60). Without relating it back to Milton's synaloepha (his metrically determined eliding of vowels), Walter Jackson Bate, in *The Stylistic Development of Keats,* notes instead the "extreme and persistent" tendency toward "hiatus" or "vowel-gaping" in Keats's early sonnets. But what of the cross-lexical shunt that moves to span this gape, this gap—or, should we say, threatens to?—even at the expense of meter, in a phrase like "thy *high* requiem"? To have ascribed that song to the nightingale, in the context of the speaker's wished-for return to earth, is to have defined it, by contrast, as "high." In this sense it is fitting (indeed, by a close phonemic fit) that the pronominal adjective seems to entail, to trail off into or be taken up by, the epithet. This is so even as the full measure of "high" (in a kind of kinaesthetic enhancement of the referential elevation) would tend with its "high" vowel to lift away from "thy" in enunciation—against the enforced prosody of Keats's own iambic requiem, where "thy" rather than "high" would take the accent. The inner speech of the body as reading site must negotiate in this way between two contradictory impulses, transegmental and kinaesthetic. If held to metrical regularity, this phrasing thus suppresses that normal hyper-articulation which might otherwise work to offset thematically the languid blurring of "a(s) sod" at the close of the line.[13] Just as the reflexive recognition of "the very word," like a bell, will help the persona recover from his death wish a stanza later, the tension here in both phrases between hiatus and elision, enforced juncture and conflation, might equally be felt to hold alert (even if under constraint) the verbal consciousness (ours by proxy for that of the "speaker"), to keep the mind and body energized at one crucial point of their intersection: in silent as well as spoken enunciation. In this, the self-conscious literariness of graphonic tension encodes the very force of its utterance as a will to (still) living speech.

The subsequent stanza now ends on the belling note "Of perilous seas, in faery lands forlorn," where the subjective admonishment slipping into the phrase through the elision of a transegmental drift—namely, the chastisement of "perilous (s)eas(e)"—registers the indolent mood of mind from which the speaker is about to rebound into the chastening echo of the next stanza. Given that the "full-throated ease" (l. 11) of the nightingale has initially led the speaker to his thoughts of "easeful" death—the latter adjective used in Keats's day, both passively and actively, for "slothful" as well as "easing"—the word "ease" has cut deep, always potentially recurrent, grooves in the poem. The lexical risk incident to a sibilant juncture like "perilous seas" is therefore all the more likely to let slip into "production" the text's more telling noun, for which "seas" is part of a figure here anyway. Against the grain of the written phenotext, that is, the phonotext has once again sounded (at the level of a suppressed matrix) the implicit tenor to a metaphoric vehicle operating at the scripted surface of a phrase.

The easy slipping in of the verbal rather than substantive form of "ease," though without the monitory overtones of the "Nightingale" ode, is even more self-enacting in the "Ode on a Grecian Urn," where "ease" carries the sense less of torpor than of aesthetic release. The synecdochic urn, silently in-scribed vessel described entirely by the sheer inscription (to recall de Man's terms) of the poem "on" it, is apostrophized in the last stanza as precisely that (quasi-textual) "silent form" which—in a self-illustrating animation of such silence—"dost tease us out of thought" (l. 44). It is just that formal second-person-singular ending ("do*st*"), insignia of direct address (of prosopopoeia in the form of apostrophe), which permits the very slip in inscription that draws off the (in context) synonymous "ease" from its less predictable variant, "tease." If "seas" edging to "ease" in the "Nightingale" ode seemed confirmed by the prehistory of that noun in the same poem, so may this climactic image from the "Ode on a Grecian Urn" be at least encouraged by comparing its earlier formulation in the "Epistle to John Hamilton Reynolds," where imagination's desired objects cannot be willed into existence: "Things cannot to the will / Be settled, but they tease us out of thought" (ll. 76–77). As noted, it is the later shift into the formal vocative case, "dost," that introduces the possibility of elision into the ode. In this sense what we find there is a Riffaterrean matrix that could be said to undergo deconstruction by its very apostrophizing inscription—but a deconstruction negotiated in the play be-tween graphic (in particular, here, ekphrastic) inscription and the "sensual ear" of the phonotext. The artifact's teasing us free of anxiety, its role in aesthetic appeasement, is indeed possible, given the urn's exclusively textual embodiment, only through the tease of inscription itself—which pretends to address the object as present to us, to give plastic face and form, shape and dimension, to its sheer imaginary status.

Another, later "closure" comes to mind. Keats breaks off the unfinished *Fall of Hyperion* with a vision of the title deity rushing past the dreaming speaker, his "flaming robes" streaming behind him. The poem then closes with a portmanteau blur of their flaring and his wayfaring, as if Hyperion were burning up distances in his speed: "On he flared." A comparable ear for the power of lexical compression is, earlier in this late poem, directed against the terrible verbal power of Moneta's awesome disclosures. Containing in their narrative the whole englobed tragedy of the Titans, her words seem shaped by the vastness and devastation on which they report. By a transferred epithet from the mythic sphere whose fallen world they evoke, her language is characterized as "an immortal's *s*phered words" (1.249). By elision and another transference, here from cause to effect, the words naming her words thus also characterize the narrator's recoil from this "feared" revelation. Such a wording on the text's part is rounded to contain its own microdrama, its own tension between utterance and response.

Mon Blanc

In just this sense of textual repletion, it was Keats who gave phrase to the rhetorical mission of second-generation Romanticism in urging that poetry should "load every rift with ore."[14] Shelley's *Defence of Poetry* may be read in part as an expanded meditation on this impulse. In Shelley, however, the rifts and crevices that must be made full are explored as the poet's natural province because of their extratextual relation to the gaps, blanks, and lacunae of lived experience, the slumps and dead spots of existence, which the poet exists to animate. The term "interstices" recurs suggestively in the *Defence*. In celebrating the poetic imagination for its "unapprehended combinations of thought," Shelley argues that these new admixtures "have the power of attracting and assimilating to their own nature all other thoughts," forming "new intervals and interstices whose void for ever craves fresh food."[15] Filling gaps in our consciousness that we never before knew existed, by linkages and surpluses never previously engaged, is the task of a poetry whose own gaps and lapses remain real enough. No poem is all sustained inspiration. The craft, rather than the genius, of poetry is the fashioning of serviceable bridge passages, a more or less "artificial connexion of the spaces between by the intertexture of conventional expressions" (504). All the rifts can never quite be swollen with gold. That Shelley here argues home his point in evocations devoted to the maneuvered interval and trace, the phonic visitant and larded interstice, does not of course in any way demonstrate that his defense of poetry is mounted explicitly as a theory of style. I am merely noticing how much his prose seems to evoke what he calls later in this paragraph, in figures again of perceptual blank and traversed interval, "the vanishing apparitions which haunt the interlunations of life" (505). Far more than his prose, the Shelleyan verse text can be found replicating these interlunations at the microlevel, finessing their ruptures, thickening their interstices with the music of his own "evanescent visitations," a play of phantom ripples and echoing traces.

With his stress on "vanishing apparitions" and "interlunations," Shelley's anticipation of Derrida's trace-under-erasure seems phonetically activated in another image from *The Triumph of Life*. The only "trace I find," says the persona, is "as of foam after the Ocean's wrath / Is spent upon the desert shore" (ll. 162–64). Rather like Keats's "become a(s) sod," though by elision now rather than reverse liaison, the collocation "as of foam" is virtually interchangeable—by way of phonemic meltdown as well as descriptive reference—with the analogic construction "as a foam." So, too, in the "Mutability" sonnet, where human life in the collective is analogous to "forgotten lyres" with "dissonant strings," the very noun "dissonance" manifested across its own transformed adjectival bond. In "Lines Written among the Euganean Hills," the "sun upsprings behind" (l. 100) on "the level quivering line / Of the waters chrystalline" (ll. 102–3). In this volatile dissolve of sound, the noun "sun" seems to have merged into a fuller subject, "sunup," before its second syllable is claimed by the verb. Moreover, the aurally overrich rhyme on "line" and "l/line" actually risks phonemic redistribution in the pleonastic rephrasing "Of the water's crystal line" — a quivering of segmentation itself, with the ambiguous "liquid" phonemes as lexical solvents. Quite apart from the motifs of quivering evanescence, Shelley's phonemic transmutability can, for instance, work toward the consolidation of an outer power through apostrophe. This fluidity thus provides yet another interfusion of representation and verbal registration. In "Hymn to Intellectual Beauty," the climactic invocation voices the hope "That thou — O awful LOVELINESS, / Wouldst give whate'er these words cannot express" (ll. 71–72). But "these words" themselves attempt to encompass such sublimity — in exactly its quality of majestic *pervasiveness* — by a sliding synaloepha at the all but double elision "th*ou* — *O aw*ful." For a moment it is as if address, exclamation, and attribute were all one suffused epithet. Indeed, the founding prosopopoeia of this invoked loveliness here seems generated, evocalized, out of a distended ablauted matrix still in the process of morphemic consolidation, a genotext still gathering the expressive force of a phenotext.

As against such swollen aurality and metaphysical repletion, barrenness and vacancy as textual conditions also, as we have seen before, phonemically impinge on the Shelleyan text. The title "Epipsychidion" refers to that projected soul which makes full the "bare and void interstices" (l. 482) of nature. Here, quite explicitly, the style and theme of the interstice are made to coalesce — as do the lexical units of the line themselves, for "bare and void" is likely to be evocalized in passing as "barren void," an anti-pun quickly readjusted by syntax. This takes place according to a logic which the poem has earlier exemplified by spelling it out in an enjambed description of the lunar cycle, "whose changes ever run / Into themselves" (ll. 278–79). So, of course, do the phonemic changes of language, as in such acoustic — if nonsemantic — elisions as "ever(r)un" (compare the first word in Joyce's *Wake:* "riverrun"). In *Prometheus Unbound,* there is the image of a geologically retarded assault, "crawling glaciers pierce me with the spears" (1.31), with its harrowing vision of suffering time spatialized as the inching forward of primordial masses. The phrase is arranged so that the temporal drift of reading itself encroaches upon the scripted logic of phonemic spacing — to create the proleptic first thrust of "spears" in "glacier*s pierce.*" Later in *Prometheus,* the loss of life's animating moments "leaves this people*d earth* a solitude" (2.17), the phonotext itself thus bewailing that very "dearth" feared by the speaker in the spiritual vacuum so portrayed.

In the context of Chapter 2's attention to the closing rhyme of "Mont Blanc," we can observe an earlier transegmental effect that cooperates in the text's resistance to void. Inaugurating the closing apostrophe to the mountain, we have heard how the "secret strength of things" (l. 139) — rhyme word for the final "imaginings" four lines later — forever "inhabits thee" (l. 141). Here is another prosopopoeia whose rhetoric is underwritten by inscription at one level and interanimated at another by phonemic reading. Indeed, in those vexed closing lines already examined, it is exactly at the point of nearest abutment between the outer world and the inner landscape of response that a transegmental restitution sets in. At the very point of enjambment, that is, in "if to the human mind's imaginings / Silence and solitude were vacancy?" the pluralized subjectivity of "imaginings," figuring their variety without enumerating it, blurs over into — takes up or is taken up by — that existential "silence" with whose signifier the previous plural will fuse and whose vacancy such multiplicity may infuse. The text itself is thus less "silent" here than it seems, energizing the very gap at the end of a line with a sibilant ligature. The unsaid matrix of this whole interrogative image is *blankness,* with its suggestion of external void but also of emotional depletion. The constitutive textual blank itself, however — in this pivotal moment halfway between the portentous chimings of "and sea" / "-ancy" explored in Chapter 2 — would defeat and repeal that implicit nullity, rendering it connective. Invocation ("thou") depends upon inscription, yes, but inscription depends upon, and may even be rectified by, the energies of evocalization. *Mon(t) blanc,* Shelley suggests in French, is never to be taken for granted in his English texts.

"A Sound but Half Its Own"

The oratorical apostrophes and incantatory lamentations of *Adonais* might also be expected to inspirit the phonic interval, to breathe life into the lacunae of its dirge. They do. The text's early invocation of the blind Milton is a call to the author of a precedent elegy, "Lycidas," a poet summoned as the "Sire of an immortal strain" (l. 30). With "strain" meaning "song" as well as "generic lineage," the monosyllable "Sire" is all the more likely to release its aspirated homophone, "sigher," both opening up and at the same time filling in an internal phonemic juncture where none exists in the scriptive form of the lexeme. A transegmental variant of such phonemic decontraction may hover as well over the image of the Muse Urania in *Adonais,* whose "distress / Roused Death: Death rose and smiled, and met her vain caress" (ll. 224–25). At this chiastic pivot, the paronomastic chiming of "Roused" against "rose" works less to enforce our instantaneous aural recognition of the second verb than to delay it. We expect more variety from the syntagmatic sequence. Instead of this etymologically related "gradience" (in the manner of Hopkins), we are just as likely to hear the antiphonal phantom phrase, "death throes." Yet even that most terrible motion native to death is beyond possibility in "the death chamber" where Keats lies stilled.

A related anti-pun in *Adonais,* again phonetically poised across a lexical juncture, and again brushing the written utterance with the shadow of a false hope—a trace of wish fulfillment in the gaps of the elegiac—appears in the clause "cold hopes swarm like worms within our living clay" (l. 351). Reversing the original effect, before revision, of Keats's juncture in "Bright Star," in the phrase "its=swarm sink," here the paronomastic inner echo of "swarm" against "worms" only encourages a more strictly alliterative parsing of the sequence as "cold hope*s* (*s*)warm." Elision thus unleashes a verb antithetical to the adjective "cold," as if the dead dream were being warmed to renewal by the very delusion these words half seem to generate. A later elision describes the "lofty thought" that "Lifts a young heart above its morta*l l*air" (l. 393), where "air" as "atmosphere"—and, by extension, the human "sphere" or "clime"—would serve only to literalize the metaphor of mundane shelter and containment in the figure "lair." In so doing, the transegmental drift might also dislodge an equally secreted pun on "air"—for the lost poet's remembered song. In an earlier image of "lofty" ascent, the dead Keats is already seen to have "outsoared the shadow of our night" (l. 352), saved thereby from "the contagion of the world's slow stain" (l. 356), a phrasing in which only a mimetic slowing of the last three monosyllables could prevent a reemphasized designation of the world's "low" contamination in its contrast to the soaring release of death.

The shifting, ephemeral power of junctural irony or of segmental indeterminacy in verse is most intriguing perhaps in the case of *Adonais*'s very title, a combination, as Earl Wasserman has argued convincingly, of *Adonis* and of *Adonai:* the Greek figure of perfection crossbred with the Hebrew name for the Lord. The first two incantatory appearances of the name, in the poem's first two lines, are deployed around an internal chime that accentuates the *is* syllable and its homology with the verb of being, here in the oxymoronic predication of "being dead": "I weep for Adon*ais*—he *is* dead! / O, weep for Adonais!" The vocative "O" renews itself, along with the internal rhyme, two stanzas later: "O, weep for Adonais—he is dead!" (l. 19). The next half dozen mentions of the proper name, distributed over three dozen stanzas, appear without that synecdochic echoing of the *is,* until the doubled anticipation of "'tis Death *is* dead, not he; / Mourn not for Adonais" (ll. 361–62; my emphasis). This last consolatory imperative is then reversed into a rhetorical question six stanzas further along: "Who mourns for Adonais?" (l. 415). Five stanzas later, the remaining five stanzas space out alternately the last three appearances of his name. First: "What Adon*ais is,* why fear we to become?" (l. 459), which abuts unmistakably with the part-echo of predicated existence. Next: "'T*is* Adonais calls! oh, hasten thither" (l. 476), a phrasing which reiterates the *is* in slightly strained elliptical grammar, amounting to "It is

Adonais (who) calls." And, finally, as the syntactically surcharged climax to the whole pattern, sparked by a double grammar itself energized by phonetic ambiguity:

> Whilst burning through the inmost veil of heaven,
> The soul of Adonais, like a star,
> Beacons from the abode where the Eternal are.
>
> (ll. 493–95)

The genealogical portmanteau that has kept *Adonis* and *Adonai* vying for lexical and semantic space in the proper name—across fifty-five stanzas inaugurated by "Adonais—he is"—is finally unpacked and momentarily re-delegated. Punctuation cannot stop it, the pull of grammatical and semantic probability being for a split second too strong; the middle line above thus reads as a momentarily stabilized and grammatically complete unit, whose verb simply posits the deathlessness of its subject in a divination (both senses) of poetic powers—"The soul of Adonai is (,) like a star." In such a phonemic reading of this line, the poet is compared to a star that "beckons"—or "beacons" (as the text has it in an anti-pun on the more likely verb). He is compared in either case to a shining exemplar, a light in darkness, a no-longer mourned artist whose refulgent genius above all, and despite the grave, is.

To audit Shelley's verse texture in this fashion is to sense that the most telling microcosmic statement of his verbal purposes may not lie primarily in *The Revolt of Islam*'s phrase for a "subtler language within language" (7.3112).[16] We might find it more specifically in the figuration from "Mont Blanc" of a river's continuous music amplified by the adjacent tumult of nature, the rushing water murmuring "with a sound but half its own" (l. 6). Given the graded cross-lexical paronomasia of "sound . . . its *own*," the phrase is indeed self-exampling, each partner in the internal slant rhyme a part-echo of the other. So "speaks," so *we* speak, the flowing Shelleyan word, tributary to other lexical sounds into which, in the phonemic stream, it perpetually feeds. As the paronomastic turn two lines earlier in "Mont Blanc" has it, each word may be found "lending splendour" to its neighbor, turning contiguity not just to equivalence (Jakobson's rule for poetic combination) but to overlap.

This phonemic layering and exchange can aspire in *The Revolt of Islam* to the highly Miltonic "road of Hell'*s s*ulphureou*s s*urge" (11.4305), with the variant recurrence of *ell* in *ul* encouraging the sense of "all-furious urge." Or it can be arrayed in a more uniquely Shelleyan vein, its evocations nearer the heart of the Romantic program. In the "Hymn to Intellectual Beauty" we hear sung the very birth of the hymnist, as well as his theme. The vocation of the Romantic poet seems materialized in the crevices of his own language. The fourth stanza begins with a panorama of evanescence typical of Shelley, where natural ephemera are arrayed at the turn of an enjambment to image the slippages and recuperations of the mind: "Love, Hope, and Self-esteem, like clouds depart / And come, for some uncertain moments lent" (ll. 37–38). This is again the lent "splendour" of inspiration, but it is contextualized here as an epiphany of commitment. Within four lines, the spirit of beauty is being lauded as a "messenger of sympathies" (l. 42), a harbinger of love, like the "winds" that "are wooing" vitality out of the earth in the next stanza (l. 56). Nature is a solicitation, the incipient poet all ears. This is, of course, nature in its undeconstructed state, or status: nature as yet unexposed as the referential figment of a vocative inscription. Apostrophized itself as voice, this image of nature helps figure in turn the attentive response of the lyric subject. Further, it is in this same stanza that the speaker describes the onset of his vocation, the moment when the "shadow" of intellectual beauty "fell on me" (l. 59), sealing an ecstatic pact. As we hear in retrospect at the opening of the sixth stanza: "I vowed that I would dedicate my powers / To thee and thine" (ll. 61–62). The text's earlier transitional image, concerned with the mutability of those elevated thoughts that are only "for some uncertain moments lent," takes on now a prescient overtone. Call it an interstitial anti-pun, or antiphone, or transegmental drift, but in any case the inner ear may well be made alert to the suggestion that it is ultimately "for summons" ("for *some unc*ertain") that "certain moments" are indeed briefly "lent" to the craving spirit. In the flux of language itself, then, esemplastically transformed, we are to hear the invitation to another life, a life perhaps dedicated to the very words that have, in every sense, shaped its *calling*.

In a famous passage from *Prometheus Unbound,* Shelley writes that "Language is a perpetual Orphic song," a "Daedal harmony" designed to unify "a throng / Of thoughts and forms, which else senseless and shapeless were" (4.415–17). Even before the flickering agrammatical hint of "swir(l)" in "s-wer," it has been precisely the resistance to such transegmental adhesion in the sibilant-laden collocation "else senseless" which is necessary to make sense of that adjectival phrase. Without language, without pertinent oppositions, without a respect for lexical borders, there would be only the swirl of sound and aimless perception. Enacting the very consolidation of the lexical out of phonemic sequence, the Shelleyan text has here mounted one of those transegmental effects that is actively, even metalinguistically, ruled out by context. Thematized in such a line, then, is the need for the kind of hyper-articulation of juncture that—turning back to Keats—would provide a further differentiation between first and second versions of "La Belle Dame Sans Merci." In the 1819 text, the phrase "The latest dream I ever dreamt / On the cold hill side" is shuffled in refrain to the possessive "And I awoke, and found me here / On the cold hill's side," a variation flattened out in the 1820 revision.

In the original version, the phonic densening of the doubled sibilant—to the point of almost unforestallable elision—seems to retard the enunciatory process in a minuscule equivalent of the knight's arrested quest, his drugged heaviness of mind in desolation.

In Shelley, however, as elsewhere in Keats as well, the transegmental temptation is usually situated so that it should be succumbed to rather than resisted. In the most luxuriantly plotted phonemic exercise in all of Shelley's work, the "Ode to the West Wind," the speaker, in apostrophe to the wind, imagines a boyhood vitality wound up to the point where "to outstrip thy skiey speed / Scarce seemed a vision" (ll. 50–51). Enhanced by the dynamic of enjambment, the syntax must outstrip its own lineation in order to round out a last strained phrase that may at the same time homophonically regroup itself to "thy sky's speed." Sense would permit this, since the wind's speed is visible as "skiey" only insofar as it pushes clouds on before it. Phonemes too, then, are outstripping themselves there. Against the semantically intriguing, albeit somewhat thick-tongued, metrical regularity of "skiey speed," the no-longer iambic rapidity of "sky's speed" scuds past. This etherial rush at last comes bearing down on the inspired present speaker for the inverted copulative clauses of "Be thou, Spirit fierce, / My spirit! Be thou me, impetuous one!" (ll. 61–62). With the first comma again "unheard," the enjambment would move to close off one possible, slightly elliptical grammar—"Be thou (a) spirit fierce"—only to have it reopened and adjusted when the tentative predicate nominative is displaced in retrospect to an appositive. The speaker's own "spirit" next takes up the grammatical slot following the equative verb, only from there to be swept up into the second appositive phrase, "impetuous one," across the vernacular solecism of "me" in the objective case. Once again, grammar deconstructs rhetoric by exposing a self still subject to—still object of—the wind with which it hopes to fuse. Yet the wind's spiritualized velocity impels identification, impels fusion—so the speaker dreams. It is an *impetus* that, once scripted as the quatrasyllabic "impetuous," introduces—by way of phonetic rebus—the pronoun "you." That encrypted pronoun is placed, and suddenly played, against the first person authorial plural of "us," though still in the objective case. It thus takes part in a swift but no less emphatic positing of subject and object that—given the spondaic precedent of "Be thou me"— blends into the phonemically lent splendor of *impet/you/us/one*. Such is a desideratum—difference subsumed to unity, lack transcended—written only in the chord progressions of a natural harmony, not traced anywhere upon the legible face of things, whether of nature or of poem. Indeed, it is produced as text only by what the next tercet reflexively highlights as "the incantation of this verse" (l. 65)—to be heard and not seen.

Romantic Interlunations

Jerome McGann, in *The Romantic Ideology,* makes claims for a stylistic component in his "revisionist critique." Stressing, first of all, a reading of texts in and against "the socio-historical ground" of their production and consumption, he is quick to insist: "This does not mean that 'purely' stylistic, rhetorical, formal, or other specialized analyses cannot or will not be pursued."[17] Few books of such frankly historicizing ambitions are so professedly open to stylistics, and so McGann's work might serve as a test case for the always elusive rapprochement between linguistic and socio-historical reading. But what kind of "stylistics" are in order? Nothing is ever spelled out by McGann, only ruled out. In order to support his sense of the radically destabilized ideological ground of Romantic assumptions in the major texts of the period, their uneasy compromise with their own contradictions, McGann resists what he sees as the *critical* compromise that takes the texts as part of a "poetry of process" (28), exploratory and irresolute. In such an (unsatisfactory) view, the exemplary Romantic texts, searching, tentative, and ambiguous, participate in their own uncertain interpretation, an approach related by McGann to the "reader-response school." In his view, any such method passes the buck. It makes over the poetry's deep self-divisions, the rifts and contradictions of its insufficiently examined purposes, into a capacious dialectic in the hermeneutics of reception. For McGann more is at stake, and at peril, in the Romantic text. What, then, might any sort of stylistics have to offer by way of elucidation? How are the fissures of Romantic ideology conveyed to, or carried by, the verbal topography and tropology of a text? The closest we get to a direct confrontation with such questions in McGann's book is his reading of the last four stanzas of *Adonais,* with their poignant tension between a sense of irreparable human loss and a consolatory "futurism" (123) of poetic immortality. Lest the reader relax into the "sentimental idea" of the latter, McGann proposes "an historical analysis" that would help "distinguish the ideological, the stylistic, and the emotional aspects of poetic work." Though issues "stylistic" are twice invoked in this culminating paragraph of McGann's chapter on Shelley, and though he quotes as full an excerpt from any Romantic text as we will find submitted to commentary in his entire study, there is no adduced evidence whatever of specifically "stylistic tensions" (123) — except, perhaps, in the closing tonal contrast between "cold mortality" and the shining "abode" of Keats's immortally fixed "star." A tension *in metaphor?* Even this is not specified.

The present discussion, of course, has earlier closed in on more strictly stylistic — or morphophonemic — details of this passage. If we were now to recast the tenor of earlier observations in terms of emotional contrasts widening to ideological contradictions, if we were to register moments when the verbal texture of the poem protests too much its own visionary resolution, we might first return to that recurrent echo of the verb of being, "is," in "Adonais." By the close of the poem, predication itself, displaced and sacralized, is absorbed into the strained and grammatically unstable plural of the last rhyming word: "The soul of Adonais, like a star, / Beacons from the abode where the Eternal are." "Beacons," as we have seen, is not quite "beckons" — indeed, not quite as inviting as "beckons." At the other end of the line, capitalized and reified, "the Eternal" might emerge as if it were an abstract singular noun, requiring (students regularly assume so) a singular verb (as in the earlier "A portion of the Eternal" [l. 340]). Until, that is — in a reader-response trajectory? surprised by sublimity? by anonymity? — we realize that Keats's single "star" is put in rhyme with, even while erased in its singularity by, the plurality, the host, of those who have gone before to their immortality. Romantic individualism in a stylistically coded tension with meliorative eschatology? Poetic eternity as cold comfort for the intensified subjectivity that attends life in the flesh? Ideology at odds with desire? And this a tension that is itself part of the uneasy ideology of the transhistorical long view?

Looking again at the final stanza, which McGann has not so much read as simply delivered wholesale into evidence, we can notice a transegmental marker of just such a gulf between human feeling and visionary schedule, between mourning and ideological manifesto:

> The breath whose might I have invoked in song
> Descends on me; my spirit's bark is driven,
> Far from the shore, . . .

The smiting loss of all that might have been is converted to the "might" of poetic inspiration, fanned by the breath of the lost Other only when internalized as the living speech of creative continuance. The comma that interrupts the more natural enjambment at "driven / Far from the shore" seems momentarily to mark the poetic "drive" in its other sense, as the thrust of literary ambition. This repeated lexical tension is prolonged by the homophonic double of "spirit's bark" (the rather quaint metaphor) in the more clichéd and predictable "spirit's spark," related to the earlier image of the poetic "fire" that "outlives the parent spark" (l. 408). For one thing, the suggestion of "spark" draws on the "breath" of inspiration descended upon the living poet earlier in the line. Second, by way of a more distant early prediction, the poem has long before imaged the sad remains of a death without poetic immortality as the "sparkless ashes" of an "unlamented urn" (l. 360) — as opposed to the urn of aesthetic permanence in the Keatsian intertext. The closing transmutation of Keats's dying breath into Shelley's new inspiration is, after all, more likely — as "spark" rather than "bark" — to fan the soul than to put wind in any sails. When this transegmental alternative, or matrix, is thus repressed by the paraphonic variant ("spark" by "bark"), what has happened is that the normal resuscitative energies of a mourning friend and poet, lifted to new confidence in the name of the Other, is graphemically recast — sobered, if not chastened — by the more ominous figuration of the bark's deathward voyage, "darkly, fearfully, afar." In short, the disturbing ideological cross-purposes of this climactic passage — wavering between an elegiac fervor converted to *furor poeticus* and a more distant philosophical consolation — are kept alive in the cross-lexical phonemic ambivalence of "spirit's spark" versus "spirit's bark."

All this said in amplification of McGann's sparse gesture toward the work of "stylistic tensions" still leaves us far from any systematic understanding of the relation of style, let alone the activity of the phonotext, to the "socio-historical ground" of literary production. Yes, ambiguities — whether understood as textual mechanisms or as reader-response signals — may negotiate (or embody or enact or thematize) various contradictions and cross-purposes. Given the self-conscious architectonics of certain texts, one might even be willing to say that a verbal cleft, a lexical blank, a consequent segmental slippage may actually replay a conceptual irruption or schism in the ideological superstructure determining a poem. But what about an ideology of the text itself, as textuality? McGann early on explains that he will substitute the term "ideology of poetry" for "theory of poetry" (10) in his deliberations. But is that emphasis meant to imply the relegation of both poetics and aesthetics? Moving even beyond the literary text, can we responsibly subordinate all of linguistics and philology to the ideology of a historical epoch as well? Here, of course, our questions verge again upon Foucault's archaeology of the human science of language. Understood in Foucault's terms, the Romantic moment — exemplified, for instance, by Shelley's expressive tensility of phrase, his romancing of the phoneme — stretches as watershed between classical conceptions of discourse as representation and the modern ontology of language as a thing in itself.

Yet this epochal turning point of Romanticism finds that its ideology of language — conceived as the means of an independently articulated armature of human communication — is an ideology, and an ideal, mediated at crucial literary turns by the lyric operation: as in itself a suppressed crisis in subjectivity, a site of anxieties less expressed than covertly enacted by language. These anxieties have, in fact, to do in good part with the relation of language to time passing, of record to history, of writing to things recoverable. In all the Romantics, history is in some sense or another rewritten as the Fall, first in

Blake, where recovery involves an at least intermittent access to the unhindered tongues of Beulah. This would entail no reversion to mere babble but, rather, the achievement of an organized lingual innocence—available to the poetic effort within and against, not simply before, the Urizenic or rationalist hegemony. If for the Romantic enterprise as a whole in one of its important aspects—as for Shelley, in particular—language is identified as "a perpetual Orphic song," the underworld to which it makes its foray and from which it retrieves its visionary treasure is the unconscious itself. This is the locus of expressible desire still in touch with a poetic impulse before symbolic acculturation, though later absorbed into it (ideally, without too extreme a denial). To dwell in these alogical depths is not only the beginning but also the end of speech; to visit there, however, in the visionary raids of Orphean adventure, is to mine that song waiting at the very root of speech, that rhythm underneath reason, that lyric pulse before linguistic ordering—in Kristeva's terms, if we choose, the semiotic stratum upon which the symbolic is mounted. But to do so programmatically could never be a matter of a poet's conscious decision from line to line. Any cogent sense of such Orphic power in Romantic poetry, therefore, resides merely in the recognized *tendency* to a certain excessive and unregimented texture, to the preferred surplus of signifier over signified, to Coleridge's "soft-floating witchery of sound" (validated by analogues in nature, to be sure: this is its most obvious ideological component). These are the resonances and reverberations that, in other terms, inflect the Shelleyan interlunations of both world and text; of world and text together, the one in the other's image: as Wordsworth put it, of nature's meanings half-created, half-received. One avowed philosophy—or ideology—of language in Romantic poetry rests just here: in a recognition that its lyric aspirations work toward a "Daedal harmony" connatural with what is visible and audible in the labyrinthine symmetries of the experienced world—a synesthesia, for instance, no more artificial than nature's own admixtures and sensory interfusions.

This program entails a more perplexed ideology, whose contradictions thus go unexamined, when it requires for lyric transmission a theory of the uttering subject, of subjectivity as utterance. This is a verbally conscious subject whose anxious discontinuities—whose psychic caesuras and ellipses, ambivalences and elisions—must also be mapped, along with the landscape of nature, onto the topography of a text. Romanticism, it may be shown, arose contemporaneously with the dawn of philology in an independent but parallel gestation, birth, and development. It continued to flourish, or at least survive, in Victorian and even twentieth-century revisions only as long as the systematic study of language, the scientific rigors of linguistics, did not threaten the cherished metaphysics of individual selfhood. Inspiriting as they were to the style of poetry as part of the generalized spirit of an age, its verbal predisposition, these linguistic investigations could thrive only as long as their rigor was kept from deconstructing exactly that lyric subjectivity, that bardic centrism, lending authority to a philologically preoccupied art of words. But the frictions that would become fissures were already apparent, even in high Romanticism, already seeking appeasement by rhetorical deflection. The ideological cleavage McGann spots at the end of *Adonais* might in this light be recast as the living poet's recognition that in the death of Keats, the death of the Author as Other, lies the innate destiny of all authorship, the fixity of a presence only within the structured absence which is any and every text. In or out of the elegiac mode, all prosopopoeia is merely figural, funereal—and on both sides of the personifying contract. As the almost dead-metaphoric "spark" of Keats's living genius is scriptively overruled, to become instead the more insistently figural "bark" of immortal destiny and reputation, something like a true "stylistic tension" has thus opened consciousness to the potentially terrifying void between even the persona's own psyche and his text, between all voice and any poem. Here, then, is an ideological irreconcilability—to be laid bare a century and a half later in Derrida's term "thanatopraxis"—which Romantic instances of the elegiac genre disclose only to contain.

If the Romantic ideology of language is such that the word is seen to absorb and transfigure experience, then the extreme malleability of language—when highlighted, for instance, at a junctural slippage—may offer a stylistic emphasis to an even more oblique metalinguistic tremor of the text. Here we may look aside for a moment from Shelley to a comparable instance in his nearest peer. There is no overt evidence in the "Ode on Melancholy" that the Keatsian persona is speaking as a literary voice, that he is writing his way into a poetic stance. For all the florid staginess of his conceits, there is, in short, no mention of writing, of the melancholic as writer. The "speaker" appears to be merely setting forth the existential rather than literary premises of the melancholic visionary, who sees, among other things, the beauty of the fleetingness of beauty. He addresses the first two stanzas in second person to a kind of spiritual advisee, if implicitly to himself at one remove. It is only by extrapolation from the "sovran shrine" of a personified Melancholy that the courted goddess may become in fact the Muse, the presiding genius of that poetic wisdom won from the bittersweet of luxuriance. Explicitly in the lines, it is merely the human agent, as "poetic" sensibility, not in particular the poetic craftsman, whose fate is sealed at the close of the poem, in a stanza that has shifted into a general third-person formulation: "His soul shall taste the sadness of her might, / And be among her cloudy trophies hung." But if Melancholy is not only a general inspiration to the Romantic spirit but, after all, the specific Muse of Keats's verbal artistry, his one hope of that bardic immortality which would enshrine forever his insights about a terrible plea-sure feeding deep on loss, then the closest hint of this may appear in a poetic warping of the final juncture: literally, letterally, the poem's last word(s). Anticipating this, it is easy to imagine a figural transference in the last line from him who can "burst Joy's grape against his palate fine," the ultimate credential for melancholic service, to the poetic use of the mouth in lyric utterance. Following from this, it is then by the overtone of a sibilant liaison in "trophie*s* *s*(h)*ung*" that the "him who" of this last stanza becomes a melan-cholic dedicant specifically *hymned* into the pantheon of spiritual insight. In our phonemic adjustment of Riffaterre's terms, to have one's achievement "sung" among those of the goddess's other adulants is the avoided cliché; to be "hung" among them, incarnate, is the more striking paraphone of that mono-syllabic matrix. Once again, phonemic reading can work to sustain the Romantic dream of verbal embodiment, the very stuff of "cloudy" and evanes-cent incarnation.

Precisely because so many of the phonotextual instances we have noted fall within the always-churning realm of the contingent, no direct ideological link can be demonstrated, except by way of the general inclination toward such a thickened, excessive, and hence polyvalent style. This is just what would doom to confusion any programmatic attempt to read off some Romantic "ideology" from the unregimented verbal flicker and phonemic slip. There is, we can readily see, an ideology (read, "poetics") of the Romantic lyric, an ideology (read, "aesthetics") of Romantic euphony therein. Both, moreover, predispose such texts to a richness given (and sometimes given over) to phonic accidents poised against the graphic grain. This predisposition is, in fact, part of the largest antirationalist bias of the period, its nostalgia for the unfallen state of nature and for its psychic cognate in the "immortal sea" of imaginary totalization. But the poetic (or, rather, psycholinguistic) counterideology – of a subjectivity neither preceding nor exceeding the letter of the text, and thus dispersed and imperiled by the text's every lapse – this must wait, long and impatiently, with an impatience warping the surface of many a text in the meantime, for the theoretical enterprise of another century.

Tennysonorities

In its Keatsian debts, the phonotext works overtime almost everywhere in Tennyson. A reader may come upon the most fleeting of transegmental effects, as in the image from "Mariana" of a "sluice" that "with blackened water*s* *s*lept," where *le(a)pt* emerges from the signified stagnancy and signify-ing sibilance as an impossible but relevant anti-pun, the pertinent antonym of the water's portrayed state. It is no accident, however, that the phonic texture of Tennysonian verse, the rhythm of voice itself as an adjunct of script, is at its most dense and crafted in the dramatic monologues. The heroic speaking subject of "Ulysses," in the stanza beginning "This is my son, mine own Telemachus" (l. 33), concludes with a dismissal of the son's "common duties" and "slow prudence"—and this in implicit celebration by contrast of his own martial exploits: "He works his work, I mine" (l. 43). The drudgery of mere "work" has already been contrasted to the image of a community of achievement among "Souls that have toil'd, and *wrought,* and *thought* with me" (l. 46), where working and thinking, objective labor and subjective purpose, are made in every sense to rhyme with each other. This is not the prudent, mundane toil of Telemachus, and so the quotidian form of the verb, in a cognate repetition, has been used only of the son—"He works his work"— whereas Ulysses has spoken more compactly of his—"I mine." Beyond the semantic pun on the verb form of "mine" as a dredging passionately in the depths of experience, this phrasing is also syntactically ambiguous even when "mine" is taken as adjectival, involving not only the grammar of ellipsis but also the phonemics of ligature. For over against the routinized and unvaried "works his work" stands the radically unalienated labor—indeed, the equative predication of being itself—in "I'm mine." The verb is not just left out; the object is lent, overlapping, to the subject, in a transfusion of self into its effects. Any potential psychic divisions would thus seem healed across the lexical breach. We might say that in this text about a defied discontinuity between youth and decline, the nostalgic speaking subject also seems to suppress, by momentarily mastering, the very consciousness of linguistic discontinuity and rupture that contributes to defining modernism and the theories of its textuality.

If this is so, then one would also have to say that the ironic counterpart to this dramatic monologue, "Tithonus," can be seen to exploit the same lexical ambiguities and cleavages for what looks, what *sounds,* much more like the dissociated sensibility of a modern identity crisis. The verbal fissures are there in both cases but seamed over in differing degrees of lexical precariousness. The fading Tithonus, lover of the dawn, is an antihero withering endlessly in the grief of his granted wish to be made immortal. He begins a stanza of excruciated retrospect with the double pun on his own identity, as ambiguously subject or object of this bleak nostalgic vision:

> *Ay me! ay me!* with what another heart
> In days far-off, and with what other eyes
> I used to watch—if I be he that watched—
> (ll. 50–52; my emphasis)

The specular gap, opened by pun, between the present bemoaning "I" and the "other *eyes*" that used to perceive the world leads us to the transegmental irony of "If I *be he* that watched." By an elision at the very turning point of predication, this textual effect subordinates even present as well as past identity to the pathos of the subjunctive: "If I be(h)e [at all anymore] that [formerly] watched." The very idea of being, once put in question, swallows the pronouns that would identify it — or at least threatens to against the sway of metrical stress. Even though usually subserving the meter, Miltonic syn-aloepha boasts no more strategic examples. Then, too, this transegmental meld reminds us that exactly what Tithonus is *not* saying in a Ulyssean vein, with that "Ay me!" two lines before, is that "I'm me" — or even "I'm (h)e that." If such anti-puns show their face on the obverse of the more apparent mor-phemic play, they remain merely antiphonal hints whose sense is banished by the semantic default of confident self-predication in the rest of the passage.

By contrast, Robert Browning — one's reading of Browning — has a different "sound" altogether, but not a stabilized one.[18] His transegmental play between syllables is certainly grittier, less melodious, than anything in Tennyson. When Browning's Childe Roland moves toward the Dark Tower over "Bog, clay and rubble, sand and stark black dearth" ("'Childe Roland to the Dark Tower Came,'" l. 150), our mind is so fixed on the desiccated topography that we are likely to hear a disyllabic "black'd earth" rather than its scripted equivalent, "black dearth." The more likely alternative, indeed, seems left to the paraphonic variant. Then there is this from "Fra Lippo Lippi": "And nip each softling of a wee white mouse, / *Weke, weke,* that's crept to keep him company!" (ll. 10–11). Around the turn of the enjambment slips the very sibilant necessary to convert this eccentric encoding of mouse noises (allit-erative with *wee*) into a closer approximation of the familiar "*s-*we*ke-weke.*" Later, asking why a painter cannot "Make his flesh liker and his soul more like" (l. 207), Lippo's comparative adjective "liker" has already anticipated the likeness to which he turns in the next line: "Take the prettiest face, / The Prior's niece." Since the touchstone of his realism will indeed be the achievement of an image more and more "like (h)er," it is as if, though metrically suppressing it, he had that sensuous beauty on his mind all the while.

In a dialogue with his dead wife in "The Householder," Browning's speaker, recognizing the revenant, answers her rhetorical question — "What else did you expect?" (l. 8) — with "Never min*d, hie* away from this old house" (l. 9). The transegmental phonemic structure itself calls out for the only departure possible, another dying away. Elsewhere, Browning is a poet of such marked consonantal imbrications that he gives us at two different points in "Love Among the Ruins" a syllabic or phonemic irony timed to enjambment. There is the hint, momentarily confirmed, of the metaphoric vehicle "pyres" hidden in the tenor of "spires," an overtone prepared for by one elision and transeg-mentally released by another: "Where the domed an*d d*aring palace shot it*s* *s*pires / Up like fires" (ll. 19–20). In addition, the poem's very first line passes over to its second as if the metaphoric verb were constituted somehow by the expanse of its application: "Where the quiet-colored end of evening smile*s* / *Miles* and miles." To the ear, the figurative verb seems twice repeated by liaison—"smiles/(s)miles"—before it cedes to an overlapping reduplication of the adverbial noun. The given alphabetic format, overlain with its phonemic other, thus generates, as if from an unwritten matrix, the overdetermined image of sunset as a pervasively insistent "beaming" across the land.

Words Listing

If, as Auden thought, Tennyson had quite possibly the "greatest ear" of all the English poets, Hopkins may well have had the most brilliantly nervous. In order to prepare the groundwork in Chapter 2 for a consideration of Hopkins's tandem rhymes, I have already taken account of the phenomenon of vocalic "gradience" in his verse, attempting to extend this principle of incremental phonemics into a transegmental phonotexture. We shall pursue this extension even farther here, since the concept of verbal "inscape" can now be seen as a late nineteenth-century English equivalent to the early modernist ontology of language in French literature described by Foucault. Survey the inscape of one word and you will find another, and another, and, in conjunction with a second scripted word, yet another—one that scoops out and instantaneously refurbishes the hollow between, the downslope of one lexeme overead as merely the upswing of its successor. The obsessive, mock-etymological word lists of Hopkins's early diaries testify in this sense to a sounding of inscape. This, for example: "*slip, slipper, slop, slabby* (muddy), *slide,* perhaps *slope,* but if *slope* is thus connected what are we to say of *slant?*"[19] Displayed here is an instinct for minimal phonic discriminations in the lexicon that Hopkins shares with Coleridge, whose notations on language can coax out a punning homophonic series from a conjunction like *thing/think,* here from the *Notebooks:* "'Thing': id est, thinking or think'd. Think, Thank, Tank—Reservoir of what has been thinged—Denken, Danken—I forget the German for Tank/ The, Them, This, These, Thence, Thick, Think, Thong, Thou."[20] This goes farther, faster, than anything in Hopkins, but the parallel is manifest: in each case a linguistically oriented poet preoccupied more with the ontology than with the strict etymology of language, more with its materiality, its thingness in the work of thinking and writing. When this interest in subterranean bonds between words begins to contour the inscape of a given textual phrase, it is likely to result in the partial telescoping of the list across a lexical break, a listing of one word into its neighbor.

We have already noted in Chapter 2 the paronomasia of "diamond delves!"/"the elves' eyes," where the transegmental ligature makes this seem like one of Hopkins's word chains rendered metrical. A simple conjunction may grammatically separate the echoing phrases a bit more, as in the next example from "Inversnaid," while at the same time transegmentally participating in their phonemic reprocessing. The iterative predicate here conspires in the evocation as well as designation of a whirlpool: "It rounds an*d rounds* / Despair to drowning." The doubled verb thus anticipates a root finite form of the line's closing participle by way of the transegmental homophone "an*d=rounds*" (including, in an ever-broader phonemic swath, the dental ligature of "I*t=rounds*"). It is as if both were portmanteau clusters combining the cause and effect of rounding to the point of drowning. Further, the kind of transegmental rhyming discussed in Chapter 2, even while absorbing lexemes into fuller, nonsemantic echoes, may still imply a referential kinship between the separated phrasings. In "God's Grandeur," for instance, since all "the world is charged with the grandeur of God," the link between the rhyming words of the next two lines — "shook *foil*"/"ooze of *oil*" — works to suggest, in an effect enhanced by the transegmental spreading of the echo, the commonality of *foil* and *oil* in the inventory of divine attestations, of transcendental witness. Origin of the world, God is also the authoring cause of its divergent tongues and terms, the poet-priest his mystic etymologist.

Such transegmental accords, collected within a single line as oblique internal rhymes, may, again, resemble the word lists of Hopkins's diaries. The sonnet "Spelt from Sibyl's Leaves" spells out seriatim the phrasing "earliest stars, earlstars," as well as the phonemic prolongation of "Our tale, O our oracle!" At another point in this same sonnet, there is an enjambed disclosure of a quasi-etymological bond between "off" and the transegmentally activated "doff": "ah let life win*d / Off* her once skeined stained veined variety." This same preternatural attunement to the inscape of the lexical declivity, earlier in this sonnet, has brought to the textual surface an echo of the swelling cause behind the overwhelming effect of "our night whelm*s, whel*ms, and will end us." It might be noted here that the logically implausible drift "l=end" that follows in this line is phonemically just as likely, lexically more complete, and yet semantically canceled by context: another instance of the accidental and arbitrary contained in reading by the cumulative, by the developing sense rather than just sensory potential of an utterance. Context is necessary to activate the latent. The octave of "The Windhover" ends with an image of the speaker's sympathetic awe before the windhover's flight, recounting a heart that is first said echoically to have "Stirred for a bird." Such paronomasia, spread across separate lexemes, is next condensed in the appositional phrase for the bird on the wing, "the achieve of, the mastery of the thing." Phonemic reading tends to inflect the "heave off" in "achieve of," as if "heave" and "achieve" (like "foil" and "oil") were filed away in some cryptic listing, their common denominators to be revealed only in the inscapes of poetic epiphany.

This is, of course, merely a special case of the general transegmental play in Hopkins's verse, which does not always recall the lexical autonomy of his speculative philological chains. In the sestet of "The Windhover," a related effect appears within a single syllable, a mere inflection of tense, without dislodging an independent lexeme. In noting devices in Hopkins that are "kinaesthetic in nature, determined by the sense of stress or muscle," Geoffrey Hartman includes among them the phrase in question: "Plough down sillion." The effect in this case is said to derive from the evocation of "neither the shining plow nor the new earth but the kinaesthetic effect of plow-breaking-through-earth."[21] What this assessment leaves unsaid, however, in its link between vocal and agricultural musculature, is the additional transegmental pressure exerted on the line by the unscripted weight of the past participle "ploughed," operating under erasure at the junctural break complicated by "plough(e d)down."

Alongside Hopkins's diary passages explicitly devoted to the topography and archaeology of the English lexicon are those that concern, in another sense, the "inscape" of the phenomenal universe, prose evocations that attempt to take the mold and contour of the world in words. Both need to be understood, separately and together, in light of the term "inscape" in its full range of designation. James Milroy, arguing that too few critics have realized the bearing of the term upon the language as well as the natural subjects of Hopkins's poetry, calls his chapter on Hopkins's diction "Wordscape."[22] Hopkins himself attempted to make clear the verbal application of his famous term in the essay "Poetry and Verse," when insisting that "Poetry is in fact speech only employed to carry the inscape of speech for the inscape's sake — and therefore the inscape must be dwelt on."[23] Stepping back to an example of poetry that is not verse, we may turn briefly for clarification to the prose poetry of natural observations in Hopkins's journals. The passage in question is the inscape of a seascape, of the sea escaping over shelves of rock in a channel. Two sentences from this 1872 paragraph divide up the two chief effects of Hopkins's phrasal inscape: the multiplication of phonic patterns across intermittent items of diction, on the one hand, and, on the other, the fusion of phonemes at contiguous borders. As we have seen, it is when the two appear together, in tandem, in tension — as they do not in this more straightforward prose excerpt — that his poetry achieves its most daring and characteristic effects. The first of these sentences from the journal passage goes like this: "The sea was breaking on all the stack and striking out all the ledges and edges at each breaker like snow does a building" (255). Water overflows and erases first the surface of the ledge, then the very edge that distinguishes it from the others in the shingled terrace of flat rocks. The second sentence at issue in this description generates two adjacent transegmental liaisons that seem arranged to evoke a fluid overlap without forming a separate lexical item: "In the channel I saw (as everywhere in surfy water) how the laps *of foam mouthed* upon one another" (255). Mouthed as vocables, with their own kinaesthetic inscape as well as their explicit referents, the word "of" encroaches upon "foam" as "foam" does upon "mouthed": an aural emblem of overlap.[24]

To combine the separate effects of these two illustrative prose sentences, so that, for instance, a word ending in *l* might overlap with "ledges" and thus unpack the implied sequential word listing compressed to a single malleable lexeme: this would be to create the Hopkins verse text as we know it. It is a text incorporating as fully as any in English that aural tropology which Hopkins, well before Jakobson, called the "figure of sound." For Hopkins as well as Jakobson, the term refers to a mapping of phonic recurrence upon syntactic contiguity—and for Hopkins, every bit as much as for Jakobson, it provides the very definition of poetry, as "speech which afters and oftens its inscape" (289). The use of the preposition "after" as verb suggests the kinetic trace, the aftermath, of one word left reverberant in its successors. Narrow the gap of succession so that it becomes overlap, and you have a special transegmental case of that "oftening, over-and-overing, aftering of the inscape" on which poetic effects depend. Understand these adverbial predications in a spatial as much as temporal sense within the dynamics of reading, and "over-and-overing" becomes something very much like that overeading with which we are concerned. In his "Lecture Notes" on "Rhetoric," Hopkins follows comments on what "may be called the *lettering* of syllables"—by which he means all the recurrences we normally identify as alliterative, assonant, and so forth, whether at the beginning, middle, or end of words—with a category of verse effect little discussed in the criticism of his poetry, perhaps because so sketchily characterized in Hopkins's own passing mention of it: "Holding, to which belong break and circumflexion, slurs, glides, slides, etc."[25] In this category we might include the transegmental drift: that holding (over) of phonemes, that gliding or skidding, that slippage and blurring of a suddenly delettered lexeme which refashions adjacent diction on the sly, the slide.

A lexical inscape rebuilt along the instep of a metrical foot, this holding over of phonic matter—produced as text through overeading—can be seen powerfully at play, at work, in Hopkins's greatest litany of ontological inscapes, "As Kingfishers Catch Fire." The poem's central premise is that "Each mortal thing does one thing and the same" (a transform by tmesis of the matrix "one and the same") or, in other words, "selves" (a verb form in context), "Crying *What I do is me.*" This is a poem that repeatedly asserts how being (rather like the condition of textuality itself) is defined in its own actualization, produced in process. The sestet arrives to cap and theologize the point:

> I say more: the just man justices;
> 　　Keeps grace: that keeps all his goings graces;
> Acts in God's eye what in God's eye he is—
> 　　Christ. For Christ plays in ten thousand places

We find here a phonemic play (Empson's "engineering" sense: a slack) in the paronomastic echo of "plays" against "plac/es." Preceding that is the Miltonic synaloepha of "In God's eye he is," with the phonological glide of /ay/ all the more likely to precipitate a gliding or "holding" that will elide out the pronoun. Since this is a poem in which every nomination is only at base a predication, a name for that being which is ultimately declared only as enacted, it is entirely appropriate that this syncopation of a whole word makes no semantic difference in the line. The just man is hereby understood to act in the sight of God what in *God's eye is,* the only thing in God's eye when justice is under scrutiny—namely, the omniscient Christ immanent in "ten thousand" worthy places. Such is the inscape—or, as Hopkins elsewhere calls it, the "instress"—of identity as a presence *to.* Which brings us back to "the just man justices," where the cognate verb, though found in the dictionary, is neverthe-less estranging enough to seem generated by another "holding," an "over-and-overing," of an antiphrasal variant, "the just man just is, is." This oddity is all the more destined for reception because the scripted "justices," unless other-wise heard, makes a weak rhyme with the verb of "in God's eye (he) is."

Returning now to the opening of the sonnet, we encounter through phonemic reading a curious bidirectional "holding" at the first enjambment, an "aftering" and retrospective elision. More explicitly sonic (at the level of the signified itself) than the effects of the sestet, this phonemic meld captures the inscape of the poem's essentialist predications:

> As kingfishers catch fire, dragonflies draw flame;
> 　　As tumbled over rim in roundy wells
> Stones ring

The enjambed lines may recall the Tennysonian ear for verse sounds—in particular, that previously treated rhyme from the openings of *In Memoriam* on "divers *tones*"/"Stepping *stones*" (st. 1). The comparable diction in Hopkins's run-on line, when submitted to overeading, elides the second sibilant across the very mimetic drop from line to line which the hissing ligature serves at the same time to defer—thus bringing out, bringing forward, the *tones* of the falling stones. It is as if the natural inscape has been weirdly plumbed, metalinguistically sounded, disclosing that "one thing and the same" which asserts itself as the auditory essence (or inevitable effect) of such natural gravitational motion.

Though nowhere to the degree we find it in Hopkins, post-Romantic American poetry of the period also experiments with that phonemic play which puts the vocable at lexical risk. Emily Dickinson's sustained system of marked hiatuses, of dashes, of rests and arrests, does perhaps tend to militate against certain elaborate ligatures in her verse. There is nevertheless a fricative "holding" to be heard, for example, in "After great pain a formal feeling comes" (J 341), an aural contouring of sequence itself. A velar prolongation appears first in the emergence of "*comes*" from the participial *g* in the first line, then, more dramatically, in the gemination of the poem's last line, "First chill, then stupor, then the lettin*g g*o." We might call this the inscape or instress of pain, the hold it has on both sentience and its expression. It is registered in a phonemic grip that must be loosened before bringing to utterance the final "o(h)" of relief and release.

Modernist "Symphonetics"

Before glancing briefly at a very few representative instances of the modernist wordplay that continues the line of phonemic density from Shakespeare through Milton to the Romantics and their direct Victorian heirs, I should say a word again on the methodology of these passive auditions. They are in the double sense phono*logical,* recuperating the sensory for the sensible, the phonemic for the semantic. Why so? To trace out the transegmental effect in context and in force, this chapter, as those before it, has repeatedly moved from merely reading such latent aural features to tentatively interpreting their effect, binding them over to certain thematic imperatives, giving them only enough play to justify themselves as restructured diction. If this is false to their function — or dysfunction — in the field of verbal contingency, false to their sheer inevitability in syntactical buildup, it is no less true to their role in literary text production. As soon as we *read,* we tend to process; we incorporate into larger and larger aggregates; we install the phonotext within a widening hermeneutic. As with Hartman's "wounds" of wording, including the extreme lacerations audited by Lucette Finas, even the most severe morphological hemorrhaging is soon staunched by the suturing force of simply reading on. Hence the tendency for this chapter's readings, these registrations of phonemic layering, to be found in close conjunction with more familiar strategies of stylistics, with reader-response theory, with analyses of conceptual and phonic figures, of ambiguities in diction and syntax, of punning, double grammar, and the shifting emphases of enjambment, with examinations of self-revising syntax and self-referential metaphors, and so on. Already embedded within a context, and certainly within an overarching grammar, the transegmental effect is likely to fall *into line;* is likely, that is—in its very flux and flexion—to fit, to make one kind of sense as fast as it undoes another. It is in the nature of reading to naturalize input through interpretation. This is the way texts are always generated in process. Phonemic reading just takes us deeper into the works, beneath and between the apparent minims of semantic sequencing.

As reading rather than writing, words have no status until produced in reception: this is a fact upon which some texts openly capitalize, and none more implausibly than a 1914 poem by Thomas Hardy that takes its title from its interrogative first line, "Ah, are you digging on my grave?" The power of this phonemically tortuous gambit consists in an utterance from beyond life that can be enunciated by the reader only like some reverse death gasp. The text seems struggling up to articulation through one prolonged inaugural phoneme that finally closes off its transegmental dilation in a recognizable word. Lending voice to the gothically exaggerated nonpresence not simply of a poetic persona but of a dead one, our evocalization of the spectral question cannot help but bestow a more formal lexical shape—the groaning "Ah are" slurred to the monosyllabic "A(h)re"—upon a posthumous cry summoned up from the grave of language itself.

With a more mellifluous case in point, the verging of contingency upon design in the transegmental generation of texts is addressed directly by John Unterecker's comments on the opening line from the second stanza of Yeats's "The Sorrow of Love," from *The Rose* volume. "A girl arose that had red mournful lips" strikes Unterecker as part of the "great craftsmanship" of the poem, though he admits that some of its "effects" may be "accidental."[26] The following comments are set off in a lengthy parenthetical aside: "That repeated 'arose' which pleased Louis MacNeice because of its abruptness delights me because it puns so accurately on the title of the section." It does so, for Unterecker, because of the lexical breakdown from verb into article and substantive. His "eyes, seeing double, enjoy the simultaneous vision of 'A girl arose' and 'A girl, a rose, that had red mournful lips . . .'; such second sight might even have entertained Yeats" (81–82). The last clause confirms Unterecker's understanding of this effect in particular as probably "accidental." Be this as it may, it is crucial to realize how no so-called double vision could operate here on its own. The lexical gap, an opening for ambiguity, would never have yawned as a possibility between the syllables *a* and *rose* if it were not for the double audition as well. Yeats may be overead elsewhere, as well, according to this same homophonic scansion, as when the heard music of nature at "The Lake Isle of Innisfree" is internally synchronized, in high Romantic fashion, with the orchestrated motions of the mind: "I hear it in the deep heart's *core.*" Or when, in the thundering paratactic redundancy of "The Second Coming":

> Things fall apart; the center cannot hold;
> Mere anarchy is *loosed* upon the world,
> The blood-dimmed tide is *loosed,* and everywhere
> The ceremony of innocence is drowned

With the emphatic repetition of the participle "loosed" attracting the preceding sibilant—to form on its trace the passive transform of the transitive verb *sluice,* for "to drench" or "to flood"—we audit a decentering of the enunciatory regime of script itself.

The foregrounding of aurality, in close conjunction with printed textuality, can be yet more explicit in Yeats. An early text, "When You Are Old," a lyric address structured around the intertwined acts of reading and enunciation, commands in the first quatrain a perusal of the very book that contains it. The former beloved is told to "take down this book" in old age "And slowly read, and dream of the soft look / Your eyes had once" (ll. 2–4). Hardened by time, these once pliant eyes are now confined (by the deadlocked rhyme of "book" with the activating "look" it requires) to the only effectual seeing left to them: a rueful backcast spurred by verse across the anagrammatic ligature of "*read,* an*d dream.*" So, lexically and mentally, would the addressee now naturally drift off; but human voices wake her—her own in particular—for she is next urged (across the same conjunctive grammar) to evoke the vanished past in a whispered lament that can only coincide with the lines she is still reading. The poem that begins in the eyeing of a text, that is, now summons its *own* muted voicing:

> And . . .
> Murmur, a little sadly, how Love fled
> And paced upon the mountains overhead
>   (ll. 9–11)

Here is where the act of reading and the theme of acknowledged loss are, one might say, somatically confronted—in as piercingly ironic an antiphone as verse can achieve. The saddening climax of a personified "Love fled," precisely when evocalized as a murmur by the aged voice of lyric reception, elegizes the woman's faded yearning to be drawn forth by Love to erotic heights ("the mountains overhead")—and so registers, in other words, the decline of a once "pilgrim soul" (l. 8) whom in the dimming years it could no longer be said that "Love led." In reviewing the first Oxford installment of the Yeats letters, Helen Vendler closes with the volume's "earliest anecdote," which "shows us Yeats at the age of four: introduced to Edwin Ellis, he asks whether Ellis is related to Cinder Ellis. Truly, poets are born and not made."[27] Those poets, at least, of the lexical drift.

Ezra Pound is at times such a poet, though in a more disjunctive modernist vein. When he speaks famously of the poetic endeavor as "the dance of the intellect among words," he implicitly catches the right balance between the spatial and the audible in the processing of texts.[28] Poetry is the choreography of conceptual signification performed upon the phonemically based gestures of wording. It is a dance among, and therefore between, lexemes. We can attend such a poetic "dance," a virtual pirouette at line's end, in the first of Pound's cantos, his recast image of the Ulyssean (partly Tennysonian) quester pressing ever beyond the "margin" of experience—as well as of textual limits:

> Then we sat amidships, wind jamming the tiller,
> Thus with stretched sail, we went over sea till day's end.
> Sun to his slumber, shadows o'er all the ocean,
> Came we then to the bounds of deepest water
>
> (1.8–11)

Three times in these lines Pound deconstructs an idiomatic phrase, once by the echo of "midshipmen" in the adverbial invention "amidships," twice by the opening up of a compound, "windjammer" and "overseas" transformed to "windjamming" and "over sea." In the context of these experiments in lexical resegmentation, there appears a remarkable flaunting of linear segmentation as well: that enjambment (despite punctuated end-stopping) across "till day's end. / Sun to his slumber." The absolute (or nominative absolute) grammar opened by the new line is never completed by a verb form (as in "Sun *gone* to his slumber"), which frees it all the more for a ligature with the line before. In this realignment we may now read Pound's complex slide of bidirectional liaisons as "we went over sea till day ('s)end(s) sun to his slumber," a momentarily continuous (because enjambed) syntax that defies the given punctuation as well as shifts into the present tense for a kind of generalized definition of sunset. Compared to this "dance of the intellect among words," this radical reprocessing of the graphic text according to phonic cues, the transegmental effect that later closes Canto 20 can seem only rather traditional. After the description of "gilded barocco" (a Joycean portmanteau) in a hall of "columns coiled and fluted," Pound's text pictures "Vanoka, leaning half naked, waste hall there behind her." Given that odd collocation of noun modifier and noun in "waste hall," what inevitably strikes the inner ear is "waste all there behind her."

Whether (in Vendler's terms) born or made, Wilfred Owen is certainly— and self-consciously—a poet of the transegmental tendency. As with Joyce's texts in prose, Owen's poems marshal as often as possible the "symphonetic" effect. That last is a portmanteau coinage (from *symphonic* plus *phonetic*) in an unfinished draft entitled "All Sounds have been as Music."²⁹ In it, we find the elliptical clause "Bridge*s*, *s*onorous under carriage wheels," as if the sibilant unfolds a near pun on "burden" for the musical and the "onerous" at once. It is a poem whose next stanza is also likely to hint of "lutes" in the "drawl *of f*lutes and shepherds' reeds." In alliterative parallelism with the phrase "*G*urgle of *sl*uicing," this same stanza is also likely to register the harsher "slap" in the "*gl*uttonou*s l*apping of the waves on weeds." The well-known experiments with "slant rhymes" in Owen's verse have their equivalence in oblique internal rhymes, these often aided by a transegmental regrouping, as in "To the world'*s towers* or *stars*" ("The Roads Also"). At other times the internal slant rhyme can warp the verse with an anti-pun, inoperable in context, the ghost of a vanished or suppressed possibility. The poem "Training" begins "Not this week nor this month dare I lie down / In languor under lime trees or smooth smile." Reminiscent of Browning, this denied smile then haunts as anti-pun the next stanza's "My lips, parting, shall drink spa*ce, mile* by mile."

T. S. Eliot is scarcely this sort of poet as a rule. The stark vernacular of his mature verse normally eschews the kind of thickening effects that are carefully cordoned off in the (almost parodistically full) transegmental chimes of the few rhyming stanzas from "Little Gidding." In that poem's "Ash on an old man's sleeve / Is all the ash that burnt rose*s leave*" (ll. 56–57), the first line's sibilant is no sooner elided to anticipate the rhyme than the ending of "roses" drifts over a line later to fill out the echo. Or there is the fuller tandem rhyme of "incandes*cent terror*" with "*sin and error*" (ll. 203, 205). In bringing *The Waste Land* to a close, "What the Thunder Said" is perhaps the best-known phonemic rumbling in modern English literature, first "DA" on one line, "*Datta*" on the next (ll. 401–2), then twice more, at narrowing intervals, "*DA/Dayadhvam*" (ll. 411–12) and "*DA/Damyata*" (ll. 418–19). Eliot's note, of course, identifies his source (in the Upanishads) for the repeated syllables issued by the Hindu divinity when speaking in tongues, as it were, through the accidental phonemic overtones of the thunder. Three pregnant *DA*s are followed by three responses generated from within the semiotic impulse of the listening interpreter. Like Saussurean anagrams, two of the responses, "*Datta*" and "*Damyata*" (to give alms; to practice self-control), may be said to be generated from the sacred syllable "DA" according to a bracketing "mannequin," while the common denominator of all three consists simply in the fact that the single, capitalized, presyllabic transcription "DA" yields up the first two letters of the next word, the primal noise incurring the human phoneme. But this is not all. In the original manuscript of *The Waste Land*, the first reverberation as well as the response appear in the same typographical format, all caps: "*DA/DATTA.*"[30] This makes all the clearer the way in which the *tripled* boom of the thunder sings out its riddling three syllables even in the sheer phonetics – quite apart from morphemics – of the very first enunciation and hymned return: *DA, DA, TTA.* The revision thus secures the sense of the thunder's threefold *DA* being pieced out across this whole climactic passage, its appearances never directly collapsing into the meaningless repetitions they would produce without the intervention of lexical processing. Never directly – and yet even across the highlighted shift in typographical format, one may also hear three times repeated, by transegmental enjambment, the name of that contemporaneous offshoot of modernism whose aesthetic role, just the year before, Eliot had minimized and dismissed, no doubt for its tendency to belittle all the revelatory fervor of art's hieratic aspiration.[31] In Eliot's modernist script(ure), that is, the defiant voice of DA/da is evoked only to be drowned out by a more resonant phonemic fiat.

A poet as different from Eliot as is Robert Frost cannot help but be overead this way in his most lexically overrun moment, the pun on *a fence* in "Mending Wall": "Before I built a wall I'd ask . . . / . . .to whom I was like to give offense." So too, if less flamboyantly, in "The Aim Was Song," about the telos of natural music passing through meter into melody, even through phonation into lyric. In its play between theme and thematized medium, this could be Frost's version of Coleridge's Eolian emblem for breathed poetic meaning. "Before man came to blow it right," the poem opens, "The wind once blew itself untaught." That last participle then recurs as a lingering instructive aftertone across a segmental break in the second stanza: "it blew too hard – the aim was song. / And listen – how it *ought* to go!" As we know from one of Geoffrey Hartman's examples of "junctural zero values" in the Prologue ("le monocle de mon oncle"), we can find such "symphonetics" in Stevens as well as Frost, and in English as well. In "Anecdote of the Jar," a passing transegmental shift accompanies a clear case of Empsonian double grammar in the opening stanza. A jar is set down in Tennessee,

> And round it was, upon a hill.
> It made the slovenly wilderness
> Surround that hill.

From the clausal format of "And round it was," we are led to expect, at least until or despite the comma, some delayed subject. It turns out, rather, that "round" is adjectival rather than adverbial ("around"), the grammar entirely self-contained in its inversion ("round it was," it was round). Its roundness, like everything else about the jar, is focal, centering. Enhanced by sibilant enjambment, the second sentence of the stanza next inscribes an almost perfect homophonic alternative for the unwritten "made the slovenly wilder-ness / *around* that hill" — with "*made* the landscape" understood in the ver-nacular sense of giving it form and focus.

Dylan Thomas is a poet whose ear runs to such crisscross lexical effects as those in "Poem in October," where the enjambed unpunctuated series "With *apples / Pears* and red currants" finds its first two items reversed two lines later for a homophonic anagram in "the *parables* / Of sun light." Words in his verse can also be fused in their given order, as when the famous lines "The force that through the green fuse drives the flower / Drives my green age" manage with their last strained metonymic figure (transferred epithet plus noun) also to suggest the single vocable "greenage" (as implicitly contrasted at the level of an antonymical matrix to a formation like "dotage"). Besides such transforma-tions of separate lexemes into the new syllabic units of a larger term, there are transegmental phantoms in Thomas that shear off a single phoneme at a subliminal level. "It's Not in Misery but in Oblivion," for example, covertly anticipates (and afterward explicitly reiterates) the noun "sin" by the fluid (lubricious?) phonic drift of "By u*s in* sin or u*s in* gaiety." The opening of "I Know This Vicious Minute's Hour" involves the phonemic imbrication of a transegmental bond in "minute'*s hour;* / It is a *sour* motion in the blood." Internal rather than end rhyme, though inaugurated in terminal position, thus enforces an adjective that seems endemic to the moment. But as soon as such possibilities for liaison are allowed by the ear, the reverse momentum is also permissible. The second line thus seems able to insinuate the inevitable equivalence between "a sour motion" and one that, by definition, "is a*s our* motion." In "Now the Thirst Parches Lip and Tongue," a stinging acid "pours away... / Into the places and the crevices / Most fit for lover to make harmony." In the accompanying clause, "the acid (d)rips," such virulence is further conveyed in a lexical crevassing whose effect — by gemination and elision — is to split open one verb to reveal a more rending one. In connection with such verbal rifts and clefts, there is a transegmental rhyme in the first quatrain of "Clown in the Moon" that one could read as an oblique thematizing of the lexicalized d/rift itself. "My tears are like the quie*t d*rift / Of petals," Thomas writes, and "my grief flows from the *rift* / Of unremembered skies and snows."

Graphonology

From Anglo-American modernism on, then, to what? Any closure brought to bear on this cursory survey of transegmental activity in the English poetic tradition since Shakespeare will be to some extent as arbitrary as its starting point. There is no reason, however, to let our modernist examples trail off without a glance forward to their theoretically oriented succession in poststructuralist poetry. In her chapter on these recent experiments, "The Word as Such: $L=A=N=G=U=A=G=E$ Poetry in the Eighties," Marjorie Perloff includes among her epigraphs, without comment, a typifying parapraxis of phonemic sensuality: "But this is a false tart, the trap door insecurely latched, a tear in the velvet curtain."[32] This run of appositives, excerpted from Ron Silliman's radical linguistic primer, *ABC*, kicks off with the transegmental absurdity of "false tart" (Shakespeare's "Trojan strumpet" by any other name) as a monosyllabic false gambit, the second lexeme getting underway a sibilant too late. This self-instancing initial solecism is indeed the lexical promiscuity as trap, an unlatching, a tear in the eroticized veil of language. If we take this instance of the phonotext rectifying the graphic slip as in some sense a quintessential instance of graphonic relativity in such experimental verse, then in the very exposure of this materiality and biplay can be felt a vestigial link to Romanticism. For this is the legacy within which verbal art increasingly aspires to provide yet more self-conscious stagings of "literature" in the very condition of its possibility. In the high modernist period, despite an ontology of the word as sign, this still meant the enactment of literature as ideality rather than of language as sheer substance—of literature, in other words, as an "ideology" of language. In this as in many respects, modernism is a phase, not a phasing out, of Romanticism.

But Romanticism relies on a more foundational myth yet: its glorification of the personalized and prophetic voice of lyric utterance. This is the reason why this chapter, though providing a desultory survey of the whole tradition of English phonemic play, has repeatedly taken focus as a theorizing of Romanticism per se. In Romantic verse, the heady privileging of the signifier is not regularly indulged at the intended expense of the referent but, rather, in purposeful homage to—and in a willed mirage of—the very density and mutability of the natural world, the thick but permeable life of things. Yet sound play is not thereby restricted, as acoustic evocation, to one delimited zone of mimesis, licensed only as the phonemic mirror of natural harmonies. Instead, Romantic textual vocalization operates at the very core of the lyric motive itself: a text's impulse to represent the voice of its own representations. Such is the myth of presence—in warrant of reference—that of course co-opts the reader as well. And in particular, the reader's passive vocal organs. This is indeed the way in which aural presence is borrowed, rather than earned, by Romantic texts. One recalls here the embattled confrontation of phonography and premodern textuality speculated upon by Friedrich Kittler in Chapter 3. Yet the fullness simulated by Romantic texts, the repletion they would impart, can only be brought to, not sought in, the surface of their inscription. For it is Romanticism's dream as well as its perpetual default to engage the very pulse of the reading body, whose palpable equivalent it would at the same time pretend to incarnate in the organic vitality of its own verses.

Let us return in closing, then, to a locus classicus of high visionary Romanticism—in order to read its reflexive fantasy of creative fabrication from within the materiality of its own production. Coleridge's exemplary fable of divination and manifestation in "Kubla Khan" becomes, instead, the admission, indeed the site itself, of an aurality ingeniously veiled and inverted. It is masked by an "ideology" of epiphanic *vision* within the complementary mode of *lyric* in its descent from the lyre. When Wordsworth, late in his career, casts into imperative grammar his invocation of the reading agency as sole oral source—"Give voice to what my hand shall trace" ("Inscribed Upon a Rock," l. 5)—the notion of engraving in solitude for some future visitor ("Pause, Traveller!") localizes the moment so that it stops far short of a general theory of Romantic text production. The indirections of aurality in "Kubla Khan" are more typical. Kubla had a dome; Coleridge a dream; posterity a poem. There was once a perfect shape decreed, decreed by the fiat of a potentate. There was also a damsel with a dulcimer once, more recently, in the living memory of the persona, the memory of his own dream. If he were to remember again here and now the full splendor of her "symphony and song," her voice and its accompaniment, then

> To such a deep delight 'twould win me,
> That with music loud and long,
> I would build that dome in air,
> That sunny dome! those caves of ice!
> And all who heard should see them there
> ("Kubla Khan," ll. 44–48)

The buried matrix of the speaker's—the lyricist's—empowerment lurks on the obverse side of a single preposition: "*in* air" as in "*out of* (thin) air." The rondure of a dome would thus emerge from melody, for which in one sense "air" is only another word. In this fashion a spatial presence would be generated out of the temporal continuum—and alliterative dilation—of a "music loud and long." A poem, in short—once more, a textual "symphonetics." But when texts are shaped out of air, out of breath, out of "inspiration" in its material agency, and then written down in ink, the tensed breath that remains to sustain them is nowhere to be summoned but from the phonic imagination of the reader—alone from our bodying forth of silence as latent vocalization. When the text suggests that all who hear the music would see the created object, would find the dome *in air,* the Romantic "ideology" is working overtime, and specifically on its linguistic front. It is using one myth of poetic articulation to cover another. An important brilliance of Coleridge's poem is how close this ruse brushes the truth, the terms simply manifested in reverse. The real dream of Romanticism is not first and foremost that, in "listening to" its transcribed oracles, we will see their visions but, more fundamentally, that, in seeing marks on the page, we will seem to hear the music of (their) words.

A music ambiguous and unstable. For at the turning point of the poem is yet another transegmental drift that captures—any way you take it—the dubiety of juncture and the paradoxes of visionary manifestation. "To such a deep delight 'twould win me." Out of the metrical telescoping of "it would" comes the decontracted multiplicity of the phrase. "To such a deep [that is, depth] my delight ('t) would win me," we may well read by way of evocalization, with the second *t* unprocessed and with "deep" therefore functioning as noun rather than adjective. In this role the word "deep" would indeed be somewhat less dead a metaphor, recalling the "chasm" and the "caves" earlier in the text: that mysteriously empowering and threatening underside of the pleasure dome. Concerning the damsel singing of Mount Abora, that ad hoc Muse chanting the highest reaches of human habitation, this production of "deep" as noun might even draw out the profundity, the unplumbable otherness, latent in her designation as an "Abyssinian maid." Into and out of the visionary "abyss" flows the power of art, coded here as the displaced vernacular matrix of inspirational "depth," the Orphic prototype of the poet's heroic trials. All this would be tacitly mobilized in that tiny secondary elision, within contraction, syncopating out that extra *t* from "'twould" and reconceiving "deep" as a noun. Short of this, however, even if we don't evocalize such a phonotextual double grammar turning on a single elided letter, we certainly do hear within the given inverted syntax the smooth overlap of cause and effect: the reverse linkage between "'t" ("it"), with "her symphony and song" its antecedent, and the creative "delight" it precipitates. It is this that enunciates the very dream it at the same time begins to fulfill—fulfill, though, only within the twofold illusion of Romanticism—the text as heard in the service of a vision seen.

In and along the untractable drift of the signifying flux, we thus confront in textual reception the relative f/utility of all reference; in Coleridge's words from "Dejection" (for natural rather than textual interanimation), we receive from language but what we give, giving only what we cannot get along without. The dismantling, in turn, of the vocal subject of such truant utterance is therefore something that the major Romantic texts already do for—and against—themselves. When Romanticism draws on the phonic register to confer aural presence, but does so with a luxuriance and manipulation that turns exuberance into excess, excess into surplus, surplus into undecidability, the overflow of full utterance into dispersed textual biplay, it has thus begun to deconstruct in its own right the logic of all that it posits in the name of prophetic voice, let alone of adumbrated visions. It is such an uneasy and beleaguered logic that nevertheless remains the deepest mythology of expressive *style* itself. It is this that phonemic reading works to account for from the (morphophonemic) ground up, even while taking it to pieces.

This chapter's concern with the microparticulars of the poetic word has meant in part to register the potential shivering of the Romantic mystification from within its grandest linguistic designs, to record the infinitesimal cracks in its monuments, in its whole cultural edifice, well before major fault lines become evident — and to do so while noting that it is upon the reader's body that the least shocks are registered. The hard gemlike flame of the literary word, let alone of aesthetic response, is not formed to be so internally obdurate after all, its intrinsic friction felt in the reading. This is especially true at the level of junctural pressure upon lexical structure, upon literality itself. Exposed by a transegmental sequencing at odds with syntactic coherence, the decentered word is schismatic at its most prismatic. Such an induced d/rift entails a shaving off of phonemic matter that makes of what is left a refractive and oblique register, an angled surface in which other lexemes glint, other phonemic clusters, alight in the unheard melodies of a sound but half their own. In prose too, as we are next to see, such are the aural facetings that overreading retrieves from the steady suppression necessitated by grammar itself.

5   Evocalizing Prose
Sterne to Dickens to Lawrence

A transegmental prose too? Can a sentence or paragraph from a novel, in any degree like a line or quatrain from a sonnet, be found to invite phonemic reading? Prose doesn't work this way, one is told. In the language of prose fiction, by contrast with poetry, less seems to go on than to go forward, less texture than direction — in Jakobson's phonological terms, less arranged equivalence than simple combination. Wouldn't, in fact, the overeading of literary prose, as against verse — given the former's very different tempo and specific gravity — amount to a willful over-reading after all? The answer, in the negative, rests with an understanding of the transegmental effect as a function, in considerable part, of chance, to which prose is as open as verse. Not ordinarily a phonological nuance consciously tuned to a hairbreadth band of registration, the transegmental phenomenon involves instead as much contingency as craft, as much equivocal slippage as exquisite precision. The graphonic in poetry — and, by extension, in prose — is rhetoric crossed with risk, a hazard of syllables and subsidiary phonemes. It is thus wordplay in a very particular sense, a gaming both with and against the odds. Prose, at least before Joyce, is often thought to be more "transparent" than poetry, assumed to give the close application of a deconstructive analysis, as before it of a New Critical reading, more trouble, less action: less scriptive thickness on the way to the described. But this assumption is no more shielded from local surprise than from theoretical disproof. Vagrant, refractory, the stray phoneme in prose can — to use a scriptive dead metaphor — still make its mark in the syntactic shuffle. Put thereby into silent play in prose fiction, though usually more at ease than in verse, are, once again, the reader's passive vocal muscles: the solicited body in the poise of its constantly shifting activity of withheld enunciation, labile and always just a little precarious.

"Undercraft" as Subtext

In that book of play, that game of a book, *Tristram Shandy,* Sterne writes that "'tis an undercraft of authors to keep up a good understanding amongst words, as politicians do amongst men—not knowing how near they may be under a necessity of placing them to each other" (7.19.502), itself a strained phrase with its own nine-word inverted displacement of "near" from its grammatical completion "to each other." In some very different cases, however, the tang of verbal propinquity can become explosive. An unguarded collocation may accidentally suffer a strange textual fate well beyond the ken of a given character, even one who may articulate part of its words. At the opening of Slawkenbergius's Tale, that story of the man burdened with an enormous length of (euphemistically designated) nose, the protagonist so endowed overhears the trumpeter's wife planning to touch the notorious organ when he sleeps. His fury is immediate:

> No! said he, dropping his reins upon his mule's neck, and laying both his hands upon his breast, the one over the other in a saint-like position (his mule going on easily all the time)—No! said he, looking up,—I am not such a debtor to the world—slandered and disappointed as I have been—as to give it that conviction—no! said he, my nose shall never be touched while heaven gives me strength.
>
> (4.247–48)

In the adamancy of his refusal, conveyed by an inverted grammar ("said he") bringing the *s* sounds into adjacency, the speaker has three times accidentally named the cause célèbre—that salient member whose mere designation will not be denied—across the recurrent transegmental slip of "*No s*aid." Even the word will out, let alone the body part. Given the regular demarcations of a fictional text, what is particularly unusual about this slippage is that it effects a transgression across the boundary of quoted dialogue and narrative discourse. It brings up into direct quotation, up from what we might loosely call the "unconscious" of the subtending text, an acoustic irony—an "undercraft"—that contaminates the uttered thoughts of a character. The protagonist speaks only his refusal; through us as silent readers, the text subverts that defiance by blurting out—right under his own nose—the noun in question, a return of the repressed under the ban of negation.

Sterne can be even more explicit about the intrigues of orthography. At one point he deliberately foregrounds the sound of the shapes of words, the phonetic articulation of written characters—before, or at the very moment of, their passing into phonemic relation with the lexeme they inaugurate. In

Tristram's alphabet of love, there is a partial list of love's attributes, each categorized by the first letter of its designation, "A gitating, B ewitching, C onfounded" (8.13.551), and so forth. It is the middle term there that is of particular interest in its teasing out the possibility of a phonetic rebus, activated only when *B* (pronounced "be") provides by elision a phonemic continuity with the word it opens. This is the bewitchment of the phonotext itself in a nervous commuting between letters as signs and letters as names. Exactly a century later, such play with letters — as not just the constituent thingness of words but as words in their own right — inflects a well-known passage in Dickens's *Great Expectations,* related in turn to Cockney humor and based on the phonetic rebus as a transitional stage on the way to literacy. The young Pip, just learning to write, scribbles a note to Joe on his chalk slate:

'MI DEER JO i OPE U R KRWITE WELL i OPE i SHAL SON B HABELL
4 2 TEEDGE U JO AN THEN WE SHORL B SO GLODD AN WEN i M
PRENGTD 2 U JO WOT LARX AN BLEVE ME INF XN PIP.'

(7.75)

Beyond the Cockney "hable" for "able," Pip traces, instead of words, both numerals ("four" and "two" as prepositions) and letters ("i M" for "I em," that is "I am"; only accidentally for the contraction "I'm"). When the novice writer gives in valediction "inF XN Pip," the letters stand for "in-eff-ection" but also, if the phonemic readout starts a split second too late, for "in f-ection," that sickness so often lurking on the underside of love in this novel.

This play with the sound of letters, related to the detachments of syllables as separate words, can make its (phonic) mark in less expected fictional contexts. Charlotte Brontë's way with words, her "undercraft," is given over to one of Jane Eyre's own central protestations in the novel. Rochester, insistently anticipating their marriage, has addressed her prematurely as the second Mrs. Rochester. In response, Jane immediately blushes, discomfited because "you gave me a new name — Jane Rochester; and it seems so strange" (24.227). The conversation that ensues, in which she refuses his offer of jewels and finery, may be read as an attempt to recover the lost integrity and singleness of an original name. It may indeed be heard to climax precisely with a disintegrating play upon both her unmarried names. Bedecked as he wishes, Jane would be unrecognizable: "And then you won't know me, sir; and I shall not be your Jane Eyre any longer, but an ape in a harlequin's jacket" (228). To which she adds in an afterthought (and after a dash), as if reflecting further on the suddenly no more than nominal self she is in danger of abdicating: " — a jay in borrowed plumes." To pronounce (upon) the name he would have her surrender is to enter upon a homophonic irony in which "Ja/ne" must resist being spoken-for (disyllabically) as a "jay/in" plumage.

Her answer—in a word—in a name—is Never. To hold to her full name as Jane Eyre, the Jane she has always been "'ere" now—the name of a woman whose continuity of spirit cannot be squandered—would after all, in an extension of the subtextual rebus inflecting this passage about the giving and taking of names, amount to being a "Jay Ne'er." As an ironic internal echo, "Jane" is therefore thrust into spiritual dissonance with "jay in"; as a phonemic allegory, we might say, the echo constitutes a syllabic degeneration of the name, recuperated only by the transegmental nudge—outside of an immediate and functioning syntax—of "Jane Eyre" toward "Jay Ne'er." If one needs a context for such rebuslike biplay beyond the multiple (and activated) puns on Jane's last name ("'ere," "air," "ire," "eyrie," "heir," including her dream of "a fairer era of life" [11.86]), one need only remember Rochester's own overt internal echo in advising her to "Dread...remorse" whenever inclined "to err, Miss Eyre" (14.120): in other words, to fear those recriminations that engulf the self is "miser/y."

In *Villette,* Brontë's verve for euphony and internal echo is developed considerably beyond even the lush, studied texturings of *Jane Eyre.* An unmistakable transegmental effect can be heard, for instance, in the passing description of a cultivated park landscape, "a well-planted round" no more symmetrically trimmed than Brontë's own prose in rendering "the green *swell* of ground surrounding thi*s well*" (33.471). Sometimes, too, the phonemic swell and overflow can be simply comic, as in the polyglot humor by which the French-speaking professor of literature pronounces "Williams Shack-spire" (28.416, 417), a phonetic "fusion" through "doubling"—here the doubling back of the surname's first sibilant to a meaningless pluralization of the first name. In the famous phantasmagoric chapter "Cloud," in which Lucy wanders alone at night in an opium-induced fog through the hallucinatory doings of a city festival, the prose is even more heightened, more convoluted: "The effect was as a sea breaking into song with all it*s waves,*" the next sentence then picking out, picking up on, the initially unbonded sibilant and *w* for the cross-lexical paronomasia of "The *sway*ing tide swept thi*s way.*" Prose of this order seems to feed on the dream logic that permeates this first-person rendering of a half-conscious, drugged cognition.

The most ingenious—or fortuitous—effect of all, perhaps, appears in the next chapter's prolongation of this opium haze, when Lucy looks on unseen at an exercise in social power on the part of her eventual fiancé, who she at this point thinks is amorously inclined toward his ward, Justine Marie. Lucy's eavesdropping finds him brushing off the petulant jealousies of a suitor with a most concise gesture of body language; in Lucy's account, however, each tiny rivalrous parry in this miniature comedy of manners takes on the proportions of an epic joust. At his most decisive moment of high-handed self-confidence,

Lucy's hero, albeit on behalf of another heroine, appears invincible, as "with the ruthless triumph of the assured conqueror, he drew his ward nearer to him" (39.565). Given the martial imagery of this phrasing, the very proximity of the desired object emerges as itself a weapon—indeed, as transegmentally suggested, a weapon as good as any sword ($s = ward$). Whether accidental or "stylistic," such displacements and condensations in the articulated responses of Lucy's waking dream serve to enunciate the released fantasies of the heroine in this episode of half-delusional projection. Prose itself, submitted to phonemic reading, thus psychoanalyzes the language of the unconscious— Lucy's or, if you will, Brontë's—beneath the neo-Petrarchan rhetoric of combative eroticism.

Sounds Switched

Before either Brontë or Dickens, Thackeray had more systematically entered the field of phonemic breakdown, through Cockney travesty, with *The Memoirs of Mr. Charles J. Yellowplush,* a "Sometime Footman in Many Genteel Families," who affects hard words in a relentless barrage of phonetic misspellings. The first installment, "Fashnable Fax and Polite Annygoats," was published in *Fraser's Magazine* in November of 1837. With much of the humor revolving around just such garblings of received English as represented by the title, the persona's frequent orthographical malapropisms— "metafizzix," for example, in the first sentence—sometimes include an unwitting punlike overtone at the syllabic level, in this case on the short-lived heady effervescence (or "fizz") of such speculation.[1] Though well past the advent of classical discourse theory in Foucault's sense, where the full arbitrariness of signifying practice was institutionalized, still colloquial comedy like Thackeray's recalls an earlier objectification of the word as malleable object, inviting subdivision into other units and combines of meaning. Malapropism of this sort indeed frequently parodies the notion behind the preclassical interdict described by a scholar of homonymics in the French language as a "prudish mania . . . in the seventeenth century, which threatened to impoverish the language by avoiding at all costs any word with an evil-sounding syllable. We can be sure that the gaulois punster had his share in that."[2] In Thackeray's *Yellowplush Papers,* the loss of one subsidiary syllabic cluster ("stances") in "circumstances," for instance, is compensated for by the vaguely risqué transcription "suckmstansies" (292), accompanied by "sins" for "since" in the same sentence. So, too, with the hint of a Cockney happiness in "appetites" contorted to "appytights" (303). This last example is drawn from "Mr. Yellowplush's Ajew," an installment which concludes with an apology for the writer's "violetting the rules of authography" (300). The title's own cross-lexical biplay at "—'s Ajew" certainly harbors a provocative second syllable in its phonetic transcription of the French noun of valediction. This is a syllable released by the tempting displacement from possessive to contractive grammar across the functional shift of the apostrophe. Such a promotion of syllable to seme, with the wrench it causes to internal segmentation and its consequent demotion of the lexeme, all but inevitably entails the adjacent risk of *syntactic* homophony, in other words, of junctural—or dyslocutionary—punning. It may well be this same ear for ironies of enunciation that later leads Thackeray, in *Vanity Fair,* to house the spendthrift, debt-ridden Sir Pitt (serpent, surfeit) Crawley at "201" on Curzon Street, Mayfair—the satiric "to owe one" getting him exactly where, as we now say, he "lives."

Three years after Thackeray's *Yellowplush,* the Victorian comic magazine *Punch* began its long publishing history, including on the second page of its first number some "lessons in Punmanship" by "Mr. T. Hood, Professor of Punmanship." The question "Why is a fresh-picked carnation like a certain cold with which children are affected?" invites the daft transegmental answer: "Because it's a *new pink off* (an hooping-cough)." As it happens, this junctural conundrum is a particularly clear illustration of *Punch's* tendency toward a lower-class London norm of pronunciation. After considering such traits as elisions, glides, and the general slurring of syllables, one linguistic study of substandard Cockney dialect instances under the heading "Grammar" the very lexical mutation by which the *n* of "an" gets attached to the succeeding syllables, as in "at a nend"/"a nold man."[3] This, in turn, serves to instance in a synchronic dimension such diachronic transformations as "a nadder" into "an adder" mentioned in Chapter 3. In literary send-ups, as in Thackeray's lexical farces, these consonantal displacements tend to operate in the same spirit as the extrusion of perverse semantic fragments from within polysyllabic words. A case in point from a narrative epistle by a Cockney maid in that first number of *Punch,* "super-silly-ous" (17), demonstrates its signified, in effect, mocked by the travesty of its own signifier. For an even more brutal murdering of the language, there is this later conundrum from the same first issue: "Why is a defunct mother like a dog?—Because she's a ma-stiff" (21).

The unspoken logic by which in *Jane Eyre* the heroine's name, already textualized by title, is then in a particular context decontracted into "jay in" (or even the unwritten "Jane Ne'er") can now be seen as the inconspicuous literary equivalent of a riddling alphabetic joke like "Q. When is a word like a bird's nest? A. When it has a J. in it." Or some such journalistic conundrum as "Q. Why won't Jane ever say yes? A. Because she thinks she's Jane Ne'er." A comparable micropoetic drift of wide ramifications for a novel's plot occurs in Emily Brontë's *Wuthering Heights,* to which Charlotte's preface offers a rhetorical clue. Charlotte writes that her sister's story is a tale of "perverted passion and passionate perversity." This very pattern of symmetrical inversion, of rhetorical chiasmus, may well have captured, in a single hinge of phrasing, some deep structural logic of the novel's plot. From a different perspective, Frank Kermode has suggested that the inscribed names discovered by the narrator Lockwood at the institution of the retrospective plot — Earnshaw, Heathcliff, Linton — become, in fact, a narrative rather than alphabetic "rebus."[4] They write in reversible sequence the passage of the first Catherine *Earnshaw* through her love for *Heathcliff* to her *Linton* marriage, while at the same time, read from right to left, they inscribe the return progress of her daughter, the second Catherine (*Linton*), back through a marriage with Linton *Heathcliff* to a restorative union with Hareton *Earnshaw*. This inverted parallelism is, Kermode might have noted, a form of structural chiasm, a crossing over and return, a switch. If the encompassing plot dynamic of *Wuthering Heights* follows the pattern of reversal and return, the crisscross of the chiasm, then a reader might expect to find this pattern evidenced even in the microstructures of the text, its subsyntactic negotiations.

This expectation is borne out, for instance, in a piece of Yorkshire invective from the dialogue of the servant Joseph. When Linton Heathcliff, Edgar's son, is first presented at the Heights, Joseph is so contemptuous of the frail thing that he suspects the creature is in fact a girl child who has been substituted: "'Sure-ly,' said Joseph after a grave inspection, 'he's swopped wi' ye, maister, an' yon's his lass!'" (20.169). Even nurse Nelly Dean calls the child a "changeling" (27.217), recalling Heathcliff himself in his original role as a kind of changeling figure, a gypsylike creature introduced into the Earnshaw family to bear "the name of a son who had died in childhood" (4.39). Given Heathcliff's role as a wild and unlegitimated surrogate for the dead heir, the idea of the "swopped" identity has immediate resonance. Though Hareton is the new heir apparent, the "'heritin'" one, as it were (like Jane Eyre, in fact, finally come into her name as Heir to a family fortune), it is precisely from the furious disrule of the Earnshaw blood that Hareton is being weaned by Cathy's softening — but to Joseph, demonic — influence. This is the influence that Joseph in his diatribe rejects with an unwitting transegmental pun, twice activated. "Poor lad . . .he's *witched*" (32.243), moans Joseph, and later, "It's yon flaysome, graceless quean, ut's *witched* ahr lad" (33.251). Across the lexical chasm passes the stray sibilant that turns the accusation of witchcraft back again to the theme of the changeling "swop" as structural chiasm — a double crossing of blood ties, a *switching* of emotional as well as genetic allegiance. Erotic magnetism mediating between demonism and familial alliance offers up the theme of the novel in the hissed drift of a single phoneme: the microgrammar of narrative.

Taken Letterally

As any cursory overview of Victorian fiction would suggest, it is Dickens, follower of Sterne and precursor of Joyce, who is the great microgrammarian of the premodern novel. His effects can be passing snags in the syntax of narration or, at times, ironic miniaturizations of an entire fictional or thematic structure. In his first novel, the Pickwick Club, philologically if not phonologically inclined, debates the supposedly mysterious runic inscription, "+ / BILST / UM / PSHI / S.M. / ARK" (11.217), adjudged finally to be "neither more no less than the simple construction of – 'BILL STUMPS, HIS MARK'" (11.228), accompanying the illiterate graffitist's "+" for X. Beyond the curious reflexive nature of this inscription about inscription, part of the puzzle for the Pickwickians in decoding this cryptogram has implicitly to do with grammatical ambiguity. Yet honoring the comma and thus reading the four monosyllables not as a transitive clause but as a possessive phrase, we encounter a transegmental slide that opens back onto the entire history of sibilance within the genitive construction. This comic example has such a classic status, indeed, that it provides, unidentified, the heading for the appendix in Otto Jespersen's *Progress in Language* on the "*his-genitive*," as in Chaucer's "Here endith the man of law his tale," a phenomenon that often becomes "practically indistinguishable" from the old flexional "*s-genitive*."[5] Though Jespersen notes that the "similarity is of a purely phonetic nature" (324), he does not go on to distinguish the effect of such a weak-stressed "his" pronunciation (in its closeness to "'s") in regard to the various nouns it might follow. In the case of his own unexplored Dickensian example, "BILL STUMP*S, HIS* MARK" abuts the *s* of the surname with the elided enunciation of "HIS." This also seems the case, for instance, with a transitional example Jespersen does not give – transitional between Chaucerian and Cockney English – namely, Dryden's "the latter part of Lisideius his discourse" in the *Essay of Dramatic Poetry,* a phrase that appears to invite, as silently pronounced, a more complete conflation between types of genitive, both pronominal and inflectional.

In view of evidence yet to come, it may not seem too much to claim that Dickens thus enters the history of the novel as the tacit and intuitive historian of language, dialect, and their convergence in the private idiolect of any reading, silent or out loud, private or communal. In a transegmental appellation that just precedes "Jay Ne'er" in literary history, from the genealogical chronicle that opens *Martin Chuzzlewit,* Dickensian comedy reads like the punch line of a conundrum out of *Punch.* Asked to pronounce with his last gasp the name of his grandfather, Toby Chuzzlewit answers – in words that "were taken down at the time and signed by six witnesses" — with the following confession: "The Lord No Zoo." The joke turns expressly upon the difference between script and enunciation, upon the ambiguities that ensue from a tension between graphic and phonic signifiers, between textuality itself and voice. We are told that searches through the titles of England subsequently produce "none at all resembling this, in sound even." This is because the sound is taken to be the garbled homophone of a proper name rather than a common idiomatic clause — to be, in other words, syntactically homologous with the expected class of answer. The zealousness of the six mortal scribes only exaggerates this farce of transcription, one which plays, as we know, on what linguistics would now term the disambiguation of segmental boundaries through stress, pitch, and juncture. Once the verb *knows* gives up a sibilant to the pronoun *who,* the nonsensical proper name "No Zoo" is precipitated from this auditory collapse. Genealogy is deconstructed by parodistic phonology; as with any fictive character in Dickens, only more openly here, origin and lineage are entirely linguistic. Since lexical conflations and displacements of this sort involve an unsettled progress across the grammatical sequence, they come to represent the lower limit of syntactic manipulation. Not wordplay exactly, nor even syllable play, they engage language at a shifting point where morphophonemic and grammatical structures intersect: the vexed juncture between words, syntax in debate with itself. What happens everywhere by accident may thus at times be admitted — made unmissable — as a scripted pun.

Or not. Dickens's phonic gestures in this vein are by no means restricted to the overt comic mode of lexical farce. In his picturesque, Romantically tinged descriptive passages, we may also find such an easing of lexical boundaries, usually in conjunction with a fuller battery of phonological effects than deployed in his comic writing. As often before in these pages, Dickens's textual mechanics seem to invite an analytic coalition of Jakobson and Riffaterre. In *The Old Curiosity Shop,* an exemplary syntactic mobilization, heavily embedded and dramatically built, sets the stage for a transegmental drift. The narrator is remembering in his troubled half-sleep the earlier sight of Nell amid the clutter, curios, and decay of her grandfather's shop:

> I had ever before me the old dark murky rooms — the gaunt suits of mail with their ghostly silent air — the faces all awry, grinning from wood and stone — the *dust* and *rust,* and *worm* that lives in *wood* — and alone in the midst of all this lumber and decay, and ugly age, the beautiful child in her gentle slumber, smiling through her light and sunny dreams.

(1.56)

Typical of Dickens, there is the impacted adjectival clotting of "old dark murky rooms." In Jakobsonian terms, its combinatory axis finds projected upon it not only the alliterating *k*'s but the abutting, potentially elided *d*'s, along with the lengthening chiastic reversal of "mur" into "room." Sub-alliterating with the *k*'s, the guttural *g*'s of "gaunt," "ghostly," and "grinning" prolong the alliteration and so bind the passage across its syntactic expansion, as does the more dramatic chiming (or Sterne-like "undercraft" again) of "dust" and "rust" or "worm" and "wood."

This last pairing, however, introduces a curious semiotic possibility of the sort that Riffaterre's terminology is uniquely adept at drawing out. The "agrammaticality" here is the unsettling echo not between "worm" and "wood" but of another collocation altogether, a variant intertext from the proverbial. In the iambic tread of this phrasing, Dickens has separated, and by alliteration set off, a verbal "paragram"—I will here be rehearsing again the whole range of Riffaterre's terminology—a paragram generated from an unsaid "matrix." This is a "variant" that "actualizes" only by "displacing" its idiomatic alternative through "conversion" and "expansion." The poetic variant performs, in other words, by evoking even while avoiding a buried "seed phrase" whose detection by the reader is the very "production" of this text, the materialized "semiosis" of its "poetry." With the openly courted Freudian implications of his method, then, Riffaterre's terms would help to explain how the redistributed cliché "wormwood," covertly naming here the bitterness of discrepancy between youthful bloom and environing waste (the compound word actually turning up in the text, in the idiomatic doublet "gall and wormwood," eight chapters further on [9.116]), is dispersed across the early syntagmatic sequence, made clausal rather than phrasal. It is a semiotic return of the repressed, a return masked but still activated. Amid such acoustic company we arrive at that last complex, suspensive phrase, "and alone in the midst of all this *lumber* and decay, and ugly age, the beautiful child in her gentle *slumber,* smiling through her light and sunny dreams." It is one thing to add the wholesale recurrence of the phonemic nexus *lumber* to the list of paronomastic bonds in the passage. It is quite another to notice the dreamlike displacement and condensation which transmute the sibilant at the juncture of "thi*s lumber*"—thus discovering, at the heart of its portrayed decay, that sleep of the just which will be spelled out a phrase later in the gentle slide of the narrator's own half-waking remembrance.

By the time such reverie succeeds to the child's living nightmare, the ferocious, stunted Daniel Quilp has been introduced as her alter ego, a figure mysteriously associated with his "wharf-side" activities, marginal, precarious, until he goes to his death by falling from that wharf. The reader is repeatedly teased by the echoic interplay of the "dwarf" (as he is incessantly called) and his "wharf" ("'The fence between this wharf and the next is easily climbed,' said the dwarf" [67.618]) — two mutually implicated lexemes whose teleologies seem destined to converge in such an inevitable (though never actually scripted) nexus as the "fated wharf." Instead, we get only the flashing memory of his last scene in the closing chapter's mention of his widow leading "a merry life upon the dea*d d*w(h)arf's money" ("Chapter the Last," 666). Just as Quilp drowns, however, Nell's virtually simultaneous death — in another part of the country and of the story — does involve a more directly insinuated cross-lexical ambiguity, one that epitomizes the double valence of her fate: not only a willing assumption of and to glory but also a willed escape. In the context of a thickening iambic alliteration — "*for* e*very fragile form from* which [Death] lets the panting spirit *free*, a hundred *v*irtues rise" — this paragraph of meditative omniscient generalization closes with an orthodox truism whose transegmental pressures bear more directly upon the specific case of Nell: "In the Destroyer's steps there spring up bright creations that defy his power, and his dark path becomes a way of light to Heaven" (72.659). Paradoxically lighting the way to heaven, the track of death is transformed to a route of divine access: that is the figurative sense of the conceit. More "grammatically" than rhetorically taken, however, and with more reference to the special case of Nell's release, the "dark path" becomes a "way," in the sense of means, "*of light*" — to but also from.

How often, and to what effect, does the Dickensian text break in this way from its graphic layout to audit its own interstices? There is a quasi-anagrammatic instance — surreptitious to the point almost of a cryptogram — in *Hard Times,* where the circumlocution of indirect discourse masks, even while implicating, the circus destination of the rendezvous with Tom. In passive, euphemistic phrasing ("caution being necessary") we read how "it was consented that Sissy and Louisa should repair to the place in question, by a circuitous course; and that the unhappy father, setting forth in an opposite direction, should get round to the same bourne by another and wider route" (3.7.211). Diversionary tactics characterize even the prose itself that hides the unsaid "circus" — in what phonology calls a "circumsyllabic bracket" — at the far edges of "*cir*cuito*us.*" Such eccentric orthographic puzzles aside, I am more interested now in effects which are heard — in one sense or another — across the normal contiguities of the syntagmatic axis. In the more calculatedly evocative prose of this same novel, we may encounter such a rugged terrain of consonants as in a phrase like "the brink of a black ragged chasm hidden by thick grass" (3.6.202), where the underground deeps disgorge their own inverted steepness across the phonemic grade "bla*ck (c)r*agged." In a more markedly dramatic moment, at the climactic confrontation between the heroine, Louisa, and her intolerant father, Mr. Gradgrind "saw a wild dilating fire in the eyes steadfastly regarding him" (2.12.166). What the reader hears rather than sees, well before we find the noun "eyes" written out, is the clichéd phonemic matrix "wild-eye(d)" glinting into audition on the way to its own phrasal dilation or circumlocution.

In the lampooned mumbling of lawyer Tangle in *Bleak House*, a deferential, drawling, grammatically effaced elision creates, among other effects, his notorious portmanteau conflation of "My Lord" (otherwise "Lud") into "Mlud" (1.4). This vocative not only names the human equivalent of the elemental muck outside but offers a phonetic anagram for the psychological as well as the legal "mud(d)l(e)" into which Chancery precipitates its victims. From the language of debased literacy and power to the underworld of untaught mumbling is, as the novel's ear for dialogue inscribes, not so great a distance. The illiterate crossing sweeper, Jo, in summing up his "mental condition" by saying repeatedly that he "don't know nothink" (16.274), speaks in a double negative that produces by its final thickened phoneme a segmental collapse of the two words "no think" into the tautological "nothing" that occupies his mind. The logic of such conflations as "Mlud," of course, requires what we might call silently hearing them aloud. Since in prose fiction they are usually found in dialogue, they may thus appear to introduce no active *textual* tension between phonic and graphic expression. On the page preceding the muddied diction of the courtroom drawl in *Bleak House*, however, the narrative prose itself makes such a (lateral) move. Occulted there within the normal order of third-person syntactic accumulation from word to word falls a conflationary disruption that might well be felt to utter more than is written.

Amid the sedimenting sentence fragments from the opening panorama of November mud and fog, we read of "Smoke lowering down from chimney-pots, making a soft black drizzle." Preceding the images of fog as drooping, creeping, and "cruelly pinching," this nonmetaphoric phrasing may offer one of the earliest hints of such full-scale personification allegory, set up even earlier by the first description of the weather as "implacable" (1.1) — an elemental force incapable, like an angry deity (or juridical behemoth) of being appeased, even by human sacrifice. Pronounced by way of assonance with two long *o*'s, the participle of "smoke lowering" could only render the adjacent "down" redundant, except as a stylistic device of pleonastic overkill. More likely is the alternate pronunciation equally common in Dickens's day, even in this spelling: indicating the intransitive participial form "louring." Probabilities aside, this is a radical ambiguity at the scriptive — and, so far, entirely lexical — level. Once the second and more cogent alternative ("smoke louring" rather than "smoke lowering") is admitted, however, both in the common figurative sense of "louring weather" and in its own faint personification of the smoke as "frowning," a second, more dismantling ambiguity is introduced. It performs not only a semantic substitution but a momentary destabilization. For in the immediate vicinity of "lower" (pronounced "lour"), the closing velar phoneme /k/ of the noun in "smoke lowering" readily clings to the next word. It thus forms the synonymous slip "glowering," rephrasing the alternative verb "lower" in a more unequivocal personification yet. The two alternative phrases inhabit virtually the same lexical space, foggily deliquescing into each other. Yet the second alternative, "glower" rather than "lower," violates juncture and instantaneously reweaves the elapsed phonemic sequence upon which the syntactic chain is mounted. It is thus less scriptive, more phonemically cryptic. As such, moreover, it simultaneously confirms and extends that demolition of reference in a certain line of deconstructive reading, engaging as it does the specifically phonemic rather than generally grammic trace. The obscuring fog of this London weather emerges of course primarily as symbol, or extended metaphor, for the misty obscurantism of the court, especially its stale oratorical smoke screens. In just this sense it is appropriate (again I am returning to de Man's terms and, again, with a linguistic rather than merely textual stress) that the faint prosopopoeia which sketches the billowing pall as a personified genius loci, frowning down from the chimney tops, should be the function of a strictly verbal density turning to ambiguity – if not to downright referential murkiness. Even before the tenor of legal discourse is attached to this prolonged vehicle of atmospheric pollution, there is no glowering here, no louring, or even lowering, no "expression" at all except in the linguistic sense of mere slippery words: a sustained giving-face to blankness, satiric in this case, demystifying, corrective, but no more able to secure its referents than is the vacuous rhetoric of the court.

On the comic front again, allegorical tag names in *Great Expectations* are repeatedly the source of a morphophonemic contortion – as with "Jane Eyre" or "Hareton" in the Brontës – that plays between eye and ear in the manner of the Cockney punning in *Punch*.[6] When Pip is harangued at Christmas dinner by his so-called uncle, one Pumblechook, the next sentence describes the reaction of another guest with the words: "Mrs. Hubble shook her head" (4.57). Dickens is a master of the homophonic near-miss. Later, instead of this scene's inferred phonetic kinship between "chook" and "shook," what surfaces in Pip's revenge fantasy is the physical violence lying latent in the first two syllables of the enemy's name: "I used to want – quite painfully – to burst into spiteful tears, fly at Mr. Pumblechook and pummel him all over" (12.125). Words are again pummeled – or, in Foucault's favored term, "pulverized" – into the disclosure of their hidden subsidiaries. The loutish (and similarly named) Bentley Drummle in London is a later avatar of this pummeling violence, in its physical rather than verbal form, while his friend Startop seems named (by the narrator, of course) in a virtual phonetic anagram of "Upstart." This is a novel in which eccentric naming also provides onomastic clues to secret lines of influence or filiation. The convict Magwitch is aurally linked to his own long-lost daughter, Estella, by a flustered solecism on Joe's part, in a scene where he affects "an air of legal formality" in reporting Miss Havisham's wishes secondhand to Pip. *Which*-ing and *that*-ing in every direction, Joe transliterates the gist of Miss Havisham's message as follows: "'Would you tell him, then,' said she, 'that which Estella has come home and would be glad to see him'" (27.246). In this overreaching slip of the tongue, as in a Freudian parapraxis, the nonce value of the relative pronoun "which" (extraneous as syntactical marker) turns out momentarily to revise, in a kind of double grammar, the preceding relative pronoun "that" into a demonstrative adjective. Heard as such, it takes as its subject a homophonic pun on "witch," thus characterizing the preternatural temptress of Pip's destiny and hinting at her genealogical descent from "Mag*witch.*" It is she whom Pip has already named to Joe, by a nervous act of syllabic conflation upon which the latter is quick to pounce, as "Miss Est-Havisham" (15.139). In both cases, through a semiotic irony beneath the momentary syntagmatic collapse, illiteracy turns agrammaticality into satire. At the same time, the elision of an *h* even within the telescoped coinage "Estavisham," in recalling Joe's pronunciation of her name as "Avisham," further invokes the general Cockney latitude with aspirates.

A more distant echo of this slang, if not the farce often associated with it, may even be heard in a very different passage of evocative solemnity in *Little Dorrit*. In the famous description of a radiant and rayed sunset spreading over London like a "crown of thorns" transmuted to an aureole, or "glory," Mrs. Clennam is pictured leading Amy Dorrit through streets suddenly calmed from the day's traffic, streets where "the worry of the day had almost worried itself out, and few but themselves were hurried" (2.31.862). As everywhere in Dickensian description, and in this case through a homophonic ambivalence, the outer is the sign of the inner, here evening quiescence of mental relaxation, hurry of spiritual vexation. To evoke this, the tempo of reading seems itself thematized. As the collocation "were hurried" collapses toward—if not quite into—the rushed or slurred disyllable "w(h)urried," the anxious pace of the protagonists seems obliquely reinscribed into the phonemically activated subtext of internal rhyme ("worry"/"hurry"). Where another writer might have written simply "few but themselves hurried," Dickens has by transegmental maneuvering (or good fortune) verged upon the lax enunciation of a Cockney dropped *h* at the syncopated matrix of an anything but humorous moment in a heightened melodramatic panorama. This is not comedy, and in no way would it directly measure an incursion of Cockney slang—or the satire thereof—into Dickensian rhetorical practice in his own narrative voice. Yet both Dickens's parodic slurrings and his melodramatic elisions together share a common intertextual backdrop. This is that popular journalistic mode of sound play that may well have heightened the awareness of his Victorian audience to phonological aberrations – or the chance of such – falling well this side of overt puns.

Alphabedding

We have, so far, ranged between that potential breakdown in lexical segmentation under syntactic pressure which is always latent in the narrative "voice" (whether Pip's or his author's) and those less *textually* unsettling effects which, though based on the same tension between lexicon and sequential enunciation, are still readily naturalized as the mere transcription in dialogue of a given character's slips and eccentricities. In *Our Mutual Friend* such phonogrammatic slippages, between words as well as within a single lexical boundary, again gather particular weight and force around the illiteracy of a single character, Mr. Boffin, and the farcical expertise of his tutelary minion, Mr. Silas Wegg. Coming into a fortune, Mr. Boffin has decided to compensate himself for the deficiencies of his education by purchasing at once the two functions of literacy: both a secretary for writing and a "literary man" for reading. In Boffin's attempt to explain to Wegg where his new money comes from, a mild contretemps ensues from his malapropism about the "will of a diseased governor," a phonetic stab at "deceased." Naturally enough, this prompts a question from Wegg about the sick man's fate – "Gentleman dead, sir?" – which triggers, in turn, an inappropriate expletive in Boffin's rejoinder: "Man alive, don't I tell you? A diseased governor?" (1.5.94). The intense *design* of such slips raises an issue more generic than simply linguistic. When Bakhtin charges that "Stylistics has been . . . completely deaf to dialogue," he means that it has not traditionally been able to absorb the mixed nature of reported speech, its play of private idiolects and dialects, within the overarching "voice" of the novel when conceived as a monolithic inscription, "a hermetic and self-sufficient whole, one whose elements constitute a closed system presuming nothing beyond themselves, no other utterances."[7] Two things need to be said in this regard about the Dickensian comic prose under scrutiny here. Not only does a sense of Dickensian stylistic ingenuity invade dialogue from the precincts of so-called omniscience, generating what we might call a "dialogism" between a character's slip and the textual (the authorial) motivation behind every malapropism; even within quoted speech, a single word may be seen divided against itself in a metalinguistic oscillation of alternatives. One could further argue, following Bakhtin's terms, that an unconscious pun quoted from a character models the double-voiced nature of the novel at its encompassing structural level, the word in dialogue with its own double take.

Dickens, and he is not alone among novelists in this, goes farther. In a knotty anticipation of modern linguistics, Dickens often renders morphology itself dialogic through his homophonic echoes and lexical slippages. In that last passage from *Our Mutual Friend,* for instance, he does so through a foregrounded irony of miscognition, the word "diseased" jostling both phonic and semantic paradigms at once with its unvoiced but intended double, "deceased." It is not that the alternatives are explicitly bandied about in an overt dialogue format. It is not even that Wegg mishears Boffin's word. It is rather that the word itself emerges into voice, into *parole,* by an accidental dialogic slide within the imperfect *langue* of the speaker. The slip from *c* to *s* does not take place transegmentally but, rather, within the same morpheme, the same syllable; it is nevertheless as illustrative here as Jane Eyre dialogizing her own first name with "jay in." Read as a reductio ad absurdum of the entire notion of dialogism, Boffin's intended utterance is outered as its own other to begin with. This point has a methodological corollary: as against familiar stylistics, the graphonic reading of dialogue — just as of other prose and poetry — is dialogic by definition. In such reading the phonotext is found generating its own evocalized feedback.

In that same scene from *Our Mutual Friend,* Boffin, impatient, moves on to explain how it is impossible for him to master reading at this late stage in his life. He does so in a passage carefully worked over by Dickens at the manuscript stage: "'Now, it's too late for me to begin shovelling and sifting at alphabeds and grammar-books. . . . But I want some reading — some fine bold reading, some splendid book in a gorging Lord-Mayor's Show of wollumes' (probably meaning gorgeous, but misled by association of ideas)" (1.5.94).[8] Rarely does a manuscript variant lay open so completely the laboratory of Dickens's compositional processes. Even that earlier and more purely homophonic malapropism, the horticultural rather than morphological "alphabeds" for "alphabets," seems (if I make out the changes correctly) to have been revised at the draft stage. The latter appears crossed out in favor of the former as if by "association of ideas" from the no longer dead metaphors of "shovelling and sifting." Then, too, these very metaphors are elsewhere associated with the activity of raking through the novel's symbolic dust mounds, those piles of litter, debris, and excrement that command a considerable price on the scavenger's market. In any case, Boffin's is a homophonic slip on the dentalized phonemic closeness, despite alphabetical distance, of /d/ from /t/. In literary-historical terms, Boffin's malapropism anticipates Joyce's twofold punning in *Finnegans Wake* on the collective noun of English lettering, first "allaphbed" (18.18) and then, a few lines later, "allforabit" (19.2). That last version puns, Boffin-like, on the ill-sorted bits and pieces that make up the alphabetic system, while also, with an added twist of Joycean etymological irony, capturing the synecdochic naming of the whole ("all for") by the mere "alpha" and "beta" that lead it off.

Another example from *Our Mutual Friend* moves as close as the novelist gets to the cross-lexical punning of *Punch*. Lawyer Lightwood means to be correcting Mr. Boffin about a London locale, whereas Boffin assumes him to be filling in the name of Lightwood's companion, taking "Doctors' Commons" as "Doctor Scommons" (1.8.136). The designated place is heard as a proper name in this multiple impropriety, violating the complete range of graphic signifiers at once: punctuation, capitalization, and lexical segmentation. It is the rupture of literacy by a lingual energy not unrelated, again, to Dickens's own style, for ex nihilo it generates a potential fictional character on the spot, risen from the blank crevices of the said. At the same time, this par-thenogenesis from the baffled head of Boffin is a metalinguistic joke on the elevation of a "Common(s)" to a proper noun. In the comic genealogies of Dickensian wordplay, Doctor Scommons's — true ancestor is the Lord No Zoo. He or it, Scommons the name as lapsus, is also directly akin to the brand of conundrum punning in *Punch* which happens to increase in frequency and lexical ingenuity in the early 1860s, just as Dickens was composing *Our Mutual Friend* (published serially, 1864–65). If George du Maurier's contri-butions to *Punch,* beginning in 1860 and given greatest fanfare with his collected parodies of Cockney French in "L'Onglay a Parry" (14 January 1865), converge suggestively with Dickens's staging of the confrontation of Podsnap and the "French gentleman" in *Our Mutual Friend* (1.11), then it is just as likely that other linguistic ironies in *Punch* may help to account for the increased incidence of transegmental illiteracies in this novel. One does indeed find numerous indirect precedents for Doctor S. scattered through the 1863 *Punch Almanack,* a volume appearing at the start of each publication year. In the "Answers to Conundrums" segment ("Questions, by some acci-dent, have not yet occurred to us"), we find not only the onomastic play on "Victor You-Go," himself a master of the holorhyme, but also "A weeping Will (oh!)" (3). Farther along in this number, we may well think of the mud-ling Jo from *Bleak House* in connection with the "Con by a Poor Crossing Sweeper. — Why is a birch-broom like a weeping willow? Because it's a thing as (s)weeps" (10; with the elision typographically marked). Evidence of Fran-glais punning, also depending on elision, appears two pages later, when the French drama critic is accosted by the English civil engineer who propounds that "the railway locomotive was the greatest '*succes de steam*' that he had ever known" (12). The subsequent number for 3 January 1863 offers the following example of junctural ambiguity, turning on the highbrow habit of accentuated *t*'s: "The Effect of Dining Out. – SMITH hearing JONES remark that their host BROWN talked 'like a book,' exclaimed, 'Why yes, of course he does, isn't he a tome?'" (9). Equally far from lowlife Cockney punning, there is the "Easy French Translation" of 21 February 1863: "'MON PETIT CHOU.' A Term of Endearment first addressed by *Cinderella* to her glass slipper" (73). More in the Dickensian spirit of such a one-word-into-two homophonic malapropism as Ham's "drowndead" in *David Copperfield* (3.83) is "the gentleman" in the 17 January 1863 issue of *Punch* suddenly understanding the literary cliché "the moaning of the tide" when, once arrived at Brighton, he realizes (breathily) how the "sea sighed" (29). In the *Punch Almanack* for the very year in which *Our Mutual Friend* began serialization, in fact, one of the recent series of conundrum answers that go begging for questions is a Cockney pun on "novel" itself: "The difference is merely that the one is an-ut, while the other is an-ovel" (12).

Back, then, to the textual environs of Doctor Scommons. He is misbegotten in the same chapter that begins with Mr. Boffin approaching the lone and underemployed clerk ensconced in the "dusty eyrie" of Lightwood's office. That dehumanizing noun "eyrie," for nest, lends itself to a homophonic collapse into its own preceding modifier – producing the suddenly foursyllabled portmanteau term "dustiary." This coinage not only renames the clerk's confine or keep of dust, but further – through etymological associations with the *ary* of brevi*ary* or besti*ary,* for instance – faintly evokes the product as well as the labor of transcription in the context of this very book of dust. We shall shortly return to *Our Mutual Friend* as the ironic "dustiary" of London life, concentrating finally on the lexical pulverizations that compose the unspoken matrix of the entire novel: the liturgical formula "ashes to ashes, dust to dust" as a principle of linguistics as well as of biology and economics, a principle of radical disarticulation. We shall do so, however, only after a desultory audition of related transegmental effects in those Victorian and early modern novelists who hold the place – at the literary level of what we might call "applied linguistic history" – between Dickens and Joyce.

Before this, another earlier – and prototypical – example from Dickens. Perhaps no episode in his novels, or in any novel before Joyce, mobilizes the transegmental possibilities of prose discourse more notably than does a proleptic moment in *Great Expectations*. Mobilizes them in connection not just with textual traverse but with the slippages and misshapings of the unconscious-structured-like-a-language. In a novel whose very pattern of characterization seems to play out the possibilities of dream projection, with figures like Orlick and Drummle the dark avatars of Pip's desire, the narrative discourse itself undergoes a displacement and condensation that provides a paraphonic matrix of one entire plot line. It does so in a way that not only derives as directly from *Punch* humor as anything else in Dickens but that in the process restructures such verbal farce within a context even more explicitly concerned with that difference between read and enunciated language which in its own way redoubles the textual condition itself that conveys the joke. The sequence of effects in question begins with a sight-reading of the said. There are words Pip doesn't know; but in the company of his harsh and carping wife, Joe is afraid to instruct the child too openly. Instead, he silently mouths the answers to Pip's also shaped but unspoken first question: "What's a convict?" The result is that "Joe put *his* mouth into the forms of returning such a highly elaborate answer, that I could make out nothing of it but the single word 'Pip'" (2.45).[9] In the dream logic of the novel's displaced and subterranean guilt (phonemically activated as much as is that opiated, dreamlike first-person report of Lucy Snowe in Brontë's *Villette*), this is of course one good answer in and of itself. In a manner cognate with the process of receiving the text as a whole, any text—the process, that is, of registering the visible signs of a "suppressed" articulation—Pip tries again to read the shape of Joe's lips. The question this time is about the source of the guns being fired, and the answer attempted, we later find out, is "the Hulks"—or prison ships. "At this point," however, all we are told is that "Joe greatly augmented my curiosity by taking the utmost pains to open his mouth very wide, and to put it into the form of a word that looked to me like 'sulks.'" Since this gets Pip nowhere, he finally asks Mrs. Joe, who answers gruffly "From the Hulks!"—at which point, like a Cockney riddler, Pip queries "And please what's Hulks?"—reiterating his previous misapprehension in the form of a homophonic (transegmental) pun on "What sulks?"

This isn't any longer what he *means* to ask, merely what is said at the level of the phonotext—and answered four times over in the course of the novel in the described person of Bentley Drummle, agent of Pip's unconscious retaliation against Estella. Described explicitly as "sulky" in all of his early appearances (25.225; 26.234, 237; 38.327), Drummle is the "answer" to Pip's earliest questions about criminal violence, the reification of the boy's unconscious slip of the tongue—indeed, a character described as boasting in his own right "a large awkward tongue" (25.225). On the way to Drummle's later appearance in the text, this early transegmental irony about "what-s = (h)ulks" is mediated in transit at the appearance of Pip's other brutal (and tongue-associated) counterpart, Or*lick*, after the first act of violence committed against one of Pip's enemies. Orlick has just returned to town from his bludgeoning of Mrs. Joe with the criminal's leg-iron linked by association to the guns originally fired from "the Hulks." We don't know this yet—but it is spelled out by the text, one might say, even before it is disclosed. This verbal inference takes place when—by narrative accident, as it were, but discursive stratagem—we are reminded of those earlier guns by the "mere" atmospheric fact that the "signal cannon broke upon us again, and again rolled *sulkily* along the course of the river" (15.146). By such echoes is the discourse of the unconscious kept up in this novel: the return of the transegmental repressed. Kept up—and brought up, uncannily, into the haunted present of the narrator's retrospective vantage. For "rolled sulkily" and "rolls hulkily" are separated at the phonotextual level only by the least distinction in the junctural force of a dentalized sibilant. Carried phonemically, the auditory memory does indeed break "upon us again, and again," time out of mind, mind out of time.

"The Other Side of Silence"

From *Adam Bede* forward, there is a general—and generally disregarded—sound texture in George Eliot's most expository style, let alone her dialogue. Whether "intended" by Eliot in the jovial spirit of the dramatic moment or not, certainly the context of the harvest supper in *Adam Bede* prompts a thick-tongued pun at the conclusion of a rowdy communal drinking song: "Then drink, boys, drink! / And see ye do not spill. . .For 'tis our master*'s will*" (53.564), the last a contemporary term for liquor good or bad. At the earlier inception of the book's seduction plot, textured by a more muted internal echo, there is the fateful kiss between Hetty and Arthur that recalls "Eros himself, sipping the lips of Psyche" (13.182); or there is Hetty described "like a child hugging its *toys* in the beginning of a long *toil*some journey" (15.203), a phonemic disassemblage of the lexeme itself within an image that anticipates the later "Journey in Despair" chapter. Even at the book's tragic turn we recognize Eliot's analytic ear for the "dileck" (2.60) in Adam's bitterness against Hetty's seducer, who has "been false to me, and 'ticed [an assimilative fusion for "and (end/t)ticed"] her away" (39.453). In the subsequent confrontation between Dinah and Hetty, the latter's heart is opened with a prayer that begins by invoking the deity who has seen to "the depths of all sorrow" (45.496). Well before this climactic moment, however, another, more preternatural fusion of reduplicating phonemes may eerily be heard to augment the denotative, connotative, and etymological associations of the sufferer's last name, Sorrel (the "sour" or bitter herb); I refer to the predic(a)tive undertone of a grief fated from the start of the narrative to descend upon her in her selfishness, the anticipated sound of "all sorrow" chiastically reversed, as it were, to the ominous and open-ended "sorrow 'll." In this way do words "sinnify" (18.234) in Eliot's moralized textual weave. Thus is foretold the destined grief that, by every imperative of story, *will* come, that must in one form or another have its will of her—whatever sorrow 'll also do in the long run, within Eliot's punitive economy, by way of redemption.

In *The Mill on the Floss,* George Eliot's penchant for internal echo and muted paronomasia remains very much in evidence. It is especially apparent in those moments of representational duplication when the play of signifiers is aligned with the signified of an explicitly auditory experience. Philip Wakem can deploy his own vocal harmonics, for instance, in saying that "Certain *strains* of music affect me so *strang*ely" (5.1.266). Similarly, narrative voice has earlier harmonized both vowels and consonants to evoke the heroine's response to the mill's "resolute din, the unresting motion of the great stones, giving her a dim delicious awe at the presence of an uncontrollable force" (1.4.26). The verbal shape of "resolute" echoes against its approximate synonym in "unresting," while the adjective "great," modifying the rumbling of the stones, reverberates by a kind of anti-pun with the *grating* which it transmutes into solemnity, a transformation framed by the consonantal gentling of "din" into "dim." The climactic phrase "dim delicious awe," beyond its frontal alliteration, may also borrow some of its quiet force from the phantom transegmental gemination of an unwritten *d* in the aural ambivalence of "dim(me*d*) *d*elicious awe."

Middlemarch continues Eliot's experiments with internal echo and its thematizations. At one point the narrator quotes Shakespeare's "to hear with eyes" sonnet (27.183) as a prototype for the divinization of another's unsaid longing. This paradoxical image provides the kind of auditory metaphor for intuition established earlier with the famous account of that unworkable hypersensitivity which would cause us to "die of that roar which lies on the other side of silence" (20.135). Once alerted to the proliferated sound play of Eliot's prose, one may come to suspect that the complex paronomasia, reversing and overrunning itself, of such a line as "di(e) . . . li(e)s . . . sid(e) . . . sil(e —)," in its crossing of chiasmus with alliteration, may not simply be stationed to instance a kind of textual hearing-with-eyes. It may further be designed, at a metanarrative level, to model the whole discursive logic of internal echo, recurrence, and repetition-within-variation: as the linguistic equivalent of those filamented layerings of felt correspondence in the represented world of the novel, those hidden patterns and detonating convergences too intense for direct apprehension. Echoism and phonemic mutation in *Middlemarch* can be particularly striking in passages of negative characterization or satire, as in the paragraph summarizing Dorothea's marital entrapment after the honeymoon in Rome, where a transegmental drift serves momentarily to echo, at the semantic level as well this time, the metaphoric trap of the heroine's entire marital life. Dorothea finds herself submitting to "a moral imprisonment which made itself one with"—was, in other words, repeated in—"the chill, colorless, *nar*rowed landscape" (28.189). Only for a moment, and only in (phonemic) passing, Eliot has named that insidious ensnarement which is the result of all psychic narrowness in this novel.

A later passage, more satiric than melancholy, orchestrates just as fully what we might call the "aural subtext"—the phonotext—of Eliot's patterned discourse, its auditing of the phonemic rumble on the underside of silent script. Its transegmental effect offers, in fact, the perfect occasion for recasting its phonotextual dynamic in terms familiar from the most influential of earlier stylistic commentaries on this novel in the general context of prose fiction and its poetics. In "Fiction and the 'Analogical Matrix,'" Mark Schorer discusses the tendency for subdued or dead metaphors in Eliot, as in both Jane Austen and Emily Brontë before her, to draw strength from an underlying figurative network that highlights them by alignment with others of their kind. Among the many such figural filiations in *Middlemarch,* Schorer suggests, are those that accumulate to the proposition "Consciousness is a stream."[10] Metaphors of current, depth, flow, channeling, muddying, and so forth, cohere within this pattern, under an analytic scrutiny that is a clear Anglo-American forerunner to the operation of the "matrix" in Riffaterre's semiotics. The ordinarily neutralized or buried metaphor in Schorer's treatment, animated by a larger figural context, may in Riffaterre's later vocabulary be read as the "paragram" of such an unsaid cliché: in the particular instance at hand, of "life is like a river." Anticipating a modernist insistence on the "stream" of consciousness—even a poststructuralist inscription of such process in the metonymical cascade of syntax—such figuration operates, in the following description of Rosamond Vincy, within the recast transegmental semiotics of a matrix/"paraphone" structure: "Shallow natures *dream* of an easy sway over the emotions of others, trusting implicitly in their own petty magic to turn the deepest *streams*" (76.536). The internal echo is so close that it renders the first phrase proleptic, at least in retrospect. This late in the novel, no sooner does the dead metaphor "shallow" surface from its "analogical matrix" than its associations wash across the plural inflection of "nature*s*" to generate, however subliminally or subvocally, the suddenly metaphoric "stream" out of the sibilant ligature with "dream." The metaphor thus precipitated is semantically outlawed as anything but the paradigmatic alternative and accusatory other to the vanity of Rosamond's stagnant dreaming—a term, in other words, inoperable except as anti-pun, or antiphonal variant. Yet such a metaphor nonetheless raises the daunting specter of those "deepest *streams*" that get phonically deepened in the subsequent phrase—in all their implied dominion over Rosamond's desire to reroute them. Such transegmental irony, as it cuts up and across words, can thus cut both ways. Whereas in Dorothea's case her conjugal immurement may be as pitiably snaring as it is narrowing, a daydreaming nature as "shallow" as Rosamond's is only mocked rather than commiserated in being momentarily misread as powerfully "streaming."

With Eliot's style working, in such undercurrents, with and against the apparent contour of script—its surface rippled with euphonic emphases above and beyond the manifest expository flow, its phonotext given to drifts as well as echoes of sound—her novels provide a sustained test case for a graphonic reading of prose fiction. As we have seen by now, however, this contrapuntal reading is aural rather than oral and is thrown into relief by such a very different stance toward literacy in action as that demonstrated by her early hero Adam Bede. In direct proportion to his identification with the characters in the Bible about whom he reads, to his phenomenological engagement with the "world" of the text, his own silent enunciation is lifted through lip movement toward voice. When he is caught up by that sacred text which provides him at once with "history, biography, and poetry," there are passages, we are told, where "his lips moved in semi-articulation—it was when he came to a speech that he could fancy himself uttering, such as Samuel's dying speech to the people" (51.542). As if his marginal literacy returns him to that state—and stage—of cultural transition from oral to silent reading discussed in the Prologue, Adam reverts to an epoch when all narrative was theatricalized, declamatory. The drama of Eliot's narrative texture, of course, is of a different order, its articulations repressed rather than partial, sub- rather than semi-vocalized.

At the same time, the whole question of articulation can be threaded back into the thematic of Eliot's fiction as part of the dramatic irony of characterization. This is made plain, for instance, amid the continuing phonic experiments of Eliot's prose, by the treatment of Grandcourt's speech defects in *Daniel Deronda,* the "broken discourse" and "toneless drawl" of his emotionally impaired mutter, with its "languid inarticulate sound" (29.362). Grandcourt's not even clenched, merely desiccated, inner speech surfaces in measured pauses and blanks, an effete depreciation of all converse that persists at one point until he "ceased his slow delivery of sentences" (30.393). Within a page we hear again of the resumption of "his low voice" (30.394). Between these two phrasings, taken as "languid articulations" in the slack spirit of the man himself, emerges the transegmental irony that renders the very specification of his utterance redundant, "his slow delivery" inevitably characterized by "his (s)low" speech. (In the self-exampling nature of this flaccid articulation, Grandcourt is the reverse counterpart of the forthright Dorothea in *Middlemarch,* who attempted to speak up to her husband in "hard distinct syllables" [20.139], as hard as those required by the enunciation of that first dental juncture.) Grandcourt's penmanship, too, is of a piece with his aristocratic "drawling," for when he deigned to write, he *"scrawled with ease"*

(25.332) in an "indistinct handwriting" as uninvigorated as his monotone. According to a subsequent description, the "little pauses and refined drawlings" (27.347) of that monotonous talk are described, as with the clipped phrasing from *Middlemarch* just above, so that an extreme articulation — this time contrary to the enunciation described — is necessary on the reader's part to mark the juncture between those last two words. If we submit to this textual impedance and its attendant labors, we have in other words momentarily redeemed ourselves from the charge of slackness leveled against the villain in the phrasing at issue. In this way, his utterance and inscription are not simply rendered as the antithesis of the narrative's *flow;* they set up a contrapuntal drama in our own processing of the phonotext. At the same time, it is just as likely that the quick pace of our own reading will generate elsewhere an opposite, if related, irony against the grain of script. In Grandcourt's tired sketch for Gwendolen of his previous life, we hear his tedium and torpor indicated (and transegmentally indicted) across the terrain of his phrases — if, that is, we respond to his manner in satiric kind this time, with anything less than a hyper-articulation in our own silent voicing: "His answers to her lively questions about what he had seen and done in his life, *bore d*rawling very well" (29.371).

Polarized by Grandcourt, Gwendolen's neurotic inwardness is charted in part by similar microlinguistic registrations, description burdened by the unsaid: "Hers was one of the natures in which exultation inevitably carries an infusion of dread ready to *curdle* and *declare* itself" (31.404). Not only do the compound verbs "curdle" and "declare" seem to implicate each other by an almost anagrammatic logic of consonants, but the "infusion of dread" that precipitates this reaction presses upon the phrase of latency, "ready to"; by an overlapping internal echo, it thus generates a shudder of redundancy bursting the seams of sequence — "infusion of drea*d ready*." Coming even closer to a fully activated lexical mutation through transegmental drift is a clause like "Gwendolen's will had seemed imperious in its small girlish sway" (35.477). The expected idiom "in its small (girlish) way" — or, alternately, "in its (small) girlish ways" — almost manages to assert itself by an (imperfect) elision between *sh* and *s* in "girli*sh s*way," a tongue-twist of phrase that does not quite come off. It is just this sway that is balked by Grandcourt's willful negations of desire; at which point consciousness turns further inward, perverse, and this novel concerned with "the language in which we think" (19.247) begins to read like its streaming transliteration.

Climaxing in this very manner the fateful story of Gwendolen and Grandcourt, there is a distracting lexical collapse in Gwendolen's trembling account of his drowning, a narrative elicited from her by Deronda's sympathetic hearing of her plight. Recalling the virtually mortal panic that led to her failure to save Grandcourt, Gwendolen says hauntedly, in an accent and cadence not her own: "I had stept into a boat, and my life was a sailing and sailing away—gliding on and no help—always into solitude with *him,* away from deliverance" (56.760). Judith Wilt has argued persuasively that the italicized male pronoun refers not to Grandcourt alone, the obvious antecedent, but to memories of the abusive stepfather whose entrapping presence Gwendolen had just a moment before been comparing, in effect, to Grandcourt's.[11] This is not the only odd double inflection in the passage. Unless its predicate is taken to include a compound and redundant substantive, the strange wording of "my life was a sailing and sailing away" encourages the unsettling shift from gerund to participle—from the noun phrase "a sailing" to the adjectival form "a(-)sailing." This probable phrasing, though, is neither colloquially convincing in Gwendolen's dialogue nor grammatically stable even as an intrusive rhetorical heightening. It makes sense, it *reads,* only as a dislocated verbal symptom of a traumatic disturbance. It is thus a phrasing in two ways retrogressive: temporally (as a returning memory) and segmentally (as a junctural reflex, one word turned back upon its predecessor). My life, Gwendolen means to say in at least every sense but the lexical, was "assailing and sailing away," at once punishing and vanishing, both an assault upon and a desertion of desire. The death of the violating male was her only way out, her only way back.

In a very different fashion, in *Jude the Obscure,* an idiomatic compound of article plus verbal form inscribes—writes, that is, though at the level of the phonotext alone—an equally devastating irony in the last conversation, before his suicide, between Sue Bridehead and her prematurely morbid teenage "stepson," nicknamed "Father Time." Though she has just explained to him that they will soon have yet another mouth to feed, she remains, in a typifying irony, too prudish to explain further that this has not come about entirely by free choice. The narrator having recently mentioned that the boy "had learned to use the Wessex tongue quite naturally by now" (5.7.246), we are doubly alert to such densities and accidents in his speech as noted with Joseph's extreme Yorkshire dialect in *Wuthering Heights.* Thinking that it is a deliberate cruelty on Sue's part to increase the family misery with another hungry being, the boy groans out, "O God, mother, you've never a-sent for another" (6.2.264), meaning, of course, that she "should never have" voluntarily "sent for" a new child. At the subtextual level of ironic malapropism, however, his objection to her "assent" scores against her entire life with Jude, with whom she has grudgingly succumbed to sexual intimacy in order to keep him from returning to his first wife, the boy's own mother.

"The Vulgarization of Our Tongue"

Farther from Dickens than Hardy or even George Eliot in the spectrum of Victorian novelists, at the opposite pole from a popular and fluent narrative style, falls the mannerist prose of George Meredith. From the dialect of minor lower-class characters to the most orotund reaches of the narrative voice, transegmental thickenings inflect his text and complicate its phonemic reading. The titular hero of his first novel, *The Ordeal of Richard Feverel*, anxious about detection after a rick-burning episode, casts his adolescent fears into paronomasia: "I wish you hadn't given them the *scent, though*. I like to look inno*cent*" (4.37) – and this in a chapter whose title, "Arson," seems to pun on his own status, Our Son, as scion of an ancestral line. Even his former nurse, Mrs. Berry, speaks with overlapping internal rhyme in bemoaning women's lot: "The best of women's too soft. . .more's *our sor*row" (37.413), where the lament sets in even before the plural pronoun has been traversed. At the very center of the novel, the parodistic evocation of love on the wing gathers to a head in the image of Richard on his wedding day bursting in his pride like "a cock-robin in the dress of a gentleman, big joy *swelling* out his chest" (29.289; my emphasis). A sentence later, in a deliberate twist of idiom, the transegmental capper: "All *is s*well" – redolent of the Cockney joke from *Punch* "All's swell that ends swell" (see note 6). Meredith's high-toned verbosities often draw strength from a secret affiliation with the "undercraft" of the under-classes, his humor sociolectic as well as lexical. In *The Egoist,* the learned avocational linguist, Dr. Middleton, brings this to a quirky focus in his split verbal personality, delighting in Cockney puns while fortifying the bastions of "correct" enunciation. Making fun of his daughter's stumbling effort to warn him of a rift between herself and her intended, Dr. Middleton takes only pedantic verbal heed of Clara's cryptic "We have differences" when followed by her elliptical "He and I – I accuse myself," a truncated phrasing in which the second "I" has at last, and at least, managed to assert itself free of the unwanted coupling. But Dr. Middleton hears only sloppy speech: "And let me direct you, for the next occasion when you shall bring the vowels I and A, in verbally detached letters, into collision, that you do not fill the hiatus with so pronounced a Y. It is the vulgarization of our tongue," he concludes in a metalinguistic travesty, "of which I y-accuse you" (19.149). As Robert Martin Adams glosses this moment in his edition of the novel, "Where she speaks her heart, he hears only phonemes" (149). Elsewhere, however, Dr. Middleton shows himself a master of that transegmental punning designed to tamper with hiatus and coerce new junctures. Alluding to the comic sayings of "Joe Miller's jest book," an earlier Victorian compendium of low wit, Sir

Willoughby's phrase "Joe Millerisms" is revised by Dr. Middleton, in a homophonic jostle reminiscent of Dickens's "Doctor Scommons," to the more Irish sounding "O'Millerisms" (29.247; Meredith's emphasis). Hierarchy, patriarchy, can contain the "vulgate" only when it is voluntarily deployed, an ironic intertext rather than an accidental lapse induced, for instance, by female anxiety in the face, and grip, of male privilege. But while Dr. Middleton is hoist on his own petard of preciosity, Meredith has it both ways.

The convolution of Meredith's prose, with its simultaneous tendency toward the dense and the rarefied, is never more unremittingly worked in its wit than in the late novel *Diana of the Crossways* (1885). This is, in fact, the story of a female novelist of extraordinary stylistic dexterity and finesse, whose style often sounds indistinguishable from Meredith's own. It is a style unabashedly given to the ironic possibilities of internal echo, as with the long *u* sound in the first description of the heroine's regrettable husband, Warwick, portrayed with "eyes of that half cloud and bl*ue*, which make the kind of *hue*less grey, and are chiefly striking in an authoritative stare" (6.60). The *h* of "hueless" is certainly weak enough to be folded into what amounts to a chiastic pattern of assonance and alliteration, even as the transegmental adhesion from the consonant in "o*f*" creates a homophonic alternative in "*v*iewless grey," thus anticipating the blank stare of his irresponsive authority. The husband of the other heroine in the novel, Diana's friend Emma, also comes in for a satire turning on the play of a single phoneme, in a passage augmented by Meredith in revision. In a long speech of remorse over his infidelity, Sir Lukin's "All I can do is to pray" is preceded by three sentences of expletive added at the manuscript stage, the last and nearest being the self-accusatory "A Common donkey compared to her!" (26.247).[12] In the immediate vicinity of "donkey," the term "pray" is contaminated by that all but onomatopoetic sound called "braying," an antiphone of subliminal derision. Of the heroine, Diana, upon her reentry into society, we hear that she "gathered its current topics and scattered her arrowy phrases" (39.369). Beyond the partial rhyme of "gathered" and its antithetical "scattered," there is the cross-lexical (and entirely pertinent) hint of *rare* in "he*r arr*owy phrases." We shall find one such phrase alluded to shortly in a comment on her suitor, Redwood, a reticent man warmed in his matrimonial hopes by recalling how Diana "had once in his hearing derided the unpleasant hiss of the ungainly English matron's title of Mrs." (41.386)—as if indeed it were spelled "Miss-hiss." The heroine's own maiden name comes under fire as well when attempts are made to patronize her with it. Rousing her strength for a political struggle in the midst of personal hardship, Diana rejects the sympathetic and conciliatory nickname "Tony," based on her middle name, Antonia. In reaction, she forges an obscure pun on the noun "atony," for languor, want of tone, enervation—presumably in this context for a sense of being out of sympathy, out of patience, finally out of tune with those who would curtail her passion: "Tony me no Tonies; I am *atony* to such whimpering business now we are in the van of the struggle" (29.290); Meredith's emphasis). With its play on lexical if not vowel "hiatus," such rebarbative punning is worthy of Dr. Middleton in *The Egoist*, especially since her "arrowy" jest comes to an even sharper point if and when one knows that "atony" is not only pronounced with a short *o*, rather than the long *o* of the unsaid antiphrase "a Tony," but that it has a specifically linguistic denotation as well. Referring as it does to a lack of syllabic stress, the term "atony" thus becomes a self-illustrative near-homophone of the article plus proper noun. A similar lexical maneuver operates against the textual grain — but very much in keeping with the metaphoric gist — of a climactic phrase from Meredith's "Ode on the Comic Spirit": "the music of the meaning of Accord." Where harmonized meaning is figured as music, the resulting "accord" gets figured at the same time in lexical terms as "a chord," a dyadic phrase in its own right that picks up the earlier, twice-reiterated (anapestic) beat of article plus noun. This is the "music of the meaning" of any prose, too, that is attuned to textuality in its phonic as well as graphic — its graphonic — overtones.

"Shadow and Adamant"

We are concerned here with the bedrock of syntax under alleviation by the shadow play of the lexicon. But not all style invites phonemic reading in this way. There are only rare moments in Henry James, for instance, when the sound shape of words is recruited for something like an overt rhetorical effect. The explicit mention of a "droll" sound in *The Ambassadors* seems to give special point to a phonemic biplay verging on the anagrammatic as well as chiastic form, when "with a sound half-*dolor*ous, half-*droll* and all *v*ague and equi*v*ocal, Chad buried his face" (11.1.288). The Janus-like pattern by which "dolor" and "drollery" mutually reconstitute each other at the level of the signifier adds verbal texture to the tragicomic dimensions of the scene. For the most part, however, James is not likely to roll words around on his tongue so much as thoughts — or, at least, not phonemic clusters so much as diction. His shadows and adumbrations are largely semantic, his primary means syntactic. Even a Jamesian variant of the transegmental syllabic effect is likely to be more directly cerebral — or metaphysical — than those in George Eliot, for example. When Brydon in *The Jolly Corner* is brought face-to-face with the ghost of his former self, his recoil, his instinctual disavowal, is phonotextually mediated. The ghost moves his hands away from his face to reveal a "bared identity . . . too hideous as *his*" (476; James's emphasis). With the aspirate itself a ghostly function, phantasmal but no less accusatory, the idiomatic "as is" is thereby cross-lexically asserted as the surfacing of a repressed matrix, through an elision that actually posits and predicates the protagonist's spectral existence in the Other.

On the subject of the actual death moment, rather than its supernal afterimages, the drifting phoneme may often mark a mortal transgression as well. Death scenes in the Victorian and modern novel, with their complex recruitment of fictive tropology, their sheer *style* on the verge of the unevidenced, are quite likely to exert a peculiar torsion on the combinatory logic of word sequence.[13] Jude the Obscure's penultimate despairing utterance, "And I here" (6.11.320), is a declaration of presence that turns to a self-willed imperative of absence, of death, across the transegmental slide of "And die here." Without such a manifest lexical regrouping of sound clusters, there is still a peculiar densening and interplay of syllabic matter in certain renderings by Conrad of the death moment. When the helmsman in *Heart of Darkness* is fatally speared through the chest, "the luster of inquiring glance faded swiftly into vacant glassiness" (47). Conrad's phrasing produces a paronomastic gradience that suggests fatal blankness as merely a hairbreadth away from the stare of life, and this even at the textual surface – as if death were the transition precipitated by the "lance" hiding in the elided noun of "inquiring glance." After the murder of Verloc in *The Secret Agent,* when one of the knife thrusts administered by his wife at last finds its lethal opening in the rib cage, the narrator stands back for a generalization about such a fate that is also a roulette spin of contingent syllabification: "Hazard has such accuracies" (11.212). In Conrad's most famous death scene, again from *Heart of Darkness,* the last half-dozen syllables of Kurtz's death gasp are "The horror! The horror!" (71). With all the narrator's emphasis on Kurtz's voice, the incarnate presence of the man in his portentous enunciations, their mystery and unaccountable force, and indeed given the narrator's later lie to Kurtz's unnamed Intended that "the last word he pronounced was – your name" (79), we may well hear Kurtz's last utterance phonemically displaced into a continuous thought: "The whore or the horror!" In the now-indistinguishable alternatives of desire and depletion, and with all seductive idealism prostituted for power, this hearing would also figure the doubling of Kurtz's jungle consort with the deluded mourner back home. Such is the potential "accuracy" of a phonic "hazard."

Ford Madox Ford is certainly not what one would call a syllabic or phonemic stylist, and yet the inevitable elisions of the English language can occasionally play into his hands. In *The Good Soldier,* the bloodless narrator, Dowell, describes his own role in relation to his ailing wife as that of a "sedulous, strained nurse" (8), where the very notion of professional qualification in the more familiar adjective, "trained," is an anti-pun written off by the prolonged tedious fact of his makeshift responsibilities. By contrast,

E. M. Forster is frequently inclined to a euphonic, though often ironic, chiming of syllables, even in his nonfictional prose. He writes in *Aspects of the Novel,* for instance, about those "divings into and dividings of personality" (112) that characterize "fantasy." Divided from within, the first participle is wedged open into the name of the very operation that produces it. This is the poetic in Forster's prose, his plastic way with diction. He, in fact, defines the poetic impulse in this broad sense in his 1907 novel, *The Longest Journey,* where in a self-exampling fusion of syllabic matter he writes of "the union of shadow *and ad*amant that men call poetry" (15.154). The bond of the ferrous and the ephemeral is held there in the blended emphasis that makes the second noun a kind of phonemic portmanteau, telescoping material from both the preceding noun and the conjunction that yokes them. A similar syllabic realignment of the conjunction "and" appears in *Howards End* as the passing shadow of a not quite so adamant transegmental meld. Margaret Schlegel is coming to recognize the gap between classes; though culture has "worked" for her, "during the last few weeks she had doubted whether it humanized the majority, *so wide and so widening* is the gulf that stretches between the natural and the philosophical man" (14.115; my emphasis). A syntactic increment seems calibrated there to evoke a signified increase. In a transegmental drift, that is, the disyllabic sequence "*wide and*" offers the first partial enunciation of the participle "*widen*ing" to follow. If we borrow the phrase "the union of shadow and adamant" to characterize such phonological blendings — with the scripted words holding the place of the adamant, the inalterable, while spectral phonemes seem to play across their surface and blur their boundaries — then the union of the inscribed vocable and its aural equivocation, of text and silent enunciation, lends Forster's definition of poetry a morphophonemic as well as a metaphysical cast. Or to borrow from Conrad again, it might be said that in the poetry of prose "hazard has such accuracies."

Forster as prose poet is of course outstripped, among his great contemporaries, by Lawrence as well as by Joyce and Woolf. In a passage explicitly devoted to the "so wide and so widening" play of concentric rings on the surface of water, Lawrence's own prose achieves a rippling overlap of phonemes in the transegmental mode. In the famous "Mooney" chapter of *Women in Love,* the reflection of the moon on the water, imaged as a "ragged rose," is repeatedly shattered. As its image reintegrates itself at the center, "the rays were hastening *in in* thin lines" (19.239), where the threefold repetition of "in" as or within a syllable is matched by the transegmental blur of "*were has*tening." Telescoped there by an elision of the *h* (recalling the Jamesian "as [h]is") is the phantom aftertone, the phonic wake, of the verb "race" as well as an auditory radiation of "rays." Similarly, amid the massive (and arguably visible as well as audible) alliteration in the immediately preceding image of the scattered moon, we note the *fl* alliteration transforming itself into something more like the anagrammatic diphone of Saussure:

> *fl*ying asunder in *fl*akes of white and dangerous *fi*re. Rapidly, like white birds, the *fi*res all broken rose across the pond, *fl*eeing in clamorous con*fu*sion, battling with the *fl*ock of dark waves that were *fo*rcing their way in. The *fu*rtherest waves *of l*ight, *fl*eeing out, seemed clamouring against the shore for escape.
>
> (19.239; my emphasis)

The recurrently successive but suddenly noncontiguous pair of letters actually bridges a lexical gap in the penultimate italicized instance: to form—by liaison rather than elision this time, and in anticipation of "fleeing"—the phrase "*of light.*" At this level of phonotextual pressure, there lies between *The Old Curiosity Shop* and *Women in Love* no wider a gap than the lexical one their own phonemes are able to overleap.

For all the sporadic modernist activity in the way of transegmental drifts, it may still be that no single text before Joyce's *Ulysses* brings lexical dispersion into such direct thematic consideration as does Dickens's *Our Mutual Friend,* as we had begun to see. There is, though, a curiously Dickensian moment early in the first act of Oscar Wilde's *The Importance of Being Earnest* that should—with its harking back to the *Punch*-style alphabetic humor of Thackeray as well—serve to route us round again for a final look at the "shovelling and sifting at alphabeds" in Dickens's last completed novel. When Ernest Worthing attempts to reveal that his name is really "Jack," his friend Algernon six times objects, in as many sentences, that "Ernest" is his incontrovertible essence. "It's on your cards," he adds, in a definitive last stroke. "Here is one of them . . . Mr. Ernest Worthing, B. 4, The Albany." As part of a theatrical phonotext, the "B. 4" can well be heard by an audience as a phonetic rebus for that time "before" the present reversal, that time when Jack's pseudonym was still in service. In this way, Wilde's designation of the Room of One's Other reminds us by homophonic irony that the past efficacy of a ruse never survives the moment of its exposure.

Dickens's Dustiary Revisited

The *New Yorker* cartoonist who pictured a wide-eyed Dickens in profile on a publike barstool, under hanging beer tankards and over the caption "Dickens' First Encounter with a Martini," looking bemused at the bartender's question "Olive or twist?" (27 September 1987) may well have thought he was making his own kind of joke, not Dickens's. In the context of this chapter, however, Boz's double take of authorial recognition would be itself twofold, on grounds not only of storytelling but of punning, of naming and wording together. We left off our initial investigation of *Our Mutual Friend* with the slurring of "dusty eyrie" into "dustiary." With this symbolically freighted collapse in mind, a word more is in order about Victorian wordplay outside the precincts of major fiction, especially about the contemporaneous ambience of Cockney humor. In 1865, during the second and final year of the serialization of *Our Mutual Friend,* the 28 January number of *Punch* ran "A Cockney's Epitaph," a perfect epitome of the thematized accidents to which transegmental malapropism can lead. Facilitated by both the dropped *h* phenomenon and the junctural slippage of *n* before vowels, a single sliding consonant guides the irony along a syntactic arc representing life's temporal duration: "Think! 'From the cradle to the grave!' my brother, / A nurse take you from one, an 'earse to the t'other." This exceeds the linguistic bounds of the *Punch* epitaph for the Cockney cook, "Peace to his hashes," for instance, which is simply a pun on a single butchered lexeme. In the rhyming epitaph above, the segmental ambiguity between *an nurse* and *an hearse* — almost a textbook example, beyond Cockneyism per se, of what linguists debate as the proper disambiguation of juncture, as in "a name" versus "an aim" — involves a syntactic conundrum at the smallest compass, a question of when exactly one word cedes to its successor.

Nearer yet to the thematic material of *Our Mutual Friend,* and far enough back in time to be a conceivable influence on Dickens's comic style, is a Cockney music hall song of the sort we know the young Dickens to have won approval from his father by performing.[14] Singer Robert Glindon (1799–1866) included among the ditties that made his reputation a song called (no less) "The Literary Dustman," published for the first time in 1832.[15] Boffin's eagerness to become not only the "Golden Dustman" (in the titles to chapters 4 and 5 of book 3) but a literary one as well (if not literate, and if only by proxy) lend special prophetic point to this earlier composition, where the speaker boasts a "liberal *hedication*" (his emphasis on the Cockney pun), learning "all my letters" from a "turnpike man," and finds it odd — "a co-in-side-ance queer" — that the name of Adam, who "vos the fust man," is also his own, "the fust of Dustmen!" Here is Wegg's semiliterate braggadocio, as Dickens will separate it off from Boffin in their symbiosis of ambition. Here, too, is even the sense of a given name whose "coincidence" invites speculation (though Wegg-of-the-wooden-leg will later refuse to speculate on his). In addition, by that associative logic of syllabically apt malapropism which characterizes much of the humor in early Thackeray or *Punch,* as well as that of Wegg later, the song-text's italicized "*hedication,*" along with the typographically inflected "co-in-side-ance" in the chorus, may be said to put, respectively, the head ("hed") back in learning and the adjacency ("side" by "side") back in fortuitous convergence. Dickens's "drowndead" is only one of many later counterparts.

In returning to similar lexical disintegrations in the "dustiary" of *Our Mutual Friend,* then, we can examine them further as part of a deliberate congeries of social fragmentation and splintered utterance, the shavings and leavings of a rendered empire in decline. As a matter of fact, the ironies of "dust" and debris in the novel are closely concentrated around the linguistic comedy between Boffin and Wegg in the precincts of the dust mounds themselves. Such effects are associated there, in part, with Wegg's bodily dismemberment, his own limb cast off into a circuit of waste and reclamation. In the chapter wryly titled "Mr. Wegg Looks After Himself" (1.7)—meaning both the idiomatic "looks out for himself" and, more literally, "goes in search of his lost limb"—a manuscript addition clarifies a similar pun: "I shouldn't like to be what I may call dispersed, a part of me here, a part of me there, but should wish to collect myself like a genteel person" (1.7.127). Dickens had originally stopped the joke at *collect myself* but pressed it further into affectation with "like a genteel person" above the line.[16] This works to underscore the idiomatic connotation of "collectedness" as an air of composure, while highlighting all the more by contrast the starkly literal sense of attempted recomposition of Wegg's very body through the recovery of the disarticulated member.

Mr. Wegg, of the amputated leg, sells it to Venus, the "articulator of human bones" (1.7.128), and when he is later able to arrange the sale of his own verbal articulation to the inheritor of dust, Mr. Boffin, he wants to use the money he gets in return for his words to rearticulate his body with the missing leg. This is money symbolically unburied, in turn, from the same partly fecal heaps that are passed on to Boffin in the Harmon will and in which another version of that will is rumored to be buried. Remarkably interknit in their symbolic complicity, these details can be seen to triangulate with one another as follows: partly organic debris linked with money (filthy lucre) along one axis, money with language (ill-gotten literary gain) along another, and language with organicism and anatomy ("articulation") and its breakdown along the third.[17] Formed here is in fact a grid isomorphic, as we will further see, with that triumvirate in the so-called human sciences—biology, economics, and linguistics—that is so crucial for Foucault's sense of the nineteenth-century "Sciences of Man."

Elaborating the axis of filth and money in *Our Mutual Friend* is a set piece that performs its satire not only by invoking shredded paper as legal tender but by involving as well the additional disintegration of words inscribed upon another kind of paper currency known as text. In a passage augmented by several manuscript insertions (as italicized), Dickens is describing the air of London streets thick with litter:

> That mysterious paper currency which circulates in London when the
> wind blows, gyrated here and there and everywhere. Whence can it

come, whither can it go? It hangs on every bush, flutters in every tree, *is caught flying by the electric wires,* haunts every enclosure, *drinks at every pump, cowers at every grating,* shudders upon every plot of grass, seeks rest in vain behind the legions of iron rails.

(1.12.191)

The second two additions contribute to the personification of this flying detritus, and together the three inserted verb phrases, along with the five others in series, accumulate with the inevitability of the collected and distributed debris they portray. The metaphor that transforms this whirling matter into "paper currency," into the circulating currents of an economic model of free exchange, is the most explicit mention in the novel of that waste which *is* money, rather than just of the scene of heaped incidental wealth (the mounds). Framing this paragraph is a refrain that links the "paper currency" more explicitly yet with the euphemistically named "dust" mounds. "The grating wind sawed rather than blew; and as it sawed, the sawdust whirled about the sawpit. Every street was a sawpit," and so on. Then, right after this paragraph about "currency" as the dusty leavings of a violent wind, we read again: "The wind sawed, and the sawdust whirled." Thus routinely repeated, the internal echo of the monosyllabic "sawed" against its homophonic extension into "sawdust" works to suggest the latter as building upon an elided, sawed-off, shaved-down, or otherwise disintegrated version of the former — "sawdust" thereby emerging as the transegmental double of "sawed dust." Anthropologist Mary Douglas has argued that the cultural concept of "dirt" should be taken to cover not just residue but the residuum of all categorization, less refuse or leftover than that which is conceptually refused by a given society.[18] In this sense, Dickens's symbolic dirt, his mounded and mounting dust, figures ultimately the residualization of the human organism itself — in the liturgically familiar ashes and dust that survive the vacated life of the body. When, in turn, language falls to pieces into an association with dirt and money, not only is its material basis pulverized but its communal function is excluded, escaping that categorization known as normative linguistics. The stretch of narrative prose we have been reading is far tamer in its verbal demolition than more drastic collapses elsewhere, of course. Yet the phonemic splintering of a lexeme here — the frictional erosion at the mutual border of the implied matrix phrase "sawed dust" — does give evidence of morphology, of structure itself, caught on the trace of its own disintegration, however much domesticated in this case by the social consensus of an idiomatic contraction.

This same degenerative logic continues to pursue and traverse the linked symbols of Dickens's novel. If dirt is extraneous, if language reverts to dust and dirt, or at least to molecular leavings, and if other, more familiar kinds of dust are designated as refuse even while being returned to circulation for their exchange value as currency, and, further, if anatomical debris (such as a superfluous limb) is the stuff of rearticulation for profit—then the question arises whether articulation in the other sense, as language, is also part of that monetary nexus analyzed by economics. Wegg would be the first to hope so, as he designs to sell his words. And Boffin would seem to think so as well, given his eccentric financial metaphor on the subject of his marginal familiarity with the English alphabet: "I don't mean to say but what if you showed me a B, I could so far give you change for it, as to answer Boffin" (1.5.94). Words beginning with *b* are for Boffin a paradigm that can be shaken down, separated, made to pay. Like economics, linguistics concerns a system of exchange, as indeed do the life cycles of biology. The body, money, and language—in Foucault's terms, biology, value theory, and philology (organic science, economics, linguistics)—thus converge upon Wegg the reader-for-pay in his association with Mr. Venus, the corporeal articulator. It is in the latter's shop, too, that the disarticulated limbs and organs of his inventory are called the "human warious" (1.7.126), a Cockneyism that itself brings together mortal anxiety ("wary") in a portmanteau articulation with "various." The reciprocal logic is complete: if dust, figured as money, can be personified as wayward windblown agencies in the London streets, then people, itinerant or otherwise, can be reduced to the flux of exchange value.

The denouement of humanist investigation in the conjoint epistemological crises of (1) biological, (2) economic, and (3) linguistic discourses in the late nineteenth century, as Foucault argues, may thus be satirically witnessed in *Our Mutual Friend* by the fact of (1) a body part being (2) sold off to (3) the (figurative) articulator. The commodification of the biological or anatomical structure of the living organism, the microeconomics of the body itself, is here carried to parodic lengths in the marketing of skeletons for schools of art—to be used, in ironic turn, as models for representation. This travestied economy by which pieces of organic life pass as commodities into the realm of aesthetic reproduction is also matched at the level of metafictional irony by the manner in which the "literary man," Wegg, retails his linguistic powers, such as they are, through an economy of verbal dissemination in which words, whether or not one can be given "change" for them, do have their price. Then, too, in their unwitting play, such words can be made to pay out more than expected. Like the syllabic malapropism of Thackeray's Yellowplush three and a half decades before, Wegg's misplaced "authographic" stabs can strike gold, as when his version of Gibbon, "Decline-and-Fall-Off," hits upon a homophonic pun in the preposition. By discovering the word within the word, he thus brings to light all that (shortly restated) "declining and falling off" that lays empires low (1.5.96).

In the masterly comic scene that sends Wegg on his way to strike his devil's bargain with Boffin, the vocal production he is about to market is, in fact, momentarily shattered. His words are broken down into other words, disintegrated into subsidiary—and subversive—fragments of lexical sense. The dismembered antihero becomes once and for all the disarticulated voice, a shambles of syllabification that ends up speaking in tongues the darkly coherent truth. Central here to the satiric agenda of the novel, its attack on the money ethic of Victorian society, is a play-by-play displacement of words—a lexical splintering into phonemic shards—that anticipates by over a decade the journalistic ingenuity of rhymes like these from the Cockney poem, "Echo's Answers," in the *Punch* number of 18 August 1877:

INQUIRER:	What's the first requisite for taking pleasure?
ECHO:	*Leisure.*
INQUIRER:	The second (for a slave to matrimony)?
ECHO:	*Money.*

The Dickensian setting for a related lexical farce has Wegg taking a convulsive coach journey to visit Mr. Boffin near the former residence of the miserly John Harmon, a residence called disparagingly in the neighborhood "Harmony Jail." Wegg struggles valiantly to get out his questions about this odd name:

Mr. Wegg's conversation was jolted out of him in a most dislocated state.

"Was-it-Ev-verajail?" asked Mr. Wegg, holding on.

"Not a proper jail, wot you and me would get committed to," returned his escort; "they giv' it the name on accounts of Old Harmon living solitary there."

"And-why-did-they-callitharm-Ony?" asked Wegg.

"On accounts of his never agreeing with nobody. Like a speeches of chaff. Harmon's Jail; Harmony Jail. Working it round like."

"Doyouknow-Mist-Erboff-in?" asked Wegg.

(1.5.98)

And so forth. Even the twice repeated nonidiom "on accounts" suggests the obsessive ledger keeping of the miser in question. The phrase "dislocated state" was added in the manuscript to introduce the hyphenated dyslocutions to follow, even as the hyphens suggest a slurred continuity within the cantering

resyllabifications. Nowhere does Dickens more intriguingly mark the phonically bridged gap that always joins phonemes, no matter how clearly they are
segmented into lexemes. In this and other such lexical emergencies, the
accentual discriminations of pitch, stress, and juncture are reduced to the
accidents of physical discomfiture. Out of such violence in this case, finally,
breaks the satiric truth.

Syllabically divided against itself, through false gemination of the /v/, the
phrasing "Ev-verajail" releases perhaps a faint trace of the "veritable," answered at once by the explanation that the term was only figurative, a "species"
of nonsensical wordplay, or "chaff." But, of course, Dickens's own chaff, his
linguistic spoof, has "worked round" the word "species" to the (in context self-
referential) "speeches." It is at just this point — with "callitharm-Ony" — that we
come upon a quintessential moment of disarticulation in this novel symbolically preoccupied (notably through Mr. Venus, the boneman) with literalized articulations. Like a Cockney echoist, Wegg brings out the "harm"
(rather than the money, but then the one is the other) in "Harmony." It is a
species of revelation chafing at the phonemic overlap of two unsaid nonetymological components. Cued by the mercantile pun behind the mangled
idiom "on accounts," the matrix of the whole passage — in Riffaterre's terms,
the unsaid moralistic cliché behind the irony of "Harmony" — is the harm
rather than peace, the imprisoning fixation rather than freedom, that money
brings. The semiosis of this comic poetry is thus glimpsed in the interstices of
the narrowest agrammaticality, the violated succession of the syntactic nexus
itself. "Harm" and "money," imbricated within a single phonemic span,
encode the paired sins that at one and the same time cannot speak their names,
cannot be simultaneously verbalized. They are there in the text not as a written
but as a silently overheard interdependence, a reciprocal satiric indictment
plumbed beneath or between inscriptions, in both senses *sounded* without
being said. As with Boffin before, though here to Wegg's own active an-
noyance, dialogism assaults his utterance from within, divides and conquers
intent, rends the blurted question to render its own answer double-voiced
despite itself. Once again in Dickens the syntagmatic axis snaps at its lower
limit, speaking in tongues from the lucky breaks of lexical segmentation.

If this suggests a more radical reading practice entailed by Dickensian
fiction than criticism ordinarily supposes, guided by less complacent assumptions about a textual system by no means entirely exhausted by graphic
signification, even though positing no grounding authorial voice behind its
phonic play, if in fact this destabilizing play appears born of a syntax at odds
with the very words that constitute it on the skid, and if all this, despite the
debts to Victorian humor, sounds more like Joyce than like Trollope, then we
are ready for a further contextualizing of its verbal farce. It is time to locate

more precisely this late but typifying achievement of Dickens, this symbolic text of articulation and its discontents, within Foucault's "archaeology" of literary history in relation to linguistic science. In the section of *The Order of Things* on "Articulation," there is an unspoken anticipation of that linguistic principle eventually formalized as "double articulation," the twofold system of relational differences between sounds as well as words. Such are the categorical or paradigmatic distinctions whose emergence in the nineteenth century serves to explode a classical philosophy of discourse into the first stirrings of modern philology. Foucault traces to this point what we might call the representational imperative seen to govern classical attitudes toward language. The axiomatic assumptions of this attitude are found to carry an unquestioned confidence about language's signifying power into the smallest fractional units of the word, whether fragmented or regrouped. In this representational episteme, syllables, even single letters, were read as referential, in order that "all analysis of verbal signs . . . be retained within discourse itself."[19] As mentioned in the Prologue, this amounts to "a search for the obscure nominal function that was thought to be invested and concealed in those words, in those syllables, in those inflections, in those letters that the over-generalized analysis of the proposition was allowing to pass through its net" (101). Every word, no matter how utterly—or unutterably—splintered into its constituent elements, still concealed "dormant names" (102). These subsidiary agents in discourse's "immense rustling of denominations" would, according to Foucault, once silenced by the philological revolution, reemerge again only as counterrevolutionary agents in a modernist poetics. They appear there with a renewed sense of the given word inflected by its hidden verbal undersong, its singing of cryptic names in counterpoint, its thinging of language. The glory of articulation, though called now its "enigma," is seen again as an invincible "pulverization" in which every disintegrated structure produces a new integer, every rupture the nub of another utterance.

In briefly following out Foucault's periodization of linguistic "science" across the last three centuries—by way of those British literary landmarks (or "archaeological" strata) considered so far in this chapter on the accidents and "undercraft" of prose—we can indeed conveniently begin with Sterne. An entire verbal episteme is on display in Tristram's alphabetical list of love's attributes (including the transegmental glimmer of "B ewitching"). To read such a textually reflexive moment as Sterne's self-conscious nod at an eighteenth-century discoursing on (and of) the letter, however, would in no way oblige us to find in Dickens's verbal disintegrations—thematized as disarticulation—some nostalgic or regressive gambit at the metalinguistic level. If Dickens follows in the tradition of Sterne, he is also forging the tradition of Joyce. On the evidence of Dickens's sublexical punning, Victorian language theory (in comic practice), having moved beyond a philosophy of pervasive discourse into the realms of philology—and having been virtually allegorized as an "anatomy" of utterance in Dickens's last novel—appears there to press at the very threshold of modernism. Which is a way of saying that the sketch of the nineteenth-century linguistic episteme that Foucault has drawn, when transposed to Victorian experiments in comic prose, provides not just the archaeology of a philological epoch but a far more circumscribed theory of what that era came to know as the "portmanteau." It is a concept mastered by Dickens, named by Lewis Carroll, and passed spectacularly to Joyce. Smash one word and you emancipate another, pulverize and you eventuate, dismantle and then manifest anew. In Wegg's case, when his self-serving questions are disarticulated under pressure, the text reticulates in response a cryptic truth: "And-why-did-they callitharm-Ony?" This voluble amputee, trafficker in an impaired verbal facility, becomes more obviously than ever—and precisely on this symbolic quest to "collect himself"—the prophetic decentered voice of that prose-poetic dismembering that defines "modern" writing not as discourse but as sheer text. The imperium whose decline and falling off he most notably chronicles, therefore, is an empire of signs, and he does so as the "literary man" whose explosive powers have always resided silent in writing's assault on literacy.

The interests of Dickens the intuitive philologist here converge with those of Dickens the empiricist of talk, of oral expressiveness. Language as voice is the meeting ground of both these signal late-Romantic preoccupations. And Wegg's coach ride is their allegory: a miniature picaresque of vocalizing. We are all of us Weggs in motion, readers for "profit" if not for monetary gain, jostled by the fits and starts of language in our attempted engagement with plot. The vehicle that transports us in the service of a motivated reading, a reading whose locus in another sense we already inhabit and define from the start, is a complex engine of verbal sequencing that now and then exposes the jog trot of evocalized textuality, of graphonic processing. Taking fractured dictation from the virtual unconscious of the text, Wegg's disarticulated stammering turns the enunciating body from single source into conflictual site. It is a site whose delegated occupation by us as readers requires in turn the substitution of our own voicing bodies, querying through Wegg's proxy the name assigned to the very space of secondary reading—his reading out loud, and haltingly, to Boffin in the environs of "Harmony Jail." It is *toward* such a designated scene of reading—yet one at the same time already in process, already reflexively staged—that both the signifying as well as the signified activity of this very "passage" ushers us by our own silent "delivery." To attempt an extreme localization of Bakhtinian terminology, one might say that the "chronotopicity"[20] of Wegg's ride—the space-time relationship of his race across the urban cobblestones of mid-Victorian London — is redoubled by our own reading pace across the lines of print. It is our *textual* chronotope, in other words, that dialogizes his language — double-voices it, voices its doubles — in sync with his own segmental syncopations. Novel by novel — or, more accurately, text by text — Joyce will turn such a farcical picaresque of articulation into the linguistic epic of a speaking tribe.

6   "An Earsighted View"
Joyce's "Modality of the Audible"

What has Joyce to do with the novel, and what is the novel to him? If Dickens is not indisputably the greatest novelist of the nineteenth century in English, he is surely the greatest writer of the novel in the period, preeminent stylist of prose fiction, the ultimate writer of prose as itself a dynamic system with a plot and momentum all its own. Dickens in his late prose made Joyce inevitable. And Joyce made the novel expendable. After over two centuries of experimentation in the language of fiction, Joyce reinvents the fiction of language, the book of words. It is, finally, not a novel at all that he writes, that is so remorselessly written, under — and over — his name but, rather, beyond genre, a verbal text in extremis. Joyce authored two recognizable novels before this, however, and some stories, as well as poems and a play. In the earlier prose works, *A Portrait of the Artist as a Young Man* and *Ulysses*, as in *Our Mutual Friend* before and behind them, the agenda of *Finnegans Wake* is adumbrated. Words are at times mobilized by textuality to enwrap or unfurl only other words, to splinter into syllables and reconstitute themselves, to vibrate, snap, and shatter even while they bond and reverberate anew, gather and regroup. As never so evidently before, the textual work seems to generate its own stylistics along with the production of its style. At the microlevel, the smallest impulse of linguistic articulation becomes the real shape-changing protagonistic urge of the *Wake,* whose dreamplay encodes the encyclopedia of experience in a polyglot storm of alphabetic "characters."

The Joycean Wake of words, novelistic or not, is the subject to which Chapter 5, on prose fiction, has inescapably led, as well as one unmistakable point of convergence for any broad-ranging speculations on the "phonotexture" of literary writing. Like Shakespeare, Joyce is the name not so much for an author as for a textual field, a field of effect. Joyce is the place where words won't stay put, don't put stays on each other, can't settle down to expression:

where what is written is never the last word. Joyce's the place where language abrades writing, upbraids it, operates its unraveling. His is the semiosis that never gives itself over wholly to code, that leaks, drains, recoagulates. His the drift that no typography can integrate, only grapple with. Under the lens of Derridean deconstruction, Joyce thus names that associational signifying practice that lays the ghost of authorial voice forever. Yet Joycean writing takes place in the space of its own undoing, its refusal of an exclusive or even predominantly graphic function. The Joycean text exceeds the writing that marks it out as much as it exceeds the speech whose univocality it mocks. Joyce's signifying process thereby solicits its own disintegration in the act of reception, sets the traps that any reading will spring.

This is the greatest comedy of discrepancy in his great comic work: that the writing and the text do not fit flush to each other. Reading won't have it. In text production, in the operation of the phonotext as we have been exploring it, there is always with later Joyce, in the *Wake* especially, that subvocal phonemic throb whose risk is that, at any turn, it may in all mirth rob writing of its given words, substitute its own, sewn into the gaps, sowing semantic dissension. Writing is there to enchain the system of wording. But reading breaks links — or relinks breaks with detached phonemes, melding new hallucinated possibilities. In reading Joyce we see through writing to its very origins. By an inversion of logical sequence, it would seem that reading Joyce serves to derive not writing from language at large but originary language once more from writing, wording again from words. Wording polyglot and incorrigible: a continuous contra-diction. Accompanying this process is a corrosion of grammar as well, for grammar *is* the process of leading on from one word, settled upon, to its next in line. By the time of the *Wake*, the Joycean phonotext prods and complicates this process to the point of lexical and syntactic delirium. If, for instance, the first words of Joyce's last text can be taken (inverting, as they do, the formulaic word order "Adam and Eve") to leave behind the protagonist of the two earlier novels — with the transegmental overtone of "Stephen" in "riverrun, pa*st Eve an*d Adam's" — then the prominence of a newly elusive and suspicious alphabetic "character" is at the same time enshrined. The Stephen Dedalus books, both his *Portrait* and the story that includes him in *Ulysses,* have each in their own way heard this coming.

There is a perplexing moment at the Christmas dinner scene early in *A Portrait of the Artist as a Young Man,* a moment of strangely self-conscious dialogue from Mrs. Dedalus: "For pity's sake and for pity sake let us have no political discussion on this day of all days in the year" (31). What? Why the redundancy, or whatever it is? Out of the mouth of this modest woman, it would seem, comes a vernacular instance of an entire principle of Joycean lexical erosion, a principle not to find comparable expression anywhere else in this early novel. Representative of the folk voice, the mother tongue, Mrs. Dedalus seems to display a vernacular instinct for phonic ambiguity. From her comic tautology, we infer her intuition that, because of the elision of sibilants in "pity's sake," the phrase commonly falls on the ear as "pity sake." To cover the bases, she gives it emphatically, both ways. She gives it, that is, phonetically rather than conversationally, as a play not of exclusive alternatives (either/or) but of still active variants (whichever). Each term of this auditory differential takes on a status comparable to that of referential autonomy, and therefore each needs to be appealed to separately.

Not until the phantasmagoric transformations of dialogue in the "Circe" episode of *Ulysses* will Joyce return to a comparable segmental ambiguity by way of a third route, an adjacent lexical rut or groove that was not directly exploited by Mrs. Dedalus. Says Bloom: "For old sake'sake" (444). At first glance, the apostrophe works like a hyphen, separating identicals. In fact, this is one of the few Joycean compounds that, in telescoping the lexical break, does so at a possessive juncture. What can be reconstructed from the junctural breakdown in this case is either an elision of one *s* and its spacing ("sake's sake") or a homophonic pun ("sake's ache"), the latter a possibility implicit in the drift of Mrs. Dedalus's redundancy as well: for "pity's sake" and for "pity's ache." And this transegmental slippage has its own literary precedent, its own orthographic and typographic history. In *Jude the Obscure,* for instance, the singular possessive form before a word beginning with a sibilant is suppressed in the phrase "old acquaintance' sake" (1.1.10). That phrase is given in dialogue suggests an attempt to render the inevitable dropping away of the first *s* in spoken English. In Joyce's own vernacular delegation of possessive wordplay to the dialogue of a character within plot, namely to Stephen's parent as maternal forebear of the young artist's own later ingenuity, the novelist is there listening in on her joke as the implicit historian as well as custodian of English linguistic culture.

"Nonce Ends": Words Kidding Around

When Joyce in the *Wake* writes transegmentally of oneiric "nonsense" as the "nonce ends" (149.22) of things, he has indirectly given us a phrase for the fraying ends or borders, the canceled closural certainty, of diction itself in its dream dislocations. It is the noncing of juncture in "nonce" as enunciated that precipitates its skid, by liaison, into "(s)en-" and a comparable homophonic negation of the written that unravels the end of "ends" into the dentalized "ence." Along with such another transegmental effect as "for pity('s) sake," this junctural play with sibilance is related to those punning jokes for which Dickens shared a taste with the Cockney rhymesters and riddlers of *Punch*. Indeed, long before the *Wake,* the first specifically signaled homophonic riddles in both *Portrait* and *Ulysses* draw on this kind of lexical disintegration. Half a dozen pages before his mother's vernacular ambiguity, Stephen encounters the first outright joke in the novel, inculcating principles of orthographic and phonemic wordplay that will only have grown programmatic in Joyce by the time of *Ulysses*. Stephen is asked a riddle, "Why is the county Kildare like the leg of a fellow's breeches?" The solution: "Because there's a thigh in it. . . . Athy is the town in the county Kildare and a thigh is the other thigh" (25). The doubly localized site of this joke is the topographical play on "in it," the space both verbal and geographic. A comparable moment early in *Ulysses* is capped by the interjection "See the wheeze?" – like "See the joke?" in *Portrait* (25) – after Lenehan's riddling in the newspaper office: "What opera is like a railway line?" The answer: *"The Rose of Castille.* See the wheeze? Rows of cast steel. Gee!" (134). The homophonic pun is, of course, based on a lexical breakdown of the mispronounced Spanish place-name and the elision of one or the other *st* clusters in "cast steel." Part of the joke in both texts may involve the fact that this is just the sort of "wheeze" or "joke" one could in fact never "see," for it is based entirely upon a phonic rather than a scriptive coincidence.

Yet as a textual activation, this aural punning has to be produced in print by precisely the "rows of cast steel" (or of iron, with lead letters) responsible for the book's own typographic generation, thereby rendering graphic the difference upon which the surprise of sameness is based. This linotype process, patented in 1885 – "at the center of the decade," Hugh Kenner reminds us, "when the instigators of High Modernism were born" – lent textual spacing in print both a predictability and a palpability; such spacing was now identified with the precise width of a rubber increment, a standardization that "bypassed all the skill with hairline spaces for which master compositors had earned respect."[1] With lexical demarcations thus routinized by machine, it may be possible to understand Joyce's defiance of expectation in their regard as a reaction against the wholesale instrumentation of textual norms in the boundaries and respites of printed diction. In this sense the "cast steel / Castille" pun is just the sort of play with spacing (among other things) that might appeal to a worker in a newspaper office, minion of the linotype. Kenner's approach to literary modernism through such industrial implementations of voice and script as the telephone, the typewriter, the linotype machine, and the calculator might lead us to read Joyce's play with juncture as a self-consciously erratic "technologizing" of the lexical break against the move toward uniformity. In the new methodology that eclipsed typesetting by hand, "matrices would slide down from magazines onto a moving belt for delivery to the line's incrementing array; and between the words wedge-shaped spacers would be pressed, which in squeezing everything out toward the boundaries would make all the spaces in any line identical" (8). Though Kenner makes no suggestion of this sort, it would seem as if Joyce's segmental hairsplitting (rather than "hairline" precision) in a phrase like "For old sake'sake" might well be a modernist countermove against the updated workings of textual dissemination itself. In this sense, too, it might hark back to those still shifting typographic conventions of possessive grammar manifest in the late nineteenth-century example from Hardy. In any case, Joyce's phrasing was certainly an assault on the patience of his printers and proofreaders. And they too, as we shall see, had their revenge on Joyce.

A junctural ambiguity like "cast steel" is a low drollery in many ways central to the high modernist dislocations of the Joycean text. Margot Norris's professed "structuralist analysis" in *The Decentered Universe of "Finnegans Wake"* discusses such slippages in terms very close, at one point, to those of the present study. In her chapter "Technique," Norris is attempting to account for the "substitutions and freeplay" that "deconstruct the language itself," and she mentions in passing the typical case whereby Joyce "disrupts linguistic structure by ignoring internal junctures." Such "junctures," she continues, understood as "the meaningful pauses between words," are "treated as suprasegmental phonemes in modern linguistics because they function to distinguish the meanings of otherwise identical units"; beyond Joycean examples, she offers a joke from W. C. Fields's *The Dentist,* where there is prolonged confusion over his daughter's dating either "an ice man" or "a nice man."[2] The Dickensian legacy is again glimpsed through a journalistic intertext—in this, for instance, from the 1864 *Punch Almanack:* "Song for a lazy winter lie-a-bed—vs. his friends who'd have him get up: — "They say 'tis an ice day" (23). Norris's own example from the *Wake* itself—"an earsighted view" (143.9)—not only provides the Joycean equivalent of this phonemic ambiguity but offers (though Norris does not consider this) the most strikingly condensed comment in his work on the very reception of such produced textual bucklings. They become reading effects, in this case actually naming the ear's scanning that alone can unfold such a transegmental alternative.

Polysyllabax

Joyce may have given us another term for such effects as well. Based on "parallax" in astronomy, the phenomenon whereby the distant movement of an object is determined by triangulation with two points of vantage, the *Ulysses* text coins in passing, by direct echo with "parallax" a line before, the cryptic "polysyllabax" (512). The *Oxford English Dictionary* defines "parallax" as the "apparent displacement, or difference in the apparent position, of an object, caused by actual change (or difference) of position of the point of observation." The relativism of difference and displacement invites linguistic analogy.

In the domain of transegmental reading, "polysyllabax" suggests, in particular, the zone of shifting evocalized bonds: the apparent spread of functional sound units across the space between words. Like parallax, this phonemic drift is in fact a difference at the point of perception, of reception—only a relational phenomenon, only a fix, a take, a reading effect. The differential phrasings, for instance, of "an earsighted view" and "a nearsighted view" are each the acoustical, rather than optical, illusion of the other when listened to aslant from different textual positions. Or, if another optical metaphor is allowed, they constitute a phonemic anamorphosis, where difference would not manifest itself unless the listening ear, the earsighted view of the phrase, were to evoke—to evocalize—the alternative spelling.

Such difference, such polysyllabax, can be great enough in Joyce to defy the probabilities of print itself. In the edition of *Ulysses* that I, like so many of us, went to school with, Molly Bloom, about halfway through her closing soliloquy, is worrying about a possible fart that might wake her husband, even as she is imagining the emission of controlled breath in her singing act. Infiltrating her rumination is the distant rumble of a passing train. The more than four-page paragraph ends with "Piano quietly sweeeee theres that train far away pianissimo eeeeeeee one more song" (763). Since she has already been thinking about the familiar ballad "Loves old sweet sonnnng" (754), we read *in* the *t* later in the "sweeeee," mending the apocope (or dropped last letter). At one point in the bedeviled printing history of the novel, this word-note was actually typeset to close off with the *t*. In one of the seemingly less debatable restorations advanced by the newly "corrected" edition, it appears that Joyce had in fact written "*sweeeee* theres that train far away pianissimo *eeeee* one more *tsong*" (my emphasis).[3] Stretched out pianissimo along the train of syntax is the full spelling, the full voicing, of *sweetsong*, as if it were a Joycean compound disbanded for a singer's emphasis across a long legato line, ending in the ligature or tie of *tsong*. That thickened monosyllable is almost in its own right an exaggerated phonetic transcription of an arch vocalistic enunciation, even while the *t* is the grammatical trace of an adjective for which the deferred substantive has been oddly long in coming. A polysyllabax whose displacements are almost beyond detection, such is the Joycean textual tsong in a quintessential instance, perhaps inadvertently normalized in previous versions of the imperfect text.

This is, of course, Joyce the textualist more than Joyce the novelist, exactly the obsessively impersonal *writer* with whose breaks from the rules we are here concerned. The phonic and graphic shapes of language, superimposed upon each other in the *letter*, are not in Joyce subordinated to the word but pass into the textualized stream of consciousness as functions thereof. The syntagmatic sequence is no longer assigned the strict management of the lexicon. It is charged instead — both senses — with the channeling of phonetic and graphic matter along a circuit where neither is entirely discharged in word formation, sending off instead stray sparks, rays, cross-lexical arcs. No computer "spelling check" could control misprints in the sprints and vaults of the Joycean text, for the contradictory principles that govern the eccentric alphabetic trajectories are sometimes phonic, sometimes pictographic. The letter is no longer an alphabetic character solely but a double agent even in the text, a freer agent, a free reagent — phonic aftereffect at times to its own graphic cause. In the permutations of Joyce's textual system, the phonetic sensorium displaces the regimen of phonemic sense, and this within the government of a typography as much as an alphabet, the law of the loose letter as well as of the lexical increment. His is a typography that concerns the blank and the capital, concerns mark, space, and boundary, all as functional equivalents of the letter, as part of that perpetually breached continuum which the word itself does not exclusively occupy and exhaust. It is the exact, however various, relation of the phonic to the graphic trace, or the phonic resonance (rather than residuum) within the graphic, that this chapter seeks to explore. One purpose in doing so, finally, must be to resist a too hasty and unexamined assimilation of the Joycean text to a narrowly conceived grammatological model.

Compbounding

We can begin our inquiry into Joycean segmentations with the most innocuous and least disruptive of all space marks, the silent stitch of the hyphen. Joyce's early experiments with the dropped hyphen, the blanking out of the blank in enforced lexical compounds, should direct us toward a fuller account of the elastic gap in both phonic as well as typographic aspects of his style. The Joycean compound elides the hyphen while foregrounding its very status in absentia. Whenever a hyphen appears (even its disappearance reminds us), it is the mark of difference itself under partial erasure, of juncture and disjunction at once, a linkage that retains distinction. It is the horizontal sign of a lateral process of break and pause, what Joyce himself in the *Wake* calls the "blotch and void" (229.27) of script. The hyphen is thus a sign that also binds over such a break, in the process fusing a semantic amalgam that stops short of lexical collapse. Merely remove the punctuating link, leaving the lexical segmentation intact, and you lose sight of the hyphen's double service. On the other hand, collapse the adjacent lexemes into one and you throw the (canceled) hyphenating function into relief as the lexical ligature it always half is: a sign of cleaving in both senses, *of* and *to*. Either way, it is a crisis of juncture at the narrowest scope.

The earliest dis-hyphenations in *Portrait* are virtually negligible — for example, "carriagelamps" (19) or "pierhead" (35). Composite forms of this sort, however, quickly grow more striking when the deletion of the purely graphic signifier opens the morphophonemic floodgates. They come thus to resemble the later compounds of *Ulysses* and the *Wake* where eye and ear seem to play tricks on each other. In "telegraphpoles" (20), for instance, the near proximity of one silent (diphthongized) and one pronounced *p* is graphically disconcerting, in a way that a hyphen would have forestalled. This is all the more true in a compound like "ironingroom" (19), where an extraneous third term ("groom" rather than "room") lurks insurgently in the coinage, irrelevant but momentarily assertive in the unfamiliar word's claim on the eye.[4] In the dozen or so compounds in the first half-dozen pages of *Ulysses*, we find such facile examples as "gunrest" (3) and "guncase" (4), as well as such more notable coinages as "snotgreen," "noserag" (6) and the ingenious "scrotumtightening" (5), the last a mimetic instance of typographic contraction. Far more than in *Portrait*, the *Ulysses* text indulges in geminated (twinned) consonants as the cement between compounded words, as in the odd-looking "dressinggown" (3) or "lumberroom" (29) and the more suggestive mirroring replication of "lookingglass" (6). In general, double letters highlight the unavoidable phonic elision that the redundancy of their script pretends to deny. In the particular case of "lookingglass," the reciprocally elided but still visibly inscribed *g*'s suggest that sameness within difference, that otherness on the trace of identity, which is not simply emblemized in a mirror but emblemized ideally in that "symbol of all Irish art" provided by the "cracked lookingglass of a servant." We actually see there, though instantaneously smoothed over, one of those cracks in signification that Joyce will raise to a high art in the pantheon of Irish style. Other compounds in *Ulysses* have a more openly semantic meld, including the yoked segmentation of "strandentwining" (38), indeed of "yokefellow" (43) itself. Not to mention the reflexive play on dirty language, as well as on the phallus, in "naughty night*stalk*" (78). "Sweetoned" seems to name its own deepening and rounding of "sweetened" (23), and in this same vein of self-referential coinages there is the almost pictographic enactment of an inward curvative in the rickety lexical composite "knockkneed" (32). All of these odd bondings are in a sense knockkneed conflations that play out at the least disruptive level a sudden malleability of spacing where the hyphen once was. Either this, or, under pressure from the evacuation of the hyphen, the collapse of lexemes into a forced syllabic bond seems momentarily to displace juncture itself, forward or back, along the lettered succession.

In this sense, perhaps the most illustrative of all the compounds born of an elided hyphen in *Ulysses* is to be found, though also found wanting authority, in the familiar edition of the "Lestrygonians" episode. Bloom is surreptitiously fondling "a slack fold of his belly," and by possibly an equal slackness in the printer's transmission, we have always read "I know its whiteyellow" (182). Beyond the possessive adjective where we would expect the apostrophe of contraction ("it's"), converting "whiteyellow" to a nominal form, that last shifting coinage has a further Joycean look — but only at the expense of an even more Joycean sound. The "corrected" edition gives it as two words, "whitey yellow" (149), inviting a liaison at exactly the border where one tint attenuates into another. Since "whitey" was too rare an adjectival form to break free from the melded coinage in the typesetter's (reading rather than just seeing) eye — at least so one may speculate, with those medieval scribes from the Prologue in mind — what we have for decades been reading in the bipartite version of the phrase can now be metatextually reread in play with its alternative, there in one sense all along. This is just what, at the level of a phonotextual response, is so fascinating and fertile in the debates about the "authoritative" *Ulysses*. In connection with lexical eccentricities, the experts attempt, again and again, to adjudicate on the strength of manuscript evidence what remains, by the force of receptual effect, always an open question as we read. Such sustained ambivalence bears witness once again to those phonemic fusions by which the flux of speech inevitably (we shall soon use Joyce's word "ineluctably") proceeds. Such, he might have said, are the earrata of the typograph/vocal slip.

The dis-hyphenated conflation is one of those rudimentary experiments in lexical adhesion that will eventually result in the highly pressurized transfusions of the *Wake*'s portmanteau terms, one word not just enjambed with but slamming into another, overlapping and interpenetrating it, sometimes superimposed upon it in a way that not only erases but overleaps the gaps between words. Following loosely Joyce's own self-referential coinage for a similar kind of overlay — the imbrication of *superb* with *superpose* in "superpbosition" (299.8) — one could dub such a lexical "combine," one that amalgamates words into a single lexical mass, a "compbound" (or of course "combpound"). It is a device that functions therefore as the lower limit of junctural transgression in the general category of the portmanteau conflation. Without such a blatant transposition, such a superposition of switched letters, a nonetheless extreme imbrication in the fifth paragraph of the *Wake*, for instance, dovetails an unhyphenated *multi* with *multiple, multiply,* and *applicable* in "multiplicables" (4.32). Here, again, is a polysyllabax of overlapping internal displacements. Such inventions operate transegmentally, by reversible elision, across a lexical break they have already erased to begin with. Within one of the canonically remarked elements of the Joycean style, the portmanteau syndrome, they seem to compress — by lexical compression itself — an entire phonotextual program that has received too little, or the wrong sort of, attention.

More obviously than the merely disheveled or dis-hyphenated compound, these "compbounds"—involving binds and bounds, pounding fusions and leapt gaps—insist with instructive clarity on the phonic dimension of writing not within but athwart the graphic. At the very point of overlap, the "multiplicable" is decoded partly by the reconstructive ear—as it fills-in the invisible blank under cover of that very "superpbosition" which defers the fulfillment of one lexeme by the encroachment of the other. What is unseen by definition, telescoped out of the orthographic puzzle, is heard-as-missing. What the eye scans in such cases will always leave unseen, and audible *as deleted,* the ultimate trace of each constituent element's sudden difference from itself, from its normal lexical autonomy. The peculiar Joycean portmanteau—what I am calling the "compbounded" lexeme—is thus not only a test case for signification as difference but for such difference as manifestly a play between eye and ear. It is this same portmanteau comb-pounding that produces the impacted overlaps in the very title of Joyce's postmorphological carnivalesque, *Finnegans Wake.* This title contains not only "Finn" but the French word for "end," *fin,* as well as the prefixes of negation, "ne" and "nega," followed by a disyllabic homophone for "again" in "egan," plus the archaic form *gan* for *go.* On top of this is the ambivalent slippage between a plural subject—for the tribe of all Finnegans coming awake—and a possessive form either for the funeral of one by this name or for the trace left by him in life or death, "wake" there rather in the sense of "track." Finally, even within the possibly suppressed sign of the genitive apostrophe, there could reside a further deletion: *is* (rather than the implicit possessive) not only contracted to *'s* but followed in turn by an aphaeresis muting /ə/ as first syllable of the adjectivalized verb form *(a)wake,* thus reading "Finnegan's 'Wake."

In pursuing such microlinguistic details, this chapter has started small in order to develop a model for Joyce's signifying program at large. At its fullest realization, the Joycean text follows a wholesale agenda of estrangement. His prose alienates the normative by its recombination, wreaking havoc with the axes of paradigm and syntagm at once. Word *by* word, Joyce's writing at its most extreme aspires to continuous neologism; from word *to* word, it courts a self-sustaining agrammaticality (in every sense, not just Riffaterre's). But these two radical dispensations are more closely interrelated than has been noticed. The interim case (part invented diction, part vestigial syntax) of the hyphenless compound, at least in its roughly vernacular forms, raises the very issue of segmentation as itself the borderline between diction and syntax. It raises it by demonstrating the extent to which segmentation is at the mercy of a play between vocal temptations, on the one hand, and the rules of script, on the other. Moreover, when moving from the simple compound to the overlapping compbound, that minimal portmanteau conflation, we find that the motive of neologism has invaded syllabic integrity itself in a way that furthers the divergence—within what we read—between what we see and what we hear: see as fractured regrouping, hear as morphophonemic vestige.

The most rudimentary cases, however, remain the most illustrative. The least striking hyphen may remind us not just that language, as Derrida has it, is a function of spacing but that spacing is a function, a variable, of textuality. Once allow for its collapse within the reading effect, and you have thrown open the lexeme not only to collisions but to incursions, to amalgams and transformations under pressure of contiguity, to *drift*. Because we do not hear the space girded by the hyphen in the first place, the ear is untroubled by its removal. The eye's surprise is thus mitigated by an inner voicing. If, however, the spaces regimented by hyphens are expendable, so too, perhaps, are those other segmental markers, those ordinary gaps between words, that are also more or less ignored by the ear even while honored by the eye. The elided hyphen would then provide the invisible index to an inaudible, and thus fluctuating, semiosis of the blank. In so doing, it would offer a wry defiance of those determinant rubber wedges between lexically bordering letters on the linotype machine. The invisible hyphen, the unwritten but still operable trace of difference-plus-relation, is thus the smallest registrable integer (not inscribed at all, except as absence: a true infinitesimal) in the calculus of Joycean transformation. As in no text production so openly before his, this is a transformation by which the axial, and axiomatic, difference between lexicon and grammar begins to break down.

When the lexicon gives, grammar does not always take. As the logic of compounding and disbanding, of compbounding and disintegration, escalates in Joyce, new models of phrasing are introduced. His textual activity reconceives our notion of voicing and sequencing, of wording in the sense both of diction and its serial articulations. One preeminent model of such phrasing is drawn from the practice of music, of song, but drawn to the breaking point in its tension with the textual precondition of a work as book. In moving from Joyce's conflationary stylistics of the dis-hyphenated polysyllabic bond to the more elaborate blendings and staccato dismemberments of a textual episode explicitly devoted to the musical analogue, the "Sirens" segment of *Ulysses,* we must monitor the Joycean text all the more closely in its play between the written and the read. For in this play lie the text's enunciatory *annotations* of script as score. In the "Sirens" episode—which everyone agrees is the earliest sustained departure in *Ulysses* from the normal referential function of fictional language, the most concerted breakdown in lexical and syntactic coherence (in favor, so the argument usually runs, of melodic continuities)— such neatly packaged homophonic jokes as "base barreltone" (270) are less frequent than a more undulant dilation of syllables. Sometimes it is a musical onomastics, here transmuting a noun and two pronouns, *Bloom* and *him* and *whom,* into the threefold indirect object of "Winsomely she on *Bloohimwhom* smiled" (264). It is a case, as the text itself has it elsewhere, of "Bloom looped, unlooped, noded, disnoded" (256). This phonic elongation of the central vowel, a further opening and swelling, leads directly to such homophonic inflations (rather than conflations) in *Finnegans Wake* as "there are trist sigheds to everysing" (299.1–2). Not only is "thing" sung there as "sing," but "sides" is stretched to the homophonic expiration "sigheds," a vocalic self-exemplification that is also reminiscent of that Cockney pun in Chapter 5 on "the sea sighed." In the "Sirens" episode of the earlier novel – staging in part, as it does, the luring of language toward its own dissolution into pure tonality – we again find the name of "Bloom" precipitating an expanded vocable within a far more standard compound: "Bloom sighed on the silent *bluehued* flowers" (268). That assonant vowelizing may strike the inner ear as one long, modulated, transmuted *u,* creating an apocryphal past-participial form of *blue* itself.

In the "Sirens" segment the quantifiable measures of such music are called its "Musemathematics" (278) – in other words (in the other words thereby compbounded), the inspired musical semantics of a mathematical thematization. "Words? Music? No: it's what's behind" (274). For an example of such a subtext we can return to the ambivalent straying of a single phoneme on the episode's first page: "A sail! A veil awave upon the waves" (256). The ship is "asail" but represented synecdochically only by "a sail," a sail that is a wave of sorts, undulant and rhythmic as it flutters awave upon the rolling of the sea. Juncture is both fused and breached, fluid, wavering, as in the later erotic pulse of "Throb, a throb, a pulsing proud erect" (274), where the ear hears "athrob" against the visible indication of a separate article and repeated noun. To remember Gwendolen Harleth's "a sailing and sailing," with its contextually insinuated pun on emotional assault, is only to recognize the possibilities of literary history as linguistic history upon which the manipulations of the Joycean text open back.

Following "A sail . . . awave" on the first page of "Sirens" is another conflation of aural material in "Ah, lure! Alluring."[5] The last is not just a phonemic compendium of the preceding two vocables but a new compbound of its own, compressing "all" and "luring" as well. There is an even more symptomatic sound play on this opening page of "Sirens." What might well be heard as the farthest seduction by music away from language occurs in the metrical dismemberment of a hypothetical matrix phrase like "Good God, he never heard in all his life" into the garbled syllabic paragram of "Goodgod henev erheard inall" (256). One certainly does not discount the scriptive dimension of such textual eccentricity; this is, in fact, all that is eccentric about it. Yet such a departure from the norm is precisely an accession to the phonic (if not exactly the musical) within the linguistic, the metrical within the discursive, the note within the word. Unlike the overt homophonic joke or pun, where visual notation is wed to aural surprise, in these mathematical permutations of quasi-musical voicing, disjunctive rhythms are in every sense spelled out, made marked by the marks of script. The vernacular warping of "Good God" into a single word "Goodgod" (all attributes of the Logos drawn to its primal nomination) is the complementary opposite of the fission that rends the remaining words. In both cases, the rules of the lexicon are subordinated to articulation, whether "natural" or more artificial yet. In this chapter of inveigling orality, concerned with the alluring lilt of textual musicalization, even the deaf Pat is not immune. In a textual clue to the reading effects of the entire episode – and only as they perform a certain kind of distillation of the novel as a whole – this character, once cut off by dysfunction from the music of the world and of the spoken word, must read that world as if it were a text: "He seehears lipspeech." In a novel so thoroughly premised on the programmatic lapse, this is at the same time to "seehear slipspeech." It thereby speaks obliquely of the listening g/lance that slices across the lexicon and reformulates Joycean script for the inner ear of reception.

This textual effect is no less operable in our eavesdropping upon Molly, listening with her own inner ear to the vocalization of that old "sweeeee . . . tsong," than it is when we confront deaf Pat decoding the shifting shapes of speech without sound. They are both *reading* effects, drawn from melody or silence. Molly is their analyst as well as their purveyor. A dozen pages after her "(t)song," she warmly remembers Simon Dedalus's "delicious glorious voice" as he intoned the familiar lyric: "dearest goodbye sweetheart he always sang it not like Bartell dArcy sweet *tart* goodbye" (774). This woman of the trained ear thus articulates a vocal preference by a segmental emphasis and a sexual pun. In so doing, she also epitomizes the Joycean method within a few pages of the text's close. In the articulation of a single word, a musical treatment can deconstruct and reinflect sound – and so meaning – in a manner that passes the stray *t* along the syntactic chain and across the lexical breach, rather than merely reduplicating it at the point of internal juncture. This latter would be the mode of the ordinary homophonic pun, which Bartell's arch musical phrasing serves to generate. A more drastic play with external juncture, with lexical segmentation and syntactic contiguities, is found in Joyce's systematic extension of the process beyond the internal syllabic framework of a single word. As I have suggested before, his textual play in fact de-privileges the word in favor of the letter that potentially demolishes as well as composes it.

Phonemanology

If there is one literary text that urges upon Derridean deconstruction a certain recalcitrant phonological pull, that text is *Finnegans Wake*. Certainly, for all its stress on Joyce's letteral manifestation, on the *bookishness* of his text, Derrida comes as close as anywhere in his work to acknowledging the pressure, however phantasmal, of pronunciation upon script—or at least the play between them. This recognition of a dialectic between eye and ear, sometimes suppressed in deconstructive commentary outside of Derrida's own work, therefore invites close monitoring. First, though, let me clarify the position toward which the preceding textual examples in this chapter have been aimed. The later style of Joyce, the style of the so-called dreambook, is not the style of some subjectivist transcription. Nor is this the case with *Ulysses* either. Joyce's style is not a record but a construct. Mind is not captured by text, the stream of language in the flow of consciousness, an ultimate record of the inner life in language. Rather, and in every sense, the text is brought to mind—foregrounded and reconstituted there, in the reading. The text, produced, induces. It generates our own waking dreamwork, not that of author or characters. Like its title, *Finnegans Wake* reverberates—I use the dead metaphor of sonority advisedly—between the encoded and the construed, the impressed and the processed.

This might be too obvious to need saying if it were not both deceptively simple and increasingly denied. An entirely grammatological *Wake,* for instance, would rule out a reception theory that alone might delve the complications implicit in the text when read as a phonic instrumentation *in the mind*—or in "the mind's ear," as Joyce himself calls it in a punning passage (on "mare," "marine," and "mer") whose phonemic contours also evoke a wavelike metalanguage very close to that of Woolf's *The Waves:* "The mar of murmury mermers to the mind's ear" (254.18). Not to the mindseer but to the mind's audition. So too with the mar or scar, the "blotch and void," of script rather than marine rhythms. Neither before nor after all, but rather *between* the written and the read, falls the phonic provocation. "Derrida would probably object that Joyce achieves his polyglot or palimpsest effects by driving to the limit the privilege accorded to the oral within the written, and proceeding logocentrically, word for word"—thus Geoffrey Hartman in 1981.[6] So almost everything in grammatology would indeed lead one to suspect, to predict. But this is precisely what Derrida does *not* argue when he eventually turns to Joyce at some length. In avoiding the angle of attack that would paint Joyce into the corner of logocentrism, however, Derrida is at some pains to find a deprivileging of the oral in the operation of the Joycean text. What is so instructive in his work on the *Wake* is that the phonological component of this text remains insistent enough to prevent any demotion of the aural register beyond a leveling parity with the graphic or, rather, a virtually instantaneous oscillation between the ascendancies of eye and ear. Derrida's generalizations, though, if not his fullest readings, do tend to elide the dialectic—rather than theorizing the graphonic elision, for instance—that keeps voice active and at work against the graphic: our voice, not Joyce's, but ours, like Joyce's, never to be heard. In demonstrating the impossibility of a univocal reading of the *Wake*, Derrida implies that he has extricated the text from all myths of voice whatever. Instead, the processing of Joyce's later style, its production as text, should be read to depend on what we might call a polyphonic cerebration. Though no one, even to oneself, can of course say two sounds at once, even though prompted by a single letter, any of us *is* able to register, by phonic rather than graphic deferral, what amounts to an aural rather than scriptive palimpsest, an overlapping of phonemes. Indeed, it can't be helped. This is the registration (of a specifically phonemic *différance*) that Derrida, confronting the *Wake*, does for once almost allow—and all but theorize.

Yet again, as in the Prologue and in Chapter 3, I shall be using one Derrida against another, the reader against the theorist, the pragmatist of free association (without peer, or even many imitators, as a surveyor of linguistic materiality) against the deconstructor of metaphysics and its textual manifestations (widely subscribed to and emulated). I do so specifically to rethink, to *re*theorize, Derrida's liberated critical practice within a fuller apprehension of the literary phonotext: that level of literary manifestation where "writing," as a name for a process rather than a labor or even a product, is finally achieved only in the reading. Derrida concentrates in his essay on the famous passage in the *Wake* ending with the transformation of the Lord's Prayer, a mutation turning on the metavocalic pun on Lord as "Loud" (259)—as if sprung from the previous homophonic spelling of *applaud* as "Upploud!" (257.30). Within this passage, he focuses on the innocuous-looking monosyllabic sequence that caps a brief biblical allusion: "And shall not Babel be with Lebab? *And he war*" (258.11–12; my emphasis).[7] Derrida would suggest that this sentence—in English—means both (elliptically) that he, namely, *He*, the Lord, *is* war (the predicate functioning under erasure) and also (by a solecism of number, the transitive activation of this thought) that *He wars*. The war would seem enacted for Derrida in the text itself, in the verbal skirmish by which Babel is reversed to its lexical mirror image in Lebab. The latter word is related to the Gaelic for "book" (*leabhar*) and hence further serves to encrypt this reversion—this inversion—of tongues to a primal writing. In this, we are moving all the while toward Derrida's sense of the passage as a metatextual parable. A decentering deity, the original grammatologist, wars with and overturns—turns around—the very name for the original site of polyglossia. He thereby discloses the text or inscription that actually founds it, the Babel that is always and already booked. In the beginning, the word as written—enunciated, however, by anagrammes on the (supposed) imperative to listening rather than reading in the words "he war" once undone: "Everything around speaks to the ear and of the ear: what speaking means but first what *listening* means: lending one's ear (*e ar, he ar*) and obeying the father who raises his voice, the lord who talks loud" (152). This is the fathering impulse whose voice is itself the war, the assault. Nothing could seem farther from the gramme, the scripted differential. Here loudness speaks by and of itself as the enunciation of presence. Read this way, the passage would seem to allegorize the site, or citation, of the founding Logos through a phonocentrism that predates the linguistic diaspora symbolized by Babel. Before the dispersion and dissemination of tongues — whose glossolalia is now preempted by such localized textual punning, both letteral and quasi-homophonic, as Joyce's on the Loud as Heard — there existed at origin the world as volume, the voice of full presence.

Derrida's essay is at this point overdue for a more dramatic subversive move against this (albeit satirized) mythology. We don't have to wait much longer. As it happens, the ground of the Loud's pun-ridden originary *parole* is seen to be undercut by not staying put in one *langue* at a time. Occulted here, beyond "ear" and "hear" in "he war," is the Hebrew for the Lord as Warrior, the hint (by anagrammatic transposition) of the vowels of "YAW EH." This passage from English into Hebrew is accompanied as well by a Babel-like displacement into the mispronounced German "he war." Layered over the additional echo of the German "he wahr" (for "he true" [with a /v/]), we also find in play a solecism of predication ("he were"), related (Derrida may be implying) to a low-dialect response to the preceding question, almost a Cockney joke again: "He war" for "he was." While Derrida does not explicitly recall this passage from *Portrait,* his reading would work to deconstruct the chauvinist linguocentrism of Stephen's belief that, though "*Dieu* was the French for God," and though "God understood what all the people who prayed said in their different languages," nevertheless "God's real name was God" (16). For Derrida the whole issue of translation explodes not only this myth but the phonocentric assumption itself. How, he asks, with his own pun on Joyce's Shem the Penman, can the Word of God, the Logos, undergo "dishemination" when only the sensible plenitude of the word, its presence, can incarnate God? The Logos dissipates in confrontation with homophony, with the homology between separate tongues, or with any punlike superimposition of two meanings upon the same word. Derrida has written earlier in the essay that the "audiophonic dimension of the divine law and its sublime height is announced in the English syllabification of *he (w)ar*" (152). But with the introduction of the Hebrew and Germanic traces of this trace (let alone the Cockney *v* for *w*), all Babel upends itself to the Book where such multiplicities can be assimilated. Translation is therefore a "graft (and without any possible rejection) of one language onto the body of another."

As much as in Shakespeare's sonnet 15, a narrow acceptation of this "grafting" trope would take the issue out of earshot altogether. Leaving aside the contorted Saussurean anagrammatism by which "He war" congeals to "hear," even such a strictly sequential bonding as the transegmental hint (taken by Derrida three sentences later in the passage from the *Wake*) of an "Anglo-Saxon god" (Got) in "Go to" (154) may be said, given divergent pronunciation, to be more visible than audible. This cannot, though, be assumed as the inevitable priority of eye over ear, and especially not for such transegmental drifts. The specific phonemic differential behind the ambiguous *parole,* because ambiguous *langue,* of w/*var* (not to mention associated cross-lexical effects) directly teases the auditory imagination. This is the para-vocal excitation Derrida wrestles down by too quickly redefining its terms. He admits of the *Wake* "this book's appeal for reading out loud," yet insists that "the Babelian confusion between the English *war* and the German *war* cannot fail to disappear—in becoming determined—when listened to. It is erased when pronounced" (156). But what about listening with "the mind's ear," as Joyce recommends?

In using Joyce's comic prayer as witness against the logophonic myth of divine fiat, as well as against all subsidiary shibboleths of voice as presence, the leverage of grammatology, for all its gains in the demystifying of metaphysics, has in fact backed Derrida's argument into an impasse on the score of Joycean polyglossia—or, at least, a contradiction. For just a moment more, however, Derrida's line of attack seems to sustain the explanatory force of a dialectic. It is true that for him linguistic *différance,* however much determined by the phonetic alphabet, rules out the phonological *basis* altogether. The Joycean turn in question becomes the primal scene of an exclusive—and exclusionary—inscription. But Derrida rephrases it this way: "The homography retains the effect of confusion, it shelters the Babelism which here, then, plays between speech and writing" (156). Here, then? Where else? When otherwise? Even while acknowledging that something is indeed going on "between speech and writing," Derrida would insist that such play, such interplay, is foreclosed by any attempt at phonic determination. This case of Joycean "translation"—between homographic but not homophonic inscriptions—gives Derrida what he takes to be the supreme instance of a grammatological confirmation at the very inauguration of the Word's war on Babel, a war booked and brooded over by Joyce. Since listening is excluded, only inscription can take up the slack between pronunciations, a difference reduced to the sheer gramme of *différance.* Yet this passage from the *Wake* may also be singled out as a test case for a revisionist approach to a postgrammatological "stylistics"—a test case, in short, for phonemic reading. In this sense it highlights the recovery of a *graphonic* trace in the reading *effect* of textuality.

It is just because there is no difference in script between German and English *w* that the graft is not entirely graphic, that one must "seehear lipspeech" in order to activate the pun, to recognize the "translation" at all.

Against a too insistent grammatological reading, one might lodge the implications of Joyce's own portmanteau coinage in the very passage under discussion by Derrida, the virtually performative self-enunciation "phonemanon" (258.22)—not, importantly, the more predictable "phonemenon." Mentioned briefly by Derrida (153) in tacit allusion to his own conjunction of speech and phenomena in the book by that title, the anagrammatic twist actually encodes a more suggestive point about the voice in relation to the phenomenon of a phonetic alphabet disposed as text. By this compbound of transposition and abbreviation, Joyce seems to signify a system of signification that has no roots in an authorizing voice. It is a process that is nevertheless textualized and decentered only through the *heard* play of the *phoneme anon.* The author is dead and gone, but the banding and disbanding of words plays on. Such is the anonymous (*anon.*) trace of pronunciation (rather than record of enunciation) not kept in play (from some voiced origin) but rather (sourcelessly, ceaselessly) *put* in play by the differentials of script.

In direct contrast to a Derridean approach, it is instructive to see how one of the most verbally alert recent scholars of *Finnegans Wake* thinks he can defend a thematics of such slippages only by rejecting the whole poststructuralist approach to Joyce. For John Bishop, as we learn from the title of his study, the *Wake* is "Joyce's Book of the Dark," a nighttext, a dreammode of audition.[8] For him, the "subject" of the text, the dreaming Earwicker, lends a quasi-psychoanalytic rather than narrative authority to all its verbal play—by focusing it continuously around oneiric mechanisms and motifs: the counterlogical transmutations of dreamspeech, whether generated or overheard in the register of half-conscious imagination. Freud is repeatedly adduced, but never his particular approach to the condensation and displacement of jokes as well as of dreamwork—those mechanisms of wordplay examined in the Prologue as a revealing analogue for the reciprocal phonic incursions and junctural overlays of the transegmental drift. Even this aspect of Freud seems too anarchic for Bishop's position, which stiffens itself against all notions of the Joycean text "as a free floating scud of signifiers disengaged from contact with the concrete" (299). The real, the "concrete": few terms could more completely beg the question, when it is precisely the concretized, if impalpable, materiality of the signifier itself, opaque and often intransigent, that is most profoundly at issue in the arguable divorce of Joyce's text from any transparent representation of reality.

No critic before Bishop has more avidly cataloged those instances of homophonic punning—including, without special notice, many transegmental effects—that bear on the thematics of dream audition, while few have had less to say on the linguistic implications of Joyce's coinages and portmanteaus. But what better example of the free-floating "scud" of signifiers, only fleetingly attached to reference, could a reader otherwise inclined hope to adduce than one of Bishop's most often cited puns on the paradox of death and wakefulness in the novel's title, the "trope" of sleep figured by a head nodding off so decidedly that it looks like the last slump of a corpse: "tropped head" (34.6; Bishop 29). Joyce's text is in just this slippery way audible, an "auradrama" (517.2; 270), its voicings "auracles" (467.28; 298), its waked subject the embodiment of the "earopean" (310.21, 598.15; 276) consciousness subject perpetually to the "noisance" (479.20; 281) of garbled language in a confluence of tongues—indeed, transegmentally again, the "tacit turns" (99.2; 265) of a laconic unconscious. "Phonoscopically incuriosited," as the *Wake* recurrently suggests (449.1, cf. 123.12–13; 286)— inciting the curiosity of eye and ear at their conjoint textual *site*—such effects are what I have been calling graphonic undulations of the materialized text, highlighted by specific disjunctures between sighting and silent hearing. They are exemplified also at the revelatory locus of decentered subjectivity in the novel: in the very nomination of its oneiric protagonist, what Bishop calls "the obliterate reduction of the *Wake*'s sleeping subject to a 'belowes hero' (343.17 ['below zero'])" (62). As we are to see in Chapter 7, with joint reference to abstract mathematical theory and to a heroine's immediate fear of numbers in *The Waves,* here too the zero interval in syntactic computation, transgressed and so activated, razes the very noun of identity. It thus writes a subject in as hero only to zero him out. Scudding or skimming, this is the drift of signification that rewrites lexicon and syntax together from within the very script that would fix them, incurring alternatives at the cost of disfigured contiguities, exploding combination by the shimmer between equivalences still differentially in play. To deny the deconstructive ramifications of what Bishop so acutely observes in the Joycean text is at once to disperse and curtail the force of his findings, to dissipate them in the name of the "concrete" world with which these effects are supposedly in touch.

For a last pair of "phonoscopic" examples that work against the preferred referentiality of Bishop's reading, we can look to phrasings explicitly concerned in the *Wake* with the vagaries of language in functional process—even as they manifest the lateral detachment and redistribution of the single letter as single phoneme. Most suggestively, at least for a transegmental reading of Joyce's text, we find invoked those "lines of litters slittering up and louds of latters slettering down" (114.17–18). The coinage "slittering" may hint at "slithering," but "slettering" is a neologism of pure phonemic displacement. As in this case, so later in "whose sbrogue" (581.16)—a slipspeaking about speech itself. By the transegmental migration of the possessive sibilant over to the term "brogue," Joyce has, typically, plumbed to a polyglot etymological depth, springing undertones of both "spoke" and "sprach." From such lexical oscillation in the *Wake,* we can return now to the birth throes of this preeminent modernist idiolect in *Ulysses,* where the dialectic between graphic and phonic is first put thematically as well as stylistically to work.

"Aural Eyeness": A Protean Modality

Near the close of "Proteus," we read how "lips lipped and mouthed fleshless lips of air" (48), with the lapsus "slip" twice slung across the segmental interval. The apocalyptic speech so characterized envisions the "road of cataractic planets, globed, blazing, roaring wayawayawayawayaway," an onomatopoetic reverberation of some such idiom as "way far away." If the Hebrew God "Yaweh" was present for Derrida (by a phonetically crisscross anagram) in "he war," how much more, in this primal astronomical thunder, is the ana*phone* of this sacred name to be heard four times repeated in the looped, iterative portmanteau "way*away.* . . ." Here, in protean recurrence, is a graphic metamorphosis by which the *deus absconditus* is audited in withdrawal from within roar of his own created "chaosmos" (*Wake,* 118.21). Manifested only by the reflexive logos of a phonemically ambiguous neologism, divinity is to be heard and not seen. The lexical misrule that lords it over the text in this way can be expressed by the punning anagram-like twist on "royal highness" in the *Wake:* "aural eyeness" (623.18). In terms sketched out in the "Proteus" episode of *Ulysses,* what we have been considering as the *graphonic* interdependence of textual signifiers honors not just the "ineluctable modality of the visible" but the "ineluctable modality of the audible" as well. This pivotal early episode in *Ulysses,* with its famous scene on the Sandymount Strand, develops a textual negotiation between these two irrefutable claims of eye and ear. It thus demonstrates the deep structuring logic behind Joyce's footnoted portmanteau pun in the *Wake,* "words all in one soluble" (299n.3). These are letters dissolved in the volubles of their syllables, in the latent enunciation of their segmental process.

The first line of "Proteus" is taken up mostly by that "mouthful" of a noun phrase, "Ineluctable modality of the visible," asserted and not demonstrated (except as we read with our eyes this self-substantiating substantive). The line then adds: "at least that." As we read, since we read, we are constrained to agreement. Reading becomes, in fact, the explicit semiological trope for the remainder of this paragraph: "Signatures of all things I am here to read." The phenomenal world is awash with "coloured signs." But what else? The paragraph closes with a paradoxical turn of phrase, the turning inside out of an idiomatic dead metaphor of sight: "Shut your eyes and see." Not *our* eyes, though. By way of indirect discourse, Stephen is talking, that is thinking, to himself. If *we* closed our eyes, there would be no next paragraph at all. Yet what we do find there is not altogether visible in its effects:

> Stephen closed his eyes to hear his boots crush crackling wrack and shells. You are walking through it howsomever. I am, a stride at a time. A very short space of time through very short times of space. Five, six: the *Nacheinander*. Exactly: and that is the ineluctable modality of the audible.

(37)

The one-thing-after-another of audibility, of sound as duration, is opposed a few sentences further on in this paragraph to the *Nebeneinander*, the one-thing-next-to-another, of visible contiguity. Like the phonological basis of language, the world mediated through closed eyes and thick boots is the world of the ear. Stephen does not feel what is beneath his feet but hears it, does not feel the "wrack" (whether meaning "kelp" or "strewn wreckage"—or both at once) but hears the sound of it. In this first instance of a purely heard world, the ineluctable modality of the Joycean phonic subtext is recruited to offer—as befits the description—an auditory effect before the assigning of any other material cause. In the *Nacheinander* (or sequencing) of phonemes, what Hopkins might call the after-ing of syllables and sounds, the phrase "crush crackling wrack"—by a holding over of the /ŋ/ and then by "dynamic displacement" of the /g/ from within it—ends up sounding like the iterative "crush crackling *wrack*" (or, in a word, *crack*). It is thus processed as rendering no more and no less, through a syntactical onomatopoeia, than the crush of bootbeats on the shore. This is the way sound works in and as text, a continuous modality of auditing not entirely marshaled by the contrary modality of script.

When Stephen begins talking to himself—"You are walking through it"—the text must as always, to make its *meaning,* order itself by demarcation, by signaled contiguities, by the *Ne/ben/ein/an/der* of one-thing-next-to-another under constraints of lexical and syntactic demarcations. Without this, we would have only the modality of the audible to guide us. We would then be likely to hear in the above passage, without interruption, the phrase "I am astride" rather than the cogito of "I am, a stride," the latter punctuated twice over by a comma and a lexical gap that enact the tread of identity in the world of touch. Schismatic at base, subjectivity is hereby mounted upon the break into speech and the breaks between it. It is constituted by the introduction of a determinate lexical rhythm into an ambivalent phonic pulse: in Kristeva's terms, by the emplacement of the symbolic upon the undulations of the semiotic. Of this there is yet another, fainter suggestion in the immediately following sentence. This comes with the transegmental trace of a pluralized and contracted "I am" — "*I'ms*" — in the fissured lexical tissue of "very short (t)*imes* of space." When, near the close of this chapter, Stephen again speaks to himself in the imperative mood, invokes his own audition, it is to hear the language of nature, of otherness, as a syllabic play, a delineation of seaspeech: "Listen: a fourworded wavespeeech: seesoo, hrss, rsseeiss, ooos" (49). This is the ineluctable modality of the audible as an oscillation of cryptophones, a sign system "forwarded" (a homophonic pun on "fourworded," like "sea's" in "*see*soo") in such a way that it evokes the verging of the world's semiotic plenum upon the human symbolic, the churning of sound toward and into language. The opening disyllable, if more than sheer onomatopoeia, is an echo of the seesaw motion it locally enacts, a rhythm to which the last syllable offers a chiastic response ("soo" into "ooos") — even as it phonetically calls up its phonemic variant in "ooze." With the incremental iteration "rss rsseeiss," there is not only the hint again of "sea's" but the cadenced overlap of the sea's "*reced*ing," without ever "*ceas*ing" its motion. This is the speech before language waiting in the "signatures" of the phenomenal world. Echoing Ponge, here is the world's "gnature" when processed by and as text — a world always, in yet a third valence of Joyce's homophone, "foreworded." Such is the ineluctable semiosis both reproduced in textual play and generated by it as a reading effect.

S/lipspeech

If such a passage appears to yield nature's s/lipspeech as inscribed by the Joycean text, it is only within the reciprocal modalities of reception. The "sonorous silence" of the text, before it can be extrapolated to anything like the "science" thereof (*Wake*, 230.22), is voiced only, as it were, visually: evocalized. At the end of *Joyce's Voices,* Hugh Kenner suggests that Molly emerges as the voice of the Muse passing unnarrated into sleep as the "pure composing faculty."[9] Molly's utterance, transcribed but unmarked as text, is thus the last of Joyce's voices, none of them really acknowledged as such by the text. It is the one that erases every storyteller's convention, every intervention (even "said Molly to herself") in order to produce voice itself, inevitably deputized but supposedly unmediated. Hers is the gnomic omniscience not of narrative principal — or narrational principle — but of consciousness itself in registration. The technological emphasis of Kenner's more recent book, in which Joyce's scrivening is understood in light of printing innovations, leads him to a radically different position, one that surfaces only briefly in a passing early aside. In *The Mechanic Muse* the voices are no longer read as Joyce's at all, nor do they belong to the characters. Technology having demystified text production, the typewriter and the linotype machine having served to expose the delusion of the speaking voice incarnate in print, the result is that Joycean voicings, robbed of their phenomenality as overheard speech, have resurfaced into phonology as the reader's activation of the text. For Kenner, both Joyce's city and his book are "haunted by the shades of people," the novel in particular by "a vast roster of people whose voices, even, we may think we hear though it's we ourselves who silently supply them" (76). Nothing in Kenner's tone signals the critical emergency of this recognition. Nonetheless, in a single remark, the presuppositions of his previous study are swept out from under him. The technologies he finds informing modernism have led him, quite without his admitting it, to an impasse: an acknowledgment of the voiceless mechanics of textuality for which he has no further theory in reserve. In giving up more than he knows, however, Kenner also allows more than he illustrates. His understanding of the Joycean text leaves it precisely where we have taken it up. Joyce is voices, but the text's alone—in production. The Mechanic Muse cedes authority to this verbal drive, and through it, to us; our reading bodies its wake, supplying the only "volume" ever displaced by the path of its signification.

At one point in Molly's closing episode, folded away in the overtly musical contours of this singer's silent monologizing—and, it is now claimed by the new editors, smoothed out at some point in the passage's deviant transmission into print—is the vocal phrasing "dear deaead days beyondre call" (627.874–75). Molly's half-asleep inner phrasing turns the adjective "dead" into an elongated dirge all its own. In addition, the subsequent syllabic stretching involves the dismemberment of an adjacent lexeme, her thoughts fusing the preposition with the iterative prefix of the next word (a process normalized to "beyond recall" in the 1961 edition [762]). The variant wording ("beyondre call") would thus serve to dismantle in advance the lost possibility it mourns, further distancing the past with the surfaced etymological hint of "yon" (or "yonder") in "beyond." What is indeed called to mind here, and perhaps recovered from oblivion by the new edition, is certainly not Joyce the maker of books exclusively nor, on the other hand, Joyce the transcriber of a singer's internal melody. Returned to us in this tiny moment, among a multitude like it even before the *Wake,* is the Joyce whose verbal slips and lapses, whose transegmental ambiguities turning to psychological ironies, whose polysyllabax—in short, whose textuality—manages to speak, by being not just written but read, of the unconscious-structured-like-a-language. Voiceless itself, but in a continuous evocation of the enunciating function, the Joycean text plays out those condensations and displacements that enact in articulation the slippages attendant on desire as s/lack.

In the contrasting section just before Molly's sustained stream of consciousness, we encounter the "musemathematics" of an antithetical stylistic mode across which, nonetheless, something of the same phonotextual energy is manifest. Into the reasoned stretches of a categorical and analytic style, a discourse stripped of rhetoric and flattened by relentless terminology, bursts a complex lexical mutation carried on the irrational "wavespeech" of ebbing and fluctuant subject-positions. In "Ithaca," the penultimate episode, Bloom and Stephen, urinating side by side, enter upon a wordless hush that is not just a mutual but a textually reciprocal silence. Beneath the suspended conversation of the scene, and the silence of the script that represents it, seethes a graphonic metamorphosis that refuses to settle on any new constitution of psychic boundaries, rippled impertinently with the slide and denial of pronomination itself: "Silent, each contemplating the other in both mirrors of the reciprocal flesh of theirhisnothis fellowfaces" (702). Few moments in Joyce's novel more fully justify the poststructuralist work that has been done on the relation between consciousness and signifying practice in its pages. Nor does any moment in *Ulysses* open this 1922 text more directly to the motivated lexical mayhem of its 1939 successor. Looked at in one way, according to the prevailing scientism and parodic precision of the "Ithaca" format, "theirhisnothis" might be (simply?) an idiomatic (and grammatically questionable) plural for "each other's" — that is, "their" — corrected by specification to a parsing of pronominal reciprocity itself: "their, or rather his and at the same time not his." Instead, looked at askance, the phrase (word?) scans in the manner of the *Wake* as a virtually schizophrenic designation convulsed by an indeterminacy lexical because psychic.

In this sense, the phrase is found erupting into the discourse of science as its Other and its annihilation, the end of precision in the breakdown of *-cision* itself. For once read, silently enunciated, the compbound begins immediately to unravel and reloop. As an unabashed stumbling block in the hypertrophic prosiness of "Ithaca," this hybrid of lexicon and syntax, this word-phrase, works free of any tripartite adjectival determination to take on a textual life of its own. To begin with, "Theirhis" registers as a phonetic exaggeration of "theirs," while also (therefore) of the predicating "there is" in the composite lexeme when construed as a clause: "There's no this." Which is only to say that, as is the case with "theirhis," the attached "nothis" is bound by no junctural law (neither phonic nor graphic) — but merely inclined by parallelism — to read as "not his" rather than "no this." Yet in the strained latter case, the phrase makes acceptable ("reciprocal") sense as well — at least when registered as instantaneously reformulated from the point of view of either self in turn. With the grammatical shifter "this" detached from any set antecedent, each self is lost to a stable subject-position in the text's process of denominating the other's. Demonstrative grammar, in short, can no longer demonstrate the site of the subject. There is suddenly no "here" there where "this" can take hold, neither in the signified space of reference nor even in the signifying chain. In such a radical collapse of possessive upon demonstrative grammar, the textual ironies of segmentation and juncture in this fourteen-letter collocation figure the disjuncture and interchange between the dis-positions, the continuous dispossession, of self-consciousness itself. Nowhere before *Finnegans Wake* will a collision of homophony ("theirhis"/"theirs"/"there's") and homography ("not=his"/"no=this") bring what we might finally call the profound "spaciness" of Joycean verbal tactics more strategically to the fore. In the remarkably layered and stunningly unpoetic lexical knot of "theirhisnothis," that bastard offspring of scientific refinement and psychotic contradiction, Joyce has pushed so far beyond the domain of traditional stylistics that almost every letter of this textual compress has become, in short, a phonotextual free agent.

No less dismembering, except on the written face of it, is probably the most recognizable utterance from *Ulysses,* lexically discrete until read. I speak of that sensualized murmur of eros and acquiescence in the book's last line, Molly's famous reiterated affirmative: "and yes I said yes I will Yes." Out of the sheer expiration of this sibilant breath, the inner speech of Molly as "auracle" (*Wake,* 467.28) designates the condition of its own unspoken, its own unconscious, utterance. It is as if language were urging itself toward the surface of the almost sleeping body in the form of the very word transegmentally named by its emergence. This is the "sigh" that punctuates her remembered desire between the monosyllable of self-surrender and the identifying pronoun of its retrospect: "yes sigh said yes sigh will Yes." With the iterative sequence evocalized in this way, the whole self as (pro)nomination – the "I" – is passed over and away into a phrasing of the very sound which that self is complicit not only in making but in producing – by naming – as a reading effect. Then, too, one thing leads to another in the phonotext. At the other end of this phantasmal monosyllabic hiss is a potential pluralizing ligature with the sibilant of "said," which serves to render all the more syntactic a phonemic reading of this speech about repetitive speech, with the "sighs" as grammatical subject rather than punctuation or filler: "yes sighs said yes." Can it be doubted that the treatment of such an utterance in *Finnegans Wake* would be entirely likely to spell out this punning alternative in so many letters? And that those letters would thus count as a passing gloss, by exaggeration, on a homophonic latency in that whole literary and even linguistic prehistory upon which a work like *Ulysses* first turned not its back but, rather, its analytic machinery?

On the subject of just these last lines in *Ulysses,* in fact, a revealing moment in Derrida's approach to textuality as a whole, as well as to Joyce in particular, appears in the essay, "Ulysse gramophone: oui-dire de Joyce," accompanying the previously translated essay on the *Wake* in the original French volume.

The second essay, more recently appearing in English as "Ulysses Gramophone: Hear Say Yes in Joyce,"[10] is preoccupied in good part with Molly's "yes," especially in its last capitalized appearance, "the last word, the eschatology of the book" (86) as it circles round to the opening capitalized "Yes" of her monologue. Like word breaks and punctuation, as we have seen before in Derrida, the "majuscule inaudible" (86) — the capital seen only, not heard — becomes in this context a quintessential gramme. It is, we are told, activated only "dans l'oeil de la langue" (86).[11] As usual, despite the duplex "Gramo/phone" of Derrida's present title, the gram(me) remains privileged, at least in rhetorical emphasis, over the phone — without always the qualifying admission, as there was in his discussion of the *Wake,* of the play "between."[12] Beyond its being exclusively privy to the "eye of the language," hence to the reader's eye rather than ear, Molly's "*yes* dans les *eyes*" is thereby defamiliarized by Derrida into a partial anagram of the organ that sees just such letteral play: sees at this point, in other words, an unsayable but operable alphabetic shuffle.

In this sense, Derrida reads the Joycean text at hand as if it were in itself a parable of any text's affirmation only through the eyes that produce it — produce it within his own version of an "ineluctable modality" of inscription. Again, to rescue Joyce from the phonocentrism of which Hartman expected that Derrida would accuse him, the Joycean text is rewritten wherever possible under Derrida's gaze, rewritten as sheer script. In the present case, however, to isolate this exclusive "eye"-ing of the "yes" without passing the latter through the incremental "graphonic" generation of the text as phenomenally processed is to miss even such a further and directly relevant insinuation (or "phonemanon") in the actual syntagmatic succession of the passage as "yes eyes said yes." This is a symptomatic oversight in Derrida precisely because such a transformation, unlike his associated sense of a graphic switch (or ana-gramme), could emerge only as a "modality of the audible," an aural modality even in the mode of silence. Illustrating what I have earlier characterized as the recurrent deaf spot of deconstruction when too programmatically applied, such is also the case with that other overlooked homophonic — and, so to speak, metaphonic — alternative educed above from Molly's closing "enunciation": "yes sigh(s) said yes sigh/I will Yes." Entirely through the "productive" medium of the text as process, the language of the body's desire is here sighed forth by the (in one sense only) breathless, the entirely passive, body of the reading agent. Read according to a genuine gramophonology rather than grammatology, then, the differential principle of the simultaneously protensive and retensive trace would find in Joyce its most relentlessly phonemic experimentation. The tacit question lodged at such a moment in regard to the "site" of textual processing, or again "phonoscopically incurio*sited,*" is one that Joyce will later pose explicitly, but already nearly a decade after Woolf's 1931 experiment in consciousness as evocalized stream. With or without *The Waves* as intertext, the *Wake* takes time out, amid its wash and wake of phonemes, to ask of itself the question: "what are the sound waves saying?" (256.23–24).

7   Catching the Drift
Woolf as Shakespeare's Sister

Before Virginia Woolf's *Waves,* there were those of Gerard Manley Hopkins. The sketch and caption reproduced as frontispiece show Hopkins — it is almost irresistible to put it this way — writing the world. He inscribes the inscape and instress of the sea's rippling tracery in a hand curled and fluted like the froth it details, first in iconic, then in symbolic lines. By the latter array of finely etched characters, Hopkins actually models the principle of undulation, crest, and reversal under analysis, evokes it in script while evocalizing it in the "lettering" (his special sense) of junctural fold and overlap. The phrase "a network *of f*oam," for instance, invites a layering in its own phonic rather than scriptive medium. Further along, the script itself, in sheerly graphic terms, and if only by an "accident" of handwriting, repeats and compounds this effect with the lexical aberration of "only *amass* of foam." The use of "amass" as substantive was obsolete by Hopkins's day, and the participial form "amassed" is present only by arrested association. Whether or not this orthography departs from dictionary logic to form a new word (and new prepositional idiom: "amass of," on the partial analogy of "awash with," say), Hopkins's handwritten notation has, on the very face of it, curiously amassed its constituent alphabetic characters in a single irregular gesture of registration. To insist that the article and noun of "a=network" earlier in the caption seem almost as closely bonded by the eccentricities of Hopkins's hand — as if this point would entirely rule out the graphic interest of the scrawled "amass" — is to refuse Hopkins full self-consciousness about the physical basis of his transcriptive enterprise in this verbal "sketch." In any case, within the fragmented grammar of the passage, however inscribed, there remains an active, if only instantaneous, aural ambiguity — between a phantom participial phrase, "amass(ed) of," and its (immediately revised) substantive sense — an ambiguity whose onset, whose pressure point, is the segmentally uncertain juncture of "a" and "mass."

Intentionality and manuscript evidence aside, the phonemic microdrama produced by the phrasings "of foam" and "a/mass of" finds its own ideal characterization in this brief text's final image of marine backwash — with one word after another, much as one wave, caught "upon the point of encountering the reflux of the former." There is scarcely a more evocative description to be found anywhere, as it happens, of the linguistic subject to which *Reading Voices* is addressed. The transegmental drift is indeed the "reflux" of one junctural phoneme upon its predecessor. Woolf's own most self-illustrating phrase for the verbal fluctuation that permits such effects comes from her 1931 novel, *The Waves,* and comes bearing a trace of the original working title, *The Moths:* "the silver-grey flickering moth-wing quiver of words."[1] However troped, this is the oscillation of words as sonic waves, the quiver and flux, the flux and reflux, of silently voiced phrasing. Woolf's *Les Mots,* by any other name. If at the draft stage, therefore, the "moths" of the provisional title referred to the lexical divisions of utterance, it was not this ultimate referent, only the working metaphor, that was altered in the change to *The Waves.* Evoked thereby are the figurative waves whose "flickering" and "quiver," in all their difference from Joyce's equally transegmental "wavespeech" before them, shape the subject of this final chapter — where they will be subjected to the work of a fuller interpretive operation than these pages have yet attempted.

While at work on *Mrs. Dalloway,* Woolf in 1924 bestowed on her diary the following confidence: "As I think, the diary writing has greatly helped my style; loosened the ligatures."[2] The word "ligature," of course, as it has occasionally found its way into these pages, is a technical term from music: for those "ties" that bind together a phrasing, those holds and prolongations that can be readily transferred to the linkages of an alphabetic text. In this sense, stylistic advances of the kind we know Woolf to have been making at the time of *The Waves* might better be said less to loosen ligatures than to allow them their full play in loosening the rule of diction. The novel which Woolf came to feel was "my first work in my own style!"[3] — and which Yeats singled out, along with *Ulysses* and Pound's *Cantos,* as one of three "typical" modernist works in which language conveys "a deluge of experience breaking over us and within us, melting limits whether of line or tint; man . . . but a swimmer, or rather the waves themselves"[4] — is certainly one place to test the fluidity of "ligature" against the narrative crises of emotional blockage which such writing wants at one and the same time to analyze and, at least for the reader, to assuage. Reading the novel for its psychological as well as linguistic ligatures, their tenuous strain and occasional failure, can discover in Woolf a resolute but never irruptive modernism continuous with the literary history of which she was so sensitive a reader and critic. Quietly culminating the tradition of phonic play in the English canon, without going beyond to its multilingual deconstruction as did later Joyce, a novel like *The Waves* offers a molding of the "masterly" to the pen of a writing woman. Woolf's resistance to the high style of the fathers often takes the form of a textural resistance, a thickening or impedance of syntax, an intrusion of the phonic into the scriptive. As inferred in the Prologue from her essay about disease and sickbed reading, Woolf at times appears to favor an ill-locutionary mode of textual processing dependent on what we might call a slowed phonic pulse. Woolf's explicitly antipatriarchal style is thus designed to render opaque the received, authoritative handling of literary diction and syntax. This is the poetry of her prose. At the same time, of course, in Shakespeare or Milton, not to mention in Father Hopkins, as of course in many of the novelists down through Forster, let alone Joyce, the practice of literary phrasing has always generated not just a facility and power but a curious phonemic fluency as well. It is just this that Woolf must work to maximize in a strategic feminist blend of homage and departure.

Separable Ligatures

It should by now be expected that the verbal phenomenon this chapter will be listening for in Woolf's *The Waves* isn't really there. Or, to be more exact, it is neither here nor there in any given unit of prose. It falls, or flashes, between words, as something they can be said to keep between themselves in enunciation, as, for instance, in the doubled phoneme – become ligature or bridge – between "wing" and "quiver." We have come to understand this aural, not necessarily oral, phenomenon as a mode of ambiguity – but one whose doubleness is not primarily semantic. The ambivalence in question subtends not two senses of a word but two senses of the reading body. It divides between eye and ear, between script and a tacit voicing fractionally out of phase with it, overlapping the boundaries between written words. At such moments, Woolf's prose is more permissive than expressive; it lets in as lingual disruption the stray reverberations ordinarily contained or suppressed by the marshaled effects of literary style. Woolf's phonic counterpoint to the rank and file of script, her syncopated collaboration between the written and the read, creates a poetic resonance that is at the same time a dissonance within the logic of inscription, of textuality itself. In vibrating upon the inner ear, this conceptual discord between the graphic and the phonic matter of words appears to reroute the written text through the palpable, the palpitating upper body, its passively engaged organs of articulation. Not *back* through the body, as if voice were the privileged ground of all language. Rather, once again we find the body providing not so much the recovered origin as the secondary medium of poetic

262 ▲ Reading Voices

utterance. This chapter will return for a final consideration of the reading body as the ultimate field for the poetic irregularities of Woolf's late style. In the meantime, we will need to examine the relation of Woolf's prose to the life and death of her suicidal heroine, Rhoda, the character who is quick to figure what is most unforgiving and disruptive in temporal consciousness as a precarious linguistic terrain and to find textual metaphors for the unyielding succession of her clocked, disjunctive moments. If Woolf's prose is in any functional sense to be read as an appeal to the articulating, tactile body, then we must note the manner in which such sensual apprehension fails at the same time, even by analogy, to anchor the novel's doomed female character in a meaningfully eased sense of temporal succession. Even when a given effect cannot be semanticized, its guiding logic may still be more generally thematized: hence the culminating place of this chapter in a theory of reading drawn inevitably toward interpretation. In a diary entry dated 7 January 1931, while Woolf was at work on *The Waves,* she wrote, "I want to make prose move—yes, I swear, move as never before."[5] But movement, negotiated duration, is the very thing that terrifies and defeats her character Rhoda, who is tortured by scriptlike intervals that provide no respite, torn by the knowledge that getting on with it is always a getting over of the dead spots. Rhoda's recurrent prepsychotic lapses and eventual suicide may thus seem to embody in a single fictional character the notions of linguistically based subjectivity and its traumas prevalent both in poststructuralist theory at large and in the particular bearings of its feminist (or, at least, gender-oriented) investigations. My general procedure thus far of isolated audition will now gather, provisionally, toward a more comprehensive reading of a literary narrative as it takes focus around such a distraught psychology. The reading will attempt to suggest what psycholinguistic options for the maintenance of subjectivity Woolf's feel for verbal duration as pulsional drive might seem to hold out, even as this one narrative withdraws its recurrent promise of rhythm and fluidity from the ruptured consciousness of a single female character.

In Woolf's last novel, *Between the Acts* (1941), the heroine, Miss La Trobe, retreats after the staging of her play into a crowded pub, where indirect discourse retreats further with her into a reverie on the nature of language. The printed version of the passage goes like this: "Words of one syllable sank down into the mud. The mud became fertile." But Woolf had originally thought to write: "Words copulated; seethed, surged. Phrases began shoulder-ing up from the mist," with "mist" at once changed, even at this stage of composition, to the more fecund "mud."[6] One is tempted to generalize from this passage, even though Woolf later euphemized it, to say that in Woolf's late style words shoulder each other as well as up, and in so doing, interlock, couple, give, and blend. Such an erotics of style is nowhere so directly referred to in Woolf's published prose. Yet what implications might it have for that implicit "woman's sentence" she seems to call for in *A Room of One's Own*?[7] In view of the shattering, linguistically figured experience of Rhoda, what kind of sensual charge, what yielding, what abandon, what giving way between the acts of wording, so to speak, would serve to feminize or diffuse the insistent syntactic drive of a male-preempted mother tongue? Or is this sexual differentiation, this gendering of utterance, a false lead even in Woolf's own dream of something beyond the "man's sentence"? Might language perhaps lay claim instead to a sensual component apart from gender, where the rhythm of phrasing is itself sexualized without being co-opted by one sex or the other, where words "copulate" with each other, abrasive, fertilizing, well before they can be commandeered by the forces of sexual politics?[8] If so, this frictional pulse of language must nevertheless, in the interlinked silent soliloquies that compose the text, also be taken to compose the articulate self, to found subjectivity itself. In this structuring of story by inner discourse, *The Waves* demonstrates more strenuously than any other novel by Woolf how the stream of consciousness, in its expressive projections, is licensed only by a simultaneous act of the unconscious — one that must attempt, often vainly, to posit, and position, a subject behind all such verbal energy. The drama of constituted identity is thus played out within the soliloquies by the pressure of language exploiting its own clefts, ruptures, elisions, and deflections, its subjective continuity riven and recontrived, breached, appeased, or radically reconceived.

While other characters, for instance, "cannot follow any word through its changes" (42), or sense themselves "tied down with single words" (16), Bernard — alter ego for Woolf in her androgynous verbal imagination — insists, by contrast, that "we melt into each other with phrases" (16). As a novelist he is therefore "dabbling always in warm soluble words" (68–69), seeking out "the hot, molten effects," the "lava flow of sentence into sentence" (79), by which language, dissolving under its own pressure, will burn away the borders of received distinctions. Even his occasional skepticism about language manages an unconscious celebration — a recuperation by the very language of the unconscious. Toward the end of the novel, for instance, Bernard has actually come to despair over the power of words to achieve identity with what they would designate, to convey rather than just name experience. Despite its plasticity, the opacity of language always sabotages its referential intent. "There are no words" sufficient to his task, none transparent enough. "Blue, red — even they distract, even they hide with thickness instead of letting the light through" (287). Reality is masked, rather than manifested, by words. Unless, of course, at the metalinguistic level, this phonic veiling, this lexical thickening and gathering, is precisely what such words are sometimes attempting to represent. A transegmental nexus like "with thick-ness" merely exaggerates the inevitable overlapping of phonemes either by an almost irresistible elision or by the labored emphasis necessary to forestall it. This offers a clue to the entire mimetic premise of Woolf's textual effort, where prose, never transparent to reality, often abstracts and reduplicates its structure in the *form* of words. The sort of phonemic clotting audible in "with thickness," for instance, can elsewhere suggest a merger or bleeding between semantic units, as when in an italicized interlude "*all the blades of the grass were run together in one fluent green blaze*" (149). Framing the whole clause is the phonemic matter of "blades" displaced to the undentalized, slightly com-pressed acoustic echo of "blaze," not to mention the echo of "were run" in "one." At the same time, the entire verb phrase itself, "were run" (not just "—run"), slackened and rushed enough in enunciation, is pronounced as one swift blurred "run." At most, however, this is only an acoustic collapse into a part term of the complete phrasal verb. The lexical segmentation succumbs at its border, but no new word emerges, no third term wrung from contiguity or stretched between its scripted units.

The reflexive "wi*th th*ickness" phenomenon can, of course, also occur in mimetically or thematically irrelevant contexts, as with Jinny's fantasy of "a thin dress shot wi*th red* threads" (34)—unless this double stitch in the transeg-mental prose (what phonetics, again, calls "dynamic displacement") is taken to figure the metonymical anticipations of the unconscious itself. More often though, and more directly, the transegmental drifts of Woolf's text seem contextualized to enact processes homologous with their own operations, as here the oddly hued and diaphanous folds of lexical accumulation: "Our eyes seem to push through curtains of color, red, orange, umber and queer ambiguous tints" (135). In that profusion and confusion of color, the ordinary sequence would have unveiled, after red and orange, the dark orangish yellow of "amber." This expectation is suppressed in that blending of the phonemic palette which softens the overt paronomasia of "amber" grading to "ambigu-ous" with the earthiness of "umber." As we move through Woolf's veiling and layering of overtones, we may even suspect a cloaked pun in "curtains"—for chromatic "shades." In any case, the word "curtains" provides a metaphor for the opacities "whi*ch y*ield like veils" only to remind us—by what phonetics calls the "fusion" produced by an intruded "glide" sound—of the "shielding" that must precede its own visual and, indeed, phonemic yielding. Certainly, Bernard the writer would appear to be summing up Woolf's textual experiment with a final transegmental play in the last soliloquy. His flagging faith in language suddenly recovered, we hear that "loveliness returns as one looks with all its train of phantom phrases" (287), the host word "train" coupling itself with the preceding sibilant to form upon its trace the new noun "strain."

To hear such a strain on the nexus of syntax in Woolf is to attune ourselves to a reading unpledged to the eye, an active realization of the phonotext.

"Intermitten(t/ce) Shocks"

It is at just such a juncture, such a conflicted sense of lexical juncture, that the psychology of Woolf's novel addresses and is answered by its very textuality. Woolf's prose discourse transcends the strict limits of syntax in a novel whose suicidal heroine is shackled by such limitations. In an apostrophe to life itself, Rhoda bewails "how you snatched from me the white spaces that lie between hour and hour . . . and tossed them into the wastepaper basket" — as if they were scrap paper, without a shred of useful meaning. "Yet those were my life" (204). She lives for, and in, the interstices of duration imaged as the white blanks of a text. And she does so having addressed life itself, reified it in the vocative case, "given it face" by prosopopoeia, as if it were nothing more than the textual ground of inscription, the neutral base for the ups and downs, the starts and stops, of any particular story — as, of course, in prose fiction it is, even when consciousness is not explicitly figured as transcription. Only by hiding out in her coveted gaps, those all too infrequent remissions in the inexorable logic of sequence, can Woolf's heroine bear the rhythm of intermittency that would pummel her with sensation. Reaching her breaking point, Rhoda goes to her death to avoid the further punishing disruptions of temporal existence, the chief analogue of which, for her as well as for Woolf, is the nature of script as a series of differential notations and recurrent blanks.[9] Rhoda, in short, cracks over the breaks between words, even while she yearns for their supposed nullity. At the same time, the metalinguistic implications of Woolf's fluent style work to bind and heal these very fissures, attempting this within a complex plot that keeps other lives in motion around the violence of Rhoda's existence and the vacancy of her unenacted death.

Concerning the irregularities of her temporal existence, Rhoda realizes that "we have invented devices for filling up the crevices and disguising these fissures" (64). The silent soliloquy continues: "So I detach the summer term. With intermittent shocks, sudden as the springs of a tiger, life emerges heaving its dark crest from the sea." Language and duration here coalesce once again in Rhoda's imagination. The temporal unit "term" becomes itself an admitted lexical term, to be etymologically and paronomastically embedded in its successor, "intermittent." A mounting acoustic density now presses finally toward the actual shearing of a lexeme. In the phrasing "dark crest," the rest between words, the fissure that separates them, loses the cutting edge of its crevice, as it were. Out of quiescence comes energy; out of submergence, emergence; out of the leveled, the heaving. That seems to be Rhoda's sense, but we also sense the seams — and the anarchic textuality of their elision — into

whose contingencies she herself cannot relax. At the chiastic juncture between "dark" and "crest" a lexical dissolution appears that allows the ear to
hear in the rendered swelling a "dark rest" — a death? — brought turbulently to
light, as if from the undulant *langue* beneath the scriptive intermittence of
parole. This acoustic flux in language is not a drift with which Rhoda can
synchronize her mind. Neither is she capable of managing the intermittencies
of lived duration, whose shocks grow unendurable, whose lacunary spaces
become at last unsurvivable. She cannot, in short, assume her fictional
birthright as a function of Woolf's sliding, elided, resilient, and rippling style.

Ciphering Time

And in a formative scene we are to see why. Early in the novel's first section, at
the end of a lesson in Latin grammar, Woolf shows Rhoda emerging into voice
at precisely the moment of her exclusion from written discourse, her in-
comprehension of the lesson going forward on the blackboard and in the
copybooks of her friends: "But I cannot write. I see only figures" (21). Only
graphic shapes, that is, not their possible meaning. Here is the otherness of
language stressed as the language of others, an accession to the symbolic
whose rite of passage, whose writing, Rhoda, alone among her peers, cannot
achieve. What Rhoda "cannot write," as it happens, are after all not "figures"
as alphabetic characters to be bunched together into words but, instead, the
cardinal "figures" of numerical ciphering, whose logic of representation and
combination she cannot master. The inculcation of Latin grammar has
shifted, in other words, to a lesson in arithmetic, yet the Arabic notation is for
Rhoda even more of a dead language. "'Now Miss Hudson,' said Rhoda, 'has
shut the book. Now the terror is beginning. Now taking her lump of chalk she
draws figures, six, seven, eight, and then a cross and then a line on the
blackboard'" (21). Beginning with the "six" that sums up her place alongside
the major otherness in her life (her five present friends), the challenge for
Rhoda is to generate continuity out of that precipitating integer within a
signifying chain of numeration: 6, and then what? She cannot meet that
challenge. "The figures mean nothing now," she says. "Meaning has gone.
The clock ticks."

Confusing the circular clockface with the curvilinear figures of mathematical script on the board, not realizing that numbers can calibrate without
containing time, Rhoda says to herself, "Look, the loop of the figure is
beginning to fill with time." In so doing, it would seem to siphon off all
temporality from the space Rhoda woefully inhabits. Whether belonging to
the 6 or to the 8, for instance, the loop she mentions yawns as the cipher of an
empty plenum, the zero of evacuation. As in all writing, only more dramatically here, Rhoda is cast outside the signifier she has been asked to set down.

But for her the loop that inscribes this fact also sketches her lack of access to the potential signified of human time. If the circuit of the hours can be drawn closed as a loop, then, as Rhoda says climactically, "I myself am outside the loop; which I now join—so—and seal up, and make entire" (21). By these words, and the letters that form them, the linguistic and mathematical parables of this episode slyly overlap in a conjoined argument about a "writing" to whose circuit the self is at best tangential. For that inscribed adverb "so" in "which I now join—so—" also contains in the second of its characters a loop of its own, the rounding off of the "o." In this context "so" becomes a quasi-performative locution that closes off by enacting the graphemic gesture it names, reflexively instancing the sealing shut of a transcribed letter rather than a described integer or loop thereof. Then, too, what the zero-loop and the circle of the letter *o* have in common is that for enunciation they both require a sound that is elsewhere the signifier of exclamation itself, "O." No sooner has Rhoda rounded off the loop of "so," than she recognizes how with exactly that gesture she must confront the fact that "the world is entire, and I am outside of it crying, 'Oh, save me, from being blown for ever outside the loop of time!'" (22)—as if the very *O* (or the chiastic reversal of "so" in the lurking pluralized *O*'s of "*Oh, s*ave") were the vocative object(s) of her prayer.

Though figured (out) by arithmetic in one sense, time is also figured in another by the rigors and irregularities of inscription. Numbers may mark time, add it up, but their own enciphering as lines and spaces, every bit as much as in linguistic writing, may also trace visual metaphors for the forward toil and voiding gaps of temporal succession. Since the loops of numbering have become by the end of the classroom passage the graphic holes in the scriptive characters themselves, since we have thus passed from arithmetical back to alphabetical writing with that symbolic but also hieroglyphic "so," a major question remains about this schoolroom lesson. Apart from its thematic links with other modes of writing as attempts to order duration, why has arithmetic been introduced in such direct psychological terms, its unmastered disjunctions staging the scenario of Rhoda's first major crisis?

Zerography

The start of an answer, before it returns us to linguistic particulars, might be found in Lacan's use of the number theory of Gottlob Frege, an attempt to bring abstract logic to the aid of psychology. To follow out the considerable complications of this line of thought, we can turn to an essay by Jacques-Alain Miller that explores at some length the applicability of Frege to Lacan in terms of the "suturing" process whereby the subject is sewn into its own discourse.[10] Since logic demands that any object be identical to itself, each object is therefore identified singly by the number "one," naming not wholeness but the concept of being one of itself, one with itself. If, according to Frege, "one" thus names the number assigned to the concept "identical with itself," and that concept subsumes one of everything taken singly, then what would name the concept "not identical with itself," and what object could it possibly subsume? Since this concept is a logical contradiction, it subsumes among possible objects exactly "none." Thus the zero is engendered. As the number that names a concept having no object, zero is paradoxically the first "one" among the series of numbers but is represented there not by the numeral "1" but by the arithmetical "0."

Zero thus oscillates between an inauguration and a naught, a cipher in both senses, an integer and its own negation, logically engorged by the sequence it institutes. This "zero lack," as Miller has it, produces "by the alternation of its evocation and its revocation the zero number" (30). We are reminded here of the Derridean notion of writing *sous rature,* designation under its own erasure as mere trace. The zero lack, counted as the 0 number, surfaces into inscription as the trace of an absence—both a void and the necessary disappearance of that void from the concept of sequence—an absence or lack placed under erasure as one among the numbers, the first. Rhoda was asked to draw, and couldn't, what she knew not, but intuited: the loop that inscribes a lack even as it introduces a unit of succession, the trace of an absence not entirely masked by a signifying presence. In his account of Frege, Miller introduces the concept of "suture" as that seaming over of the lack by a number (to start with: of nothing by zero) necessitated by the stitching together of a logic of succession. Tamed here is the lack behind not just the number one but all numbers that proceed from it. Once this zero lack has been taken up as number in order to anchor the chain, its nullity must next be neutralized from step to step in the sequence, canceled as lack "in each of the names of the numbers which are caught up in the metonymic chain of progression" (31). Hence, to add one more to any number is to subsume the zero once again in each unit of addition.

Following Lacan, Miller then asks rhetorically, "What is there to stop us from seeing in the restored relation of the zero to the series of numbers the most elementary articulation of the subject's relation to the signifying chain?" (31). This is the critical sticking point in recent rejections of suture theory as a false importation of subjectivity into the realm of number. But even if this aspect of the Lacanian project does "disfigure" Frege, as has been argued,[11] it might well gloss Rhoda's fate in *The Waves* (24); Woolf's heroine makes no claims to a purity of perception, no promises to keep subjectivity out of arithmetic or any other subsequent "writing." Let us grant that zero marks the rupture where suturing must make its start. In Lacan, however, suture cannot obscure the "deconstruction" or splitting of the subject taking place in the very process of its constitution. If the subject must somehow come first in order to institute the metonymy of the zero, suturing it, then the "I" which stands in this place can only instance the very principle "not identical with itself." We can thus summarize the paradox, and potential crisis, as follows: the subject is sutured into discourse without benefit of identity. There may even be a distant hint of this logic in the "Proteus" section of *Ulysses,* when Stephen conjures the telephone number that would "link back" to his Adamic source: "Put me on to Edenville. Aleph, alpha: nought, nought, one" (38.4–5). In the shift from alphabetic to numeric characters, he seems to imagine an incremental zero between each of the cardinal numbers, even between nothing and one, while at the same time punning on the psychic emptiness ("nought, not one") which defines the supposed originary "self" at the non-self-identical point of origin.

Take again the case of Rhoda, who sees only abstract numbers on the board, knows nothing of counting, has as yet nothing to count, and therefore, in a manner of speaking, can count on nothing. In her desperation it is as if she sees the gap of the zero opening not merely before and between the sequence of numerals but actually gaping from within the loops that compose them. Mistakenly, one may say, but all too vividly, she also seems to envision an inescapable relation of the subject to the signifying system in mathematics, as well as to the chain of speech. In any such metonymic system, the self is zeroed out by what Miller calls that alternate "evocation and revocation" of the subject which is necessary in order for any "I" to enter upon succession. Rhoda's recoil from language as system, from writing as sequence, is only a measure of her expulsion from it at its point of origin. She is one of the first characters in the modern novel to recognize in this way the self's native effacement.

But what about the novel's own sense of language, of style? By mathematical analogy, a theory of displaced lack within succession may begin to elucidate the transegmental phenomenon of Woolf's acoustic wavelengths as themselves engendering a stylistics of the *phonemic* zero, of that ambivalent juncture between silence and sound at the edge of certain lexical bondings. This is the border between absence and the differentiations from that absence (in the first place, and thereafter) by which speech is raised upon a silence into which it repeatedly fades back. If, in other words, the zero in arithmetic must logically be held to as a preliminary as well as eliminary point of departure, and then held off from there on, canceled from integer to integer as a principle of negation and converted to one of augmentation, may we not perceive a comparable logic of intervals in transcribed speech? From word to word a ceaseless yielding to and then abolishment of phonemic lapse? Especially when the apparent phonemic interruption between words has been called the "zero allophone"?[12] Suture may thereby preserve for semiosis those moments or nodes that seem merely to keep silent, keep silence in place, make room for wording. In this sense suture may be found to negotiate the rules and ambiguities of lexical closure and adjunction, allowing for the very seams between words, the apparent gaps that are in fact ligatures, the nonce values covertly enounced into auditory sequence. Phonemic suture would therefore be analogous to the Lacanian paradox of a subject, to use Miller's phrase, "flickering in eclipses" (34) in its own discourse, a now-you-see-it-now-you-don't phenomenon comparable to the disappearing act of the zero in the chain of numbers. But Rhoda's is a mentality "outside the sequence" (155), we hear, exiled from it, in danger upon return of excision by it. This is the fate ultimately figured in her suicidal jump, itself elided from direct representation in the novel. Her death figures by its very narrative absence her refusal to strive for continuity any longer, an embrace of the blank space, a plunging into the gap. We have already noted how Derrida understands the textual *blanc* — the white as blank — as a check on all possibility of "phonic plenitude" or "presence" in writing.[13] Rhoda's traumatic failure of acculturation into the mysteries of script bears in this sense upon Derridean notions of textual spacing, the break that is also a signifying join. Rhoda would choose to lose herself in the lateral as blank, surrendering to it as sheer lack rather than availing herself of its freeing slack between words. Woolf's novel, however, hints at another view of language, instances a verbal energy not entirely bound to the symbolic, to the file and defile of semantic succession.

R/evocalizations

In any attempt to place Woolf's verbal innovations in the representing of consciousness — and, within them, the symptomatic case of Rhoda's break-down — against recent theoretical developments in language and psychology, the linguistic work of Julia Kristeva is particularly illuminating. As we noted in Chapter 3, there is in Kristeva's terms a semiotic activity well before any accession, or capitulation, to the symbolic — an unlettered tongue not yet given over to words, syllables, phrases, and sentences but content with the uncoded signs of rhythm and phonic free association, with vocalized harmonies and intonations. Kristeva claims that this is a "maternal" utterance of the generative hum and murmur rather than the regimented word.[14] Such intuitive semiosis has not yet succumbed to the laws of number, division, grammar, discrete sense. It is "mobile, amorphous," hence premorphemic. Melodic rather than syntactic, this modulation of sound is the very pulse of voice before it becomes talk, pulsional though not yet circulatory. It generates a tremulous destabilization by means of which, well after the acquisition of language, instinctual and lingual energies may still erupt into the linguistic and deconstruct it, inserting in its cracks — its defaults — a reminder of voice first entering upon its motor function before the regimentation of rational segments. When Woolf speaks about the desire to make prose "move as never before," she indeed prefigures Kristeva by imagining the range of such motion on a scale from (in Woolf's words) "chuckle" and "babble" to "rhapsody."[15]

Exploring such fractured and fantastic gabble in Woolf, Sandra M. Gilbert and Susan Gubar instance the rhythmic moaning of the ancient "crone" opposite the Regents Park Tube station in *Mrs. Dalloway,* for them a prototypical case of the female voice absconded — or cast out — from patriarchy. In the still pulsional flexion without articulate inflection of her "frail quivering sound," it is as if the Shakespearean seventh age of human life has again circled round to the first, the superannuated mutter at one with a child's first utterance in this "voice of no age."[16] In their brief mention of this chanting female, this "battered woman — for she wore a skirt," Gilbert and Gubar not only follow Woolf's lead, naturally enough, about the sex of this figure (though a paragraph of the novel has gone by without determining the gender of her ancient "shape") but also seem to take Woolf at her word about the "absence of all human meaning" when they remark on her "famously enigmatic song." Yet when we first hear her voice, her song, it is said to be "of no age *or sex*" (my emphasis), "running weakly and shrilly and," yes, "with an absence of all human meaning into" the twice quoted two bars "ee um fah um so / foo swee too eem oo — ." Even assuming the first line to be more like a rehearsed musical scale than a private code, nevertheless in the interrupted *fa* (or *fah*) *so* transition, given what is soon said about this as a lament for "her lover, who had been dead these centuries," we may well hear the anagrammatic plangency of "so far." Taken in this way, the passage would not represent some weird introversion of the female voice in a spurt of decrepit baby talk but almost, instead, a distillation of Woolf's own syllabic fluencies in the impersonal alembic of an entirely desocialized voice. In any event, the fact that "she crooned" of love appears to contradict the narrator's own mention of "no human meaning" or, at least, to suggest the possibility of a significance without ordinary signification. This latter possibility seems quite likely to be impinging upon the incoherencies in the second line of her refrain. Indeed, it would match exactly my sense of the junctural leaps of lexical succession in Woolf's own late style to discover even in the nonce-sense of this toothless voicing, this tired speaking in tongues, an encrypted poetry beneath the cackle, perhaps even a "rhapsody" beneath the "babble," some bent remembrance of a season long past when this now-withered sybil of the semiotic itself could once have found it in her strength as well as in her heart to have been "foo" (full?), maybe even foolishly, "swee(t) to(o) (h)eem (wh)oo . . ." In this "running weakly . . . into each other" of her broken sounds, the phonemic ligature at "swee t" may indeed seem to mark in its loosened, exhausted bond the bittersweet trace of a lost liaison: Molly's "swee . . . tsong" in refrain.

Out of the prose format as well as the narrative sequence of *Mrs. Dalloway,* this indented, isolated poetry breaks free, "the voice of an ancient spring" not only spurting up amid the plotted sounds of London commerce but blurting out its semiotic chaos within the symbolic monopoly of prose discourse. My sense is that the latent energy of similar irruptions, though not stationed so visibly on the page, churns frequently beneath Woolf's prose from *Mrs. Dalloway* on. Call Woolf's access to such language (along with that of the male modernists Kristeva discusses) an erosion of the partriarchal order and ordering of language or not, in any case it is just the received regime of segmentation that Woolf's style around its edges, precisely around its lexical edges, resists. Rhoda's fate in *The Waves* is simply that she can neither maintain this resistance nor survive without it. How then does Woolf sustain it, and what does the voice of such resistance actually sound like?

Sproken Words

One guess is that it will be *felt* to take its wavering tonalities from some primal flow, from the "ancient spring" of desire in *Mrs. Dalloway,* for instance. Such is an energy glimpsed elsewhere only under constraint or erasure, flickering, as it were, only in eclipses, in the crevices of the unsaid. All writing can be said to start from scratch, from the first mark of inscription, but textuality as a system must reach back axiomatically to the initiating blank encroached upon by that first scratch, recapturing the differential authorization of absence from word to word. When that differentiating blank starts slipping along the chain of signification, however, an effect, say, like Woolf's "whi(ch / sh)(y)ield" skid may emerge, a lexical enjambment to be heard and not seen. In Rhoda's terms, this phonic event deflects the "crevice" of script with the "device" of inflection. Such sliding or splaying—such dialogizing of the monosyllable—is induced by an oblique friction between the lexeme and the phoneme that, to borrow Rhoda's verb, can be said to *fissure* into a semantic redistribution without thereby erasing the original sense. This is the give and so take of succession, the lending as blending, that might ultimately help to construe sequence as continuity—for all its wounding lapses. Bernard knows that "for pain words are lacking" (263), with a play on the idea of "lack" itself, since to communicate such pain there should be "cries, cracks" and—Rhoda's own two obsessional words again—"fissures, whiteness," in short, an "interference with the sense of time, of space" (263), including the time of lexical spacing. Bernard knows also that this "lacking" in words applies as well to pain's supposed contrary, desire fulfilled in love, since there too he yearns "for some little language such as lovers use, broken words, inarticulate words, like the shuffling of feet [in part metrical feet, an inference highlighted by transegmental alliteration (*of feet*)] on the pavement" (238). One suspects that this "little language" of the emotions, microphonically calibrated along the contours of such s/lack, can be glimpsed, even across the (debatably audible) comma, in the differential ambivalence of a plosive drift at "lovers u*se, broken* words." A similar example, also in connection with the passage from thought into language, and again triggered by plosive ambiguity, surfaces in the silent voicings of the text's other maker of texts, the poet Neville, who remarks on how "we sit silent, or perhap*s be*thinking us of some trifle, suddenly *speak*" (145). Shortly before the *spe* cluster, there emerges a suballiterating and just barely perceptible liaison between the closing sibilant of the conjectural "perhaps" and the prefix of the archaically reflexive "bethinking us." Put another way: *if* there emerges any such unbinding link, it would provide the first surge of denotation for that "speaking" which is to bubble up from this crucible of thought and which, when it does, will of necessity be an attempt to articulate a continuity across the lags of consciousness. With or without the transegmental emphasis, what we hear discoursed upon is the origin of all discourse, what we might call the very pressure to speech.

Addicted as Bernard is to "solacing myself with words" (184) in just this way, many of his laments find amelioration in their very wording. Even the "lacking" of his depleted self-image may turn on the play of an acoustic irony, a phonemic halftone, as well as on a visual recognition. This we discover, farther along in his final soliloquy, when we come to the novel's second mirror scene of sorts, answering to Rhoda's earlier terrified avoidance of the mirror at school. Hiding behind Susan as if to occlude the identification with her own gaze, Rhoda boasts in her evasion: "I am not here. I have no face" (43). Since she has already been painfully initiated into the symbolic through her schoolroom routines, the mirror would have only revealed this faceless non-entity to her as well—but not as a contingent, rather as an exigent, fact of subjective (em)placement. When the "I" is still an image, not yet a linguistic subject, it can still seem authorized as object by perception; once passed from the imaginary into the symbolic, however, once uttered as "I," it is effaced as signified object, even if there were no one blocking this particular mirror. Furthermore, the vexed locative in Rhoda's "here I have no face" becomes in the double process of record and reception—here then, in the story's subvocal transcriptions, here now in our reading of them—a metatextual admission; the adverbial shifter "here" designates a textualized speech act (however silent) that evacuates presence not only from any and all mirrors but from the two-dimensional plane of once written, presently read page as well.

In Bernard's climactic mirror scene, by contrast to Rhoda under cover of Susan, there is no one blocking his line of sight—and no one in it at all, perhaps, but himself as Other. Whether or not Bernard is still in the company of a temporary companion at his last supper, during which his inner voice has been buzzing with reverie and regret, in any case he is at least in part addressing his own reflection as alter ego when he catches his image in the restaurant mirror. "Oh, but there is your face. I catch your eye. I, who had been thinking myself so vast, a temple, a church, a whole universe, unconfined and capable of being everywhere on the verge of things and here too, am now nothing but what you see—an elderly man, rather heavy, grey above the ears, who (I see myself in the glass) leans one elbow on the table, and holds in his left hand a glass of old brandy" (292). For all the suspense of Woolf's typical periodic grammar, dilating here until all at once strategically contracted, the most striking suspension in this passage is not syntactic at all but phonemic. Across the homophonic echo between "eye" and "I" at the turn of the second into the third sentence—between an organ of subjectivity and the name of a subject, each the other's object—is a difference within repetition that constitutes the self on the very trace of an otherness, whether that otherness be a second-person addressee (again, the text by now seems deliberately ambiguous about this dinner partner's presence) or the self's own image. This sense of repetition as simultaneously a phonic and psychic trace is, we might note, an effect achieved in redrafting. After "I catch your eye," Woolf had originally written "There is no escape. No no immunity. No end it seems to the eternal struggle." At which point she continued with the initially unpunctuated "I who had been thinking."[17] Even the comma after "I" in revision sets the pronoun not only off but back, fractionally more attracted into the vicinity of the homophonic precursor "eye."

When the redrafted version of this passage hits upon the contracted "I catch your eye. I," the scene's narrated mirroring seems translated to script as an echo. The imaginary oneness, as it were, the self's unitary image in the mirror (or the eye of another caught and held) cedes to an inevitable symbolic divergence at just the point where script is necessary to differentiate sound from like sound. Identity is thus the function of a pun diverged from mere repetition, a word broken loose from its double. The phrasing verges, as we hear, on yet another transegmental blend. But, of course, what phonetics accounts for as the *y*-glide of the syllable "eye" creates a kind of disyllabic diphthong that must be renewed rather than merely prolonged in order to engender its unelidable repetition as the pronoun "I." Self-and-Other remains a dichotomy instituted by the breakdown of the imaginary field into its symbolic differentials. What is more, this primal dichotomy is held in place by a phonemic integrity that resists elision in the name of those very boundaries in Woolf that so often need alleviation. If the phonemic law of transegmental gravitation is a rule to be honored exclusively in the breach—in or across the repeated breach between words—then Bernard's language in this passage has worked to hold tense against this breach, if just barely. As much as in Lacan, therefore, the recuperation of an at least hypothetical subject can be tracked down to an analogy with the smallest increments of pertinent linguistic opposition, the difference that founds—or, in Bernard's case, finds again—the language of identity.

In an earlier wordplay that straddled the crucial distinction in *The Waves* between an inhabitable and a merely serviceable language, between words that fashion and those that can merely express a self, Bernard had written "I shall enter my phrases" (36), meaning both that he will compose them and that they will encompass him. This is the Woolfian ideal given scope in one character while denied to his suicidal counterpart, the woman who is blown forever outside the figures she is called upon to draw. Rhoda's suicidal slippage reverses Bernard's success in inching to identity through phrase. For Rhoda's battle against the rigidity of sequence, a language would be needed that loosened script back to the looped play and continuity of vocal overtones, a language whose necessity is theorized and even exemplified in the novel's own streaming of consciousness—and preserved, if fitfully, in the voice of the novelist hero through to the end. The transegmental phenomenon would be one such gesture of a softened differential writing, its junctures more forgiving, its borderlines relaxed. When, near the close, an awesome "space" of wordless silence is suddenly "cleared" like a vacuum in Bernard's consciousness, its yawning void does not appall or swallow him up, as it might have Rhoda. Words, failing, have simply fled, and the lifelong creature of phrase enters this new acoustic vacuum at the very moment when "the rhythm stopped: the rhymes and the hummings" (283). Described here, of course, is a dead space that Bernard must somehow have gotten past in order even to put it this way in retrospect, since once again we hear the lava flow of his gift for phrasing. By a syncopation of spacing and acoustic pacing, and in what phonology would call a loosening diphthong sequence, the disyllabic "rhyth(u)m" is at first glance syllabically dispersed into the "rhymes" and "the hummings" of which it is comprised. That final collocation of article and gerund also reveals a phonetic prolongation of *thm*'s lingering hum into the faintly engaged transegmental elision of "*th(e h)*ummings," hinting in turn at its own part-echo of the "th(r)ummed" vocal cords that produce it. Without this echo there is only the drift of phonation itself, tending toward a sound— "thumming"—that is not even a word, only a vocalized murmur. Spanned here is a breathing space between words whose medial aspiration does not aspire to articulate discourse, an ever-deferred echo from the undifferentiated matrix of speech, a mimesis of semiosis itself in embryo. It is the onomatopoetic rhythm of signification without the sign. It is Woolf the writer, in the inwardly voiced consciousness of her delegated verbal artist Bernard, silently speaking in tongues across the bridged abyss of the phonemic zero, across a silence pregnant with meaning but still undelivered of it.

For Kristeva this rhythm and thrum would exemplify the virtual definition of the poetic quotient of literary language, the irruption of the underlying semiotic (in Kristeva's special sense) into a symbolic system mounted to contain and repress it. Such irruption is the "effraction"[18] or breaching of the signifying chain by phonic play, the breaking and entering of syntax by the subversive laxities of a sublexical music. It sounds intriguingly close to what Woolf imagined, without exampling, in *A Room of One's Own,* an uninhibited language – beyond the "man's sentence" – whose diction would involve "those unsaid or half said words, which form themselves, no more palpably than the shadows of moths" (88). The novelist of such a sentence would have "to hold her breath," would have to get at somehow, without necessarily getting down, those "words that are hardly syllabled yet" (88), words whose ordering not only breaks up the masculinist assurance of classic sentence but the syntagmatic "sequence" itself. All of this is to come about, according to Woolf, in order to bring to voice, if not to ordinary articulation, a woman's expressive potential within the proper androgyny of art. Rhoda, her surrogate, is scapegoated to the fragility of this hope. She has trouble learning to add, trouble learning to write, because she cannot abide even those analogies in discourse for the constitution of subjectivity, those irruptive equivalents, that she finds also, and more piercingly, in the existential discontinuities of a life in time. To sustain herself across the "shocks" of such "intermittence" – the shock waves of consciousness – Rhoda would have to submit, without succumbing, to something akin to that freedom of "blank pages, gaps, borders, spaces and silence, holes in discourse" which recent French feminism has seen as the touchstone of *écriture féminine.*[19] In fearful recoil from the rigidity of the symbolic order, in full recognition of the need for some controlled preschizophrenic release through what Kristeva calls the "pulverization" (51) of discursive language, Rhoda, incapable of this release, vanishes instead into the temporal blank of death, a vanished death at that.

Bernard, who can write, who can even finally accept his own phasing out within the very articulation by which he abides, comes through ordeal to another fate: the return to continuity. Rhoda, by contrast, leaves the novel as the most extravagant avatar of discontinuity in modern fiction, her death scene syncopated out of plot entirely in Bernard's elegiac reconstruction. We sense the voice of the Other, typical of the heightening and thickening of Woolf's language in the rendering of death,[20] breaking through his soliloquizing retrospect: "I . . . feel the rush of the wind of her flight when she leapt" (289). Sensing only intermittency and rupture, Rhoda leaves the novel in one of those white spaces so terribly familiar to her, an unspecified gap in the text that is only retroactively filled in by Bernard's mournful retrospect. In her last set of speeches in the penultimate section of the novel, Rhoda seems to sum up her lifelong attitude toward temporality and its sonic contours by regretting "how short a time silence lasts" (226), itself an irrefutable rule of phonic juncture. The female character at once drained by endurance and rebuked by vacancy is to encounter in her pending death the only sustained silence Woolf has to offer her: a lapse in representation itself, a long stretch without any mention. Yet in Bernard's ultimate allusion to her death, many pages later, its violence can just barely be heard to reemerge in the *blanc,* the blank, the empowered white *lateral,* of the very language that elsewhere mirrors for Rhoda the punitive disruptions of life. Beyond the precipitant cadence charted by those doubled "of"s ("the rush of the wind of her flight"), what is so grueling and at the same time elusive about the phrasing is the flickering displacement between the "rush" and the preposition that places it, that ascribes it to Rhoda. A fissure into which falls, or is plunged by its own momentum, the doomed self in flight: gone out of sight in a fatal crevice wedged open within time itself, a hole incapable of any but merely verbal suturing. Between "rush" and "of," in other words, in quite another word, flashes in eclipse the very "shoving" off that brings her to her death. Overheard, that is, in the interstice, flung between monosyllables, is the phantom reshuffling: "ru*sh of.*" Though the verb "shove" can be intransitive, it usually takes an object; yet the ghostly hint of some unspoken external agency here — someone shoving *her* — remains just that, phantasmal. It is immediately internalized by the fact of self-murder, the spectral assault vanished in a sort of schizoid rift, or phonemic schism, within the linguistic play itself. Though ungrammatical, because too fast for the logic of syntax, nevertheless this recasting of the lateral does at the same time implicitly name the push of succession, finally become fatal, which charac- terizes the metonymic chain and permits the transegmental drift in the first place. Dying by ellipsis, Rhoda is mourned by ligature — as the very repeal of intermittency that might have offered her reprieve.

Catching that D/rift

And so, once again, we are prompted to suspect that the form of the novel models a continuity that can at any given moment fail its characters. The crevices that permit language, if they are to be traversed rather than merely vanished into, terrify the astylistic consciousness of Rhoda, who suffers a virtual paralysis of syntax. Woolf's style is there to pose an alternative from within its own diagnosis of this condition. The primal disjuncture of the self or split subject, in its passage into the symbolic, is ordinarily not just mirrored in the separation anxiety of inaugural self-image but mirrored also, and forever after, in the gaps of language itself, those severances that not only violate the imaginary but eventuate in the symbolic, that explode wholeness into the parts and particles of speech. Continuity, at the textual level, can emerge only from a sense of language that assuages these gaps, turns them to segues, stretches across their rents a harmonizing reverberation, cleaves them only with the leavings of a previous sound still carried on the air of silence. This is the sound that makes the white spaces between hour and hour, number and number, word and word, a never utterly evacuated space, a duration no more voided than the ambiguous blankness of white noise. Since Woolf's Rhoda is unable to claim her right to a mother tongue instinct with rhythmic ligature, what galls and daunts her about utterance taken up into the regime and regimen of spacing, about "writing" in the rudimentary form of numbering, for instance, is that it feels, it looks, so much like the psychic life she has come to suffer, all manic fits and starts and stops, arbitrary, abrupt, and discontinuous, an oscillation of blacks with lacks. The other side of that "little language" such as lovers might use, gaping at times across the surface of its "s/broken words," is thus the voice of death: the lateral as void. Woolf's verbal fluidity cannot directly counter or sanitize this view, only open it to other rhythmic possibilities, releasing paranoia into relaxation and capaciousness.

But to what extent, finally, is this writing a body language – and whose? In our promised return to this question, we can also usefully return to Kristeva. In an essay closely related to her work in *Revolution in Poetic Language,* she borrows Mallarmé's phrase, "the vibratory uncertainty of language," to cover in part those moments in "a *strongly ambivalent* if not *polymorphic semantics*" when "phonemes reacquire what the sounds lost in becoming the sounds of a given language"; when, that is, "they reacquire the topography of the body which reproduces itself in them."[21] Though the return of this nurturant and "maternal" phonic vibrancy in adult language, including literary style, is not necessarily a gendered phenomenon, it is not sexless either. Rather, it seems more like a polymorphous eroticism of the voice escaped for a split second from the circuit of lack and its designations in ordinary discourse. Unlike signifying language, this pulsional body language in a sense satisfies its own desire, not by naming it but by utterance itself, a vocal play ultimately devolved upon the alert, the *listening* reader. This does not, of course, return the reader to some prelinguistic euphoria, but it does set up a sensory overload whose momentary force is a kind of giddy synesthesia between eye and ear. Touched by this, writing and its reading emerge once more at generative odds with each other, phonetic impulses slipping out from under the visible rhythm of script. As with Joyce's "earsighted view," this is again a partial discipherment of writing into phonotext, a process going forward in and across that reading which produces its text *glancingly* off the ear.

It is Woolf's more radical peer in feminist modernism, Gertrude Stein, who recalls our own point of departure in this book in the "hear with eyes" sonnet – when she stakes her sense of literary language on the reciprocal definition of graphic and phonic energies in the poems versus performance pieces of the "Shakespeherian rag." For in the cryptic wordiness of her formulation, "Shakespeare's plays and Shakespeare's sonnets even when they are all here are different to the eye and ear. Words next to each other are different to the eye and ear. . . . Words next to each other make a sound to the eye and the ear. With which you hear."[22] Even when the words are "all here," as for instance here before us as text rather than there on stage, we are all ears for them. Yet what they offer is not sound but the occasion thereof. The point bears repeating, as Stein does in her next paragraph: "Oh yes *with* which you do hear" (125; my emphasis). She has also made this explicit a few paragraphs earlier in a wording that seems a direct allusion to Shakespeare's (Bottom's) "The eye has not heard" speech, since for her "words next to each other . . . sound different to the eye that hears them or the ear that sees them." The "sound" they are later said to make is not audited, then, but provides instead the material, the "with which" and the wherewithal, of visual hearing: in other words, evocalization.

In Woolf's case, the polymorphemics of reading generated by the unique "sounding different" of graphonic evocalization – stretched unsteadily across the shifting granules of a syntax in dissolution – is likely to recall the emphasis on the androgynous *jouissance* of the body in Roland Barthes, where an ecstatic interference with the logic of transmitted meaning releases language beyond all clear-cut oppositions, including the dichotomy male/female. The year before Kristeva published *Revolution in Poetic Language,* Barthes brought *The Pleasure of the Text* to very similar conclusions, more explicit if not more specific. He called there for a "*writing aloud*" that "is not expressive; it leaves expression to the pheno-text, to the regular god of communication; it belongs to the geno-text, to significance"[23] – to what Kristeva would call semiosis. It may be maternal in origin but for Barthes its effects are neither male nor female. "Pleasure is a *neuter* (the most perverse form of the demoniac)," a categorical "suspension" that rejects the presumption of the clearly signified for "the sumptuous rank of the signifier" (65). In the penultimate paragraph of his book, however, Barthes concedes too hastily, perhaps, that such "vocal writing (which is nothing like speech) is not practiced," even though he wants to "talk about it as though it existed." On the contrary, I think we can find it, in a unique and allusive concentration, on almost every page of Woolf's late fictional prose – find it as a writing that amounts to a virtual rereading of the whole English literary tradition, its sensuist impulses and its missed chances. For Barthes such writing would be an "erotic mixture of timbre and language . . . the art of guiding one's body," sustained primarily by "pulsional incidents." Given Empson's sense, as we saw in Chapter 3, that the polyvalent skein of poetic language "has the character of the flesh of an organism,"[24] for Barthes—as, in a sense, for Louis Marin as well—that organism is no metaphor, but ourselves. Sent into play by the opposing tugs of an ambiguity all its own, the tensions in Woolf's style between script and sound attain frequently, it would seem, to what Barthes envisions as a "language lined with flesh" (66). If Woolf's writing does not produce the sustained "carnal stereophony" of which he dreams, nevertheless it does depend, at least intermittently, upon "the *grain* of the voice"—and this often against the grain of the script, sounded between and across discrete words, luxuriating in the precincts of the betwixt. What leads Barthes to think of such writing as not yet having been realized is doubtlessly that, in pure form, it would have to replace all normative procedures of meaning by an undercoded "signifying" at the level of the "geno-text." Defined as "not phonological but phonetic," this sounded writing would unharness a lingual energy not fully bound back into phonemes, into syllables, into words. When functioning as part of narrative prose, however, with all semiotic impulses in tow to a continuous symbolic organization, unspoken vocalizing could only remain a surplus of the discourse—in excess of, and in tension with, the very language that releases and impels it.

If we provisionally attend in *The Waves* to this dialectic between discursive language and the undulations of a semiotic pulse, we can further see how such verbal interplay foregrounds again the logic of Woolf's text in its arrangement as a network of soliloquies. The quoted passages are not spoken really, yet they can still be said to be "said," as one might say something to oneself rather than declare it. The "speeches" are not whispered or muted enunciations either, not uttered at all or even intoned, but somehow inflected—inflected into a zone between verbalization and vocalization, between phrased impression and overheard expression. In other novels, interior monologue, when dictated to the page in the format of dialogue, is often interrupted by the predication "felt," as in "felt Bernard," say, or "felt Rhoda." Though not signaled in this way, what is "felt" in the monologues of *The Waves,* as in the italicized descriptions that take their flavor from them, becomes sensory as well as sentient, the sinuous heft of words half-bodied into articulation along a given line of thought. Barthes talks of "writing aloud," but in our reception of these speeches we encounter a vocality without sound. In its unique tension between graphic and phonic signification, however, the transegmental drift does seem particularly apt as a conjectural (hardly exclusive) illustration of what Barthes might mean to infer by a vocalized inscription. Woolf, believing she had "not yet mastered the speaking voice" in *The Waves,* planned extensive revision of the novel, to be guided by "reading much of it aloud, like poetry."[25] Without transcribing any such authorial voicing as a recoverable dimension of the novel, of course, she nevertheless charged the text with the latency of just this enunciation—displaced upon her readers' reading to themselves.

What I am suggesting about Woolf's language is that it subscribes in its lingering junctures to the liquid transitions of an unprogrammatic music, even as it necessarily takes part in the cohesion, even the wit, of a reading effect. In the ripple of lexical overlap, there is a perceptible but not immediately processed ebb to the phonic flow. Between the written and the reread, between two scripted units as they oscillate in the release of a cryptic third term, opens a moment of extraneous pulsation—before the regularizing provided even by conceptual ambiguity. This moment is not produced by an Edenic innocence speaking through the text, trailing filaments of prephonemic glory, but it does precipitate a certain freedom between beats of the reading brain. It does so, however, not by repositioning the deconstructed textual subject as the consolidated "I" of the reader. Rather, it transmits textual energy along the momentarily ungendered and nonsignifying body of a vocal agent without identity, whose subvocal cooperation alone spans the recesses within that combined cerebration and subjectivity known as reading. To remark this in Woolf is in no way to champion the unfallen prattle of infancy, and certainly not to associate women's verbal originality with such a vocal sphere. It is simply to respect the sensual determinants of one kind of verbal play, one kind of freedom from the given, the dictated, the pre-scribed: a freedom that speaks, speaks up, against the normal constraints of discourse, if only for the split second before a second *thought* sets in. Between the instant when an *antiphone* is heard and the immediate regrouping of its inscribed or imagined letters into a new semantic claimant, between truant sound and its segmentally de-cisive assimilation to meaning, fall away the sign-bound operations of a reading subject into the palpable fund of sheer, of shearing, sound.

We are not induced by the cooperation of Woolf's language and narrative format in *The Waves* to think that we somehow hear the characters behind their transcribed words but, rather, that our own private reading takes place somewhere between thinking (reading) and hearing (voicing). To apply Barthes's term "vocal writing" (*Pleasure of the Text,* 67) without qualification here would certainly be misleading. The passive enunciation of a reader must be distinguished from anything that goes on in the act of writing. Given Barthes's stress elsewhere on the writerly text as cooperative with its active, productive reading, his account of "writing aloud" seems too quick to conflate textual generation with its processed effects. Surely "the art of guiding one's body" in such "writing" must be understood in part as the art that guides our own bodies (silent, silenced) in the act of reading. Voice no more *inheres* in such writing, conferring presence, than in any other text. The felt voicing of

Woolf's style is not a residuum of script, nor, in reverse, is the writing a deposit of voice, an impress of body. Containing nothing of organic origin inherent in it, Woolf's writing—epitomized by her deployment of the transegmental drift—does, however, *incur* the body through a disturbance in the process of reception, an "evocalization" of the reader's own physical presence. On the page, the characters are gone from us and from themselves, even as an existence kindred to theirs finds silent voice in the sympathetic vibrations of another reading—of an other, reading. It is through no embodiment other than the disposition of the reading body, then, that the oscillating drift of Woolf's style can serve to flesh out her text. "Oh yes," to recapitulate Stein, "with which you do hear." Throwing ourselves into *The Waves* in this way, we yet again realize the phonotext, recognize and activate it, as a true theater of reading.

Epilogos:
The Decentered Word

The eye of man hath not heard, the ear of man hath not seen...
A Midsummer Night's Dream, 4.1.208–9

In some happy bafflement of eye and ear, might Shakespeare's sister, as imagined and mourned in *A Room of One's Own,* just possibly have survived after all under the name of Virginia? And have done so in service to a literary reader always potentially working within a receptual mode not only fantasized by malapropism in Bottom's dream but canonized as literariness itself by the work of its author, whose textual intensifications we cannot help but "hear with eyes"? If so, *The Waves,* revised as it was by being read aloud, "like poetry," and destined for reception in an equivalent retardation by the inner ear, is an experiment in feminist modernism inevitably continuous with the "modernity" of Shakespearean practice. Through it all, *The Waves* is a book, barely a novel — a writing — audited by the "earsighted view" of readers whose textual progress is a continuous analogue for the temporal stamina of its characters. Such is Woolf's testimony, both as narrative artist and as *writer,* on the unconscious structured like a language.

The six chapters preceding the last on *The Waves,* in their alternation of theoretical postulates and textual exempla, were building all the while toward an effort at that third sort of critical thing: a reading. Nothing, though, depends on it. The audition of the phonotext need not claim anything more than the intermittent activation of phonemic slippage. Such listening does not have to exert interpretive leverage. In fact, the activated phonotext may be said to put the interpreter in his place: as one more somatic reader. Pursuing this line of thought, I brought the theoretical overview of Chapter 3 toward a speculation about the epicentered stance of textual reception. The reader is, on this showing, always placed above the text in a position entirely oblique to authorship and its intentions. Reading to ourselves is an activity of the upper body, motivated but constrained, an activity that often goes forward, in inhibited pronunciation, against the grain of the script. Such internal enunciation locates the only founding Word of textuality, its generation of signifiers at the receptual site of reading. It thus points to what we might now call the epi-Logos of Woolf's late style. The phonism involved is ours only in silence, centerless. It is a peripheral de-ciphering of written words through the sound clusters they serve to evoke without ever manifesting. In the sense that the preceding chapters have mounted a resistance to the exclusive privileging of modernism as a first, late break with the significatory—in favor of the sheer signifying—force of language, nevertheless the true radical aspiration, the dreamed breakthrough, of Woolf's modernist prose remains to be acknowledged. In its urge to sever its bondage to the grand tradition, only in fact to culminate it, the attempted androgynous wording of Woolf's prose offers, at the close of this book, an exemplary recirculation of traditional currents in literary phrasing.

In "Literature, Oral-Aural and Optical," I. A. Richards once mythologized a period for which Woolf's style might be heard to activate a similar nostalgia. Beginning his essay with remarks on that particularly pungent homophony of "oral" versus "aural"—rather like that *différance* of Derrida's that cannot be phonetically processed as different—Richards seeks to assess the distance between the text-bound culture of just such distinctions and the preliterate perception of an entirely oral language flow.[1] He speaks of literature's prehistory, however, in a way that can be interestingly transposed to Woolf's late modernism, since "for the pre-literate's *ear* words in discourse are not separate items, open to time-free contemplation, they are crests or troughs in a stream, parts of a wave pattern. It is arguable that the pre-literate could swim, as it were, in the sea of meaning while we only paddle and splash along its edges" (203). To hear such latent orality in the "optics" of Woolf's prose is to confront Wellek and Warren once more on the supposed "illiteracy" of any vocal rather than entirely silenced (that is, syllabic, for instance, rather than lexical) reading. Whether or not her prose is read as an attempt to write back, somehow, to the sound of a liberating mother tongue, a power of utterance fallen away in the prehistory of the patriarchal Word, there is no doubt that Virginia Woolf listened hard for something beyond the "man's sentence," that hallmark of classical discourse. Woolf sought something sensuous and pliable, fluttering and wavelike. But such a language was not finally to be found, for it was nowhere spoken whole. Instead Woolf herself was impelled to devise it, piece by piece, strand by filament, a "little language" where units of speech would be reducible to one syllable, detached in hearing, serried, permutable. Not finding such utterance sustained on any tongue or in any text, Woolf fashioned it, that is to say, piece by piece by splice. She molded it out of the excess, luxuriance, and perpetual insurgence of a received literary language which, even as it stiffened into the discourse of the man's sentence, on the one hand, was always undercutting its own coherence, on the other, with the countervailing tug and undertow of acoustic undulations.

The "path of a sound through the air" in this book's opening epigraph from Coleridge, his trope for the undulant and epicyclical progress of reading, is implicitly Woolf's trope too. Across the surface of her scripted texts, that sonic path cuts an invisible swath, its wavelengths in perpetual interference with the crests and valleys, the marks and blanks, of print. This path, this wave motion, this sinuous way of reading, is one she might have found in certain Coleridgean moments of soundlike power alighted in scripted texts, or in George Eliot later, with her man's name, or before them in Milton, or in Shakespeare, the brother. This phonic drift, crossing athwart the patterns of inscription in a signifying wavelength all its own, is not only there by definition in the contingencies of language, but there—by deliberate literary surplus—from the outset of the English tradition. For Woolf, it no doubt seemed lurking in the language of the Fathers as its saving grace, the deconstruction of patriarchal utterance from within the deployment of its inherited modes. What Woolf's voracious reading must thus have shown her everywhere, well before its systematic modernist exaggerations, was the syncopation of received literary form by unmastered linguistic shape. Such is the pull of mutter upon utterance, the backwash of waved sound.

Writing of this kind, both fluent and polyvalent, might serve to rescue the standards of prose discourse from the stranglehold of insistent cerebration, from the march rather than the flow of phrasing. By contrast, of course, there is always the masculinist ideal, dredged up by indirect discourse from the self-reverie of Mr. Ramsay, rationalist and philosopher, in *To the Lighthouse* (1927): "It was a splendid mind. For if thought is like the keyboard of a piano, divided into so many notes, or like the alphabet is ranged in twenty-six letters all in order, then his splendid mind had no sort of difficulty in running over those letters one by one, firmly and accurately, until it had reached, say, the letter 'Q.'"[2] One might follow Riffaterre's method in detecting in this partly ironic encomium the suppressed cliché of "scaling the heights," only to find that such a punning trope, combining the horizontal gradations of music and the vertical stages of ascent, is undercut by its own internal logic. The analogue of mind installed in this passage is the mechanism rather than the sound of music, the keyboard rather than the scale or chord (or even note). This leads naturally to the linguistic analogy of the alphabet rather than the word, the spatialized train of graphic units rather than their fused effect, whether phonemic or semantic. Ramsay's mind moves across the terrain of letters "one by one," firmly, discretely, without lingering or variation, without rhythm. "He dug in his heels at Q. Q he was sure of. Q he could demonstrate." Woolf would seem to have arranged this alphabetic figuration of his mind so that he is found blocked at the familiar abbreviation for questioning (Q), indeed on the verge of a phonemic rebus for Q(h)ED. He cannot therefore proceed to that letter which, not separately considered but rather motivated as part of a continuous discourse, might begin to spell out his own identity: the first letter of "Ramsay" itself. In any event, what Woolf portrays here is an ironic conjecture — "if thought is like the keyboard . . . or like the alphabet" — to which the implicit rejoinder is that it is not, or need not be.

A mode of mental operation far afield from this passage in *To the Lighthouse*, one projected outward onto a very different sense of alphabetic characters in sequence, has been explored in Woolf's preceding novel — and with direct implications for her own text's relation to the alphabet. The link between the mind's character and the scripted characters of language is rendered in *Mrs. Dalloway* (1925) not by an extended conceit of the sort we have just considered in *To the Lighthouse*. Instead, it is conveyed by a sustained reification of alphabetic characters sharing the same space with the perceiving mind, not just figuring forth the limits of its operations. It is conveyed, in other words, by the active reading of such letters within the narrative — and not just "one by one," either, but as increments of phrasing, of voicing. In the novel which is always seen to mark a major advance for Woolf toward the incremental fluencies of her characteristic late style, *Mrs. Dalloway* thus stages, early in its plot, an explicit scene of reading in which the desiderata of her own muted, polymorphous style are adumbrated: a language that has, we will eventually find, "soared beyond seeking and questioning and knocking of words together."[3] It is very much a style of porous borders met with blurred interstices. The scene that encodes it is the first major set piece of the novel, and it can be read to evidence and subdivide the otherwise inseparable components of textual reception: not just writing and reading but, on one side, script combined with a sonic metonymy of its supposed source and, on the other, the voice and subjected body of the reader. The scene is stretched out over more than a dozen pages, from the moment when London foot traffic is arrested first by the Prime Minister's car passing, then by an airplane overhead, until the point where the activity of the plane is mentioned for the last time. Since that activity is none other than skywriting, this scene serves to enact the process of inscription as well as of decipherment, a conjoint parable of the mechanics of text production.

Woolf's prolonged tour de force on the spectacle of aerial writing and "pedestrian" bafflement extends in effect the technological paradigms of high modernism examined in Hugh Kenner's *The Mechanic Muse*. If the spatialized textuality and actual spatial transports of *Ulysses* take their cultural bearings in part from the linotype machine and the tram system of urban transit, then Woolf's high flights of style in this passage may be read to figure themselves on the model of postwar skywriting, a new form of mechanized inscription and mass-media transmission. If there were any doubt that this aerial doodling enters the novel as a trope for the text's own etherealized and evanescent style, the earliest full description of the overhead writing is carried out by the carrying on of a sentence full of syntactic acrobatics and mimetically timed inversion, Woolf's text itself performing the vertiginous feats of signifying it evokes: "Dropping dead down the aeroplane soared straight up, curved in a loop, raced, sank, rose, and whatever it did, wherever it went, out fluttered behind it a thick ruffled bar of white smoke which curled and wreathed upon the sky in letters. But what letters? A C was it? an E, then an L?" (29). A sentence before, the overhead tracery, already apparent without yet being shaped into alphabetic characters, is linked by verbal nudge to its engineered cause. By the aura of a false etymology shading an internal echo, the effect of lettering is verbally aligned with the cause of exhaust smoke: the plane "*letting* out white smoke from behind, which curled and twisted, actually writing something!" (my emphasis). In both excerpts it is the smoke rather than the aircraft that offers the only grammatical antecedent for the action of letter formation, in verbs transitive as often as intransitive ("which curled and wreathed [itself]," "which curled and twisted [itself]"). Entirely self-contained, if not self-generated, the raw material of writing forms itself into signification, released ("let") to the process of its own lettering—"upon the sky" as upon a page.

The text's first spume is the alphabetic discontinuity of *A C,* followed by the still lexically unproductive *E* and *L,* the four letters together providing at best a fugitive (phonetic) misspelling of the first two syllables of the plane's own "acceleration." In indirect discourse, we then encounter musings about how "the aeroplane shot further away and again, in a fresh space of sky, began writing a K, an E, a Y perhaps?" (29). Maybe, but this still offers no KEY to the message or the motive. The letters looped in series simply refuse at first to form themselves into words. Woolf's text at the same time parodies the interpretive urges of the craning onlookers in their clumsy guesses: "'Glaxo,' said Mrs. Coates in a strained, awe-stricken voice, gazing straight up," followed by "Kreemo," uttered by "Mrs. Bletchley, like a sleepwalker." The writing seems to project a collective metropolitan unconscious of mercantile slogans and product trademarks. In the long run, this ephemeral text does indeed appear to be spelling out an advertisement for a candy company: "'It's toffee,' murmured Mr. Bowley," as confirmed a moment later in indirect discourse: "It was toffee; they were advertising toffee, a nursemaid told Rezia. Together they began to spell t...o...f..." (31). We never see more; the lexical ambition of the gaseous script, the very grouping of the letters, must be taken on faith.

Most important, it is Rezia's psychotic husband, the hero Septimus Warren

Smith, whose instinct it is to retain the mysterious and inviolable otherness of this airy script, this "signalling to me" in vaporous exhortation. "Not indeed in actual words" does the signal come; "that is, he could not read the language yet; but it was plain enough, this beauty, the smoke words languishing and melting in the sky and bestowing upon him in their inexhaustible charity and laughing goodness one shape after another of unimaginable beauty" (31). Texture, tumescence, delicacy, weightless free modulation: these are the attributes of a language exuded from the machine, an exhaust that is far from wasted, a boon and a beauty, paradoxically "inexhaustible," whose "smoke words" can be heard (by the reader) to draw the melting spirit "smokewards." For Septimus, though, this is a writing still other, not yet to be read and internalized by silent enunciation, a writing still entirely pictographic — until the nursemaid speaks within his hearing of further letters in formation. It is at this point that the phonemic stratum of this parable is made apparent. "'K R' said the nursemaid, and Septimus heard her say 'Kay Arr' close to his ear, deeply, softly, like a mellow organ, but with a roughness in her voice like a grasshopper's, which" — paronomastically — "rasped his spine deliciously and sent running up into his brain waves of sound which, concussing, broke" (32). The words are intoned so "deeply" that they seem taken up, taken in, by his own body, felt along the spine. Barthes's textual "grain of the voice" is registered here as if it were the flexion and rumble of one's own inner voice suddenly surging to enunciation.

In what amounts to a schizophrenic instance of reading — channeled along what we saw Deleuze characterize in the Prologue as the fluid, amorphous body of the psychotic speaker — text production is transferred here to the listener at one remove. It is for him, for Septimus, that the sky's text is transmitted in a vocalized format. The outer writing, distanced and inde-cipherable — when once mediated by the reading body, whether of self or other (here the "nursemaid" of a new mother tongue) — must then make its necessary cerebral connection. This happens as, again, it "sent running up into his brain waves of sound," itself a wavering phrasing. Its imbricated grammar turns on a dislodged direct object ("sent . . . waves") dovetailed with an object of the preposition instantaneously transformed to adjectival function in a momentary compound ("into his brain/waves"). Inner and outer, reception and phonic input, meet there at a segmental conflation, an Empsonian double grammar verging on phonotextual slippage. Another double grammar fol-lows, again located to negotiate between acoustic cause and mental effect: "Sounds made harmonies with premeditation; the spaces between them were as significant as the sounds" (33). The collocation "with premeditation" performs either as a phrase of agency, naming the motive or cause of the "harmonies," or else it names the object in phase with which such harmonies are achieved—namely, that meditative inwardness set in echo by external phonemic patterns, especially by the enunciation of a diaphanous writing in the morning sky. In the alphabetic cryptograms of these cloudy plumes of smoke, "the spaces between" are wholly "significant"—signifying, differentially functional, pregnant in their pauses, gaps, leaps.

In this vein, an encrypted graphonic example of such articulation happens to occur later in connection with Septimus. This shell-shocked World War I veteran cries out at one point in unacknowledged erotic longing to his dead comrade, Evans, whose haunting presence figures for him the death he at once fears and desires in the body of the Other. In so evoking the past, he actually enunciates an occulted transegmental "paraphone" of his own name's origin in the mystic number seven. Through a schizophrenic dialogism, that is, a "great revelation took place. A voice spoke from behind the screen. Evans was speaking. The dead were with him" (140). With Evans in his resurrected power? With Septimus in the form of Evans and all those others who did not come back? Woolf's pronouns in this indirect discourse are slipping undecidably between the consciousness of self and other, even as this both ecstatic and torturing ambivalence yields to the climactic utterance as overheard by a servant girl, an utterance which she assumes to be "Mr. Smith...talking aloud to himself." Indeed so, though in code. We hear twice over at this point—across a phonemic liaison—the slurred name of the dead alter ego blending into that of the morbid survivor. With the repeated "Evans, Evans!" tending to evocalize, that is, the shadow of suicidal self-recognition in "Evan-S=even(s)," dialogism is transformed once again to a lexical dualogism. As if from beyond the grave, identity returns from the unconscious, calling itself up (and out) in the very name of its surrender to another. To read this cry transegmentally, however, is not, like Septimus, to hear voices. It is to voice silently the textualization of his utterance—in a way that ventriloquizes its double through an auditory homoerotics of the different-as-same. Had his summons gone out from a skywriting machine, its letters could scarcely have been more mutable, more polymorphous.

We left off that earlier skywriting passage at the very point where Septimus himself is attempting to decode its lettering through the intermediary voicing of the nursemaid, as if he were being weaned again from the semiotic into the symbolic. The sense, indeed, that all allusions to sounds and significations in this narratively dispersed skywriting passage are linked back to the aerial script and its translations—as a master trope for text production—is attested further by a striking and curious description of the plane, along with its wake of letters, disappearing from view: "It had gone; it was behind the clouds. There was no sound. The clouds to which the letter E, G, or L had attached themselves moved freely...then suddenly, as a train comes out of a tunnel, the aeroplane rushed out of the clouds again, the sound boring into the ears of all people" (30). As the misty letters lose distinction against their vaporous background, by what logic does the sound of the engine disappear, a sound aeronautic, of course, rather than phono-graphic? Baffled perhaps, partially muted, by atmospheric blockage, why should the sound be gone altogether? By the same logic, we must suppose, that has introduced this engine of textual generation and momentum into Woolf's novel in the first place: its figural recasting of the novel's own textual maneuvers, where enunciatory sounds are in fact inseparable from the letters kept in process only by distinctions from each other and the backing page. The sound that "bores" and burrows into the consciousness of the attentive Londoner has at once nothing and everything to do with the letters it announces; it indexes their condition without in any way lending them definition. The skywriting is neither sonic nor phonic in its own right, any more than is script in more earthbound texts. Ordinary writing is, of course, not accompanied by sound at all, but it is, Woolf would suggest, associated with it: not with the buzz of a distant engine but with a far nearer murmur, secondary, reactive, bodily, to which this scene's mechanical noise puts at least one hypersensitive reader below, Septimus Smith, on alert. Then, too, the phonologic dimension of this parable is only further secured by a phonetic coincidence that brackets it. The rasping, visceral enunciation "Kay Arr" that plays so powerfully upon the body of the hero happens almost directly to echo, in its translation of the unauthored writing on high, the novel's own attempt to capture a stray sound in the phonetic transcription of its own letteral code. This is the burst of dialect that begins this whole exercise in urban semiosis, a passing Cockney's guess that the state vehicle stopping traffic just before the skywriting begins is indeed "The Proime Minister's kyar" (20). From the phonetic transcription of "kyar" through the nonsyllabic, nonlexical nexus, "K," then "E," then "Y," on through the granular enunciation of "Kay Arr," this section is paced by extremities of articulation. In its fanciful thematic of wide dissemination and perplexed but ecstatic interpretation, Woolf's passage is, in short, repeatedly animated by the play of ear against eye.

But that play in a sense plays itself false, induces the reversal of its own terms. The looped script in the sky, accompanied by the sounds of its (unvoiced) source and hailed from below by almost liturgical bursts of oral response, turns out to figure in its visual attenuations the phonemic rather than the graphic basis of reading. This grows only slowly clear. A page after we have encountered that loaded generalization about sounds and "the spaces between them," the narrative seems no longer concerned with the actual skywriting. That episode has been converted, instead, to a metaphor. Septimus's wife, finding herself alone, finds also that she has thrown away her words. "There was nobody. Her words faded. So a rocket fades" (34). Enacted previously by the skywriting, Woolf's complex allegory of text production is thus turned inside out near the end, so that an airborne missile becomes now a mere figure for speech. It is eight more pages until another random pedestrian, one Mrs. Dempster, is smitten with the returning sight of the actual plane's lift and plunge; and, after her, Mr. Bentley: "Away and away the aeroplane shot, till it was nothing but a bright spark; an aspiration; a concentration; a symbol" (41). As symbol, the skywriting technology is next linked to the symbolic structure of cathedral architecture, with its upward ethereal thrust. St. Paul's beckons, and the emblematic linguistics of the aerial script is now merged with the cathedral as a conjoint figure for transcendence itself, as figured synecdochically in turn by "an altar, a cross, the symbol of something which has soared beyond seeking and questing and the knocking of words together and has become all spirit, disembodied, ghostly" (42). Hence the question "why not enter in?"—literal in reference to the cathedral, figurative (and more idiomatic) in relation to the communal faith it enshrines.

It is a faith in the very "communication" which is the central theme of the novel. Associated with the cathedral in its architectonics of the Risen Word, the symbolic ascendancy of the skywriting falls nevertheless as far from a transcendental signified as Woolf could make it. It is, rather, an analysis of the material basis of one kind of subjective communion. The whole scene has unfolded within parameters defined by lettering, acoustics, speech, and the body. It cannot be said to have produced their convergence—and is illustrative for just this reason. It brings the fourfold terms of Woolf's metalinguistics (as those of this book) into a pattern of complementarity that reifies, in order better to define, the coordinates of textual production. At the same time, the nature of these letters, airy and vanishing, bears far less relation to normal script than to those silent enunciations, those inferred sounds rather than conferred sights, which traverse it, those evocalizings which nudge and buckle the implied billowing sprawl of phonemes even without changing their transient *look* as letters. In Woolf's parable, the diaphanous becomes in the long run a metaphor for the phonational. Figured by graphic signifiers, the material basis of phonetic language determines a writing sensitized to the plasticity of enunciation, a writing where words will always be too feathery, too mothlike, too much on the wing, or in other terms too susceptible to wavering "reflux"—let us say, too *diaphanous*—ever to knock and jostle one another, ever to collide without some give and blend.

To enter upon both an expressive and a hermeneutic ambience beyond "the knocking of words together" is therefore to participate in a textuality fluent and permeable, whose letters—but only as heard integers—either dissolve into each other in the very formation of words or disperse into the signifying zone of the "spaces between." Stretched streaming, then, above quotidian London for all to read, not exactly printed but technologically produced, is Woolf's dream of the modernist text ex machina. It is a text rescued by subjectivity, by reading, from the affronts and co-optations of advertising itself, of unaesthetic writing, of prose for hire. And we can now be all the more certain about why the source of the floating, fluctuant script is, wherever unseen, therefore decidedly silent as well. The new writerly fluency of such text production, in its materialist disclosure, generates its object out of thin air. The subjective phonic existence of such a text, as located at the site of reading and interpretation, is always dependent on the visual register, on the corporeal eye of the decipherer, whose inner ear is only then and thereby engaged. A roaring biplane gone (noiseless) behind clouds is one image; a smokescript potentially merged with its equally opaque background is a second: together, silence finds its specular correlative in the blurring of plume within or against cloud, the depthless space of white on white—a figuration, in turn, of textuality's blank page. Noise and optical trace, though separate in origin, are so linked and reconceived here as to become bonded in reception. This is doubly the case when they are understood at the level of metalinguistic parable, since the tenuous visual script is conveyed in its own right as a secondary figure for the phonemic mutability and meld of utterance. One way or another, only when the ear is activated by association with the graphic can any text, however aerial, however ethereal, be said to go into production. Words brushing and yielding, thinning and flowing into each other, and in their wavelengths registering on the brain, words phonemically encroaching upon rather than knocking against each other—words indeed lapsed to the phase of sheer wording, diffuse and mutable—demonstrate yet again, and no less than in Joyce, the ineluctably linked modalities of graphonic writing. This has been our story. It is the theoretical as well as literary-historical narrative that devolves from the fact that, rather than the act of, reading voices.

Notes

PROLOGUE

1. See, especially, Francis Barker, *The Tremulous Private Body: Essays on Subjection* (London: Methuen, 1984); and two special issues of *Representations*—"Sexuality and the Social Body," *Representations,* no. 14 (Spring 1986), and "The Cultural Display of the Body," *Representations,* no. 17 (Winter 1987).

2. See J. L. Austin, *How to Do Things with Words* (Cambridge, Mass.: Harvard University Press, 1962), p. 120; hereafter cited in the text.

3. W. H. Auden, Introduction to *A Selection from the Poems of Alfred, Lord Tennyson* (Garden City, N.Y.: Doubleday, Doran and Company, 1944), p. x.

4. I use the vernacular "plus" here (rather than the debated phonemic signal $/+/$), and indeed the term "segmental," in a way that warrants some explanation at the outset. Concerning the history of the junctural phoneme— or $/+/$—devised by linguists to account for both the internal and external borders of lexical units and the long-standing arguments on its utility, see Stephen R. Anderson, *Phonology in the Twentieth Century: Theories of Rules and Theories of Representation* (Chicago: University of Chicago Press, 1985), pp. 298–304. In view of my investigations into the workings of ambiguous juncture, I repeat a revealing anecdote rehearsed by Anderson concerning Leonard Bloomfield's desire to save for phonology the concept of "the word," insisting as he did on "grammatical boundaries as potential conditioning factors" for those "subphonemic differences" by which word division is linguistically secured: "Bloomfield, Hoijer, and Hockett lunching together in Chicago. Hockett proposed that when it is impossible to hear word-boundary there is no justification for representing it by a space (or otherwise) in a phonetic transcription. Hoijer, with Bloomfield's obvious

approval, says that that is just where the space is most needed. Subject changed" (p. 267). Given the urgency of junctural signaling, I should further clarify at the start that I deploy the coined term *trans-segmental* in these pages primarily in reference to the formative procedure known as "segmentation of the chain" in structural linguistics—closely akin to syllabic demarcation—rather than to the notion of the unitary phonemic "segment" (the single distinctive sound feature) and its "suprasegmental" complements. For a discussion of lexical "segmentation" as distinguished from "segmental elements"—in other words, the morphemic versus phonemic categories—see Oswald Ducrot and Tzvetan Todorov, *Encyclopedic Dictionary of the Sciences of Language,* trans. Catherine Porter (Baltimore: Johns Hopkins University Press, 1979), pp. 17 and 176, respectively. It remains the case, however, that a sliding phoneme transferred across scripted word boundaries—or, in other terms, putatively displacing the / + / of external juncture—might be said not only to confuse the morphological "segmentation" within or between words but to produce a trans-formation, as it were, of its own "segmental" elementation of the phonemic cluster, now "pertinently opposed" in one lexical frame of reference, now in another. My coinage can thus be taken to evoke both definitions of "segmentality" after all.

5. Sigmund Freud, *Jokes and Their Relation to the Unconscious* (1905), *The Standard Edition of the Complete Psychological Works of Sigmund Freud,* trans. and ed. James Strachey, 24 vols. (London: Hogarth Press, 1960), 8:19, 22; hereafter cited by page number in the text.

6. Gilles Deleuze, "The Schizophrenic and Language: Surface and Depth in Lewis Carroll and Antonin Artaud," in *Literature and Psychoanalysis,* ed. Edith Kurzweil and William Phillips (New York: Columbia University Press, 1983); hereafter cited by page number in the text. This essay originally appeared in *Logique du sens* by Gilles Deleuze, translated and condensed in *Textual Strategies: Perspectives in Post-Structuralist Criticism,* ed. Josué V. Harari (Ithaca, N.Y.: Cornell University Press, 1979).

7. Roland Barthes, "Listening," in *The Responsibility of Forms: Critical Essays on Music, Art, and Representation,* trans. Richard Howard (New York: Farrar, Straus and Giroux, 1985), p. 245; hereafter cited in the text.

8. Although Barthes's "The Grain of the Voice" is collected along with "Listening" (see n.7 above) in the subsection entitled "Music's Body," it has explicit bearing on the somatic dimension of writing as well.

9. Julia Kristeva, *Revolution in Poetic Language,* trans. Margaret Waller (New York: Columbia University Press, 1984 [originally published in French in 1974]).

10. Barthes, *S/Z: An Essay,* trans. Richard Miller (New York: Farrar, Straus and Giroux, 1974 [originally published in French in 1970]), especially pp. 3–6. An earlier suggestion of this concept appears in his *Writing Degree Zero,* trans. Annette Lavers and Colin Smith (New York: Farrar, Straus and Giroux, 1967 [originally published in French in 1953]), where Barthes

explains in his terms "why there is room, between a language and a style, for another formal reality: writing" (p. 13).

11. Jacques Derrida, *Of Grammatology,* trans. Gayatri Chakravorty Spivak (Baltimore: Johns Hopkins University Press, 1974 [originally published in French in 1967]), p. 59.

12. See Michel Foucault, *The Order of Things: An Archaeology of the Human Sciences* (New York: Random House, 1970 [originally published in French in 1966]); hereafter cited in the text. What follows is an extremely condensed summary drawn from the whole sweep of Foucault's argument.

13. Marshall McLuhan, *The Gutenberg Galaxy: The Making of Typographic Man* (Toronto: University of Toronto Press, 1962), p. 92. In "Silent Reading in Antiquity," *Journal of Greek, Roman, and Byzantine Studies* 9 (1968): 421–35, Bernard M. W. Knox, beginning with the famous anecdote about Augustine and Ambrose, explains Augustine's astonishment at silent reading as the result in good part of being "an African provincial from a poor family" (p. 422). (The passages quoted from Augustine in my text are from the *Confessions,* trans. Edward B. Pusey [New York: Random House, 1949], bk. 6, pp. 98–99). Knox proceeds to demonstrate – against previous scholarly suppositions – that the practice of silent reading must have been fairly widely practiced in fourth- and fifth-century Athens and in Italian imperial circles of the same period. Yet Knox does not deny that earlier readers relied on the predominantly oral perception of textual meaning. From a less rigorously historical perspective, H. J. Chaytor's influential study "Reading and Writing" in *From Script to Print* (Cambridge: Heffer, 1945) implies that the reader's primary dependence on voice lasted well into the medieval period, so that "the common manner of reading to oneself meant whispering or muttering" (p. 14). Chaytor quotes a medieval scholastic on "the interior force of reading," which was often beleaguered – indeed by "devils" – who, making him pronounce the words out loud, denied him complete mental comprehension (p. 15). Even for the modern habits of fully interiorized reading, Chaytor follows certain perceptual studies in positing "a half-felt tendency to articulate the word, a feeling known to psychology as a 'kinesthetic' or 'speech-motor' image" (p. 5), adding the curious anecdotal remark: "It is said that some doctors forbid patients with severe throat affections [*sic*] to read, because silent reading provokes motions of the vocal organs, though the reader may not be conscious of them" (p. 6).

Drawing on philological research, McLuhan pursues the implications of an original oral reading in view of the subsequent erasure of "scribal culture" (*Gutenberg Galaxy,* p. 108) by the advent of "typographic man." He stresses that only "the phonetic alphabet makes a break between eye and ear, between semantic meaning and visual code; and thus only phonetic writing has the power to translate man from the tribal to the civilized sphere, to give him an eye for an ear" (p. 27), a transition involving in part, from the seventeenth century forward, the "levelling of inflexion [*sic*] and of wordplay" (p. 233).

Beginning as my study does with Shakespeare, my claim for this same modern epoch is that literature itself, among the mass productions of language, keeps these eccentric aural contours in mind (though safely out of sight) within the normalizing tendencies of print culture.

14. *Hegel's Philosophy of Mind* (pt. 3 of the Encyclopedia of the Philosophical Sciences, 1830), trans. William Wallace (Oxford: Clarendon, 1971), p. 218.

15. See Paul Saenger, "Silent Reading: Its Impact on Late Medieval Script and Society," *Viator* 13 (1982): 316–414, an essay demonstrating that texts "regularly divided into words" began to be common on the continent "over the course of the ninth, tenth, and eleventh centuries" (p. 377), a century later than in England and Ireland. "Saxon and Celtic priests," Saenger maintains, "living on the fringes of what had been the Roman Empire, had a weak grasp of Latin and needed spaces between words to recognize them in order to pronounce liturgical texts correctly as they read aloud" (p. 377). But he also claims that word breaks permitted the spread of silent reading, transcription, and composition: "It is therefore no coincidence that the first textual evidence to document the practice of silence in the scriptorium dates from the British Isles when word-blocks and word division became common in Insular manuscripts" (p. 378). About the gradual effects of the "inner solitude" (p. 411) of silent reading on composition (rather than self-dictation), Saenger notes that it was not until the fifteenth century that "the word *écrire* became synonymous with composition" (p. 407). A brief overall sketch of the history of punctuation in regard to the shift from orality to literacy has recently been provided by James Thorpe in *The Sense of Style: Reading English Prose* (Hamden, Conn.: Archon Press, 1987), pp. 17–36, in connection with his emphasis throughout on the oral "performance" of expository prose.

16. "Most twelfth- and thirteenth-century miniatures continued to show people reading in groups. To read in groups was to read aloud; to read alone was to mumble. When a single reader was portrayed, a dove was placed at his ear representing the voice of God, again suggesting audial communication" (Saenger, "Silent Reading," pp. 379–80).

17. See L. D. Reynolds and N. G. Wilson, *Scribes and Scholars: A Guide to the Transmission of Greek and Latin Literature,* 2d ed. (London: Oxford Univ. Press, 1974), p. 201, where this passage from chapter 43 of the *Satyricon* is discussed.

18. Reynolds and Wilson, *Scribes and Scholars,* p. 209.

19. René Wellek and Austin Warren, *Theory of Literature* (New York: Harcourt, Brace, 1942), p. 132. My own sense of even subvocal text production is closer to the kinetic microshocks suggested by Walter J. Ong, S.J., in his chapter "Auditory Synthesis: Word as Event" in *The Presence of the Word* (New Haven, Conn.: Yale University Press, 1967), where he insists that "words *are* powerful. We take them in tiny doses, a syllable at a time" (p. 112). It is just such a principle that explains why in silently reading the first clause of

this very sentence from Ong, without a decisive spoken inflection to disambiguate its twofold "power," we may well momentarily read "take them in" as a verb phrase, before revising its third monosyllable so that it merely attaches instead, as preposition, to the not quite synonymous "take them [by way of]," the designated "reception" in this case not conveying the idiomatic sense of internalization. In the larger framework of his discussion, the sensory presencing effected by language in "oral-aural" culture is not, on my account, somehow reproduced by texts but instead made available for the first and only time in the latent sound waves of silent reading. If this constitutes a resistance to the "visualist" regime from the "verbomotor" instincts (pp. 174–75), it is accomplished nonetheless without that resacralization of the word implied at times in Ong's discussion.

20. Virginia Woolf, "On Being Ill," *Collected Essays,* 4 vols. (New York: Harcourt Brace, 1967), 4:200.

21. John Russell, *Style in Modern British Fiction* (Baltimore: Johns Hopkins University Press, 1978), p. 212.

22. Stanley Fish, "Literature in the Reader: Affective Stylistics," *New Literary History* 2, no. 1 (Autumn 1970): 123–62; hereafter cited in the text. (Fish's essay was reprinted as the appendix to *Self-Consuming Artifacts* [Berkeley and Los Angeles: University of California Press, 1972].) In something like a poststructuralist updating of reader-response theory for the 1986 presidential address to the Modern Language Association (carried in *PMLA* 102, no. 3 [May 1987]: 281–91), J. Hillis Miller called for a return to the material specificity of reading. In an epoch of cultural critique, Miller finds that "a frontier topic for literary study these days is precisely [the] distinction between base and superstructure" (p. 288). He further insists: "In literary study the first material base is the words on the page in the unique, unrepeatable time of an actual reading" (p. 288). Left at that, however, his definition begs – or, anyway, leaves open – a crucial question. For within his formulation inheres, unacknowledged, a further distinction, one to which the present study is directed. In nominating the "words *on* the page" as the material base, Miller's subsequent preposition, "in," also further positions them. They are not, his language might be taken to imply, just there to be read but there only in the reading. That "unique, unrepeatable time of an actual reading" during ("in") which these words are realized is part of the "first material base," then, in the sense of providing the field for its activation by a complementary "materiality," a body, of considerably more weight and gravity than any such words on whatever pages. To refashion Miller's definition in terms already developed in the preceding discussion, we may stress again that in "literary study" the "compound material base" of any reading "is the words on the page" only as they are produced as text – materialized, corporealized – by the silent or speaking body across the "unrepeatable time" of each engaged and generative reading.

23. Geoffrey Hartman, *Saving the Text: Literature/Derrida/Philosophy* (Baltimore: Johns Hopkins University Press, 1981), p. 156.

CHAPTER 1

1. This Eliotian line gives the title to a recent essay, and volume, by Terence Hawkes, *That Shakespeherian Rag: Essays on a Critical Process* (London: Methuen, 1986). Drawing on Barthes's notions of textual *jouissance* and Bakhtin's theories of dialogism, Hawkes uses Eliot's line as a filter through which to rehear Shakespearean dramatic poetry as a "play-text" full of "paralinguistic" signals that depend upon "the manner of their *voicing,* over and above their overt meaning" (p. 79). The quasi-musical power of the Shakespearean text, as hinted by Eliot, is designed to invoke our articulatory investment in a manner that, Hawkes closes his essay by stressing, "turns us, even as we read, from spectators into participants" (p. 90). Though his emphasis is on the performance text, his generalizations about literary language at large bear directly on the work of my opening chapter: "As the site of competition between different ways of reading, the play-text stands, not as a different kind of text, but as the occasion which calls into question some of our presuppositions concerning the activity of reading all texts. That is its value" (p. 77).

2. Stephen Booth, *An Essay on Shakespeare's Sonnets* (New Haven, Conn.: Yale University Press, 1969), pp. 174–86, cited hereafter as *ESS,* and Stephen Booth, ed., *Shakespeare's Sonnets* (New Haven, Conn.: Yale University Press, 1977), pp. 155–58. Subsequent quotations from the sonnets are from this edition; Booth's commentary on the sonnets is cited hereafter, by page number, as *SS.*

3. Stanley Fish, *Surprised by Sin: The Reader in "Paradise Lost"* (London: Macmillan, 1967).

4. Booth is harking back here to Roman Jakobson and Lawrence G. Jones, *Shakespeare's Verbal Art in "Th' Expence of Spirit"* (The Hague: Mouton, 1970), where the authors borrow the phrase "figure of sound" from the journals of Gerard Manley Hopkins to account for the way in which "perjured" in the first quatrain of sonnet 129 chimes against "purpose" in the second, "proposed" in the third (p. 304). Booth takes comparable note in sonnet 15 of the echoes "among *When, When,* and *Then,* among *consider, perceive, conceit,* and *con-, con-,* and *incon-*" (p. 157).

5. Jakobson, "Linguistics and Poetics," in *Essays on the Language of Literature,* ed. Seymour Chatman and Samuel R. Levin (Boston: Houghton Mifflin, 1967), p. 303.

6. Booth has also taken counsel in this vein from David I. Masson, "Free Phonetic Patterns in Shakespeare's Sonnets," *Neophilologus* 37 (October 1954): 277–89 (quoted in *SS,* p. 193). For other essays by Masson, see below, Chapter 2, n. 12.

7. See Michael Riffaterre, *Semiotics of Poetry* (Bloomington: Indiana University Press, 1978), and *Text Production*, trans. Terese Lyons (New York: Columbia University Press, 1983); hereafter cited, as *TP*, in the text.

8. See Chapter 3, n. 8.

9. See Riffaterre, *Semiotics of Poetry*, chap. 3, with its subsections "Expansion" and "Conversion," pp. 47–80.

10. Paul de Man, "Hypogram and Inscription: Michael Riffaterre's Poetics of Reading," *Diacritics* 11 (Winter 1981): 17–35.

11. Geoffrey H. Hartman, "The Voice of the Shuttle: Language from the Point of View of Literature," in *Beyond Formalism: Literary Essays, 1958–1970* (New Haven, Conn.: Yale University Press, 1970), pp. 337–55. "Reading a poem is like walking on silence" (p. 342), writes Hartman, and this leads him to consider various eruptions of semantic value out of the most silent of all components in the textual membrane, the nonce value of juncture: "Juncture is simply a space, a breathing space: phonetically it has zero value, like a caesura. But precisely because it is such a mini-phenomenon, it dramatizes the differential or, as de Saussure calls it, diacritical relation of sound to meaning" (p. 341). Within three pages, however, Hartman has moved on to another figure not so directly bound up with a strictly linguistic silence of diacritical opposition: "From juncture, usually represented by a slash, it is only a step to the grammatical figure of tmesis, best represented by a dash" (p. 344). I assume it to be quite in the spirit of Hartman's pathbreaking essay *not* necessarily to follow him in taking such a "step" until the full suggestiveness of junctural "micropoetics" itself has been exhausted. Similarly, in his book-length meditation on Derrida, *Saving the Text: Literature/Derrida/ Philosophy* (Baltimore: Johns Hopkins University Press, 1981), Hartman singles out, within the whole range of ambiguity, the way in which "Derrida relies heavily on one device of *coupure,* that of tmesis or variable juncture" (p. 22). Indeed, in precisely the mode of Hartman's analyses in "The Voice of the Shuttle" (its title alluded to on the penultimate page of *Saving the Text*), a reading of Donne's lines about the debated moment of death—where some lookers-on say "now, and some say no,"—is used as an instance of Derridean "thanatopraxis," whereby the "mere breathing space between 'now' and 'no' is the economy of death as a principle of phonemics, the subtlest 'glas' [death knell]" (p. 26).

12. In *The Force of Poetry* (New York: Oxford, 1984), Ricks borrows the term "flicker of hesitation" (p. 98) from Donald Davie to describe the passing ambivalence of certain enjambed lines, but he then applies the notion far more widely to those "intended flickers of warring possibilities" (269) that animate the "potent absences" (p. 268) of the "anti-pun."

13. Jan G. Kooij, *Ambiguity in Natural Language: An Investigation of Certain Problems in Linguistic Description* (Amsterdam: North-Holland Publishing Co., 1971), p. 19; see also my discussion of related matters concerning phonetic "fusion" at the start of Chapter 3.

14. Jakobson, *Six Lectures on Sound and Meaning,* trans. John Mapham (Cambridge, Mass.: MIT Press, 1978), p. 11.

15. Henry Fielding, *A Journey from This World to the Next,* vol. 5 of *Works* (London: John Bumpus, 1822), p. 39.

16. All quotations from Shakespeare's plays are from *The Riverside Shakespeare,* ed. G. Blakemore Evans (Boston: Houghton Mifflin, 1974); citations are to scene, line, and act.

17. Dell Hymes, "Phonological Aspects of Style: Some English Sonnets," in *Essays on the Language of Literature* (see n. 5 above), pp. 33–53.

18. According to Booth in one of his glosses on the sonnets, the negative connotation of *censure*—meaning, to judge *unfavorably*—was "only just emerging in Shakespeare's time," which might mean that Hamlet's pun has a neutral as well as an ironically antonymic face. Booth would perhaps be more likely than elsewhere to credit such an example of segmental sleight, since he himself indulges in a nonetymological dissection of the verb's appearance in sonnet 148: "Note the accidental presence in *censures* of the sounds of two words generally pertinent to the sonnet's topic: 'sense' and 'sure'" (*SS,* p. 520). The instance in *Hamlet* goes one step further by rendering the punning matrix grammatical. A similar homophonic interplay between two words and one is taken up, though as an isolated instance, by Margaret W. Ferguson in "*Hamlet:* Letters and Spirits," in *Shakespeare and the Question of Theory,* ed. Patricia Parker and Geoffrey Hartman (New York: Methuen, 1985), when she turns to the editorially vexed response of Laertes to Claudius after the latter's description of the "gentleman of Normandy" (4.7.81)—Laertes' exclamation, "Upon my life, Lamord" (4.7.91). Erupting here is a proper name (Lamond in the second quarto) which Ferguson follows Harold Jenkins (the Arden editor) and Harry Levin in reading as a pun on *la Mort* (p. 301)—thus personifying death, and doing so through what I would call a transegmental disengagement of monosyllabic integers. She even suggests that the utterance doubles as well for *l'amour,* a transformation which would involve the standard French variety of those elisions elsewhere on view in the English lexical displacements of Shakespearean verse.

19. See Chapter 4, p. 158, for Keats's allusive revision of these lines.

20. Fausto Cercignani's *Shakespeare's Works and Elizabethan Pronunciation* (Oxford: Clarendon, 1981) is the first definitive advance over Helge Kökeritz's *Shakespeare's Pronunciation* (New Haven, Conn.: Yale University Press, 1953). On the basis of Cercignani's findings, it does seem probable that such modern English rhymes as Keats's of "adieu" with "songs forever new" ("Ode on a Grecian Urn") or Tennyson's of "adieu" with "true" (*In Memoriam*) would have been less likely in Elizabethan English than Shakespeare's own "adieu"/"Montague" from *3 Henry VI* (4.8.29), derived more directly from the word's French origin. Cercignani attempts to correct the tendency in Kökeritz to place undue weight on internal echoes rather than on rhymes as philological evidence, precisely because paronomastic effects are often more

effective—and hence more likely—when subtle and inexact. This logic, provided with the specific evidence about "adieu" as "adyew," may militate against a perfect pun in the line. But the same logic would argue all the more in favor of a homophonic slippage: the wavering relevance of an anti-pun comparable to a collapsed or superimposed paronomasia. In the present case, therefore, of "into a dew" (as a possible supralexical play on "adieu"), whatever a philological reconstruction takes away from this line of the play conceived as performance text, it gives back to a subsequent moment. Quoting the ghost's last admonition, Hamlet enjoins himself: "Now to my word: / It is 'Adieu, adieu, remember me'" (1.5.110–11). Given the received philological wisdom about "adieu" rhyming with "Montague" or "due" (rather than with *dew*), the comma in "adieu, remember" is likely to give way to the supralexical shadow of a doubt: "adieu, a-*d'you remember me*(?)." In general, though, Cercignani's explicit discussion is aimed at disproving certain previously assumed puns, including at one point a segmental wordplay that must be disallowed because of too great a difference between the sounds transcribed by *o*: "As for *common-come on* 1.1.57–9, it cannot be accepted as an actually intended jingle" (p. 121). The same applies (though without specific mention) to wordplay I had always assumed to be operating (as it does in any modern production) in Hamlet's first encounter with the ghost: "Be thou a spirit of *health* or goblin damned, / Bring with thee airs from heaven or blast from *hell*" (1.4.40–41). To the modern ear, the opening phrase would thus, in a vanishing moment—the split second of a splintered lexeme—name by homophone the antithetical possibility of origin here under inquiry: "spirit of hell." Yet Cercignani's researches suggest that the Shakespearean, or late Middle English, vowel sound in "health" was related more to the long *e* of "heal."

21. It was Karen Cunningham who first called my attention to this sibilant anti-pun.

22. Cercignani, *Shakespeare's Works and Elizabethan Pronunciation,* p. 61.

23. James Joyce, *Ulysses* (New York: Random House, 1961), p. 191.

24. Pun intended, this line happened to provide the title for an historicist lecture by Lisa Jardine at Princeton University (Spring 1988) on *Othello* and Elizabethan adultery laws. She opened by noting that this salacious aside in *Othello,* unlike its counterpart in *Troilus,* is never glossed in editions of the text.

25. In Godard's 1987 *King Lear* the disjoint play of sound against visual track helps foreground the explicitly vexed distinction between "image" and a narrower sense of analogy, and this as indirectly related to the play's own thematics of withheld speech. The "violent silence" of Cordelia (so described in Godard's own English-speaking voice-over) is contrasted with the sovereignty of a king named (in intertitle) "l-E-A-R." This is arguably Shakespeare's own pun, aural as well as graphic, since Lear is first addressed by name in the play during Kent's attempt to check his rash plan for the division of

the kingdom; once rebuffed, Kent tries again for a hearing from the "Roya*l* Lear" (1.1.139; emphasis added). In Godard's film, a further route into the text's metalinguistic density is opened up in a later intertitle playing both typographically (again) and also phonemically this time on the transegmental drift of "King Lear: a cLEARing" (with the velar /ŋ/ becoming /k/). Finally, the sound track itself engages a transegmental ambiguity in its summary account of the nonrepresentational "image" confined neither to mimesis nor to metaphor: "An image is true only because it is born outside of all limitation and all resemblance." Hearing this voice-over as a strictly oral text, we know that what we may well alternatively have heard is "all imitation" rather than "all limitation," the two negatively interchangeable in their supposed transcendence by "image."

26. See Anthony Easthope, *Poetry as Discourse* (London: Methuen, 1983), a study which resembles Foucault's broad periodizing of discourse. Designated by Easthope as a founding moment for subjectivity in the lyric, Shakespeare also marks an early stage on the road toward modernism. Similarly Joel Fineman, in *Shakespeare's Perjured Eye: The Invention of Poetic Subjectivity in the Sonnets* (Berkeley and Los Angeles: University of California Press, 1986), sees the constitution of subjectivity as a verbal field negotiated in the development of the sonnets from a specular to a linguistic paradigm or, in other words, from presentation to representation.

CHAPTER 2

1. Mentioned in passing by James Milroy in *The Language of Gerard Manley Hopkins* (London: Andre Deutsch, 1977). This is one piece of Milroy's evidence in his critique of Hopkins's editor, Robert Bridges, whose dismissal of such effects proves that he "did not really know how to read the poems (with the ear)" (p. 133).

2. See William K. Wimsatt, "One Relation of Rhyme to Reason," in *The Verbal Icon* (Lexington: University of Kentucky Press, 1954), pp. 153–66; Hugh Kenner, "Pope's Reasonable Rhymes," *ELH* 41, no. 1 (Spring 1974): 74–88; and John Hollander, *Rhyme's Reason* (New Haven, Conn.: Yale University Press, 1981).

3. Jacques Derrida, *Dissemination,* trans. Barbara Johnson (Chicago: University of Chicago Press, 1981), p. 277.

4. Debra Fried, "Rhyme Puns," in *On Puns: The Foundations of Letters,* ed. Jonathan Culler (Oxford: Basil Blackwell, 1988), pp. 83–99. Her essay is prefaced with a brief overview by Culler, whose intriguing title, "The Call of the Phoneme" (from Fried's essay, p. 88), seems less to the point of his comments than the pun on "letters" in his subtitle. Phonemic matters are given no particular stress in his remarks, except in the most general sense of homophonic punning, nor are they explored per se in any of the later essays to the extent to which Debra Fried takes them up. Nonetheless, the notion of the

reader as "juxtologist," highlighted in Culler's introduction (pp. 8–9) and developed in the essay by R. A. Shoaf that coins the term, "The Play of Puns in Late Middle English Poetry: Concerning Juxtology" (pp. 44–61; esp. p. 60), might well have particular bearing on the phonemic sequencing of the syntagmatic chain—if, that is, the term were taken to refer more literally, more narrowly, to textual juxtapositions and junctures rather than merely to intertextual convergences and semantic collisions. Pursuing this emphasis, Fried at one point raises important doubts about Anthony Easthope's claim in *Poetry as Discourse* ([London: Methuen, 1983], pp. 110–21) that (in her paraphrase) "Augustan poetics reins in the dangerous materiality of words" by deploying end rhyme so that its sound play "is consistently written off to convention," a sense of the phonic "so scrupulously licensed that it cannot affect its neighbors," even though they are "equally a jostling of like and unlike sounds" (p. 88). Fried doubts that "the infectious, babbling echolalia of the phoneme" can be so easily "put . . . into quarantine." So, of course, do I in this chapter and this book, the former isolating in particular rhyme's own inability to "inoculate" its most nearly adjacent "neighbors" not only against associated sound play but against more of the very same rhyming span.

5. Published well before *Rhyme's Reason,* John Hollander's earlier consideration of phonetic iteration, "Rhyme and the True Calling of Words," is reprinted in *Vision and Resonance* (New York: Oxford University Press, 1975), a collection concerned, as the title implies, with the difference between the "poem in the eye" and the "poem in the ear." Hollander illustrates his version of accretive echo with lyrics from Cole Porter and Lorenz Hart that rhyme across three words, "wreck to me"/"neck to me," and then across the syllables of a single lexical unit, "appendectomy" (p. 126). He connects this phonic comedy to such fractured rhyming as Marianne Moore's "could not/ pilot-" (p. 128), where the lexically and syntactically requisite *ing* after "pilot-" is enjambed onto the next line. He does not, however, examine the opposite sort of phonemic enjambment between the gap of words themselves, rather than lines, an overlap that bonds further echoing matter to already rhyming syllables. When he argues, for instance, that rhymes like *nick/flick/ tick/lick* tend to imply a "hypothetical morpheme" like *ick* ("I shall not follow linguistics in calling it the 'phonestheme'" [p. 120], he adds in parentheses), his commentary stops short of following out the complementary process by which single phonemes or phonemic clusters—without the quasi-morphological, quasi-syllabic nature of a false root like *ick*—might repeatedly invade from the left and extend the rhyming nucleus, whether or not the accretion could stand alone as a monosyllable. This is what I have called a *polyphonemic* rhyming, a pattern with no particular allegiance to syllabic demarcation.

6. John Hollander, "Dallying Nicely With Words: Poetic Linguistics," in *The Linguistics of Writing: Arguments between Language and Literature,* ed. Nigel Fabb, Derek Attridge, Alan Durant, and Colin MacCabe (New York:

Methuen, 1987), p. 129 (rpt. in Hollander, *Melodious Guile: Fictive Pattern in Poetic Language* [New Haven, Conn.: Yale University Press, 1988], pp. 180–93).

7. John Hollander, *The Figure of Echo* (Berkeley and Los Angeles: University of California Press, 1981), p. 32.

8. Walter Redfern, *Puns* (Oxford: Basil Blackwell, 1984), p. 100.

9. Wimsatt, "One Relation of Rhyme to Reason," p. 164; Kenner, "Pope's Reasonable Rhymes," p. 80.

10. Donald Wesling, *The Chances of Rhyme: Device and Modernity* (Berkeley and Los Angeles: University of California Press, 1980), p. 21.

11. In correspondence about these lines from Pope, Marie Borroff has suggested a "kinaesthetic" dimension as well to what I hear as a latent drift from "maxims bring" to "maxims spring." She calls attention, in a thematizable upswing or upspring, to the phonetic "rise" within sibilance from the heavier /z/ of "maxims" to the /s/ of "spring," this differential enunciation in keeping with the comparable voiced-to-unvoiced shift from /b/ of "bring" to the lighter /p/ of "spring."

12. David I. Masson, "Free Phonetic Patterns in Shakespeare's Sonnets," *Neophilologus* 37 (October 1954): 277–89. See also Masson, "The Keatsian Incantation: A Study in Phonetic Patterning," in *John Keats: A Reassessment,* ed. Kenneth Muir (Liverpool: Liverpool University Press, 1958), pp. 159–80.

13. The example from *Beppo* appears in Susan Wolfson's "Couplets, Self, and *The Corsair,*" *Studies in Romanticism* 27 (Winter 1988): 507 n. 26. I am grateful to the author's correspondence for the *Don Juan* example, and to Jocelyn Marsh for pointing out that the manuscript version of the first of these rhyming lines was originally "And all mouths were applied unto all ears!" — with "all mouths" changed to the eliding "all lips" as if to anticipate the reverse slippage at "all (l)ears."

14. Answering Kingsley Amis's charges (in "The Curious Elf: A Note on Rhyme in Keats," *Essays in Criticism* I [1951]: 189–92) against this "hopelessly inadequate," telltale "Cockney" rhyme, William Keach (in "Cockney Couplets: Keats and the Politics of Style," *Studies in Romanticism* 25, no. 2 [Summer 1986]) concentrates on the predecessor of this rhyme, as cited by Amis as well, in defending the political ramifications of Keats's virtually decentered notion of self in *Endymion.* The early rhyme, with no transegmental "justification" this time: "The journey homeward to habitual self / A mad pursuing of the fog-born elf" (276–77). Keach on its behalf: "Readers more interested than Amis apparently was in Keats's brooding about the self as a construct at once deceiving in its significance and yet hauntingly persistent may find that the rhyming precipitation of 'elf' out of 'self' (it's like a miniature of Blake's 'spectre' and 'emanation'), far from being 'hopelessly inadequate,' is intrinsic to Keats's thinking through the issue of poetic subjectivity" (p. 192). In my reading of the subsequent, more "conservative" rhyme from the Night-

ingale ode, it is more the deceptive nature of fancy, as it inflects but cannot wholly encompass the poetic self, that must be not just precipitated out but separated off from identity.

15. Donald Reiman, Shelley's "The Triumph of Life": A Critical Study (Urbana: University of Illinois Press, 1965), p. 97 n. 15.

16. William Keach, Shelley's Style (New York: Methuen, 1986), p. 200.

17. Milroy, The Language of Gerard Manley Hopkins, p. 148.

18. James Joyce, "A Flower Given to My Daughter," Collected Poems (New York: Viking, 1957), p. 49.

19. Vladimir Nabokov, Pale Fire (New York: Vintage, 1962), l. 736; the four-canto poem that begins this work hereafter cited by line number; the subsequent "Commentary" by page number.

20. John Hollander, "Summer Day," New Yorker, 14 August 1989, p. 28.

CHAPTER 3

1. R.-M. S. Heffner, General Phonetics (Madison: University of Wisconsin Press, 1950), pp. 175-202. The types of such phonetic "fusion" include "dynamic displacement" ("dynamic" implying the sequential pressure of "motor context"), as when a phrase like "all but universal" tends to be pronounced as "all bu(t) tuniversal"; "doubling" (where the "back stroke" of one word becomes the "beat stroke" of the next), as in "have various" or "and degrees"; "reduction" (an unwritten contraction), as in "extraordinary" when enunciated as a five- rather than six-syllable word, or in "th' eternal"; "omission" (the contractive forms of aphaeresis, syncope, and apocope when graphically indicated by apostrophe); "glides" (related to "dynamic displacement," but involving the introduction of an adventitious transitional sound), as with "don't chew" for "don't you"; "linking" (a bridging of hiatus either through retention or insertion of a consonant), as in the strict form of such French liaisons as raconte-t-on des histoires; "adaptive changes" (shifts that alter the enunciation of a speech sound either to match—by anticipation or continuance—or sometimes to avoid reduplicating a proximate sound), a tendency often related to "doubling" in consonant conjunctions like "hip boots," "red tie," or "big cake." In Heffner's own account of these categories, however, no likelihood emerges of any real morphophonemic—hence lexical, hence semantic—ambiguity, unless one could imagine a context, say, in which "Don't chew?" (the negative imperative cast into an interrogative fragment) could be misheard for "Don't you?" According to Heffner's meticulous phonetic transcriptions, the phenomenon of "fusion" is ultimately prevented between "speech measures, or phrasal groups" (p. 200), inhibited by the nature of speech rhythm itself; and between morphemes by the self-signaling "initial element" (p. 201), pronounced as it could never be in the position of a terminal feature (a phonetic difference, therefore, within the same functional phoneme). The "cessation of the commingling of movement patterns at the

end of a speech measure" (p. 200)= the arrest of fusion – thus also obtains at the boundaries of a morpheme; most potential fusions are therefore suspended by "intonational and accentual patterns" (p. 201) – what linguistics elsewhere calls "suprasegmental" features – if not by clear phonetic distinction.

2. Ibid., p. 3.

3. Jacques Derrida, *Of Grammatology,* trans. Gayatri Chakravorty Spivak (Baltimore: Johns Hopkins University Press, 1974), p. 63, quoting Saussure (see *Course,* p. 66, cited in n. 6 below).

4. In her Translator's Preface to *Of Grammatology,* Gayatri Spivak stresses this as the very principle of the written trace, or *gramme,* "the name of the sign 'sous rature,'" calling "grammatology" the "science of the 'sous rature'" (1).

5. Jacques Derrida, "Différance," in *Speech and Phenomena,* trans. David B. Allison (Evanston, Ill.: Northwestern University Press, 1973), p. 132. In engaging with the Derridean sense of such issues, I am attempting a very different level of textual reception than the more traditional approach, for instance, of Raymond Chapman in *The Treatment of Sounds in Language and Literature* (Oxford: Basil Blackwell, in association with Andre Deutsch, 1984). With a dozen chapters devoted to the linguistic representation of sounds, he only then turns to the sound of representation itself, the phonological aspect of scriptive signification. In his chapter "The Sound of Literature," he admits that the "implications" of the question "how far is sound inherent in written language" do "lead towards areas of literary criticism which would go far beyond the present study" (p. 210). In regard to the "counterweighting of possibilities" (p. 217) between eye and ear, he offers a brief section on how the "study of rhyme is illuminating for the relationship between sight and sound in language" (p. 215), with subsequent commentary on onomatopoetic devices and closing remarks on poetry in oral performance.

6. See Ferdinand de Saussure, *Course in General Linguistics,* trans. Roy Harris (La Salle, Ill.: Open Court Press, 1983).

7. See Jean Starobinski, *Words upon Words: The Anagrams of Ferdinand de Saussure,* trans. Olivia Emmet (New Haven, Conn.: Yale University Press, 1979), and Sylvère Lotringer, "The Game of the Name," *Diacritics* (Summer 1973): 2–9, reviewing the French edition of Starobinski on Saussure.

8. The generative model of this eccentric theory anticipates the tenets of a more sustained later methodology. Whereas Saussure saw an incantatory or ritual motive behind the encrypted name of the god or hero, Michael Riffaterre substitutes an entirely secularized logic of explanation in his encoded semiotics of poetry. As we have seen, the indirectly voiced core of the text is not, for Riffaterre, a "theme word" necessarily but often a fuller sense of a thematic idea. Literary language is in this way found to develop motifs that cannot speak their names – because to do so directly would be to fall from originality, to lapse into cliché. The unsaid matrix of a poetic text surfaces in

paragrammatic variants that are the virtual equivalent of Saussure's "hypogram" (a term Riffaterre also uses at certain points). Further, the "model" in Riffaterre – first and guiding form of the variant, which sets a pattern for ensuing conversions and expansions of the theme – would seem to have derived its own model from Saussure's "mannequin" or *locus princeps:* "a tightly drawn sequence of words which one can designate as especially consecrated to that name" (*Words upon Words,* p. 33) – consecrated, that is, to the theme word. The "mannequin" closely resembles what a phonologist like Masson calls the "bracket," with the Saussurean example "*Prima* qui*es*" yielding up, for instance, the first and densest suggestion of the name "Priamades." Framed or bracketed by the mannequin, in this case, are the structuring pieces of the name, modules known as "syllabograms." Paul de Man has also mentioned, more briefly, the derivation of Riffaterrean semiotics from the Saussurean anagrams in his omnibus review of Riffaterre's work, "Hypogram and Inscription: Michael Riffaterre's Poetics of Reading," *Diacritics* 11 (Winter 1981): 24.

9. To borrow Saussure's own example of a diphone as base unit (with annexed monophones), the coded cluster TAE can be given by TA + E, T + AE, or TA + AE; but since it cannot be given TA + TE – which would require the letters "to be amalgamated outside time, as could be done with two simultaneous colors" (*Words upon Words,* p. 30) – neither can the diphone be overthrown altogether, as would be the case with T + A + E.

10. Gilles Deleuze, "The Schizophrenic and Language: Surface and Depth in Lewis Carroll and Antonin Artaud," in *Literature and Psychoanalysis,* ed. Edith Kurzweil and William Phillips (New York: Columbia University Press, 1983), p. 329.

11. Otto Jespersen, *Language: Its Nature, Development, and Origin* (New York: Macmillan, 1922), p. 8. In line with childhood's illiterate transformations of the language as studied by Jespersen, one must confess that solecisms based on junctural ambiguity can creep into almost any written utterance; indeed, it was only in a late redrafting of one of the present chapters that I finally noticed how I had taken down in phonemic dictation from myself – and many times reread without correction – "making could on."

12. This seems to me what Barthes is suggesting as well when he asks rhetorically, "Is not the entire space of the voice an infinite space?" – adding, "No doubt this was the meaning of Saussure's work on anagrams" ("The Grain of the Voice," p. 272; see my Prologue n. 8).

13. Jonathan Culler, *Ferdinand de Saussure,* rev. ed. (Ithaca, N.Y.: Cornell University Press, 1987), p. 134.

14. Jacques Derrida, *Signéponge/Signsponge,* trans. Richard Rand (New York: Columbia Univ. Press, 1984).

15. Christian Metz, *The Imaginary Signifier: Psychoanalysis and the Cinema,* trans. Celia Britton, Annwyl Williams, Ben Brewster, and Alfred Guzzetti (Bloomington: Indiana University Press, 1977), p. 240.

16. Walter Redfern, *Puns* (Oxford: Basil Blackwell, 1984), pp. 78–79, quoting Leiris's collection, *Mots sans mémoire* (Paris: Gallimard, 1969).

17. Paul de Man, "Shelley Disfigured," in *Deconstruction and Criticism,* ed. Harold Bloom (New York: Seabury, 1979), p. 60.

18. Michel Foucault, *Death and the Labyrinth: The World of Raymond Roussel,* trans. Charles Ruas (Garden City, N.Y.: Doubleday, 1986), pp. 38, 31. Foucault explores another example from *Chiquenaude* (1900), where the multiple meaning of *doublure* (understudy, lining, rehearsal) underwrites a more complex homophonic play (p. 27). After the early mention of a theatrical piece called *Red Claw the Pirate (Forban talon rouge),* the play's title returns, through metamorphic recirculation, as the phonemic doublet *fort pantalon rouge.* As with *billard/pillard,* the "metagram" turns once again on the alternative plosives /b/ and /p/ from the phonemic paradigm of secondary articulation, but it projects them onto the syntagmatic axis as latently copresent alternatives this time, the trace of alternation itself. Quite by coincidence, the most sustained Rousselian experiment I know since his writing, in a relentlessly farcical vein, is the Nabokov-like parody of a found manuscript dutifully transcribed and meticulously glossed without the fictionalized pedantic editor recognizing that the recovered verse fragments under examination are nothing more than Mother Goose rhymes in ludicrous French phonetic transcriptions. The absurd contortions of glides, elisions, and liaisons in Courtlandt H. K. van Rooten's *Mots d'Heures: Gousses, Rames* (New York: Grossman, 1967) amounts to a checklist of effects by which the Rousselian "metagram" was negotiated. Here Humpty-Dumpty is rechristened "Un petit d'un petit" (p. 1), Peter, Peter, Pumpkin-Eater, emerges as "Pis-terre, pis-terre / Pomme qui n'y terre" (p. 8), Jack and Jill are fused in "Chacun Gilles" (p. 11), the Baker's Man buried under "Pas de caïque, pas de caïque, bécasse, mâne" (p. 17), and the whole rounded off with "TIENS, DE" in place of "The End."

19. Raymond Roussel, *La doublure* (Paris: Jean-Jacques Pauvert, 1963), pp. 45, 46.

20. See frame enlargements from Duchamp's *Anemic Cinema* in Arturo Schwartz, *The Complete Works of Marcel Duchamp* (London: Thames and Hudson, 1969), pp. 319–28.

21. Marcel Duchamp, *Rrose Sélavy* (Paris, 1939).

22. Louis Aragon, *Paris Peasant,* trans. Simon Watson Taylor (London: Jonathan Cape, 1971), p. 102.

23. It is a muted form of this same aural preoccupation that appears implicitly in Virginia Woolf's essay, "On Being Ill," her approach to the alogical force of poetic sonority at which we glanced briefly in the Prologue (see n. 20). When Woolf quotes two lines of Rimbaud without further specification of effect— "*O saisons ô châteaux / Quelle âme est sans défauts?*"—who, she asks rhetorically, "shall rationalize the charm?" (p. 200). Not Leiris, certainly not Roussel. But their work can nonetheless be taken to

analyze, even to systematize, the mysterious seduction of such phrasing. In doing so, such work, as if according to the very definition of modernism, places under intensive scrutiny the irrational machinations of language itself out of which poetry from any period has always drawn a part of its force. In Woolf's example from Rimbaud, we find the Leiris-like internal rhymes of "*saisons*" with "*est sans,*" the latter, when reversed, a sly chiastic belling of the former (given the liaison of "sans est"). Exaggerating the euphonious recurrence of poetry in general, it would be more like the radical modernism of Roussel to tease the double liaison of "*Quelle âme est sans*" into an irrelevant semantic echo of *la maison* — in contrast, somehow, to "*châteaux.*" In this line of willful homophonic effects, there also appears in Leiris's glossary just the sort of encompassing lexical slippages that — if separated by other textual material inserted to "process" the transition from one to the other — might well have been found in one of Roussel's experimental exercises: "AMEN — âme mène" (p. 74); "OCEAN — eux et ans" (p. 102). In the closed system of *langue,* with its fluid depths like an opaque "lagune" indeed (as Leiris's earlier transform suggests), one of the most accurate "glosses" on a word — as act of wording rather than as single lexeme — is always, as Leiris joins Roussel in suggesting, the transliteration of its constituent phonemes, the parsing of its material base.

24. These are terms drawn from Peter Brooks's chapter "Freud's Masterplot" in *Reading for the Plot: Design and Intention in Narrative* (New York: Knopf, 1984), pp. 90–112.

25. De Man, "Hypogram and Inscription," p. 22. The example given of Riffaterre's "phenomenal" — hence, in part phonological — criterion: "The French novelist and occasional theoretician Ricardou is reproved for claiming to discover the anagram 'gold' in Poe's phrase 'right hol*d*ing,' despite the fact that the 'g' in 'right' is not sounded in English."

26. Michael Riffaterre, *Semiotics of Poetry* (Bloomington: Indiana University Press, 1978), p. 16.

27. Julia Kristeva, "The Semiotic and the Symbolic," in *Revolution in Poetic Language,* trans. Margaret Waller (New York: Columbia University Press, 1984). Without relying on the Kristevan notion of the semiotic "chora," Geoffrey H. Hartman, in *Saving the Text: Literature/Derrida/Philosophy* (Baltimore: Johns Hopkins Univ. Press, 1981), muses on the "intransitive intimacy" of certain verbal formations that bespeak "the wish to encrypt in oneself the womb — the maternal (paternal) source — of verbalization[,] . . . of chatter and babble developing into verbal thought" (p. 144).

28. From a series of lectures at the University of California, Santa Barbara, in Spring 1987, based on Kittler's *Grammophon, Film, Typewriter* (Berlin: Brinkmann and Bose, 1986), soon to be published in translation by the University of Minnesota Press. The dangers of transegmental slippage — for "practical" rather than poetic communication — are confirmed by an experience I once had in a noisy restaurant. I was trying to explain Kittler's thesis to

a friend who hadn't encountered his work, but over the din, I sounded, it seems, as though I was discussing a critic with the unfortunate name of Friedrich Hitler.

29. See Denis Donoghue, *Ferocious Alphabets* (New York: Columbia University Press, 1984).

30. John Vernon, *Poetry and the Body* (Urbana: University of Illinois Press, 1979).

31. Ake W. Edfeldt, *Silent Speech and Silent Reading* (Chicago: University of Chicago Press, 1960), p. 13.

32. M. M. Bakhtin, *The Dialogic Imagination,* ed. Michael Holquist, trans. Caryl Emerson and Michael Holquist (Austin: University of Texas Press, 1981).

33. In chapters focused on Stendhal's autobiography, Louis Marin posits the nature of discourse as "necessarily *auto-bio-phonic*" and speculates on the "ruses" and "machinations" by which space is made therein—the space of the "silence of the saying within the said"—for that unique narrational condition of discourse "called auto-bio-*graphic*"; see "The Autobiographical Interruption: About Stendhal's *Life of Henry Brulard*," *MLN* 93 (1978): 599–600. This essay appears as part of the untranslated book *La voix excommuniée: essais de mémoire* (Paris: Galilée, 1981). By "interruption" in the English title of this material, Marin intends two related meanings of "syncopation" at the lexical level: "excision of a syllable from a word" and "liaison" in the musical sense, "the end of a note in one section . . . heard at the same time as the beginning of a note belonging to the opposite section" (p. 614). Exploring the insistent refrain of certain dates in the Stendhal text, for instance, Marin reads the slippage between "*deux cent cinquante*" and "*cinquante*" as one of the revealing "rhythmic movements woven with phonic signifiers in the *written* text," movements by which, presumably, the excommunicated "saying" returns to haunt the autobiographical memorial of the "said." The interplay between phonic and graphic signifiers is even more apparent in another section of *La voix excommuniée* previously appearing in English translation, "The 'I' as Autobiographical Eye: Reading Notes on a Few Pages of Stendhal's *Life of Henry Brulard*" (*October* 9 [Summer 1979]: 65–79), where a vertical list of women's names by which the memoirist charts the arc of his desire, when later rewritten horizontally and by initials only, presents the reader with a vexing but fertile instance of the unreadable. What we encounter are "pure graphemes, mere signifiers without signifieds" (p. 75) that can only be spelled, not apprehended as words. The "two directions" of attention posed by the text at this point, in its contradictory pull between the strictly visual and the actively verbal, tend to emphasize by default the inherence of the phonic within the graphic manifestation of the latter. According to Marin, the reader resists the sheerly pictographic response, even in the vicinity of an actual drawing inserted into the text, and attempts rather to "stammer" (p. 75) out something like a continuous verbal processing: "To take now the other direction, that of

reading, what we read, or better what we hear when trying to read the letters as a word or as a name, what is uttered in the mumbling in which, suddenly and for a moment, our reading is deconstructed, is the mother's name stuttered by a child's voice" (p. 76). In the letters "v A A M A A A M c g A" (as capitalized by Marin), that is, an enunciation of *a*'s and *m*'s tends to produce a phonetic anagram as well as a babbling pronunciation of that "auto-bio-phonic" sign at the origin of all life-writing. Though Marin does not mention Kristeva, we may find in the Stendhal text, under Marin's voicing eye, a genuinely strategic emergence of the maternal semiotic in syncopation with the symbolic order of script.

Marin's approach comes even closer to the procedures of this book when he pursues moments of lexical fissure and suture within ordinary vocabular, as well as alphabetical and numerical, sequencing. Working from a cryptic and abbreviated inscription that Stendhal recalls writing on the inside of his belt— "J. vais voirla 5." for "je vais avoir la cinquantaine" (*La voix,* p. 119)—Marin submits it to a detailed linguistic analysis concerned with the syllabic "amputation" and "disappearance" (p. 124) it involves, as well as to a generalizing analysis about the "secret" recoding of script by voice in the reading of autobiography. Here the Stendhal text itself lends occasion to the most minute lexical and syntactic instances of that "syncopation" (the technical syncope, or dropped letter, as well as "liaison") and "reprise" which provide the master-tropes of Marin's theoretical introduction (pp. 21–22). The latter term is cited from Littré's dictionary as, among other more common acceptations, the "action of mending or darning torn or cut material" in which "the needle uses the thread not yet sewn by the first stitch . . . *so that the eye does not perceive the joining of the thread*" ("The 'I' as Autobiographical Eye," p. 66; Marin's emphasis). This invisible seaming of invisible rendings, this tear and repair in the weave of the graphic text, is the work of the voice otherwise *excommuniée.* This approach through "what we hear when trying to read" is to be even more intensively deployed later in *La voix excommuniée* for a listening "deconstructed" to the point of eliding the differentials of gender itself, in ways which resemble the logic of "liaison" in the verbal experiments of Virginia Woolf (see Chapter 7, n.8).

34. Lucette Finas, *Le bruit d'Iris* (Paris: Flammarion, 1978), p. 190. As does Donoghue, I will give my own brief selections from Finas in translation.

35. See below, Chapter 7, under the subheading "Catching That D/rift."

36. Christian Prigent, "Reading in Every State," *Enclitic* 6, no. 2 (Fall 1982): 44–49.

37. Roland Barthes, "Question de tempo," Preface to *Le bruit d'Iris,* pp. 7–11. English excerpts are from the translation by Annwyl Williams, "A Question of Tempo," *Oxford Literary Review* 5, nos. 1–2 (1982): 150–53.

38. Christopher Norris, in *Derrida* (Cambridge, Mass.: Harvard University Press, 1987), understands supplementation in the readily available sense, for instance, of a so-called supplement to an encyclopedia or dictionary

(Norris's example is the *OED*, p. 110). Named thereby is that extra yet necessary extension of the thing without which it would have no claim on the encyclopedic in the first place: the additive that definitively completes.

39. Roland Barthes, *The Pleasure of the Text*, trans. Richard Miller (New York: Hill and Wang, 1975).

40. William Empson, *Seven Types of Ambiguity* (New York: New Directions, 1947), p. 45.

41. See below, Chapter 6, under the subheading "Phonemanology."

CHAPTER 4

1. Robert O. Evans, *Milton's Elisions* (Gainesville: University of Florida Press, 1966), p. 2.

2. See a related sense of punning on "Angels ken" in Edward Le Comte, *A Dictionary of Puns in Milton's English Poetry* (New York: Columbia University Press, 1981), p. 10.

3. Le Comte, following Fowler's gloss (ibid., p. 38).

4. Thomas Vogler, "Re: Naming MIL/TON," in *Unnam'd Forms: Blake and Textuality,* ed. Thomas Vogler and Nelson Hilton (Berkeley and Los Angeles: University of California Press, 1986), p. 146.

5. Samuel Taylor Coleridge to James Gillman, 31 October 1821, *Collected Letters of Samuel Taylor Coleridge,* vol. 5, 1820–1825, ed. Earl Leslie Griggs (Oxford: Clarendon, 1971), p. 185; letter no. 1281.

6. See *The Notebooks of Samuel Taylor Coleridge,* vol. 3, 1808–1819, ed. Kathleen Coburn (Princeton, N.J.: Princeton University Press, 1973), p. 4124.

7. Samuel Taylor Coleridge, *Shakespearean Criticism,* ed. T. M. Raysor, 2 vols. (London: J. M. Dent, 1960), 2:103.

8. M. H. Abrams, "Coleridge's 'A Light in Sound': Science, Metascience, and Poetic Imagination," in *The Correspondent Breeze: Essays on English Romanticism* (New York: W. W. Norton, 1984), p. 164.

9. It was Susan Wolfson who called my attention to this phonemic ambiguity in Coleridge.

10. In *The Questioning Presence: Wordsworth, Keats, and the Interrogative Mode in Romantic Poetry* (Ithaca, N.Y.: Cornell University Press, 1986), Susan Wolfson has recently expanded on Cleanth Brooks's suggestion that the urn of the ode is appealing to a kind of hearing "just below the threshold of normal sound" (p. 320). She detects at one point what amounts to the junctural disintegration of "endear'd" when registering a conjoint "sight and sound" pun that "shades into 'end ear'd,'" as if "to signify audience beyond the bourne of 'the sensual ear'" (p. 320).

11. John Keats to Fanny Brawne, [?] March 1820, *The Letters of John Keats,* ed. Hyder E. Rollins, 2 vols. (Cambridge, Mass.: Harvard University Press, 1958), 2:247.

12. This is the original version of the sonnet given in *John Keats: Selected Poems and Letters,* ed. Douglas Bush (Boston: Houghton Mifflin, 1959), p. 198 n. 1.

13. Shortly preceding the earliest recorded appearance of the term "sod" as a collective noun for the material of ground cover (rather than simply for a piece of turf) — a usage first cited in the *OED* from the Romantic writers Hood and Scott — this phrasing from Keats's "Ode" may indeed have helped to instigate such a linguistic change. Tracked back to an antiphonal matrix, the normative sense of "become a sod" is not the speaker's reduction to a single square of earth but, rather (buried under it), to a condition of analogy therewith, as insensate as the unresponsive turf: "to become a(s) sod."

14. Keats varying a line from Spenser in a letter to Shelley, 16 August 1820, *Letters of John Keats,* 2:322.

15. Percy Bysshe Shelley, "Defence of Poetry," in *Shelley's Poetry and Prose,* ed. Donald H. Reiman and Sharon B. Powers (New York: W. W. Norton, 1977), pp. 487, 488.

16. See William Keach, *Shelley's Style* (New York: Methuen, 1986), p. 186.

17. Jerome J. McGann, *The Romantic Ideology: A Critical Investigation* (Chicago: University of Chicago Press, 1983), p. 3.

18. In *The Linguistic Moment* (Princeton, N.J.: Princeton University Press, 1985), J. Hillis Miller calls attention to one such verbal "moment," decentering and potentially deconstructive, which concerns the issue of translatability between languages in Browning's "The Englishman in Italy" (p. 207). Rupturing the apparent seamlessness of this English textual retrospect with the contractions and bucklings of another tongue, the mountain named "Vico Alvano" is compressed in transliteration — by both aphaeresis and synaloepha, the ellipsis of the first and the blurring of the second syllables — to become "Calvano." It functions thereby as a transegmental signal (characterized by Miller simply as a linguistic anomaly or shorthand) to keep us on linguistic alert in this poem of two cultures, two languages.

19. *The Journals and Papers of Gerard Manley Hopkins,* ed. Humphrey House (London: Oxford University Press, 1959), p. 9.

20. From a passage cited from Coleridge's *Notebooks* (without more specific reference) as epigraph to the first chapter of Geoffrey Hartman's *Saving the Text* (see Prologue, n.23).

21. Geoffrey Hartman, *The Unmediated Vision: An Interpretation of Wordsworth, Hopkins, Rilke and Valéry* (New York: Harcourt, Brace, 1966 [originally published in 1954]), p. 62.

22. See James Milroy, *The Language of Gerard Manley Hopkins* (London: Andre Deutsch, 1977).

23. Hopkins, "Lecture Notes: Poetry and Verse," in *Journals and Papers,* p. 289.

24. See the opening of Chapter 6 below for a discussion of a comparable phrasing in the frontispiece from Hopkins.

25. Hopkins, "Lecture Notes: Rhetoric," in *Journals and Papers*, p. 268.

26. John Unterecker, *A Reader's Guide to William Butler Yeats* (New York: Noonday Press, 1954), p. 81.

27. Helen Vendler, "Poets' Prose," *New Yorker*, 16 March 1987, p. 104.

28. This is Pound's definition of "logopoeia," in "How to Read," in *The Literary Essays of Ezra Pound*, ed. T. S. Eliot (New York: New Directions), p. 25.

29. "All Sounds have been as music," in *The Collected Poems of Wilfred Owen*, ed. C. Day Lewis (Norfolk, Conn.: New Directions, 1963), p. 127.

30. T. S. Eliot, *The Waste Land: A Facsimile and Transcript of the Original Drafts Including the Annotations of Ezra Pound*, ed. Valerie Eliot (New York: Harcourt Brace, 1971), p. 76.

31. In a three-paragraph article for *Tyro*, no. 1 (1921), called "The Lesson of Baudelaire," Eliot wrote that "Dadaism is a diagnosis of a disease of the French mind; whatever lesson we extract from it will not be directly applicable in London" (p. 4). The mythic force of the Thunder's enunciations in Eliot's poem of the next year represents everything Dada parodistically degrades. The only critic I have found who notes a probable allusion (without cross-lexical biplay) to such French countercurrents at the close of *The Waste Land*, Grover Smith, comments briefly: "The fable of the Thunder with its thrice uttered 'Da' may have been invoked partly to get the kind of attention that French *avant-garde* activities were drawing; moreover there is a parable in it, a moral criticism, which they could well have taken to themselves" (Smith, *The Waste Land* [London: George Allen & Unwin, 1983], p. 119). One wouldn't put it past Nabokov – whose character Hazel Shade in *Pale Fire* notices, among her other "mirror words," that T. S. Eliot spelled backward is "Toilest" (see notes to ll. 347–48) – to be hinting at the undertone of nonsense in Eliot's ponderous mythopoetic finale with his own stuttering cryptogram "pa data" (discussed in Chapter 2 above).

32. Marjorie Perloff, "The Word as Such: L=A=N=G=U=A=G=E Poetry in the Eighties," *The Dance of the Intellect: Studies in the Poetry of the Pound Tradition* (Cambridge: Cambridge University Press, 1985), p. 215. See also Bruce Andrews and Charles Bernstein, ed., *The L=A=N=G=U=A=G=E Book* (Carbondale: Southern Illinois University Press, 1984).

CHAPTER 5

Unless otherwise noted, citations from the novels under discussion here are by chapter and page or by book, chapter, and page to the widely used Penguin paperbacks, except where Norton Critical editions are available, namely, for *The Ambassadors, The Egoist, Hard Times, Heart of Darkness, Jane Eyre, Jude the Obscure, Middlemarch,* and *Wuthering Heights*. Other editions cited are *Diana of the Crossways* (New York: W. W. Norton, 1973), *Tristram Shandy* (New York: Odyssey Press, 1940), and the Vintage editions (New York: Random House) of novels by E. M. Forster and Ford Madox Ford.

1. William Makepeace Thackeray, *The Yellowplush Papers and Early Miscellanies,* ed. George Saintsbury, The Oxford Thackeray, vol. 1 (London: Oxford University Press, 1908), p. 155.

2. John Orr, *Three Studies in Homonymics* (Edinburgh: Edinburgh University Press, 1962), p. 22.

3. William Matthews, *Cockney, Past and Present: A Short History of the Dialect of London* (Detroit: Gale Research Co., 1970), p. 172. See also Julian Franklin, *The Cockney: A Survey of London Life and Language* (London: Andre Deutsch, 1953).

4. Frank Kermode, *The Classic: Literary Images of Permanence and Chance* (New York: Viking, 1975), p. 130.

5. Otto Jespersen, *Progress in Language* (New York: Macmillan, 1894), pp. 323, 324.

6. See the anthology of undated excerpts by Phil May, et al., *Mr. Punch's Cockney Humour,* ed. J. A. Hammerton, Punch Library of Humour Series (London: Bradbury, Agnew & Co., c. 1910). The egregious Cockney punning of the lampoons from *Punch* include not only dropped-aitch humor like the "Appy 'Un" rather than "Appian" Way to "'Ampton races" (p. 18) but such false plays on nonphonetic abbreviations as "op. 13" at a concert being mistaken for a dance number, "hop 13" (p. 11). More strained yet—because ignoring even more punctuation—is the case of the Cockney bed-and-breakfaster assuming that the sign for the morning meal at 9 a.m. guarantees him a portion of breakfast "'am" (p. 22). Sometimes the *Punch* joke will even feel obliged to spell itself out typographically, so farfetched are its supposed ambiguities, as with this direct descendent of the Wellerism from *Pickwick Papers:* "'He is the greatest liar on (H)earth,' as the Cockney said of the lapdog he often saw lying before the fire" (p. 16). At other times, given a more credible play with ligature and elision, Cockney punning can revise a truism into a perfect homophonic sequence, as in "All's swell that ends swell" (p. 7).

7. M. M. Bakhtin, *The Dialogic Imagination,* ed. Michael Holquist, trans. Caryl Emerson and Michael Holquist (Austin: University of Texas Press, 1981), p. 273.

8. Charles Dickens, *Our Mutual Friend,* the original autograph manuscript (J. Pierpont Morgan Library, New York City), p. 47. The last phrase and its parenthetical extension were added in the margin, with their self-consciously tagged malapropism on "gorging" for "gorgeous." Here is a syntactic accumulation that not only comes to Dickens in an associative afterthought but is then said to have occurred to the character himself by the same route: a delegation of the verbal imagination in its almost unconscious machinations.

9. There is a closely parallel modern "narrative" instance of such homophonic puns occasioned by lipreading in the story "strip" of a syndicated cartoon by Toles (c. 1989, *Buffalo News*) in response to George Bush's presidential campaign vaunt "Read my lips: No New Taxes." In the cartoon version of this speech, which takes its rhetoric at face value, the lone perplexed audience member hears only the injunction, the message itself not given out loud. He then stumbles through three guesses in separate frames, two of them turning on junctural ambiguities: "Uh...No...Nuke...Texas?" or "No...Nude...Axes?"

10. Mark Schorer, "Fiction and the 'Analogical Matrix,'" in *Essays in Stylistic Analysis,* ed. Howard Babb (New York: Harcourt, Brace, Jovanovitch, 1972), p. 347; originally published in *Kenyon Review* 6 (Fall 1949): 539–60.

11. Judith Wilt, "'He would come back': The Fathers of Daughters in *Daniel Deronda,*" *Nineteenth-Century Literature* 42 (1987): 314.

12. See George Meredith, *Diana of the Crossways,* original autograph manuscript as sent to the printer, 1885 (J. Pierpont Morgan Library, New York City), p. 606.

13. I am alluding to the central claim of my *Death Sentences: Styles of Dying in British Fiction* (Cambridge, Mass.: Harvard University Press, 1984), which I extend here into the sublexical phonology of certain passages otherwise discussed in that earlier study of linguistic negotiations.

14. See Steven Marcus, *Dickens: From Pickwick to Dombey* (New York: Basic Books, 1965), on the way in which Dickens's father "never wearied of displaying his young son's precocity" in comic singing (p. 285).

15. This song is quoted in Matthews's chapter "Cockney in the Music-Hall," in *Cockney, Past and Present,* p. 85.

16. See the manuscript of *Our Mutual Friend,* p. 66.

17. Without the present emphasis on sublexical breakdowns in the disintegrating exchange system, the link between the arbitrary signs of money and language has received extended recent attention outside of Foucault. Marc Shell's *The Economy of Literature* (Baltimore: Johns Hopkins University Press, 1978), drawing on A. R. J. Turgot's "systematic comparison of verbal and monetary semiology" (p. 6), explores the literary ramifications of these two circulatory systems, both the "poetics" of monetary inscriptions and the face-value "economy" of fictional texts. These are themes which Shell pursues further in *Money, Language, and Thought: Literary and Philosophical Economies from the Medieval to the Modern Period* (Berkeley and Los Angeles: Univ. of California Press, 1982), where he quotes Wittgenstein's analogy between the relation of grammatical wording to the thought animating it and that of "mere printed slips of paper" to the meaningful, that is negotiable, nature of the same scraps taken as currency (p. 19n.41).

18. See Mary Douglas, *Purity and Danger: An Analysis of Concepts of Pollution and Taboo* (New York: Frederick A. Praeger, 1966), p. 161, where

the complete "cycle" of dirt as the eventually decomposed Other to orderly classification is summarized: "Dirt was created by the differentiating activity of mind, it was a by-product of the creation of order. So it started from a state of non-differentiation . . . [and] finally it returns to its true indiscriminable character. Formlessness is therefore an apt symbol of beginning and of growth as it is of decay."

19. Michel Foucault, *The Order of Things: An Archaeology of the Human Sciences* (New York: Random House, 1970), p. 101.

20. See Bakhtin, "Forms of Time and Chronotope in the Novel," in *The Dialogical Imagination,* pp. 84–258, esp. p. 251: "Also chronotopic is the internal form of a word." Yet Bakhtin's emphasis here is not on the dialogical processing across the time of a reading but, rather, on the diachronic (etymological) and syntagmatic collaboration whereby "the root meanings of spatial categories are carried over into temporal relationships (in the broadest sense)."

CHAPTER 6

All parenthetical page references from Joyce's works will be cited from the standard American editions: *A Portrait of the Artist as a Young Man,* Viking Critical Library ed. (New York: Penguin, 1968); *Finnegans Wake* (New York: Penguin, 1976), where according to standard practice, line numbers will also be given; *Ulysses,* Modern Library ed. (New York: Random House, 1961), and see also *Ulysses: The Corrected Text,* ed. Hans Walter Gabler et al. (New York: Random House, 1986).

1. Hugh Kenner, *The Mechanic Muse* (New York: Oxford University Press, 1987), pp. 6, 8.

2. Margot Norris, *The Decentered Universe of "Finnegans Wake": A Structuralist Analysis* (Baltimore: Johns Hopkins University Press, 1977), p. 128. In a film from the same decade as *The Dentist,* featuring a hero even more directly in touch than the Dickensian Fields with Victorian journalistic and almanack humor, Lamar Trotti's script for John Ford's *Young Mr. Lincoln* (1939) includes an extended digression into the folk wit of homophonic wordplay in the middle of the film's climactic trial sequence. Honest Abe is the defense lawyer in a murder trial, attempting to discredit the chief eyewitness for the prosecution, a shifty character who calls himself "J. Palmer Cass." After wondering aloud what the "J." stands for, and being told "John," Lincoln asks whether anyone ever calls the witness "Jack." Hearing that they do, he presses the interrogation: "Why not John P. Cass? Anything the matter with John P.?" "No," the witness admits, and "no" is again his answer when asked if "J. Palmer Cass" is meant to "conceal" anything. "Then what do you part your name in the middle for?" asks Lincoln, proceeding by his own subsequent pun to repart it right down the middle of a new lexical juncture, to the uproar of the court: "Well, if it's all the same to you, I'll just call you Jack Cass."

3. James Joyce, *Ulysses: The Corrected Text,* p. 628. Page references hereafter will be given to the Modern Library edition (see headnote above) except where some particular divergence is being called attention to; minor discrepancies, however, will be corrected without comment according to the revised edition.

4. Among the spliced coinages in *Portrait* that similarly give pause— because of their inoperable inclusion of an extraneous morphological recombination—are such inevitable phantom pluralizations as "*hollows*ounding" (83), "*fires*hovel" (150), and "*roses*oft" (155). This sort of stray plural occludes any semantic sense in the remainder of the compound, even though potential lexical members such as "hovel" and "oft" are left hanging. The same is true of the hint of "seat" in "seatangle" (170), or, alternately, of "tangled" in "rightangled" (208), "lecturer" in "lectureroom" (208). Even more functional and tempting is the emergence of "sulphury" in "sulphuryellow" (209), arguably a true portmanteau. In pushing the principle of dis-hyphenation one step further into the suspension of all word breaks, there is a gambit more Joycean (even) than Faulknerian at the opening of Toni Morrison's *The Bluest Eye* (New York: Washington Square Press, 1972; originally published in 1970), where the routinized rhythms of a child's "Dick and Jane" primer are syntactically and lexically deconstructed in two stages, first by the removal of all punctuation, then of all word breaks. The end result is a last spliceless para/ graph that, by conflating utterance, releases it to new forms. The very enumeration of the family members pulses with the logic of its own generation in "hereisthefamilymotherfatherdickandjane" (p. 7), where "fatherdick," when read with more than the eye, turns sequence to the primal consequence of "fathered." Such is the process of morphophonemic pulsation that it seems to name its own undulant energies in a cross-syllabic run like "father-smile*seethed*ogbowwwow" (p. 8). In this neo-Joycean parodic primer, the reductio ad absurdum of childish gibberish circles round yet again, as we saw in Chapter 3, to the prehistory of word breaks in the Medieval manuscript tradition. Once more, we might say, textual ontology recapitulates philology.

5. This is one of the examples of "augmentation in echo" given by Jean-Michel Rabaté, "The Silence of the Sirens," in *James Joyce: The Centennial Symposium,* ed. Morris Beja et al. (Chicago: University of Chicago Press, 1986), p. 83. Other phrases from "Sirens" exemplify such varied rhetorical figures as aphaeresis, apocope, ellipsis, telescoping of words, anadiplosis, prosthesis, epenthesis, diaeresis, tmesis, gemination, anaphonic extension, interpolation, and so forth, all part of Rabaté's claim that this episode is better understood as an exploitation of verbal rhetoric than as an exploration of musical cadence.

6. Geoffrey H. Hartman, *Saving the Text: Literature/Derrida/Philosophy* (Baltimore: Johns Hopkins University Press, 1981), p. 45. Hartman himself has frequent recourse to the "echoland" (p. 45) of Joyce's textual terrain before generalizing later in his study that, "whereas 'the ineluctable

modality of the visible' (Joyce) has been explored, especially by analysts interested in primal-scene imagery, the ineluctable ear, its ghostly, cavernous, echoic depth, has rarely been sounded with precision" (p. 123).

7. Jacques Derrida, "Two Words for Joyce," in *Post-Structuralist Joyce: Essays from the French,* ed. Derek Attridge and Daniel Ferrer (London: Cambridge University Press, 1984), pp. 145–59, an essay reprinted as the first half of Derrida's recent volume *Ulysse gramophone: deux mots pour Joyce* (Paris: Galilée, 1987). In the same collection with Derrida's separately published essay, other position papers on the idea of a poststructuralist Joyce are less insistent about the scriptive or graphic exclusivity of his texts. Jean-Michel Rabaté's "Lapsus Ex Machina"—on the textual mechanization of the slip—takes up a position more Bakhtinian than Derridean in a passage like this: *"Finnegans Wake* is not so much written polyphony as experience of patterns of prosodic polyphones: it is woven, braided, loomed with voices" (p. 87). Such tropes of the braided weave are only drawing out the etymology of "text" to begin with, a webwork which in Joyce becomes, at least on Rabaté's reading, predominantly phonic in the origin of its puns and pregnant slips. He is interested in the lapsus, the lapse, the default of the tongue, as a slip of but also *between* letters—not alphabetical characters but letters read as phonic signifiers. More explicitly a dramatization of the conjoint work of eye and ear in Joycean textuality is the passage Rabaté passes over too quickly as his first example. It boasts a striking chiastic homophony reminiscent of the process texts of Roussel: "What can't be coded can be decorded if an ear aye sieze what no eye ere grieved for" (482.34–36). The idea of decipherment as "decording" again takes us back to the textured, the braided text, a text noded, looped, woven taut. Rabaté mentions the conflation of "ear aye" (ear ever) into the syn(aes)thetic "eareye," but he leaves the other transegmental bondings to speak for themselves. "If an ear ever grasp what no eye before missed" is what Joyce has, in (one) effect, written. By a "decording" of his verbal compressions, however, we may *read* it otherwise. Dropping out of the subjunctive, we find that "sieze" puns on "sees," the apprehension by sight, just as in a segmental ambivalence "an ear" becomes "a near," and "eye ere" conflates to "eyer." What we then have is an argument for close reading deciphered solely thereby—an argument providing its own best case in point by homophonic self-paraphrase, a lapsus from within: "If *a near eye sees* what no sight reader, no cursory *eyer* of the text, was ever bereaved to miss." The whole passage testifies—speaking in tongues as it does, in slips and lapses thereof—to what Joyce earlier designates (with unusually discursive determination) as the text's "variously inflected, differently pronounced, otherwise spelled, changeably meaning vocable scriptsigns" (118.26–28). It is in view of such passages, well before the extremes of the *Wake,* that Rabaté's emphasis on the "eye listening" (p. 98) in the reading of Joyce seems to restore not at all the audiophonic sublime of a Logos before Babel, as deconstructed by Derrida, but instead a

certain phonic differential at work in the lapses and deferments of the multi-lingual Joycean polygramme.

8. See John Bishop, *Joyce's Book of the Dark: "Finnegans Wake"* (Madison: University of Wisconsin Press, 1986).

9. Hugh Kenner, *Joyce's Voices* (London: Faber & Faber, 1978), p. 99.

10. Jacques Derrida, "Ulysses Gramophone: Hear Say Yes in Joyce," in *James Joyce: The Augmented Ninth,* ed. Bernard Benstock (Syracuse, N.Y.: Syracuse University Press, 1988), pp. 27–75, in a translation by Tina Kendall, with emendations by Shari Benstock.

11. Citations here are from the original French version (see n.7 above). Of these two quotations from the French volume, only the former appears at all, strangely enough, in the Kendall/Benstock translation; the omission of the second decidedly skews the sense. When, in other words, "l'incorporation littérale du oui dans l'oeil de la langue, du *yes* dans les *eyes.* Langue d'oeil" (p. 86) becomes "the literal incorporation [ ] of *yes* in *eyes.* Language of eyes, [of ayes]" (p. 42), the excision and inclusion both soften the emphasis on the visual, in the latter case by interpolating a homophonic pun from another part of the discussion. Here, Derrida's stress is exclusively placed on the sheerly graphic *Yes* that "gives itself up only to *reading*" (p. 42), not to hearing. As usual, though, Derrida is hard to pin down. Focusing earlier on Bloom's own fantasy of "a gramophone in every grave" ("Ulysses Gramophone," p. 44), with its pertinent but unspoken link to textual "thanatopraxis," Derrida speaks of a "gramophony which records writing in the liveliest voice . . . archived into the very quick of the voice" (p. 43). We recognize again that arche-writing of the trace. This textual "voice" is therefore constituted only in Derrida's punning sense of *ouï-dire* (hear-say). It is a voice to which one "listens" solely by producing it in the differential interplay of textual processing. This, at least, would seem to be the gist of an earlier observation couched in symmetrical paradoxes: "*Yes* can only be a mark in *Ulysses,* a mark at once written and spoken, vocalized as a grapheme and written as a phoneme, *yes,* in a word, gramophoned" ("Ulysses Gramophone," p. 36).

12. There is no denying, though, the grammatological dimension of even this last supposed mono-logue, in particular its graphemic insistence. Indeed, there is striking reconfirmation of this dimension in the Gabler edition of the novel. Molly is musing about the death of a distant acquaintance when her stream of consciousness snaps on a matter of scriptive literacy: "bereavement symp⌀athy I always make that mistake and ne⌀phew with 2 double yous in" (624.730–31), the former spelling corrected altogether in the Modern Library edition [758]. Not present in earlier printed versions of the novel, these explicit slashes of deletion are close anticipations of the Derridean *sous rature,* the placing under erasure of the trace. And they are purely graphic. No one could say them to herself; they do not represent misspellings of the mind but can only instance the grapheme itself under correction as mental script. Such is the line of thought along which one is carried by these signified

excisions of the signifier—that is, if one can accept as plausible the assumption that the slash marks were intended for print rather than just for the printer. Given the debate over ink color alone (whether Joyce's or another proofreader's) and without, in these mere slashes, a recognizable feature of alphabetic handwriting as a check, this seems a particularly risky "correction"—or metacorrection—but a tempting one in the very extremity of its textual effect. This putative instance of a graphemic bent in this most "vocalized" stretch of the novel, in the professional singer's internal monologue, would support—up to a point—Derrida's case for an "inscription" beneath all speech. The very consciousness of slip or lapse in Molly's misspellings is traced here through the alphabetic stray and its retrospective censorship. At the same time, this grammatological exaggeration on Joyce's part, this textualization of the unconscious, is complemented by the phonetic spelling of the unwanted w as "double you." The gramme comes before speech, yes, but it is not alone there, since the phone underlies—or at least "ineluctably" accompanies—such speech as well, as, for example, in the monosyllabic "you" for u when read. Joyce's writerly text, here and elsewhere, can be felt in this way not just to invite but to perform its own reading.

CHAPTER 7

1. Virginia Woolf, *The Waves* (New York: Harcourt, Brace and World, 1931), p. 215; subsequent parenthetical references are to this edition in its separate paperback issue (1978).

2. Virginia Woolf, *A Writer's Diary,* ed. Leonard Woolf (London: Hogarth Press, 1953), p. 69.

3. 16 November 1931, *The Diary of Virginia Woolf,* vol. 4, ed. Anne Oliver Bell (London: Hogarth Press, 1982), p. 53.

4. William Butler Yeats, Introduction to *Fighting the Waves* (1934), quoted in *The Diary of Virginia Woolf,* in re Woolf's allusion to "Old Yeats...writing about me" (vol. 4, p. 255n.28).

5. 7 January 1931, *The Diary of Virginia Woolf,* vol. 4, p. 4, where she is speaking, in particular, of the attempt in Bernard's soliloquy to "break up, dig deep."

6. Virginia Woolf, *Between the Acts* (New York: Harcourt, Brace, Jovanovich), p. 212; Woolf, "Longer version" of *Between the Acts,* p. 230, continued from "Typescript with author's ms. corrections, unsigned, dated throughout from April 27, 1938–July 30, 1939, 186 pp." (Berg Collection, New York Public Library).

7. See Virginia Woolf, *A Room of One's Own* (New York: Harcourt, Brace, and World, 1927), where the aspiring female writer is said to find no "common sentence ready for her use," only "a man's sentence" (p. 79).

8. Attempting to rescue Woolf's call for "androgyny" from charges of feminine defeatism, Toril Moi argues in *Sexual/Textual Politics: Feminist*

Literary Theory (London: Methuen, 1985) for a Kristevan reading of Woolf precisely because of Kristeva's resistance to a "metaphysical belief in strong, immutably fixed gender identities" (p. 13). My phonotextual approach to voicing in Woolf means to reject as completely as Kristeva does any feminine "essentialism" about voice as the unmediated language of the female body, a position one finds expounded, for instance, in the writing of Hélène Cixous, as summarized by Moi in her subsection "*Ecriture féminine* 2) the source and the voice," pp. 113–19.

More tightly focused around issues of linguistic engenderment at the level of morphology itself is the closing and title chapter of Louis Marin's *La voix excommuniée: essais de mémoire* (Paris: Galilée, 1981). The homophonic cryptogram, or inscribed cryptophone, of Stendhal's secret writing on the inner lining of his belt—especially its junctural syncopation of letters and pauses at *J(e) vais* and *voir/la*—seems to authorize in advance the concluding move of Marin's book. There, he audits the inner lining, as it were, of an operatic phrase from *Manon,* as sung by his sister, in order to mount an oblique argument about the return of voicing to text, an argument that he knows may seem like "verbal evidence substituted for the evidence of ideas" (p. 173; my translations of this closing section). The sung line in question: "Adieu, notre petite table" (p. 174). Over the course of ten pages, Marin speculates on an enunciation of the "t(e)" sufficient to forestall the liaison with "*t*able" and thus to introduce a stray vowel cluster into a new set of free-form associations. The graded run of these vocalic associations, *ti/te/ta,* anticipates, on Marin's hearing, both the iterative internal echo of "ti/tubant" (pp. 175, 180; for the "careening" of the echo's own "noise" [p. 182]) and the missing /o/ that would generate out of *peti/to/table* a virtual anagram of the "*tableau* phonologique" itself (p. 182). From such lateral counterplay is generated at any number of levels the "double difference" (p. 180) which casts "te" into simultaneous distinction from the substantive (and substantial) "table" it somehow reform(ulate)s as well as from that adjectival root it would ordinarily complete and feminize. This last is the most far-reaching aspect of Marin's reading: the "deconstruction" of "petite" (through its own hyper-articulation) leading to implicit inferences about the arbitrary engenderment of discourse and the polymorphous lexical perversity of its undoing. For Marin, there is a "force" in the "sonorous flux" that "displaces 'te'" (in its "floating between 'peti' and 'table'") and recasts it as a register of vacillation between "feminine and masculine, *in a* difference which is *the* difference, the neuter itself" (p. 181).

Marin ascribes this "secret" (p. 185) syncopation of the written text (in allusion, one presumes to the earlier "secret" on the inside of Stendhal's belt) to the productive rewriting of the written by the read. His book closes by offering—in answer to the question "how is the auto(biographical) able to engender an ex(communicated or communicable)?"—the final "affirmation: *its* Ex- has generated *my* Auto-" (p. 185). Expelled and/or expunged, exiled or excised, the absent voice of the author has produced my voice as reader. Yet in all this theorizing of textual reception, there remains a vestigial mystification, it would seem, in which some sense of aural "communion" between author and reader—rather than sheer textual generation—is still the touchstone. Reading does the voicing, yes—but then, on Marin's account, we also seem to be hearing voices, as if what is activated by the text, spun out of it, is in some sense an "echo" of what went into it. This is, again, that phantom of the "auto-bio-phonic" origin recuperated from within the "autobiographic" (see Chapter 3, n.33). Figures of origin *may* in Marin be just that, figurative, but at times something more may well seem at stake in his account than merely textual simulacra—even in the co-productive sense of syncopated vocalization. Though admitting that the "communication of self to a possible reader" is constituted by "nothing else but the tactics of writing" and that any "singular essence" and "proper sense" always "melt into literal insignificance"—hence suffer, in a word, "excommunication"—nevertheless "they remake themselves in the same movement, outside of all signifying intention, and reproduce themselves outside of all transcendental synthesis" (p. 176). They do so, however, at least so Marin is moved to add—in an acoustic metaphor(?) begging the very textual question he has so importantly located—they do so "in echo of a voice that all symbolic articulation has 'originarily' excommuni-cated" (p. 176). Part of the question is to what extent autobiography—self-writing, the very "life" of the author in words—is the privileged locus of this echo. But this question aside, Marin's work, as I suggested in Chapter 3, joins that of Finas in its insistence on reading itself as a text. If all Marin means to suggest by the "echo" of origin is that the phoneme, rather than the speaking voice, is the victim of an excommunication by the grapheme, a banishment instated at the founding moment of symbolization, but that this e-dict against the "saying" *within* the "said" (again, see Chapter 3, n.33) is rendered reversible in the reading act, then this returning (from nowhere) of the phonic to the fold of read writing is very much what my book, and what Woolf in her genderless "reprise" of one word in the next (to borrow Marin's metaphor for textual "darning"), are after. In light of Marin's own earlier work (see *Utopics: Spatial Play* [Atlantic Highlands, N.J.: Humanities Press, 1984 (originally published in French in 1973)]), this could indeed be called the return from the "utopic" space of internal difference, a return sounded, latently, upon the body of the reader.

9. Quite apart from her work in modernist poetics, Julia Kristeva has written of the female psyche in its uneasy relation to the three main modes of temporal consciousness that she finds governing Western culture. See her "Women's Time," trans. Alice Jardine and Harry Blake, *Signs* 7 (Autumn 1981): 13–35, in which her hypotheses bear directly not only on Rhoda's exile from temporal continuity but on the linguistic metaphors that figure such an exclusion in her own mind. Woolf's title, *The Waves*, happens to signal one such temporal mode: the cyclic, the time of eternal renewal so often mythi-

cally associated with the feminine. Woolf has Bernard, her novelist spokesman, evoke this sense of time – in chiasmus and in affirmation – on the last page of the novel: "Yes, this is the eternal renewal, the incessant rise and fall and fall and rise again" (p. 297). If cyclical time is associated with the maternal, the regenerative, the other pole of temporal consciousness, the one identified not with repetition but with eternity, is also linked with a feminine principle. As against cyclical time, this is what Kristeva calls "monumental time." Rather than linear, progressive, it is instead all-encompassing, potentially devouring. In between repetition and eternity, cyclicity and monumentality, falls succession, the "time of history," a temporality that, for Kristeva, "renders explicit a rupture, an expectation, or an anguish which other temporalities work to conceal" (p. 17). This is the temporality in which Rhoda, Woolf's female alter ego in *The Waves,* can never quite relax, for she "cannot make one moment merge in the next" (p. 130). It is no accident that, in Kristeva's terms, what fails Rhoda is not only the recalcitrant time of history but, by an analogous sense of successivity, the duration of language itself: the linear time, as Kristeva has it, of "noun + verb," a time which "rests on its own stumbling block, which is also the stumbling block of . . . enunciation – death" (p. 23) or, in other words, *void.* This is Rhoda's central apprehension, her panic – a recognition of that death by severance underlying the analogy between time and language, a death whose gaping blank returns as soon as it is repressed. This is because language, like time under the aspect of history, is founded (Kristeva here follows Lacan) on the separation anxiety reproduced by, if not reducible to, syntax itself. In Kristeva's view, a common (though by no means "essential") female reaction to this anxiety, exaggerated in those women psychoanalysis terms "hysterics," is "to deny . . . separation and the language which ensues from it, whereas men (notably obsessionals) magnify both and, terrified, attempt to master them" (pp. 24–25). Woolf plots a more complex story upon a similar gender grid, with the "terror" over severance and death being divided between her suicidal heroine and the male writer figure who never more than intermittently masters it.

10. J.-A. Miller, "La suture (éléments de la logique du signifiant)," delivered on 24 February 1965, to Lacan's seminar, and published in French in *Cahiers pour l'analyse* 1 (1966): 37–49; rpt., as "Suture (Elements of the Logic of the Signifier)," trans. Colin MacCabe, *Screen* 18 (Winter 1977–78): 24–34. For the technical argument upon which Miller bases his discussion, see Gottlob Frege, *The Foundations of Arithmetic,* trans. J. L. Austin, 2d ed. (Evanston, Ill.: Northwestern University Press, 1968). With a comparable psycholinguistic agenda, as indicated by the title *Desire in Language* (ed. Leon S. Roudiez, trans. Thomas Gora, Alice Jardine, and Leon S. Roudiez [New York: Columbia University Press, 1980]), Julia Kristeva chooses to overthrow rather than revise Frege, along with other twentieth-century logicians, as "ineffective within the realm of poetic language," given their allegiance to the "0–1 sequence" (p. 70). Following Bakhtin in her approach to

nonmonologic form, Kristeva's "polyvalent narrative" requires a "poetic logic" which "would embody the 0–2 interval, a continuity where 0 denotes and 1 is implicitly transgressed" (p. 70). Instead of such a wholesale evacuation of the unitary in favor of the double integer, the interests of the present discussion—and precisely in their debt to the Kristevan "semiotic" realm before symbolic regimentation—gravitate instead toward that absence-within-presence of the 1–2 sequence: never a gradation in plenitude, always an elision of the recurrent blank, the sliding cipher necessitated by incremental transition.

11. See Joan Copjec, "The Anxiety of the Influencing Machine," *October* 23 (Winter 1982): 46, a position which might legislate, in turn, Kristeva's more radical departure from Frege's theory (see n.10 above).

12. See above, Chapter 1, p. 46.

13. See above, Chapter 3, p. 104.

14. See Julia Kristeva, *Revolution in Poetic Language,* trans. Margaret Waller (New York: Columbia University Press, 1984), pp. 25–27, from which this further paraphrase of her argument about the semiotic *chora* is drawn.

15. In my essay, "Catching the Stylistic D/rift: Sound Defects in Woolf's *The Waves,*" *ELH* 54 (Summer 1987): 442–43, I consider Sandra M. Gilbert's and Susan Gubar's critique of French psychoanalytic claims about female linguistic development, in light of Woolf's stylistic ambitions in *The Waves;* see Gilbert and Gubar, "Sexual Linguistics: Gender, Language, Sexuality," *New Literary History* 16 (Spring 1984–85): 537. My essay also finds room for a fuller discussion than here of the Lacanian mirror stage as it serves to illuminate Rhoda's crisis in *The Waves* (see pp. 432–36). In a recent argument often running parallel to my own, Makiko Minow-Pinkney sees Woolf steering in her verbal experiments between "the complementary pitfalls of both feminist realism . . . and schizophrenic modernism"; see Minow-Pinkney, *Virginia Woolf and the Problem of the Subject* (Sussex: Harvester Press, 1987), p. 155. Minow-Pinkney's study appeared at the same time as the *ELH* article on which this chapter is based. Her book answers, in a sense, half the call put out by Toril Moi (see n.8 above) for a "combination of Derridean and Kristevan theory" in "future feminist reading of Woolf" (*Sexual/Textual Politics,* p. 15). Such an approach coincides with mine in finding much of the tension in *The Waves* focused around the character of Rhoda, a being "incapable of establishing the thetic subject" (p. 163). Minow-Pinkney writes that "though Woolf does not dislocate syntax, even in Rhoda's extreme assertions of psychic breakdown, she goes a long way toward *emptying* syntax of its function of articulation across the novel as a whole" (p. 172). Yet Rhoda's suicidal fate exposes the paradox of Woolf's endeavor: "Associated with whiteness and emptiness, outside time and logic, Rhoda marks out the locus of a feminine space, that non-symbolisable Other that must be repressed but none the less exist for a normative discourse to be installed." No such installation is possible, however, without selling out to the symbolic. "A

feminine discourse of the white spaces remains strictly a contradiction, impossible except as silence" (p. 183). This is where Minow-Pinkney's argument and mine part company. Among all the recent treatments of *The Waves,* hers is the theoretical investigation most drawn to stylistic issues, but her concentration on syntax as touchstone disables her from answering her own best question: "How indeed is it possible to actualise a feminine writing that is not organised around phallocentric identity and positionality, but would none the less not just be lost in silence?" (p. 186). My answer should by now be clear. Making syntax itself possible, segmentation creates the spaces that register as blanks; transegmental drifts invade and animate those gaps with a fluid continuity apart from strict "syntagmatic constraints" (p. 172). To write from, as well as across, those gaps may be Woolf's way of speaking the feminine in prose, loosening not only the "ligatures" but many of the other binding obligations of a hierarchical discourse.

16. Gilbert and Gubar, "Sexual Linguistics," p. 531, quoting the passage from Woolf's *Mrs. Dalloway* ([New York: Harcourt, Brace and World, 1927], pp. 122–23). It is interesting to note that the expository wordplay of these two authors, though far more cerebral and less "enigmatic" than Woolf's, is still lexically transgressive, a teasing of the spaces between words. See especially the sliding open of the idiom "alas and alack" into the Lacanian parody (in style as well as in substance) of "a lass and a lack" (p. 537). The passage at issue in *Mrs. Dalloway* is also mentioned in passing by Makiko Minow-Pinkney, where it is aligned with the "pre-symbolic" in Kristeva's terms; see *Virginia Woolf and the Problem of the Subject,* p. 73. More recently yet, in *Virginia Woolf and the Languages of Patriarchy* (Bloomington: Indiana University Press, 1987), Jane Marcus's introduction to this collection of her essays on Woolf concludes with a section, influenced by Kristeva, called "Moaning and Crooning: The Charwoman's Song" (pp. 10–17) in which she numbers the old crone from *Mrs. Dalloway* among those representatives of Woolf's "socialist feminist aesthetic" (p. 11) who fuse the energies of labor and language, "tunneling a channel into the obscure origins...where language follows the rhythms of the body" (pp. 12–13).

17. Virginia Woolf, *The Waves: The Two Holograph Drafts,* transcribed and ed. J. W. Graham (Toronto: University of Toronto Press, 1976), draft 2, p. 733.

18. Translated as "breach" in Kristeva's *Revolution* (see p. 247n.71).

19. Xaviere Gauthier, "Is There Such a Thing As Women's Writing?" trans. Marilyn A. August, in *New French Feminisms,* ed. Elaine Marks and Isabelle de Courtivron (Amherst: University of Massachusetts Press, 1980), p. 164.

20. The first death scene Virginia Woolf wrote comes at the end of her first novel, *The Voyage Out* (New York: Harcourt, Brace and World, 1920), where Rachel dies quietly in her fiancé's arms. As the heroine's mind is emptied out of the scene, we are drawn into the hero's with an indirect discourse, much

worked over at the draft stage, that would seem to cure the void of death with an idiomatic, a dismissive sense of "nothing." Writes Woolf for the hero: "this was death. It was nothing; it was to cease to breath." Those impacted infinitive phrases seem odd, deliberately clinical, unperturbed, until one hears them as part of a pulsional code, a counterpoint, something which the very fact of an infinitive grammar is meant to resist. The point of the passage in context is of course that death ends nothing between the lovers except Rachel's breathing. But listen to what shadows it in passing: "It was nothing. It was *to cease*..." The infinitive phrase of an action, "to cease," itself the logical negation of an action, easily collapses, even in silent reading, into the disyllabic and etymologically related noun of death itself, *decease,* hermetically sealing the very gap of scriptive difference or functional negativity that syntax, on behalf of rhetoric, is still trying to keep open. Here, as in Bernard's sentence-long rendition of Rhoda's death, I am further developing the phonemic implications of two cadenced phrasings already investigated from a different perspective in my *Death Sentences: Styles of Dying in British Fiction* (Cambridge, Mass.: Harvard University Press, 1984), pp. 263–64, 303.

21. Julia Kristeva, "Phonetics, Phonology, and Impulsional Bases," trans. Caren Greenberg, *Diacritics* 4 (Fall 1974): 36.

22. Gertrude Stein, *Four in America* (New York: Books for Libraries Press, 1947), p. 125, in an essay putatively on Henry James. My thanks to Lorrie Sprecher for directing me to these passages.

23. Roland Barthes, *The Pleasure of the Text,* trans. Richard Miller (New York: Farrar, Straus and Giroux, 1975 [originally published in French in 1973]), p. 66.

24. William Empson, *Seven Types of Ambiguity* (New York: New Directions, 1947), p. 45.

25. Woolf, 28 March 1930, *A Writer's Diary,* p. 153.

EPILOGOS

1. I. A. Richards, "Literature, Oral-Aural and Optical," in *Complementarities: Uncollected Essays,* ed. John Paul Russo (Manchester: Carcanet New Press, 1976), p. 201. This essay, nicely enough, was originally a radio talk that ended up printed in the *Listener* (1947).

2. Virginia Woolf, *To the Lighthouse* (New York: Harcourt, Brace and World, 1927), p. 53.

3. Virginia Woolf, *Mrs. Dalloway* (New York: Harcourt, Brace and World, 1925), p. 42. This "knocking of words together," which Woolf's writing courts in order to mitigate, is what Joyce more obtrusively exploits, putting at stake the technological as well as cognitive repercussions of such textuality.

In view of Joyce's notorious bad luck on this score with the transition into print, I wondered about the fate of my own pages when this book, still a manuscript, went off to the typesetters. At least none of Joyce's own pointed slips, his "knocking . . . together" of graphemes under phonemic pressure — many of them normalized long ago by printers and lately restored by editors — suffered the fate of reverse correction in my typeset account. But curiosities there were (confirming ones, I like to think), giving pause precisely where no lexical break was intended. Proofreading turned up, for instance, the following transegmental slip of transcription across the hurdle of a closed parenthesis: "common sense) ensualizes the lexical interstices" (p. 5). Further along, an intended analogy had emerged instead as a clairvoyant aesthetic preference (by backward liaison) in "Shelley likes Stevens" (p. 85). Later, "made to pay" was short-changed (by dental assimilation) in becoming "may to pay" (p. 226). More striking yet, in the discussion of a knotty passage from *Daniel Deronda*, the overtone of "assailing" in "was a sailing and sailing" had been subliminally rethought by a compositor as the eerily appropriate "was ailing and sailing" (p. 216). Judging at least from this instance, there are some throws of the phonemic dice with which a text just can't lose.

Index

Compositor:	Harrison Typesetting, Inc.
Text:	10/13 Times Roman
Display:	Times Roman
Printer:	Edwards Brothers, Inc.
Binder:	Edwards Brothers, Inc.